OCR
A LEVEL

PSYCHOLOGY
FOR A LEVEL

OCR
A LEVEL

1

PSYCHOLOGY

FOR A LEVEL YEAR 1

Includes AS

Louise Ellerby-Jones

Sandra Latham

Nigel Wooldridge

This is an OCR endorsed resource

Hachette UK's policy is to use papers that are natural, renewable and recyclable products and made from wood grown in sustainable forests. The logging and manufacturing processes are expected to conform to the environmental regulations of the country of origin.

Orders: please contact Bookpoint Ltd, 130 Milton Park, Abingdon, Oxon OX14 4SB. Telephone: +44 (0)1235 827720. Fax: +44 (0)1235 400454. Lines are open 9.00a.m.–5.00p.m., Monday to Saturday, with a 24-hour message answering service. Visit our website at www.hoddereducation.co.uk

A catalogue record for this title is available from the British Library

ISBN 9781471835902

© 2015 Louise Ellerby-Jones, Sandra Latham, Nigel Wooldridge

First published in 2015 by

Hodder Education

An Hachette UK Company

Carmelite House

50 Victoria Embankment

London EC4Y 0DZ

Impression number   10 9 8 7 6 5 4

Year   2019 2018 2017

Cover photo © puckillustrations/Fotolia

Illustrations by Barking Dog Art and Peter Lubach

Typeset in Bliss Light 10.5/13pt by AptaraInc.

Printed in India

Contents

Acknowledgements

The Publishers would like to thank the following for permission to reproduce copyright material.
Every effort has been made to trace all copyright holders, but if any have been inadvertently overlooked, the Publishers will be pleased to make the necessary arrangements at the first opportunity.

Photo permissions
Page 9: © Time Life Pictures/Mansell/The LIFE Picture Collection/Getty Images; p.11 WavebreakmediaMicro/Fotolia; p.16: With kind permission by Alexandra Milgram, Photo: © The Granger Collection, NYC/TopFoto; p.17: From the film Obedience copyright 1968 by Stanley Milgram; copyright renewed by Alexandra Milgram 1993, and distributed by Penn State Media Sales; p.25: © David Bleeker Photography/Alamy; p.36: © Spencer Platt/Getty Images; p.59: © lithian/Fotolia; p.64: © WENN Ltd/Alamy; p.74: **all** © Simons, D. J., & Chabris, C. F. (1999). Gorillas in our midst: Sustained inattentional blindness for dynamic events. Perception, 28, 1059–1074.; p.82: With kind permission by Albert Bandura.; p.89: © AVITA MEDICAL LTD; p.117: © Scott Camazine/Getty Images; p.118: © uwimages/Fotolia; p.160: **all** Courtesy Autism Research Centre, Department of Psychiatry, University of Cambridge; p.162 **all** Courtesy Autism Research Centre, Department of Psychiatry, University of Cambridge; p.166: © Moviestore Collection/REX

Text permissions
Page 169 Figures taken from 'The Army Beta Test' from Gould, S. 1982, 'A Nation of Morons'. New Scientist, vol. 6, 349–352

Introduction

Why do people do what they do, and why don't they do the same things that I do? How can they do things that I would never do, or would never want to do? Why do they think the way they do, and why don't they seem to think the same way that I do? How can people believe in things that I don't believe in? Do people feel the same things that I'm feeling?

If these are the kind of questions that interest you, then you have chosen the right subject – psychology. What psychology actually is, however, is not commonly understood. Here is a psychology teacher's story:

When I meet new people, one of the questions they ask is, 'What do you do?' I hate this question, so I try to avoid telling them, and go for half the story: 'I'm a teacher,' I say. Then, of course, their next question is, 'What do you teach?' Well, I can hold them off with the facetious answer, 'Students', but that's a bit rude, so I have to admit it. 'Psychology,' I say eventually. This is then, as often as not, followed by them saying, 'Ooh! I'll have to be careful what I say now, won't I? You're going to be reading my mind,' or they say, 'You're going to be analysing me now, aren't you?'

Typically they might ask me something along the lines of: 'I had this dream about being chased by a giant snail round a 400 m running track and it was wearing a baseball cap and calling out my name. What does it mean, then?' or 'I must introduce you to my brother, Rick. We think he's bipolar. Maybe you could confirm it for us?'

Psychologists don't tell you what your dreams mean. Psychologists don't diagnose mental disorders: that's the job of psychiatrists – medical doctors who have specialist psychiatric training. They don't offer you therapy or counselling: that's the job of psychotherapists, not psychologists. Psychologists don't read your mind. No one can do that.

What psychologists actually do is systematically investigate human behaviour and experience, with the aim of trying to explain, understand, predict or manage behaviour. It is to be hoped that what they discover helps us to live better, happier lives and make a positive contribution to human welfare. Psychologists, then, are best thought of as researchers or scientists, and never as therapists, doctors, gurus or magicians.

Psychology is considered to have begun in the 1870s in Leipzig, in modern Germany, when Wilhelm Wundt and his colleagues opened their 'psychology laboratory'. Their method of studying psychology was to take an introspective approach – asking themselves such questions as: What do I feel? Why do I feel like this? How do I behave? How does my memory work?

However, this was rejected as a way of studying behaviour on the grounds that it was too subjective, and despite Wundt and his colleagues focusing on collecting data about behaviour, their attempts to understand psychology were always going to be limited by the fact that they were just a handful of people and their interpretations of their own behaviour were always going to be biased.

Modern psychology, on the other hand, tries to follow an objective scientific methodology in investigating human behaviour. This means that theories are generated, which are then tested by gathering empirical evidence. To be taken seriously as an academic discipline, psychology has, for the most part, taken a scientific approach to studying behaviour. The aim of science is to determine causality by carrying out controlled experiments to test hypotheses. The findings from experiments provide proof for or against a theory. The findings need to stand up on replication; that is, if you do the study again you must get similar results. These features of science are important in psychological investigations and you will learn a great deal about how data are gathered and analysed as you progress through this book or through your programme of study. In fact, if you are following the OCR examination for either A Level or AS Level, you will do a whole exam paper on research methods (Unit 1).

In general terms, psychologists have investigated aspects of human behaviour in five broad areas. These are:

1. The **social area**, which investigates how the social context, including the presence and behaviour of other people, impacts on how people behave.
2. The **cognitive area**, which investigates how we think, perceive, pay attention, problem-solve and remember.
3. The **developmental area**, which investigates how our thinking changes as we mature and grow older, the development of personality and how we learn.

1

4. The **biological area**, which investigates the relationship between biology and behaviour – both how biology, especially neurobiology (the biology of the brain), affects behaviour, but also how behaviour affects biology.
5. The **individual differences area**, which investigates the differences between people, such as abnormality and mental disorders.

This sounds fairly clear-cut, but the areas are not always as distinct from each other as they might seem and, when carrying out their work within a particular area, psychologists may come at the same questions from different perspectives (e.g. behaviourist, psychodynamic, evolutionary or humanist perspectives). This all reflects the challenges of the subject as people are complicated and understanding human behaviour is difficult: unlike in Chemistry, where chemicals don't know they are being studied and don't have the ability to deliberately alter their properties, when people are being studied by psychologists they are likely to be trying to work out the purpose of the investigation and trying to present themselves in the most 'socially desirable' way. This is why psychologists use a range of different methods when studying human behaviour and come at it from so many different angles – they need to use all the tools that they possibly can! You will get a stronger sense of all this as you go along, but it will be helpful to keep the five areas in mind as they do provide a useful structure to locate research within.

The aim of the OCR A Level, and therefore of this book, is to give you a grounding in these different areas of psychology. In order to do this, you will need to look at 20 pieces of psychological research (see Table 1).

Very important note

If you are studying the AS Level course then you will only need to look at ten of these core studies – namely, the ones relating to the following key themes:

● Responses to people in authority (i.e. Milgram, and Bocchiaro *et al.*)
● Memory (i.e. Loftus and Palmer, and Grant *et al.*)
● External influences on children's behaviour (i.e. Bandura *et al.* and Chaney *et al.*)
● Regions of the brain (i.e. Sperry, and Casey *et al.*)
● Understanding disorders (i.e. Freud, and Baron-Cohen *et al.*)

Table 1 Classic and contemporary studies grouped around a series of key themes

Area	Key theme	Classic study	Contemporary study
Social	Responses to people in authority	Milgram (1963) Obedience	Bocchiaro *et al.* (2012) Disobedience and whistle-blowing
	Responses to people in need	Piliavin *et al.* (1969) Subway Samaritan	Levine *et al.* (2001) Cross-cultural altruism
Cognitive	Memory	Loftus and Palmer (1974) Eyewitness testimony	Grant *et al.* (1998) Context-dependent memory
	Attention	Moray (1959) Auditory attention	Simons and Chabris (1999) Visual inattention
Developmental	External influences on children's behaviour	Bandura *et al.* (1961) Transmission of aggression	Chaney *et al.* (2004) Funhaler study
	Moral development	Kohlberg (1968) Stages of moral development	Lee *et al.* (1997) Evaluations of lying and truth-telling
Biological	Regions of the brain	Sperry (1968) Split-brain study	Casey *et al.* (2011) Neural correlates of delay of gratification
	Brain plasticity	Blakemore and Cooper (1970) Impact of early visual experience	Maguire *et al.* (2000) Taxi drivers
Individual differences	Understanding disorders	Freud (1909) Little Hans	Baron-Cohen *et al.* (1997) Autism in adults
	Measuring differences	Gould (1982) A nation of morons Bias in IQ testing	Hancock *et al.* (2011) Language of psychopaths

By looking at two studies in relation to each key theme, hopefully it will become clear that there are many ways in which the same broad topics can be approached. This should also bring out the dynamic nature of psychology as researchers continue trying to achieve a deeper, more settled understanding of human behaviour.

It will be important for you to think critically about the research you encounter. For example, you might ask yourself whether the sample it is based on genuinely reflects the wider population as a whole. You might also wonder whether findings from controlled laboratory experiments are ever likely to reflect how people behave in more fluid, real-life settings. Crucially, you might also want to reflect on how the participants in the study were treated: if you wouldn't have been happy being a participant in a particular study, then is it acceptable that other people were treated in the way that they were? The study of psychology will nurture your skills of critical thinking.

Much of the psychological terminology that you will have to get to grips with will be in relation to research methodology and some of the wider debates in psychology. To help you with this, the next section of this chapter provides a brief introduction to some of the key concepts you will need to know about. Your understanding of these should then deepen as you progress through the book.

Coming back to the points raised at the start of this introduction, we have told you that as psychologists we cannot read your mind. However, we can infer what is going on in your mind from your behaviour. That is, if you are reading this book, then either you must be interested in finding out about psychology or you have already started to study psychology for AS or A Level.

And if you want a bit of magic, then we can definitely predict the future for you: you are going to love psychology. Why? Psychology is fascinating because it is all about people, and what could be more fascinating than us?

Key concepts in psychology

One of the big challenges of studying any subject for the first time is getting to grips with all the technical terms that are used in that subject. Psychology is no different, although you may find some of the concepts familiar from your previous studies in science. You will learn much more about all of this as you go along, but the following should help to introduce you to some of the key concepts you will be encountering.

Psychologists investigate their subject matter in many different ways. For instance, they often carry out experiments, and these can take the form of laboratory-based experiments, field-based experiments, or quasi experiments. All can be expected to have different conditions (e.g. an experimental condition and a control condition) which differ in that the experimental condition is changed in some way that the researchers believe could have a difference on results. The thing that is changed is called an independent variable, and to measure the effect that this has had the researchers build into their study a dependent variable. Researchers also need to impose controls on their investigation to ensure that the only thing that is different between their experimental and control conditions is the one thing they want to be different – namely, their independent variable – and that no extraneous variable could be affecting their dependent variable and, therefore, their results.

Laboratory experiments differ from field experiments in terms of where they are set (in laboratory experiments, participants typically come along to a controlled setting, often in a university; in field experiments, the researchers go along to the natural environment of the people whose behaviour they are studying). Quasi-experiments differ from the other two in that their independent variable is naturally occurring, rather than deliberately created by the researcher. Examples of a naturally occurring independent variable could be time of day (morning versus afternoon) or whether the participants have a particular disorder or not (e.g. people with autism compared to people without autism).

Whichever type of experiment a researcher carries out, they also have to think about the type of design it should have. These could follow an independent measures design, repeated measures design or matched participants design. The basic differences are as follows. In an independent measures design, the sample are divided into two groups – one that will go into the experimental condition and another that will go into the control condition (i.e. participants will experience one condition only). In a repeated measures design, participants will take part in both the control condition and the experimental condition, although the order in which this is done may be counterbalanced to ensure that half do the control condition first, while the other half do the experimental condition first. A matched participants is like an independent measures design except that before the participants are allocated to their condition (control condition or experimental condition) they are assessed on some relevant characteristic (e.g. their highest level of education) so that the researchers can make sure that both conditions contain similar sorts of people.

- Check your understanding of experiments as a research method by seeing if you can say what is meant by the following:
  - Independent variable
  - Dependent variable
  - Controls
  - Laboratory experiment
  - Field experiment
  - Quasi experiment
  - Independent measures design
  - Repeated measures design
  - Matched participants design

Links to methodological issues
- Check your understanding

Experiments aren't the only research method used by psychologists. For instance, they also carry out case studies (in which they examine a small number of people in depth, with these people often being unusual in some way), correlation studies (where they see if two different things are related – e.g. temperature and the likelihood of people rioting), or content analysis (where they analyse various kinds of text – e.g. looking at images used in magazines targeted at boys or girls).

In terms of how they collect their data (whether in the context of an experiment or any other research method), two frequently used methods are self-report and observation. These can also be research methods in their own right. In self-report, participants supply data about themselves in response to questions asked by the researchers. Questions could be asked in the context of a questionnaire or an interview. In observation, what researchers do is observe how people behave and keep a record of this. Both methods have their strengths and weaknesses and there are (as you will see later on) many different aspects to both ways of collecting data, but one to be aware of right from the start is whether the data collected are quantitative or qualitative. This is important: quantitative data takes the form of numbers (e.g. the number of people doing a particular behaviour), whereas qualitative data takes the form of words (e.g. quotes of things that people say).

All research in psychology requires participants – these are the people whose behaviour is studied. Ideally, researchers should identify a target population of the sort of people they want to find out more about (e.g. children aged 7–11) before obtaining a representative sample of these people. There are various ways in which psychologists may obtain their samples. For example, they may just use those people who are most readily available to them (e.g. their students) in what is known as an opportunity sample. Alternatively, they may advertise for volunteers to take part in their research – this is known as a self-selected sample. Another method they may use is to collect together the names of all the people in their target population and then select a sample of them in a totally random way (e.g. taking out names from a hat) – this is known as a random sample. Equally, they may ask the participants that they've got to suggest other people who meet their requirements – this is known as snowball sampling. If their sample genuinely is representative of their target population, then it should be possible to generalise from how the sample has behaved to how the people in the target population would behave.

On occasions, psychologists may decide that the appropriate participants for their research are not people but animals. This may be for a number of reasons, such as the faster breeding cycle of many

 Stop and ask yourself ...

- Check your understanding of *non-experimental research methods and different aspects of data collection* by seeing if you can say what is meant by the following:
  - Case studies
  - Correlation studies
  - Content analysis
  - Self-report
  - Observation
  - Quantitative data
  - Qualitative data
  - Snowball sampling

Links to methodological issues
- Check your understanding

animals or because animals are unlikely to try working out what the researchers are studying about them. You will see some interesting examples of animal research during the course (e.g. Blakemore and Cooper's study of the impact of the visual environment on cats in Unit 2; Zajonc's study of the effects of an audience on cockroaches in the sport option within Unit 3), but they will clearly raise issues of the extent to which it is possible to generalise from animal behaviour to human behaviour.

Whether research is conducted on humans or animals, a vital consideration at all times is the way in which those being studied are treated. This is known as ethics, and the British Psychological Society (BPS) lay down clear guidelines that need to be adhered to. In broad terms, the ethical guidelines require that human participants in psychological research should give informed consent to take part, not be deceived, be given the chance to withdraw from the study, be protected from harm, be debriefed at the end, and have their results kept confidential. For animal participants, the requirements are that stress and suffering are avoided or minimised, other options apart from animal research are considered, and as few animals as possible are used in the research.

Another consideration for researchers is the time period over which to collect their data. In most cases, data are collected from participants in one go (e.g. participants come along to a laboratory, take part in an experiment, and are then thanked and waved goodbye). This is known as a snapshot study. Alternatively, researchers may follow the progress of the same people over a lengthy period of time, revisiting the same participants many times to see what, if anything, has changed. This is known as a longitudinal study. If researchers want to see how people change over time, but they don't want to carry out a longitudinal study, then they may carry out a cross-sectional study in which they look at different people of different ages. This is a particular form of snapshot study that gains some of the benefits of a longitudinal study without taking up so much time, and you will see an example of this in Unit 2 when you look at the work by Lee *et al.* in which they studied samples of children aged 7, 9 and 11. The above is not intended to provide you with a comprehensive knowledge of research methods but it should, hopefully, give you a sense of some of the key concepts that you'll be encountering.

Stop and ask yourself ...

- Check your understanding of things to consider in relation to the people (or non-human animals) being studied in research by seeing if you can say what is meant by the following:
  - Target population
  - Sample
  - Opportunity sample
  - Self-selected sample
  - Random sample
  - Six ethical guidelines for human participants
  - Three ethical guidelines for animal participants

Links to methodological issues
- Check your understanding

Stop and ask yourself ...

- Check your understanding of *the difference between snapshot and longitudinal studies* by seeing if you can say what is meant by the following:
  - Snapshot study
  - Longitudinal study
  - Cross-sectional study

Links to methodological issues
- Check your understanding

Methodological issues

As you may already have sensed, there are issues with much of the above. For instance, field experiments may be more true-to-life (or ecologically valid) than laboratory experiments, but will it be possible to impose adequate controls on them? Likewise, administering questionnaires may be a good way for researchers to collect data quickly from a large sample of people, but aren't the people filling them in likely to lie and give answers that present them in a good light (i.e. give socially desirable responses)? Similarly, when they're obtaining their sample, if researchers just use the people that are available to them (e.g. students), won't they all share certain characteristics and therefore be limited in their generalisability?

Questions like this can be seen as methodological issues, and in Section A of the exam for Unit 2 you can be expected to be asked questions that test your ability to see some of the problems of this kind that the core studies encounter (see Table 2).

Table 2 Methodological issues

Methodological issue	What it's all about
Research method	Which research method has been used? All have strengths and weaknesses. For example, laboratory experiments may lack ecological validity, while it may be difficult to impose controls on field experiments. It may be difficult to generalise about case studies, while correlation studies cannot tell us anything about cause-and-effect.
Data	Has a study collected quantitative data, qualitative data, or both? The main strength of quantitative data is that data can be collected together into graphs and tables, allowing us to see patterns in behaviour quite easily. The main strength of qualitative data is that it can add 'richness', helping us to understand why people behave the way they do.
Ethical guidelines	Have the ethical guidelines been adhered to? Many of the classic (older) studies were carried out before the introduction of formal ethical guidelines, so for this reason they may be open to criticism. Even with contemporary (modern) research there may be issues as psychologists try to balance the need to treat their participants with respect against the need to conduct research that generates valid results (e.g. if participants are fully informed about the aims of the study, then will they behave 'naturally'?)
Validity	Validity relates to whether a study has measured what it is intending to measure. Features of the research that may prevent this from happening could include the use of self-report as a way of collecting data (as participants could lie in the responses they give), inadequate controls on an experiment (meaning that extraneous variables could be the reason for the results, rather than the independent variable), or the participants working out the aims of the study and adjusting their behaviour accordingly (i.e. responding to the 'demand characteristics' of the investigation). A particular aspect of validity which should be borne in mind is ecological validity, which is the extent to which a particular investigation resembles real life: as you'll see, laboratory experiments often lack ecological validity, meaning that they may tell us very little about how people are likely to behave in real-life settings.
Reliability	Reliability relates to consistency. For example, are the researchers collecting data in the same way from all participants? Is their sample of participants large enough for them to be able to claim that what they have seen is a consistent effect (as opposed to just a fluke, 'one-off' finding)? Have they collected data in a number of different ways, such that results from the different measures can be compared, to see if they are consistent with each other and 'telling the same story'?
Sample	Is their sample of participants one that can be generalised from? Factors that could limit their ability to do this could relate to the sample being quite small in number and/or of the same age, gender or cultural background. It is worth considering what the sampling method was in a particular study, as this can often contribute to the extent to which a sample is generalisable. For example, if a researcher is based in a university and they obtain their sample via opportunity sampling, then their sample is likely to consist mainly or solely of students. How typical are such people of the wider population?
Ethnocentrism	Ethnocentrism is about the extent to which findings apply to people from varying cultures. There are over seven billion people on the planet and customs, values and norms vary between different cultures, regions, towns or groups. Research is 'ethnocentric' if it claims to speak about 'people in general' when there are good grounds for supposing that it only actually speaks about people from the culture in which the research was conducted, as people from that culture may be different from people elsewhere. In this case it is not possible to generalise from what is true about them to what is true about 'people in general'. Ethnocentrism can also mean seeing one's own group as better than other groups, or only seeing the world from your own point of view, or the point of view of your group or your culture. This often leads us to believe that our ethnic group, nation, religion, scout group or football team is superior to all others (*ethnocentric bias*).
	It is important to note that research has to be done *somewhere*, and just because a study is carried out in a single culture, it doesn't automatically mean that it is ethnocentric. For example, the research may be biological (in which case it is unlikely to be ethnocentric as beneath our surface differences we all function in the same ways, meaning that it doesn't matter where a biological study is conducted), or the sample of people may all live within the same culture but they come from a wide, multi-cultural range of backgrounds. Alternatively, a researcher may decide to carry out cross-cultural research and repeat their study in a range of different cultures around the world to confirm whether their findings genuinely are true of people across the world (i.e. 'people in general') or were merely true of people from the first culture in which the study was carried out.

Debates

Something else to keep in mind as you look at psychological research will be some of the wider debates that go on within the subject (see Table 3). The various core studies can be seen as contributing evidence towards different sides of these debates, and it will be important for you to reflect on which debates they contribute to, and how. This is something that you can expect to be asked about in Section B of the Unit 2 exam and, to give you some ideas, we have included a few reflections of our own within this book. However, please bear in mind that just because we haven't commented on a particular study in relation to a particular debate doesn't mean that it has nothing to say in relation to this debate. Please feel free to challenge what we have written and to generate ideas of your own.

Table 3 Subjects for debate

Debate	What it's all about
Nature/nurture	Whether the ways in which we behave are the result of our genetic inheritance (i.e. our 'natures') or how we have been brought up (i.e. how we have been 'nurtured').
Free will/determinism	Whether we have control over how we behave (such that it can be seen as freely chosen) or whether how we behave is out of our control (i.e. it is determined for us in some way – maybe by biological or environmental factors).
Reductionism/holism	A debate about how best to understand human behaviour – either as arising from very basic causes (e.g. hormones, or particular patterns of neural connections) such that the task of the psychologist is to identify these causes through carefully controlled experiments in which variables are isolated and tested one at a time (reductionism), or as the result of many different factors interacting with each other such that models need to be developed to capture all of these different factors and how they interact (holism).
Individual/situational explanations	Whether a particular behaviour is because of factors internal to an individual (particularly their personality) or because of the circumstances (situation) in which they find themselves.
Usefulness of research	Psychological research can be seen as useful when it has practical applications that improve people's lives. However, there is a debate to be had about whether psychological research needs to be useful in this practical sense or whether it is sufficient for it to be intrinsically useful (i.e. to further our understanding and therefore contribute to psychology as an academic discipline). The methodology may increase or decrease usefulness.
Ethical considerations	It may seem uncontroversial that the ethical guidelines should be adhered to, but there is a debate to be had about whether these guidelines can prevent really worthwhile research from taking place and whether it is possible that the benefits of a study can outweigh problems with how the participants are treated (i.e. whether the end justifies the means). Is it ever justifiable to conduct research that breaches ethical guidelines?
Conducting socially sensitive research	Research can be defined as socially sensitive if it has wider (negative) implications '... either directly for the participants in the research or for the class of individuals represented by the research' (Sieber and Stanley, 1988). Examples might centre on whether parenting styles can play a role in children developing eating disorders, or whether growing up with the internet has an unalterable effect on children's brains. The debate is about whether psychologists should refrain from investigating topics that are especially socially sensitive (because of the impact their findings could potentially have), or whether doing so is the only way to challenge prejudices and arrive at the truth.
Psychology as a science	Research can be seen as scientific if it is objective (i.e. the findings are a matter of fact, rather than opinion), replicable (i.e. if the study is repeated, the same results are obtained), and falsifiable (i.e. in principle, it would be possible to prove the findings wrong). However, quite aside from discussing whether individual pieces of research meet these criteria or not, there is a broader debate to be had about whether conducting controlled scientific research is the best way to achieve understanding of human behaviour.

- Check your understanding of *debates* in psychology by seeing if you can say what is meant by the following:
  - The nature/nurture debate
  - The free will/determinism debate
  - The difference between reductionism and holism
  - The difference between individual and situational explanations of behaviour
  - Why there is a debate about whether research in psychology needs to be useful
  - The debate about adhering to ethical guidelines
  - The debate about conducting socially sensitive research
  - Features of research that make it 'scientific'

- Check your understanding

The core studies

As we have already mentioned, if you are following the A Level course there are 20 core studies that you will need to be familiar with, and if you are following the AS Level course there are ten core studies with which you will need to be familiar. In relation to each core study, you need to be able to **tell the story** of it, which means being able to say:

- Why it was carried out (i.e. its aims and background)
- How it was carried out (i.e. its procedure, including design and the use of any materials/apparatus)
- On whom it was carried out and how they were obtained (i.e. its sample and sampling method)
- What it found out (i.e. its results)
- What we have learned from the study (i.e. its conclusions).

You need to know these details for when you are asked questions (in Section A of the Unit 2 exam) about a particular core study on its own. However, you should also expect to be asked questions in the same section about how the two core studies within a pair can be **compared**.

- If asked to say how the classic and contemporary studies that are paired together are **similar to** or **different from** each other, you may find it easiest to refer to methodological issues (e.g. they are similar in terms of the research method they use, the samples they base their research upon, or aspects of their procedures) but, equally, you could make reference to debates (e.g. they are similar in terms of the position they adopt within a particular debate).
- If asked to discuss **the extent to which the contemporary study changes our understanding of the key theme**, you may feel that it changes it quite a lot, or you may feel that it barely changes

our understanding at all (e.g. it only extends it, but doesn't fundamentally alter it). The main thing will be your ability to justify the comments you make by reference to the studies concerned.

- If asked to discuss **the extent to which the contemporary study changes our understanding of individual, social and cultural diversity**, you may find it helpful to look at such aspects of the studies as where they were carried out (e.g. if they were done in the same culture) or who they were carried out on (e.g. if they were done on people of roughly the same age, gender or occupation). If both the classic and contemporary studies were carried out on people with the same personalities or with the same psychological disorders then it could be argued that the contemporary study may not change our understanding of **individual** diversity. If both the classic and contemporary studies were carried out on people of the same age, gender or occupation (e.g. students) then it could be argued that the contemporary study may not change our understanding of **social** diversity. If both the classic and contemporary studies were carried out on people from the same cultural group then it could be argued that the contemporary study may not change our understanding of **cultural** diversity.

It is also worth being aware that in Section C of the Unit 2 exam you will be tested on your ability to **apply the core studies to 'real-world' issues**. This might mean using them to help achieve an understanding of why people behave the way they do in real-life situations, or maybe using them to make suggestions about how problems in real-life situations could be overcome. There will be more guidance on this later on in this textbook (see Chapter 6), but hopefully as you go through the course, you will start to notice connections between what you do in the classroom and what you see (or read about) in the world around you.

Areas

As you have already seen, research in psychology is done in different areas – the social area, the cognitive area, the developmental area, the biological area, and the individual differences area. All have different strengths and drawbacks (some of which are outlined at the start of each chapter), and you will need to know about these for Section B of the Unit 2 exam.

You will also need to be aware of ways in which the various areas of psychology are similar to or different from each other. As you become familiar with them, reflect on such considerations as the following:

- The sorts of research method that they tend to favour
- Whether there are any common characteristics shared by the samples of participants that they typically use in their research
- The extent to which they use technical equipment
- The types of data that they typically collect
- The assumptions that they make about why we behave the way we do.

Perspectives

As we have noted, psychologists work within different areas (e.g. the social area or the developmental area) and seek answers to questions within these areas. However, in doing this, they may approach these questions from different perspectives. A perspective can be defined as a set of ideas that have been developed at a theoretical level, and psychologists use these ideas to try and explain human behaviour.

Over the years, a number of different perspectives have been developed in psychology, such as:

- The psychodynamic perspective
- The behaviourist perspective
- The humanist perspective
- The evolutionary perspective.

In this course, we need to focus on the first two of these perspectives, although you may find it interesting to investigate the other two perspectives through further reading. As with the five areas, you can expect to be asked questions about the two perspectives in Sections B and C of the Unit 2 exam.

The behaviourist perspective

This perspective was launched by John Watson in 1913 when he published his classic article 'Psychology as the behaviourist views it'. To understand the position that Watson adopted, one needs to bear in mind the context

in which Watson was writing. At that time, psychology was still a very young academic discipline – the world's first laboratory set up expressly for the study of human behaviour had only been opened in 1879 (by Wilhelm Wundt in Leipzig, Germany) – and the way in which psychology was done was through introspection, which meant the examination of one's own mental state, albeit in as calm and methodical a way as possible. For Watson, this was insufficiently rigorous, and he was clear in arguing not only that introspection should be rejected as a method but that terms like 'mental state', 'mind' and 'emotion' should be abandoned on the grounds that they have no explanatory value.

The defining features of behaviourism are as follows:

- Psychology should be seen as a *science* and should be studied in a scientific manner.
- The only subject matter for psychology should be *behaviours* which can be observed and measured, rather than internal events, like thinking and emotion.
- The major influence on human behaviour is learning from the *environment*.
- There is little difference between the learning that takes place in humans and that in other animals, therefore research can be carried out on *animals* as well as on humans.

The focus of behaviourism was placed firmly on an attempt to understand the processes by which learning takes place. Believing that humans are born *tabula rasa* (i.e. as blank slates) and that everything is learned after birth, behaviourists have proposed three processes by which learning takes place:

1. Classical conditioning (i.e. learning through association)
2. Operant conditioning (i.e. learning as the result of rewards and punishments)
3. Social learning theory (i.e. learning through observing and imitating the behaviour of others).

Pavlov's dogs: an example of classical conditioning. The dogs associated the sound of a bell with food

Table 4 Strengths and weaknesses of the behaviourist perspective

Strengths of the behaviourist perspective	Weaknesses of the behaviourist perspective
It highlights the role of *nurture* in learning, showing the important influence environment has on our behaviour.	It ignores the influence of *nature* on behaviour, failing to take account of the way in which genetics and biology can place limits on what individuals can learn.
It can be extremely *useful*, having practical applications in a range of different settings including clinical ones (e.g. it suggests ways in which phobias can be unlearned as well as learned).	The lessons behaviourism teaches us can be *difficult* to *apply* (e.g. how are we to control what our children are or are not exposed to?) and/or are open to *inappropriate* use.
The focus on studying observable behaviour in controlled laboratory experiments helps give psychology *scientific credibility*.	By favouring the laboratory experiment as a research method, behaviourist research can *lack ecological validity* and therefore fail to resemble behaviours that people might perform in real life.

You will encounter some of these processes in the core studies you will look at: for example, Bandura *et al.*'s research into transmission of aggression (the bobo doll study) will illustrate social learning theory, while Chaney *et al.*'s study with the Funhaler will illustrate operant conditioning.

The psychodynamic perspective

The psychodynamic perspective originated with the work of Sigmund Freud and focuses on the role of the unconscious mind and our past experiences as the cause of our current behaviours. Freud believed that the mind operates on three levels: the conscious, the preconscious and the unconscious. An iceberg analogy is commonly used to distinguish between each of the 'levels' of consciousness in the mind:

- Our conscious mind is what we are currently thinking about.
- Our preconscious mind can be accessed with relative ease by retrieving stored memories.
- Our unconscious mind, however, is hidden from our awareness and Freud suggests that it is very hard, if not impossible, to access it directly.

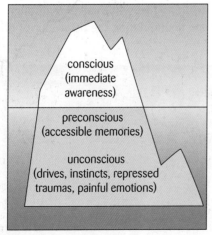

Freud's 'iceberg' analogy of the conscious, preconscious and subconscious

Freud claimed that the content of our unconscious mind is revealed in our dreams and also through 'slips of the tongue' – hence why it is so important to analyse these. Other techniques to try and access the content of the unconscious mind include free association (in which patients are encouraged to lie down comfortably on a couch and speak aloud any thoughts that come into their head) and projective tests, in which patients are presented with ambiguous stimuli (e.g. inkblots in the Rorschach test) and asked to say what they see in them; their comments are seen as a reflection (projection) of their unconscious conflicts.

In conjunction with the above, Freud claimed that we have no control over our unconscious and therefore have no free will. Behaviour is motivated from the unconscious by two instinctual drives: Eros (the life instinct) and Thanatos (the death instinct). He also believed that the personality has three parts which reside in the unconscious called the id, the ego and the superego. The id and superego can create conflict for the ego if the desires of the id (to spend unconscious energy) are disapproved of by the moral conscience, the superego. Failure of the ego to resolve this conflict (for example, by using defence mechanisms such as repression, displacement or denial) can lead to 'ego anxiety' which is, according to the 'psychodynamic perspective', the cause of mental health problems.

You will encounter psychodynamic ideas in a number of the core studies. For example, Freud's case study of Little Hans will illustrate his theory of psychosexual development, while Kohlberg will make explicit reference to Freud's theory of moral development when discussing the background to his own work. On top of this, the study by Hancock *et al.* into the language used by psychopaths will arguably invoke a number of different psychodynamic concepts, such as the unconscious, drives and ego defence mechanisms, as well as citing research that made explicit reference to psychodynamic concepts and techniques.

Table 5 Strengths and weaknesses of the psychodynamic perspective

Strengths of the psychodynamic perspective	Weaknesses of the psychodynamic perspective
It offers an explanation for why people *develop* mental disorders and, by highlighting the importance of the unconscious mind as an influence on our feelings and behaviour, Freud was the first to stress how abnormal behaviour could be caused by psychological factors.	It is *unscientific* in its analysis of human behaviour. In particular, many of the concepts central to Freud's theories can neither be verified (proved correct) nor falsified (proved wrong) – they are not open to a process of scientific testing.
It suggests ways in which people with mental disorders can be *helped* (treated) – namely, through Freud's 'talking cure' in which patients are given insight into the origins of their disorder. Although most modern therapists do not use Freudian principles, Freud's legacy is apparent in modern forms of counselling.	The evidence for psychodynamic theory is taken from Freud's case studies. The main problem here is that case studies are based on studying one person in detail and the evidence from such studies is highly subjective and can be affected by researcher bias. This puts the validity of the findings into question and makes *generalisations* to the wider population difficult.
Freud's work made *the case study method* popular in psychology. Case studies provide in - depth detail about a person or client's experiences, both current and in the past. The case study method remains popular in the area of abnormal psychology.	

 Stop and ask yourself …

- Check your understanding of the two *perspectives* by seeing if you can do the following:
  - Outline what is meant by the behaviourist perspective, as well as two strengths and two weaknesses of it.
  - Outline what is meant by the psychodynamic perspective, as well as two strengths and two weaknesses of it.

Links to methodological issues
- Check your understanding

The specification requires that you are familiar with the defining principles and concepts of these two perspectives, as well as with research that illustrates them and the strengths and weaknesses of them. On top of this, you will need to be aware of ways in which the two perspectives can be applied and the ways in which they are similar to or different from each other.

In terms of applications of the two perspectives, the key consideration to reflect on will be the sorts of people who could potentially make use of research from within the different perspectives. Examples might include the following:

- Parents
- Teachers
- Managers (e.g. of businesses, prisons, schools or colleges)
- People involved in marketing consumer products
- Those delivering psychological treatments to people with disorders (e.g. phobias).

Research on psychological perspectives can be used by people who deliver psychological treatments to help patients with phobias

When considering *who* could apply research from within these perspectives and *how* they could apply this research, you should also consider whether there are any factors that might make applying the research *difficult*. Time and cost are always relevant factors to consider, as well as the amount of training that a practitioner might require, but see if you can come up with other limitations too.

In terms of ways in which the two perspectives are similar to or different from each other, as you become familiar with those studies that draw on these perspectives, you should reflect on the same sort of considerations as apply to the five different areas of psychology. These are:

● The sorts of research method that they tend to favour
● Whether there are any common characteristics shared by the samples of participants that they typically use in their research
● The extent to which they use technical equipment
● The types of data that they typically collect
● The assumptions that they make about why we behave the way we do.

Let's get on with it!

This section of the book has contained many different concepts and you may be feeling as if your head is going to burst with all the new ideas. Instead of trying to hang on to all of this right away, the best thing to do at this point will be to start looking at research. Treat this chapter as a reference point to come back to when you encounter new terminology and to suggest ideas about how else the various core studies could have been carried out.

For now, though, let's turn to some actual research, and where better to start than with Stanley Milgam's classic study of obedience? Welcome to one of the most controversial studies in the history of the subject.

Part 1

Psychological themes through core studies

Chapter 1

The social area

In 1985, Gordon W. Allport put forward the classic definition of social psychology as 'an attempt to understand and explain how the thoughts, feelings and behaviour of individuals are influenced by the actual, imagined or implied presence of others.' This idea – that, to understand human behaviour, we need to understand the social context in which it occurs – lies at the heart of the social area of psychology and it helps to set the parameters for the research concerns of social psychologists.

However, the broad nature of Allport's definition masks the way in which social psychologists work, as what they do is to focus on one particular social process at a time and then try to achieve an in-depth understanding of it (Table 1.1). The particular social processes they examine are often triggered by recent real-world events (such as the studies we will be looking at by Milgram on obedience and Piliavin et al. on helping behaviour) but, equally, can be of relatively 'timeless' concern (such as trying to understand the relationship between attitudes and behaviour, or the reasons why we find some people more attractive than others).

In terms of how social psychologists conduct their research, a wide range of methods are used. That said, field experiments – in which an independent variable is manipulated to see its effect on behaviour in a real-life setting – have been used more often in social psychology than perhaps in other areas of the subject. We will see examples of this in the studies by Piliavin et al. and also by Levine et al. Other commonly used methods include surveys, as a means by which to find out people's attitudes towards something, and – because social psychologists are as systematic and scientific in how they approach their research as psychologists working in other areas of the subject – laboratory experiments.

The particular social studies we will be examining are outlined in Table 1.2.

Table 1.1 Strengths and weaknesses of the social area

Strengths of the social area	Weaknesses of the social area
Research within the social area can help *improve our understanding* of human behaviour, particularly the extent to which this is affected by other people.	Findings from research within the social area *may not be true for all time* (as social situations can change over time).
Research within the social area can be extremely *useful*, having practical applications in a range of different settings.	Findings from research within the social area *may not be true for all places* (as social situations can change from one culture to another).
Research within the social area often helps to *bring psychology to wider audiences*, given the way in which research often seeks to explain real-world events.	Given the socially sensitive nature of much research within the social area, it can be *difficult to stay within the ethical guidelines*.
Research within the social area is often *high in ecological validity*, particularly if it makes use of field experiments.	The *boundaries can become blurred* between the social area and, say, the cognitive area (particularly when looking at social cognition).

Table 1.2 Classic and contemporary studies discussed in this chapter

Key theme	Classic study	Contemporary study
Responses to people in authority	Milgram (1963) Obedience	Bocchiaro et al. (2012) Disobedience and whistle-blowing
Responses to people in need	Piliavin et al. (1969) Subway Samaritan	Levine et al. (2001) Cross-cultural altruism

Further reading

Bocchiaro, P., Zimbardo, P.G. and Van Lange, P.A.M., 2012, 'To Defy Or Not To Defy: An Experimental Study of the Dynamics of Disobedience And Whistle-Blowing'. *Social Influence*, vol. 7, no 1, 35–50.

Levine, R.V., Norenzayan, A. and Philbrick, K., 2001, 'Cross-Cultural Differences in Helping Strangers'. *Journal of Cross-Cultural Psychology*, vol. 32, no 5, 543–560.

Milgram, S., 1963, 'Behavioural Study of Obedience'. *Journal of Abnormal and Social Psychology*, vol. 67, no 4, 371–378.

Piliavin, I., Rodin, J. and Piliavin, J., 1969, 'Good Samaritanism: An Underground Phenomenon?' *Journal of Personality and Social Psychology*, vol. 13, no 4, 289–299.

Responses to people in authority

The relationships we have with other people can be characterised as being either *horizontal* (e.g. the relationship of equals that we have with our friends) or *vertical* (e.g. the relationships we have with our teachers or our employers in which they may give us commands about how to behave). Within a vertical relationship, the person who issues commands is in a position of authority, while the person who receives their commands can be described as subordinate to them.

Some positions of authority may be deliberately sought out (e.g. if someone actively seeks to be appointed as a manager at work, or to be elected as a politician), whereas others may just emerge (e.g. if you become a parent, you are an authority figure in the eyes of your child whether you like it or not). People will often find themselves in positions of authority in some areas of their lives (e.g. as a parent, or as the coach of their child's football team), while in other areas of their lives they will be in more subordinate positions, having to respond to those in positions of authority over them (e.g. their boss at work).

When, as subordinates, we agree with the commands issued by people in positions of authority, there are few problems. However, what if we disagree with something that a person in a position of authority instructs us to do? This is when problems can arise.

There are many ways in which we can respond to the requests made by people in positions of authority – in particular, we can do what they ask of us (known as compliance, or obedience), or we can refuse to follow the instructions we have been given (i.e. be disobedient). Of course, there is much more to it than this (e.g. on the outside we could be obedient but inside we could be simmering with resentment; we could be obedient to the major request that has been made of us, but then try to compensate for this by disobeying more minor requests) but, in terms of how we *behave* in response to a specific request made of us by a person in a position of authority, it may well come down to having to be either obedient or disobedient.

To what extent are people obedient? What would it take for someone to be disobedient? Are some people more likely to be disobedient than others? If so, what are the characteristics of those people who are most likely to disobey the orders placed on them? These are all interesting questions worthy of investigation, but what it is crucial to note is that they are of much more than mere academic interest.

In 1933, the Nazis set up their first concentration camp at Dachau, outside Munich in southern Germany. Many more followed as the Nazis imprisoned people viewed as socially or politically undesirable and used them as slave labour. Later on, death camps were set up with the specific aim of systematically killing those groups of people of which Adolf Hitler did not approve. It was at these death camps, built mainly on occupied land in Poland, that 'the final solution' to what Hitler saw as 'the Jewish problem' was to be enacted. However, for this to happen, Hitler needed the people working in the death camps to obey orders to kill people en masse. It is to try and understand how this and other atrocities could have happened that it is so important for psychologists to investigate how people respond to those in positions of authority.

Milgram (1963)

Between 1933 and 1945, millions of innocent people were systematically slaughtered on command in Nazi Germany. For Milgram, it is a social fact that the individual who is commanded by a legitimate authority ordinarily obeys. He sought to devise a technique for studying obedience in which participants would be ordered to administer to a victim what they believed to be electric shocks; this was done in the context of a 'learning experiment' apparently set up to study the effects of punishment on memory. Milgram was interested in discovering the point at which participants would refuse to go on. He also envisaged a series of follow-up experiments in which aspects of the procedure (e.g. the gender of participants; the location in which the experiment was conducted) would be systematically varied to discover those factors that alter the degree of obedience to the experimental commands.

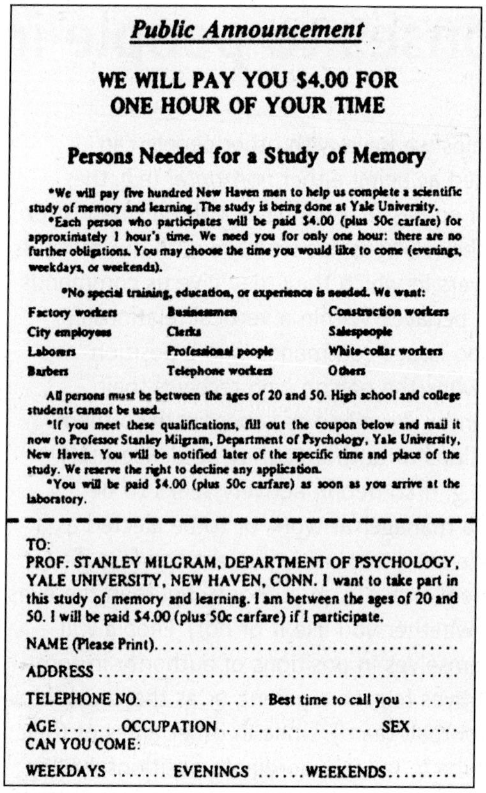

Public Announcement

WE WILL PAY YOU $4.00 FOR ONE HOUR OF YOUR TIME

Persons Needed for a Study of Memory

*We will pay five hundred New Haven men to help us complete a scientific study of memory and learning. The study is being done at Yale University.
*Each person who participates will be paid $4.00 (plus 50c carfare) for approximately 1 hour's time. We need you for only one hour: there are no further obligations. You may choose the time you would like to come (evenings, weekdays, or weekends).

*No special training, education, or experience is needed. We want:

Factory workers   Businessmen   Construction workers
City employees   Clerks   Salespeople
Laborers   Professional people White-collar workers
Barbers   Telephone workers   Others

All persons must be between the ages of 20 and 50. High school and college students cannot be used.
*If you meet these qualifications, fill out the coupon below and mail it now to Professor Stanley Milgram, Department of Psychology, Yale University, New Haven. You will be notified later of the specific time and place of the study. We reserve the right to decline any application.
*You will be paid $4.00 (plus 50c carfare) as soon as you arrive at the laboratory.

- -

TO:
PROF. STANLEY MILGRAM, DEPARTMENT OF PSYCHOLOGY, YALE UNIVERSITY, NEW HAVEN, CONN. I want to take part in this study of memory and learning. I am between the ages of 20 and 50. I will be paid $4.00 (plus 50c carfare) if I participate.

NAME (Please Print)....................................

ADDRESS ....

TELEPHONE NO. .... Best time to call you ....

AGE........OCCUPATION.....................SEX......
CAN YOU COME:

WEEKDAYS .... EVENINGS ......WEEKENDS.........

Figure 1.1 Milgram's advertisement, taken from *Obedience to Authority*

Participants

The participants were 40 males between the ages of 20 and 50, drawn from New Haven and the surrounding communities. They were obtained through a newspaper advertisement (Figure 1.1) and direct mailing. They believed that they were taking part in a study of memory and learning.

Table 1.3 shows the distribution of age and occupational types in the experiment.

Participants were paid $4.50 for their participation in the experiment. They were told that the payment was made simply for coming to the laboratory and was theirs to keep no matter what happened after they arrived.

Table 1.3 Distribution of age and occupational types of Milgram's participants

Occupations	Number aged 20–29 years	Number aged 30–39 years	Number aged 40–50 years	Percentage of total (occupations)
Workers, skilled and unskilled	4	5	6	37.5
Sales, business and white collar	3	6	7	40.0
Professional	1	5	3	22.5
Percentage of total (age)	20	40	40	

🚫 **Stop and ask yourself...**

- Why do you suppose Milgram advertised for the particular sorts of people that he did (i.e. men from New Haven aged 20–50 in a specific range of jobs)?
- Why do you suppose he settled on a sample of 40 participants (rather than have more than this, or fewer than this)?
- What was Milgram's sampling method? Why do you suppose Milgram chose to obtain his sample in the way that he did (i.e. through a process of would-be participants responding to an advertisement)?

Links to methodological issues

- Sample

- Sampling method

Personnel and locale

The experiment was conducted on the grounds of Yale University. The role of experimenter was played by a 31-year-old high school teacher of biology; he wore a grey lab-coat and remained somewhat stern throughout the experiment. The victim was played by a 47-year-old accountant whom most observers found mild-mannered and likeable.

Procedure

Each run of the experiment involved one naive participant and the victim. The experimenter explained to them that the purpose of the experiment was to find out about the effect of punishment on learning. The naive participant and the victim then drew slips of paper from a hat to determine who would be the learner in the experiment. The draw was rigged so that the naive participant was always the teacher.

The teacher and learner were then taken to an adjacent room and the learner was strapped into an 'electric chair' apparatus. An electrode (which participants were told was connected to an electric shock generator in the adjoining room) was attached to the learner's wrist, and electrode paste was applied 'to avoid blisters and burns'. In response to a question by the learner, the experimenter declared, 'Although the shocks can be extremely painful, they cause no permanent tissue damage.'

Learning task. The lesson administered by the teacher comprised a word-pair task in which the teacher read a series of word pairs to the learner and then read the first word of the pair along with four terms. The learner was to indicate which of the four terms had originally been paired with the first word. He communicated his answer by pressing one of four switches in front of him, which in turn lit up one of four numbered quadrants in an answer-box located on top of the electric shock generator.

Shock generator. The electric shock generator (Figure 1.2) was constructed with care to look as authentic as possible. The instrument panel consisted of 30 switches set in a horizontal line. Each switch was clearly labelled with a voltage designation ranging from 15 volts up to 450 volts. There was a 15-volt increment from one switch to the next going from left to right. Verbal designations were also assigned to each group of four switches as follows (going from left to right): Slight Shock, Moderate Shock, Strong Shock, Very Strong Shock, Intense Shock, Extreme Intensity Shock, Danger: Severe Shock. (Two switches after this last designation were simply marked XXX).

Sample shock. Before beginning his run as a teacher, each naive participant would be given a sample shock. This was always administered to the wrist of the teacher

Figure 1.2 Milgram's shock generator

and it was always 45 volts, applied by pressing the third switch of the generator. The aim of this part of the procedure was to convince the participant of the authenticity of the generator. The electric shock came from a 45-volt battery wired into the generator.

Shock instructions. The teacher was instructed to administer a shock to the learner each time he gave a wrong response. Crucially, he was told to 'move one level higher on the shock generator each time the learner flashes a wrong answer', and to announce the voltage level before administering the shock. (This was to remind the teacher of the increasing intensity of the shocks he was giving).

Feedback from the victim. The learner gave a predetermined set of responses to the word-pair test, based on a schedule of three wrong answers to one correct answer. When the 300-volt shock was administered, the learner kicked the wall. After that, he gave no answer to the next word-pair. At this point, the experimenter instructed the teacher to wait 5–10 seconds before treating the absence of a response as a wrong answer. After the 315-volt shock was administered, the victim kicked the wall again. After that, there was no further feedback from the victim – neither answers to the word-pair exercises nor any further kicking the wall.

Experimenter feedback. If the participant indicated his unwillingness to go on, the experimenter responded with a series of standardised 'prods', made in the following sequence:

Prod 1. 'Please continue', or 'Please go on.'
Prod 2: 'The experiment requires that you continue.'
Prod 3: 'It is absolutely essential that you continue.'
Prod 4: 'You have no other choice, you *must* go on.'

If the participant asked if the learner was liable to suffer permanent physical injury, the experimenter said, 'Although the shocks may be painful, there is no permanent tissue damage, so please go on.' If the participant said that the learner did not want to go on, the experimenter replied, 'Whether the learner likes it or not, you must go on until he has learned all the word pairs correctly. So please go on.' (Both of these special prods were then followed by prods 2, 3 and 4, if necessary.)

Dependent measures. A participant who broke off at any point prior to administering the thirtieth shock level (i.e. 450 volts) was deemed to be a 'defiant' participant. An 'obedient' participant was one who complied with experimental commands fully and proceeded to administer all shock levels commanded.

Interview and dehoax. Following the experiment, participants were interviewed. After this, a friendly reconciliation was arranged between the participant and the victim and an effort was made to reduce any tensions that arose as a result of the experiment to try and ensure that the participant would leave the laboratory in a state of well-being.

 Stop and ask yourself ...

- In what ways was Milgram's procedure different from the experience of working in a Nazi death camp?

Links to methodological issues
- Ecological validity

Predicted results

Fourteen final-year psychology students at Yale University were provided with a detailed description of the experimental situation and asked to predict how they would expect '100 Americans of diverse occupations, and ranging in age from 20 to 50 years' to behave. All predicted that only an insignificant minority would go through to the end of the shock series. (The estimates ranged from 0 to 3 per cent, with a mean estimate of 1.2 per cent.) Milgram also posed this question to colleagues and the general feeling was that few, if any, participants would go beyond the Very Strong Shock designation.

 **Have a go yourself**

- Describe Milgram's procedure to ten people and ask them what percentage of people they think would go all the way to the end of the shock series and give 450-volt electric shocks to another person.
- Ask them what they themselves would do if they found themselves taking part in this experiment.

Actual results

The obtained distribution of scores deviated radically from the predictions, with no participants breaking off before the 300-volt shock level, and 26 obeying the orders of the experimenter to continue giving shocks up to the 450-volt maximum (Table 1.4).

During the experiment, participants typically showed signs of extreme tension. Participants were observed to sweat, tremble, stutter, bite their lips, groan and dig their fingernails into their flesh. Fourteen of the participants showed signs of nervous laughter and smiling, while three experienced full-blown, uncontrollable seizures.

Comments made by defiant participants at the point at which they broke off suggested high levels of agitation and even anger:

I think he's trying to communicate, he's knocking. ... Well it's not fair to shock the guy ... these are terrific volts. I don't think this is very humane. ... Oh, I can't go on with this; no, this isn't right. It's a hell of an experiment. The guy is suffering in there. No, I don't want to go on. This is crazy. [Subject refused to administer more shocks.]

Conclusions

The conclusions reached by Milgram relate to the situation he created and its effects on his participants. First, he concluded that this is a situation that produces extremely strong tendencies to obey. Second, he concluded that the situation generates extraordinary tension and emotional strain.

 Stop and ask yourself ...

- How could Milgram's study be *criticised* in relation to the ethical guidelines? How could Milgram's study be *defended* in relation to the ethical guidelines?
- Other than in terms of obedience to authority, what other reasons might have caused 65 per cent of Milgram's participants to administer the highest level of electric shock?
- What was the *quantitative* data that Milgram collected? What was the *qualitative* data that Milgram collected? How/why does Milgram's study benefit from the collection of both types of data?

Links to methodological issues
- Ethics
- Validity
- Qualitative/quantitative data

Table 1.4 Distribution of break-off points

Verbal designation and voltage indication	Number of subjects for whom this was maximum shock
Slight shock	
15	0
30	0
45	0
60	0
Moderate shock	
75	0
90	0
105	0
120	0
Strong shock	
135	0
150	0
165	0
180	0
Very strong shock	
195	0
210	0
225	0
240	0
Intense shock	
255	0
270	0
285	0
300	5
Extreme intensity shock	
315	4
330	2
345	1
360	1
Danger: severe shock	
375	1
390	0
405	0
420	0
XXX	
435	0
450	26

Discussion

Milgram suggests nine features of the experiment that may explain the high levels of obedience observed in this situation:

1. The experiment was sponsored by, and took place on the grounds of, Yale University, which is an institution of unimpeachable reputation.
2. The experiment was, on the face of it, designed to attain a worthy purpose – namely, advancement of knowledge about learning and memory.
3. The participant believed the victim to have voluntarily submitted himself to the authority system of the experimenter.
4. The participant had also volunteered to take part in the experiment, and he felt under an obligation to help the experimenter.
5. Being paid to come to the laboratory strengthened the participant's sense of obligation to the experimenter.
6. From the point of view of the participant, it was purely by chance that he was the teacher and the other man was the learner; they both ran the same risk of being assigned the role of learner and so the learner couldn't complain about this.
7. There was a lack of clarity about what a psychologist could expect of a participant and when he could be over-stepping acceptable limits.
8. The par ticipants had been assured that the shocks administered to the learner were 'painful but not dangerous'.
9. As long as the learner continued to provide answers on the signal box (which he did up to the 300-volt level), it could be construed that he was willing to 'play the game'.

Milgram suggests four features of the experiment that may explain the tension experienced by the participants:

1. The participant was placed in a position in which he had to respond to competing demands from two people – the experimenter and the victim – whose demands couldn't both be met.
2. The demands of the experimenter (for abstract scientific knowledge) and the victim (for relief from physical suffering) were very different.
3. The experiment gave the participant little time for reflection.
4. The experiment involved participants experiencing conflict between the disposition not to harm other people and the tendency to obey those perceived to be legitimate authorities.

Evaluation of the study by Milgram

Links to methodological issues

Research method

- Milgram's study can in many ways be described as an experiment as it had a dependent variable (participants were counted as either obedient or disobedient, with them being separated into these two groups in accordance with whether they administered electric shocks all the way up to the 450 volt maximum, or not) and controls (e.g. the same shock generator machine was used each time; the same people played the roles of 'experimenter' and 'learner'; the feedback that the 'teacher' got from the 'learner' during the course of the study was the same each time, etc.).
- However, it is worth noting that, in itself, his original study *did not have an* independent variable. He would carry out a series of variations on his original study (e.g. doing it in an office in downtown Bridgeport, rather than at Yale University; doing it with a sample of women, instead of men) and, arguably, his original study became in effect a baseline 'control condition' that he was then able to compare the other versions of his study against (with the alteration he made each time acting as an independent variable in relation to the original study), but it remains the case that there was no independent variable within the first study itself.
- While Milgram's study arguably does not meet the criteria for it to be counted as an experiment, nonetheless its highly standardised procedure made it replicable which, as we'll see, aided its reliability.

Data

- The main quantitative data generated by Milgram's study comprised the percentages of participants who were prepared to administer electric shocks to the 'learner' up to 300 volts (100 per cent) and all the way up to 450 volts (65 per cent).
- This quantitative data proved immensely valuable as it meant that he would have something (the percentage of participants prepared to administer electric shocks to the 'learner' all the way up to the 450 volt maximum) that could be compared from one variation of his study to another and from one replication of his study in one country to another replication of it in another country.

- The qualitative data consisted of his descriptions of how those in the role of 'teacher' behaved as they progressed up the electric shock generator (e.g. sweating and trembling) and also the quotes of what they said as they did this.
- His study benefited hugely from the collection of both types of data as, without the qualitative data, we wouldn't know anything about the feelings of the participants as they administered the electric shocks. What the qualitative data reveals is that they may have done what they were told to do by the 'experimenter', but they seemed to do so without pleasure and in the context of great emotional discomfort.

Ethics

- Milgram's study was carried out before ethical guidelines were put in place. However, this has not stopped his study from being criticised in terms of how his participants were treated. Participants consented to take part but, as they were deceived about the true purpose of the study (i.e. to investigate obedience, rather than 'memory and learning'), it was not informed consent that they gave. They could clearly withdraw from the study – and 35 per cent of them did – but everything they heard from the 'experimenter' was discouraging them from doing this. No names of individual participants were reported in the original research paper but, when Milgram refers (page 375) to 'a 46-year-old encyclopedia salesman' being 'seriously embarrassed' by the 'violently convulsive' seizure that he experienced, it might have been possible for him to be identified – after all, how many people of this description would there be in the New Haven area? Most importantly, there is a strong case for arguing that participants were harmed by their involvement in this study: with fourteen showing 'definite signs of nervous laughter' (page 375) and three experiencing 'full-blown, uncontrollable seizures' (page 375), they were obviously experiencing very high levels of stress.
- In Milgram's defence, it could clearly be argued that, when he began his series of studies, he couldn't have known just how much anxiety his participants would experience. Furthermore, his participants were given a debrief ('dehoax') before they left the laboratory. In his book *Obedience to Authority*, Milgram writes

that each participant was also sent a five-page report 'specifically designed to enhance the value of his experience' (page 197), that those subjects felt to have suffered the most from participation were examined one year later by an impartial psychiatrist, and that (in response to a questionnaire) nearly 84 per cent of participants stated that they were glad to have taken part in the experiment.

Validity

- On the face of it, Milgram's study has high levels of face validity in that it would appear to be measuring what he wants to measure – namely, obedience. However, it is arguable that an explanation in terms of obedience alone is too simplistic and that the behaviour of his participants could also reflect their levels of empathy (with the 'learner') or their levels of moral courage. It is not obvious that obedience to authority is the only reason for why 65 per cent of his participants were prepared to give electric shocks up to the highest voltage available.
- In terms of ecological validity, it is obviously not an everyday occurrence to be instructed to give someone a series of electric shocks because they give incorrect answers to questions, and in that sense Milgram's study clearly lacks ecological validity. However, was the scenario that Milgram created similar to that faced by people working in the death camps in Nazi Germany? In many respects, it wasn't – for example, in the death camps, people were generally killed in large numbers all at once through use of gas, rather than individually using electricity, and Milgram's participants would not have feared that any negative consequences would happen to them or their loved ones if they were disobedient. (Most importantly, of course, Milgram's study was also unlike Nazi Germany in that no-one was actually killed in the course of his experiment.) That said, there were some similarities between the two situations, most notably the issuing of explicit instructions to do something that would (the people involved believed) cause suffering to another (innocent) person, the issuing of a payment to those carrying out these acts, the way in which the person/people being harmed were invisible to the person harming them, and the attempt to convince those doing the harm that their actions were serving some bigger, socially worthwhile purpose.

Reliability

- The whole procedure was highly replicable, as was demonstrated by the fact that Milgram was able to replicate it with 40 different participants. This was made possible by the standardised procedure.
- The way in which results were recorded (i.e. by seeing the highest voltage switch the 'teacher' pressed down before refusing to go on) would have led to anyone overseeing the procedure recording the same outcome (result) for each participant.
- In terms of whether Milgram's sample was large enough to suggest a consistent effect (and 'iron out' any anomalies), it is arguable that it was large enough to do this without being unmanageable in terms of the cost and effort involved to collect data from them.

Sample

- It can be assumed that Milgram selected his participants (men, aged 20–50, largely from working class and lower middle class backgrounds) to reflect the sorts of people who would have worked in the death camps in Nazi Germany. He would have been aiming to 'compare like with like', enabling him to see whether obedience to even the most destructive of orders was universal. However, as Milgram's participants were all from the same part of the same country and didn't, in the original study, include any women, his findings about high levels of obedience might only be true of the sorts of people in his sample.
- In his study, Milgram used a self-selected sampling method as his participants determined their own involvement in it by choosing to respond to his advertisement. It can be assumed that he used this particular sampling method as it was the best way for him to reach people from within his particular target population (of males aged 20–50 in everyday jobs).

Ethnocentrism

- Milgram's research can be seen as ethnocentric because it was only carried out in the one country (the USA), and it cannot be assumed that the levels of obedience seen among his American participants would reflect the levels of obedience seen among people in other cultures.
- That said, it can be argued that Milgram's study showed that obedience to authority is something that could be expected to be seen in different countries around the world as it was now seen in two countries – namely, Germany in the first instance, and now (within Milgram's study) the USA.

- Replications of Milgram's study were carried out by other researchers in other countries in subsequent years, and in general what was found were similarly high levels of obedience in most countries (e.g. Italy, Jordan, the UK, and Spain). This would suggest that Milgram's research findings ultimately were not true of Americans alone.

Links to debates

Individual and situational explanations debate

- The descriptions of how participants behaved whilst administering electric shocks to the learner make it clear that they were extremely uncomfortable with what they were doing. The fact, therefore, that 65 per cent of participants were still prepared to administer electric shocks all the way up to the maximum of 450 volts shows the power of the situation to influence behaviour. However, the fact that 35 per cent of participants were somehow able to resist the pressure of the situation and walk away before administering the maximum shock of 450 volts provides evidence that people's personalities can be an even greater influence on their behaviour than the situational pressures around them.
- To try and find out which features of the situation had the greatest impact on the behaviour of the participants, Milgram carried out a series of variations on his original procedure, altering one aspect of the procedure at a time, such as conducting it at an office building in Bridgeport rather than at Yale University (47.5 per cent of participants went up to 450 volts), having the victim in the same room as the teacher (40 per cent went up to 450 volts), and having two experimenters give contradictory commands about whether the teacher should stop giving electric shocks or go on (0 per cent went up to 450 volts). These helped to isolate which features of the situation were having the greatest impact on leading to the obedient behaviour.
- To try and find out whether there were any individual factors that those who were obedient or disobedient had in common, Milgram collected background information on participants. In his book *Obedience to Authority* (page 207), he reports the following:

Republicans and Democrats were not significantly different in obedience levels; Catholics were more obedient than Jews or Protestants. The better educated were more defiant than the less well educated. Those in the moral professions of law, medicine, and teaching showed greater defiance than those in the more technical professions, such as engineering and physical science. The longer one's

military service, the more obedience – except that former officers were less obedient than those who served as enlisted men, regardless of length of service.

- However, as Milgram makes clear in the same book (page 208), none of these findings were conclusive:

My overall reaction was to wonder at how few correlates there were of obedience and disobedience and how weakly they are related to the observed behaviour. I am certain that there is a complex personality basis to obedience and disobedience. But I know we have not found it.

Free will/determinism debate

- In many ways, the points made above for the debate about whether behaviour is best explained in terms of factors to do with the situation or factors to do with the individual can be applied to the free will/determinism debate. Thus, the 65 per cent of participants who administered electric shocks to the learner all the way up to the maximum 450 volts can be seen as having their behaviour determined by the situation in which they were. Against this, the 35 per cent of participants who walked away from the experiment before reaching the maximum shock of 450 volts can be seen as exercising free will and choosing how they act.

Usefulness of research

- Milgram's study, and the variations upon the original experiment, can be seen as extremely useful. For instance, it suggests to people in positions of authority that people in positions subordinate to them can generally be expected to be obedient. On top of this, the variations on Milgram's original experiment suggest that levels of obedience might be enhanced by keeping anyone who might be harmed by the person's obedient actions invisible to them and also by not having anyone else there giving contradictory orders. However, while Milgram's study could be put to positive use by responsible authority figures (e.g. in school, business or military settings), it also has the potential to be abused by those who might seek to get people to obey them for malicious purposes. A further use of the study, therefore, is for all of us to guard against blind obedience and to make our own minds up about whether the orders we are being given are ones we feel comfortable obeying.

Ethical issues

- Milgram's study was, as we've already noted, carried out before the ethical guidelines were put in place. It can also be seen as an extremely valuable piece of research that helped to resolve the question about whether what happened in Nazi Germany could have happened elsewhere. This is such an important question that it is arguable that the value of the study outweighs any harm caused to its participants (i.e. 'the end justifies the means').

- That said, would *you* have been happy taking part in his study? If not, presumably we can't just accept the way in which the participants in his study were deceived and caused such anxiety.
- You'll need to decide for yourself whether this is a study that should have been carried out, or not.

Links to areas/perspectives

- Milgram's study falls within the social area because it is revealing the extent to which people's behaviour can be influenced by other people around them: his participants did not want to administer high voltage electric shocks to the 'learner' but, in the face of the prods from the 'experimenter', they went against their desires and behaved in the way that was requested of them.
- However, apart from the social area, Milgram's study could arguably also be placed within the individual differences area because of his growing recognition that the same situation would not affect everyone in the same way and that the explanation for why some people would be obedient while others might be disobedient would require an understanding of factors to do with them as an individual (e.g. their political or religious beliefs, their level or type of education, or their level of military experience). However, this was not something that he was able to draw any conclusions about.

Links to the key theme

- In relation to the key theme of responses to people in authority, Milgram's study would appear to tell us that obedience to those in authority – even when they are asking us to cause harm to someone else – is much more common than we would like to believe.
- However, there are many questions that arise from Milgram's study, such as:
  - Would people in other countries show the same levels of obedience to authority figures as Milgram saw among his participants in the USA?
  - Would people still be as obedient to authority figures now as they were back in the early 1960s?
  - Is there anything (e.g. in terms of personality) that sets people who are disobedient apart from people who are obedient?

- Does it make a difference that the person Milgram's participants were being told to harm was someone they didn't know? Would they have behaved differently if the person being harmed was a friend of theirs?
- Would people be more or less obedient if the scenario they were presented with involved just one request being made of them (as opposed to a series of up to 30 requests)?
- Would people behave differently if disobedience didn't involve having to confront an authority figure directly?
- Would people be more likely to disobey if the idea that the research might not be ethically acceptable was raised during the course of the study?
- Would people be more likely to disobey if they were given time for reflection during the study (i.e. a sort of 'cooling off' period)?
- It is because of questions like this that research into obedience did not end with Milgram and, indeed, research in this area still continues today, as we will see when we turn to a more contemporary study by Bocchiaro *et al.* from 2012.

🔍 Find out more

- Use the internet to locate video footage of Milgram's obedience experiment.
- Find out more about the variations Milgram carried out on his original experiment (these are described in detail in his book *Obedience to Authority*).
- Find out about the replications that were carried out of Milgram's study in other countries by other researchers (e.g. in Spain, the UK, Germany, and Australia).

📋 Practice questions

1. From Milgram's study of obedience, describe why participants may have felt that they could not withdraw from this study. [2 marks]
2. From Milgram's study of obedience:
   (a) Describe the 'shock generator' apparatus used in this study. [2 marks]
   (b) Outline how the 'shock generator' apparatus was used to measure obedience. [2 marks]
3. With reference to Milgram's study of obedience, outline two quantitative findings from this study. [2 marks]
4. Identify two of the suggestions made by Milgram for why participants (the teachers) obeyed. [2 marks]

Bocchiaro et al. (2012)

Is disobedience to unjust authority a precondition for social progress? This is the claim made in this paper, whose authors wanted to find out whether people who disobey or blow the whistle have different personal characteristics from those who obey. To investigate this, they devised a new research paradigm (method of testing participants) based around a form of softer, psychological aggression than the physical violence paradigm in Milgram's research. The new paradigm involved participants facing a dilemma in which self-interest clashes with collective interest, and it gave them the chance to obey, disobey, or blow the whistle against authorities who were encouraging immoral behaviours. They believed this study to be the first to examine whistle-blowing within an experimental paradigm in a controlled laboratory setting.

Procedure

Participants for the study were recruited by flyers posted in the campus cafeteria at the VU University at Amsterdam. They received either €7 or course credit for taking part, and were informed before the procedure began about what their task was, the potential benefits/risks of participation, and that they had the right to withdraw at any time with no penalty. They were also assured of the confidentiality of the information collected, and they were given a (first) consent form to sign.

The main part of the study would then begin with a male Dutch experimenter greeting each participant as they arrived at the laboratory. Formally dressed and with a stern demeanour, he proceeded with a request for each participant to provide a few names of fellow students, and then presented the cover story:

Along with an Italian colleague I am investigating the effects of sensory deprivation on brain function. We recently conducted an experiment on six participants who spent some time completely isolated, in Rome, unable to see or hear anything. What happened was traumatic: all of those people panicked, their cognitive abilities were impaired temporarily, some experienced visual and auditory hallucinations. Two participants even asked us to stop because of their strong symptoms, but we didn't because such a decision would have implied collecting invalid data. In post-experimental interviews the majority said it was a frightening experience.

Now, our aim is to replicate this study at the VU University on a sample of college students. There are currently no data on young people, but some scientists think that their brain is more sensitive to the negative effects of isolation. It is difficult to predict what will happen, and I am worried about that... but I want to go ahead with this experiment.

A University Research Committee is evaluating whether to approve our study. Of course, they have high standards and know about the great suffering caused by extended sensory deprivation, so... I don't know... we will see what their decision is. In the meantime, the committee is collecting information... it seems they do not have clear ideas about what to do. That's why they are also interested in the feedback from students like you who happen to know details regarding my experiment. You will find Research Committee forms in the next room.

Having said all that, what I need is for you to write a statement to convince the students you indicated earlier to participate in my sensory deprivation study. We will send them your testimonial through email. And if this is OK, I will contact you in the future for other promotions... so this means money for you.

As you can see, this is a preliminary stage of the experiment, but it is also important to show members of Research Committee that people do not judge negatively sensory deprivation. I'll be back [the experimenter left the room and stayed out for 3 minutes in order to provide a time for reflection on the action-based decisions about to be made].

Let's move into the next room, there is a computer for you to perform the task. Of course, you must be enthusiastic in writing the statement. To this aim, it is requested that you use at least two adjectives among 'exciting', 'incredible', 'great', and 'superb'. Also, you cannot mention the negative effects of sensory deprivation [instructions were displayed on the computer screen as well]. *Begin your task; I'll be back* [the experimenter stayed out of the room for a full 7 minutes].

 Stop and ask yourself ...

- What sampling method did Bocchiaro et al. use?
- What are the benefits and drawbacks for them of using this particular sampling method in their study?

Links to methodological issues

- Sampling method

In the second room, participants would find a mailbox and a Research Committee form saying the following:

The Free University aims to promote excellent and ethical research. All research should strive to minimise the risk to participants, so that they will not be exposed to any more risk than they would encounter in their usual lifestyle. More in detail:

- *Participants should be protected from psychological harm (anxiety, stress, embarrassment, humiliation).*
- *Researchers should inform participants if they see signs of psychological problem of which these latter are unaware.*

If you think that the research on sensory deprivation violates the above-mentioned basic ethical norms please report this to the Human Ethics Committee by checking the box below and putting this document in the mailbox. Thanks for your valuable cooperation.

After 7 minutes, the experimenter returned and invited the participant to follow him back into the first room. Two personality inventories (the HEXACO-PI-R test, and a measure of Social Value Orientation (SVO)) were then administered and the participant was probed for suspiciousness about the nature of the study. After this, participants were given a full debrief by the experimenter, who had been trained to use simple language and to proceed slowly as he disclosed the true nature of the study (purposes, variables, hypotheses). Care was taken to ensure that participants did not feel uncomfortable about their performance (of being

obedient) and about the fact that they had been deceived. They were also asked not to discuss the study with colleagues and friends, to complete a (second) form giving consent for their data to be used, and were given an email address to contact in case they wanted to complain or ask further questions about the study.

Participants

The sample of participants who took part in this research comprised 149 undergraduate students from VU University in Amsterdam (Figure 1.3). Of these, 96 were women and 53 were men, with a mean age of 20.8 years. (There had originally been 160 participants, but 11 were removed because of their suspiciousness about the nature of the study.)

Figure 1.3 VU University, Amsterdam

 Stop and ask yourself ...

- Bocchiaro *et al.* faced (as they put it) the challenge of creating a research paradigm in which 'the psychological and emotional well-being of the participants' was protected while at the same time their participants were encouraged to engage in immoral behaviour and were extensively deceived. Do you think they succeeded in protecting their participants from harm? Do you think this study should have been given ethical approval?
- Bocchiaro *et al.* also wanted to create a paradigm that has 'mundane realism', but to what extent did they succeed? In what ways is/isn't the scenario that they created ecologically valid?

Links to methodological issues
- Ethics

- Ecological validity

 Stop and ask yourself ...

- In what ways is Bocchiaro *et al.*'s sample of participants good?
- In what ways could their sample be improved?

Links to methodological issues
- Sample/ethnocentrism

Measures

The researchers were interested in how participants would respond to the experimenter's request to write the statement in support of the sensory deprivation study:

- Those who complied with the request were considered 'obedient'.
- Those who refused were considered 'disobedient'.
- Those who reported the experimenter's questionable conduct to the Research Committee by ticking the box on the form and placing it in the mailbox were considered 'whistle-blowers'. (The whistle-blowers were divided further into two kinds: 'open whistle-blowers' were those who had refused to comply with the previous request to write the statement, while 'anonymous whistle-blowers' were those who had originally complied with it.)

The researchers were also interested in understanding whether those who disobey or blow the whistle have personal characteristics that differentiate them from those who obey. It was to investigate this that they administered two psychometric tests:

1. Participants completed the Dutch version of HEXACO-PI-R, which is an instrument that measures the six major dimensions of personality (Honesty-Humility, Emotionality, Extraversion, Agreeableness, Conscientiousness, Openness to Experience). For each personality trait, there are ten items, and in the self-report form used in this study respondents were asked to indicate how much they agreed with each statement – from 1 (strongly disagree) to 5 (strongly agree).
2. To assess Social Value Orientation (SVO), participants also completed a nine-item Decomposed Games measure. Based on the choices the participants made for each item, they could be classified as having either (1) a pro-social orientation, (2) an individualistic orientation, or (3) a competitive orientation in terms of the patterns of outcomes they generally prefer for themselves and others.

> **➡ Have a go yourself**
>
> Use the internet to find out more about HEXACO-PI-R and also the Decomposed Game Measure of Social Value Orientation – you should be able to locate copies of the instruments used in the Bocchiaro et al. study so that you can fill them in for yourself.

Predicted results

A separate sample of 138 students from VU University in Amsterdam were asked to imagine being in this research. They were provided with a detailed description of the experimental setting and then asked to say 'What would you do?' and 'What the average student at your university would do?' (Table 1.5).

Table 1.5 Percentage of participants describing themselves as obedient, disobedient or whistle-blower

	'What would you do?'	'What the average student at your university would do?'
Obedient	3.6%	18.8%
Disobedient	31.9%	43.9%
Whistle-blower	64.5%	37.3%

Actual results

Results from the laboratory study with the 149 participants shown in Table 1.6 revealed a very different picture.

Table 1.6 Actual results of participants who were obedient, disobedient or a whistle-blower

	Actual results
Obedient	76.5% ($n = 114$)
Disobedient	14.1% ($n = 21$)
Whistle-blower	9.4% ($n = 14$)*

*Of the whistle-blowers, 6.0% ($n = 9$) had written a message (i.e. were 'anonymous whistle-blowers'), while 3.4% ($n = 5$) had refused to do so (i.e. were 'open whistle-blowers').

No statistically significant differences were found in any of the six personality factors measured by the HEXACO-PI-R. Similarly, no significant differences were found between the groups in terms of SVO, with there being too few participants with a 'competitive' orientation to permit statistical analysis and 'pro-social' and 'individualistic' participants not being unequally distributed among the three groups. Furthermore, no significant differences were found in any of the groups in relation to gender, religious affiliation, or religious involvement. The only significant difference that was found was in relation to faith, with results suggesting a trend towards whistle-blowers having more faith (defined as a confident belief in a transcendent reality) than obedient or disobedient participants.

Conclusions

The main conclusion that Bocchiaro *et al.* reach is that behaving in a moral manner is challenging for people, even when this reaction appears to observers (the people in their comparison group) as the simplest path to follow.

Discussion

The gap between the predicted results and the actual results reflected the general belief that most of us think we are special, above average, guided by moral principles with freedom to act rationally, personally immune to the influence of powerful situational forces; it also confirms the need for experimental research of this kind, rather than relying on research in which participants are given a hypothetical scenario and asked what they would do.

Qualitative data revealed how obedient participants justified their immoral behaviour by allocating personal responsibility to external forces ('It was expected of me, that's why I continued'; 'I cooperated because the experimenter asked me to'), whereas defiant participants did not experience such an 'agentic shift', remaining fully responsible for their actions inside the laboratory ('I don't want to do unethical things, I would be very disappointed in myself'; 'I disobeyed because I felt responsible towards friends'). Within the defiant group, it is suggested that the 21 participants who were disobedient might have stayed at this level (rather than becoming whistle-blowers) because they lacked the concept, or had a too-vague one, that in certain circumstances, such as the one that they were in, something more could be done.

With regard to why the psychometric tests did not detect differences in personality between the obedient, disobedient and whistle-blowing participants, the researchers suggest that this could be because the situational forces operating on the observed behaviour were so strong as to over-ride individual differences. If the sample had been larger (i.e. $n > 250$) and more refined instruments were used, then differences might have been detected.

What this study did suggest, however, was that participants who were defiant all seemed to proceed by making the same comparison between external demands and internalised moral standards. A disobedient participant stated, 'I would be very mad and disappointed in myself if I would cooperate, because it [the experiment on sensory deprivation] is unethical and goes against my principles'. A whistle-blower said, 'I did not want to have the harmful consequences weighing on my conscience, so felt obliged to do this'. For these people, the question was not whether to obey an authority or not but, instead, which authority to obey – the one making the unjust demand or the one that would disapprove of the resulting actions.

Evaluation of the study by Bocchiaro *et al.*

Links to methodological issues

Research method

- Bocchiaro *et al.*'s study was similar to Milgram's in that it had many features of an experiment (particularly a dependent variable and controls), but it lacked an independent variable.
- Like Milgram's study, then, it may arguably not meet the criteria for it to be counted as an experiment; however, its highly standardised procedure made it replicable across its 149 participants, aiding its reliability.
- Furthermore, Bocchiaro *et al.* expressly suggest that what they hope they have designed is a new way of investigating obedience that other researchers will be able to use for themselves. If this study was replicated in another country or in the same country several years later, then either the place or time in which the study was carried out would become in effect an independent variable (with the original 2012 study by Bocchiaro *et al.* becoming the 'baseline' study against which to compare results from the others).

Data

- Like in Milgram's study of obedience, both quantitative and qualitative data were collected in the study by Bocchiaro *et al.*
- The quantitative data comprised the numbers and percentages of participants who were obedient, disobedient or a whistle-blower. The data that the researchers obtained on each participant from the two psychometric tests they completed would also have been in quantitative form.
- This quantitative data may prove particularly helpful (for purposes of comparison) if the study is replicated in other countries or with different groups of participants (e.g. non-students).
- The qualitative data consisted of the comments made by participants during the debrief about why they behaved the way that they did.
- These comments were helpful in making sense of why the participants had behaved in the ways that they did. Although Bocchiaro *et al.* attempted to group these comments together into categories (e.g. those comments in which the participant justified their behaviour by allocating personal responsibility

That said, the fact that 23.5 per cent of participants were not obedient can be pointed to as evidence of free will as these people showed themselves to be capable of controlling their own behaviour (as opposed to having their behaviour controlled for them by the pressures of the situation).

Usefulness of research

- It is arguable that, insofar as this study is of practical use, it suggests more negative uses than positive ones (e.g. bad employers could draw the conclusion that requiring employees to behave unethically would be much more likely to result in obedience to the request than either disobedience or whistle-blowing).
- However, one way in which Bocchiaro et al. would argue that it can be used is by other researchers as this represents a replicable scenario (paradigm) that could be applied in other places or at other times to see if people elsewhere or in the future are any less likely to obey than was seen in this study.

Links to areas/perspectives

- Bocchiaro et al.'s study falls within the social area because it is confirming the influence that other people can have on our behaviour (leading people to be much more obedient than they would probably predict themselves to be).
- However, it should also be located within the individual differences area as they are openly interested in trying to find out whether there are particular personality traits that are shared by people who behave in the same way in their research scenario.

Links to the key theme

- In relation to the key theme of responses to people in authority, Bocchiaro et al.'s study would appear to tell us that people are as obedient now (in 2012, anyway) as they were in the early 1960s; that people in the Netherlands are at least as obedient as people in the USA; and that people are much more likely to be obedient than they think they are.
- In terms of the extent to which Bocchiaro et al.'s study changes our understanding of the key theme of responses to people in authority, what is interesting is how little it does this. Considering it was carried out nearly half a century after Milgram's classic obedience study and in a different continent, perhaps the biggest surprise from this study is that the results are so similar to those obtained by Milgram. That said, it does introduce the concept of whistle-blowing to research in this area.

- In terms of the extent to which Bocchiaro et al.'s study changes our understanding of individual, social and cultural diversity, the fact that it was carried out in the Netherlands (when Milgram's study had been carried out in the USA) is important. However, the fact that Bocchiaro found high levels of obedience suggests that cultural background may not be a dimension on which people differ in terms of their levels of obedience. The fact that Bocchiaro's study included female participants (whereas Milgram's was all male) and that it was based on students (whereas Milgram's was based on a sample of people from the general population), could suggest ways in which groups might be different in their levels of obedience. However, with there being no significant difference between the males and females in their study in their obedience levels, and with the students in Bocchiaro's study being obedient to an even greater extent than Milgram's participants were (albeit on a less stressful task), the results ultimately suggest similarity rather than difference on this dimension.

Comparison with the classic study

- In what ways is the study by Bocchiaro et al. *similar to* the study by Milgram? In both studies, participants:
  - Were recruited in the same self-selected way
  - Received payment for their involvement in the study
  - Took part individually
  - Took part in a laboratory on a university campus
  - Were led through the scenario by a formally dressed male with a stern demeanour
  - Experienced a high level of deception.
- In what ways is the study by Bocchiaro et al. *different from* the study by Milgram?
  - The two studies were carried out in different countries.
  - The two studies were carried out in different time periods.
  - Whereas Milgram's sample was all male, Bocchiaro's sample included female participants.
  - In Bocchiaro's study, participants were left on their own for a while and given some 'cooling off' time (10 minutes in total).
  - In Bocchiaro's study, the procedure was not incremental: participants were not led into ever greater obedience in a series of small steps.
  - In Bocchiaro's study, the people who would be hurt would be known to them (presumably friends of theirs), rather than the person being hurt being someone they'd only met briefly.

- In Bocchiaro's study, the participants are very deliberately given the intellectual tools to refuse to obey the experimenter's request as they are told right from the start that the experiment of which they will be asked to write a statement in support has already had traumatic effects on participants – they are made aware that there is another way of looking upon it and so the experimenter is not just one-sided in the message he is conveying.
- In Bocchiaro's study, it was possible to be a whistle-blower without having to go through any awkward confrontation with the experimenter as participants could just place a tick in the box on the Research Committee form left out for them and place it in the mailbox that was in the room.

Questions arising from Bocchiaro *et al.*

- What questions are we left with after studying the research by Bocchiaro *et al.*? Milgram's study left a great many questions unanswered, necessitating research such as that by Bocchiaro to try and answer some of them. However, what are the questions that Bocchiaro's study leaves unanswered (and which other researchers ought to try generating answers to in the future)?
- Over to you…

📖 Practice questions

1. From Bocchiaro *et al.*'s study of disobedience and whistle-blowing:
   (a) Identify the two personality inventories completed by participants in this study. [2 marks]
   (b) Suggest one reason why the participants were given these personality inventories to complete in this study. [2 marks]
2. Outline one conclusion that can be drawn in relation to whistle-blowing from the study by Bocchiaro *et al.* [2 marks]
3. Outline two ways in which the study by Milgram into obedience and the study by Bocchiaro *et al.* into disobedience and whistle-blowing are similar. [4 marks]
4. Suggest one way in which the study by Bocchiaro *et al.* (disobedience and whistle-blowing) does not change our understanding of individual, social or cultural diversity in relation to the key theme of responses to people in authority. [3 marks]

Responses to people in need Ⓐ

There are many ways in which it is possible to respond to people in need. One response would, of course, be to offer help. This would be an example of altruistic behaviour – namely, acting for the benefit of other people without regard to personal cost or benefit. Is this, though, the typical response or the exceptional response? Faced with a person in need, helping out is not the only option – other possible responses include just ignoring the person in need and walking on by, or even taking advantage of their incapacitated state and, say, robbing them. What factors affect how we respond to people in need? What goes through our minds when we see someone in need of help?

These are important questions that psychologists first began investigating in earnest in America in the 1960s. The specific trigger to the wave of research into bystander behaviour was the murder in 1964 of a young woman, Kitty Genovese, in the Queens district of New York. She was stabbed to death over the course of 35 minutes in the street in the middle of the night. This was obviously a horrific way for anyone to lose their life, but what commentators at the time found especially shocking was that it could have been prevented, as at least 38 people were known to have heard or even seen what was going on; however, no-one called the police until it was too late. How could this bystander apathy be explained?

To try to get an answer to this question, social psychologists carried out a series of experiments. One of these was the so-called 'seizure study' conducted by Darley and Latané in 1968. They proposed that the reason why none of the witnesses to Kitty Genovese's murder had called the police at the time was because they all thought someone else would.

They called this diffusion of responsibility:

When only one bystander is present in an emergency, if help is to come, it must come from him. Although he may choose to ignore it (out of concern for his own personal safety, or desires 'not to get involved'), any pressure to intervene focuses uniquely on him. When there are several observers present, however, the pressures do not focus on any one of the observers; instead the responsibility for intervention is shared among all the onlookers and is not unique to anyone. As a result, no one helps. (Darley and Latané, 1968, page 377)

To investigate this idea, Darley and Latané set up an experiment in which participants overheard someone apparently having an epileptic seizure. The participants believed either that they alone had heard the emergency, or that one or four unseen others were also present. Results supported expectations as 85 per cent of the participants who thought that they alone knew of the victim's plight reported the seizure before the end of the fit, but when participants knew that one other person was aware of it the figure dropped to 62 per cent and when participants knew that four other people were aware of it the proportion of participants reporting the seizure dropped still further to 31 per cent.

However, studies like this were conducted in artificial laboratory conditions and the emergency was only heard, not seen. What if the emergency took place in a real-life setting, and if it was clear to everyone looking on whether anyone else had given help to the victim or if the victim had been able to help himself? Would the results from such studies be different? This is where the study by Piliavin *et al.* comes in.

Piliavin *et al.* (1969)

Whereas initial research into the behaviour of witnesses to emergencies was conducted in laboratory settings and with bystanders only hearing (not seeing) the emergency, the study by Piliavin *et al.* was conducted in the field (the New York subway) and was based around a scenario in which the emergency was both seen and heard. What difference would these features of their experiment make to the amount of helping behaviour observed?

Aims

In their field experiment, Piliavin *et al.* wanted to investigate the impact on helping behaviour of a number of different variables:

- **Type of victim.** Would it make a difference if he was perceived to be drunk or ill?
- **Race of the victim.** Would it make a difference if he was black or white?
- **Someone setting an example of helping behaviour.** Would it make a difference to the behaviour of those witnessing the emergency if someone 'modelled' helping behaviour in front of them?
- **Number of witnesses.** Would there be a relationship between levels of helping behaviour and the number of people witnessing the emergency?

Procedure

To try to obtain answers to these questions, Piliavin *et al.* arranged for a series of emergencies to be staged on express trains of the New York 8th Avenue Independent Subway. This particular line was used because the A and D trains on this route made no stops between 59th Street and 125th Street, meaning that for about 7½ minutes there was a captive audience.

During weekdays from 11 a.m. to 3 p.m. from 15 April 1968 to 26 June 1968, four teams of students — each made up of a victim, model, and two observers — would board the train, and then approximately 70 seconds into the journey, as the train passed the first station, the victim (who always stood next to a pole in the centre of the end section of a carriage) would stagger forward and collapse. Until he received help, he would remain lying on the floor, looking up at the ceiling. This emergency situation was staged

103 times, with between six and eight trials being run by each team of students on a given day. After carrying out a trial with the train going in one direction, the students would then disembark and cross over to another platform to be able to carry out the next trial on a train going in the opposite direction.

Victim. All four of the students playing the role of victim were male. They were identically dressed in Eisenhower jackets, old trousers and no tie. They were aged from 26 to 35. Three were white and one was black. On 38 trials, the victims smelled of alcohol and carried a liquor bottle wrapped tightly in a brown bag (the 'drunk condition'), while on 65 trials the victim appeared sober and carried a black cane (the 'cane condition'). Each victim was supposed to participate in both the drunk and cane conditions, alternating the conditions across days. However, as the student playing the victim in Team 2 'didn't like' playing the drunk, he ran cane trials when he should have run drunk trials — hence the imbalance in the number of cane and drunk trials. The part of the train carriage that the victim went into was known as 'the critical area'(see Figure 1.4).

Model. Within each team of four students, there was also someone described as a 'model'. This person was always a white male. They were aged between 24 and 29 and they wore informal clothes, although they were not all dressed the same. There were four model conditions, and these affected which part of the carriage (either the 'critical area', or the part of the carriage next to this — namely, the 'adjacent area') the model went and stood in:

1. *Critical area – early.* (The model stood in the critical area and assisted the victim approximately 70 seconds after he collapsed.)
2. *Critical area – late.* (The model stood in the critical area and assisted the victim approximately 150 seconds after he collapsed.)
3. *Adjacent area – early.* (The model stood in the middle of the adjacent area and assisted the victim approximately 70 seconds after he collapsed.)
4. *Adjacent area – late.* (The model stood in the middle of the adjacent area and assisted the victim approximately 150 seconds after he collapsed.)

When the model provided assistance, he raised the victim to a sitting position and stayed with him for the remainder of the trial.

🚫 **Stop and ask yourself ...**

- Piliavin *et al.* ran 103 trials in this experiment. Was that enough for them to be able to claim that what they were seeing were consistent effects?

Links to methodological issues
- Reliability

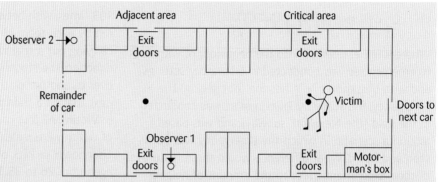

Figure 1.4 Diagram showing the layout of Piliavin *et al.*'s 'emergency scenario'

Adjacent area

Critical area

Observer 2

Exit doors

Exit doors

Remainder of car

Victim

Doors to next car

Observer 1

Exit doors

Exit doors

Motor-man's box

🚫 Stop and ask yourself ...

- To what extent was the scenario created in this study ecologically valid? [HINT: think about the times when the scenario occurred, as well as when, where, how and to whom the emergency happened.]
- In what ways did Piliavin *et al.* try to ensure that the only thing different from one trial to another was the one thing they wanted to be different (i.e. in terms of the victim, whether he appeared drunk or ill, or whether he was black or white)?
- In spite of their best attempts to make the independent variable the only thing setting one trial apart from another, what sorts of thing could nevertheless have happened that might have had an impact on the results of this study?

Links to methodological issues

- Ecological validity

- Validity/controls

- Controls/extraneous variables

Observers. The other two people in each team were the observers. They were all female, and they took seats in the adjacent area, recording data as unobtrusively as possible for the duration of the ride. Both observers within a team would record comments made spontaneously by nearby passengers, and both would attempt to elicit comments from a passenger sitting next to them. Beyond this, though, they had different roles:

- One observer noted the race, sex and location of every passenger in the *critical area*. On top of this, she also counted the total number of individuals in the carriage and the total number of people who came to the victim's aid (as well as recording the race, sex and initial location of every helper).
- The other observer noted the race, sex and location of every passenger in the *adjacent area*. On top of this, she also recorded the length of time it took (the 'latency') for the first helper to arrive and, on those trials where there was a model who intervened, the latency of the first helper's arrival after the model had started offering help.

➡️ Have a go yourself

Set your classroom up in the style of a subway train carriage and carry out a role-play of Piliavin *et al.*'s procedure. (For props you will need a cane and a [plastic] bottle in a brown paper bag; if you want to be even more authentic, you could source (from the internet) a recording of underground train sounds and even an Eisenhower jacket for the victim.) Remember which parts of the carriage the four members of the team should go in.

Participants

The participants were the passengers on the trains. Over the 103 trials, the observers recorded about 4,450 men and women in the carriages where the emergency was staged. The mean number of people per carriage was 43, and the racial composition of a typical carriage was about 45 per cent black and 55 per cent white.

Stop and ask yourself...

- What were the really good features of the sample of participants studied by Piliavin *et al.*? In what ways could their sample nevertheless be said to lack generalisability? [HINT: think about the sorts of people who *wouldn't* have been using the subway in New York at the times when the trials were run.]
- How can this study be *criticised* in relation to the ethical guidelines? Are there any ways in which it can be *defended* in relation to the ethical guidelines?

Links to methodological issues
- Sample/ethnocentrism

- Ethics

Results

Findings from the study included the following:

- **Type of victim.** The victim with the cane received spontaneous help (i.e. before the model acted) on 62 of the 65 trials, and the median latency was 5 seconds. The victim who appeared drunk received spontaneous help on 19 of the 38 trials, and the median latency was 109 seconds.

- **Race of victim.** With both the black and white cane victims, the proportion of helpers of each race was in accord with the expected 55–45 per cent split. With the drunk, on the other hand, it was mainly members of his own race who came to his aid if a victim appears to be drunk rather than ill.

- **Effects of the model.** It was not possible to conduct extensive analysis of responses to the model's behaviour because of the high levels of spontaneous helping behaviour. However, from those occasions when the model was able to intervene, it was found that while the area the model came from (critical or adjacent) had no effect on passengers' behaviour, if the model intervened early then he triggered more helping behaviour than if he intervened late.

- **Number of witnesses.** Victims were helped much faster when there were seven or more male passengers in the critical area than when there were only between one and three male passengers in the critical area.

Other findings of note were as follows:

- On 60 per cent of the 81 trials on which the victim received help, he received it from not one Good Samaritan but from two, three, or even more.

- Of the 81 spontaneous first helpers, 90 per cent were male.
- No-one left the carriage on any of the trials, but on 21 of the 103 trials a total of 34 people did leave the critical area.
- Far more comments were obtained from passengers during the drunk trials than during the cane trials. Many women made comments such as 'It's for men to help him', 'I wish I could help him – I'm not strong enough', 'I never saw this kind of thing before – I don't know where to look', or 'You feel so bad that you don't know what to do.'

Conclusions

1. An individual who appears to be ill is more likely to receive help than one who appears to be drunk.
2. Men are more likely to help than women.
3. There is some tendency for same-race helping, especially if a victim appears to be drunk rather than ill.
4. Help comes quickest and in greatest numbers when there are more witnesses present (i.e. diffusion of responsibility was not observed).
5. The longer an emergency continues without help being offered, the less impact a model has on the helping behaviour of others, the more likely it is that individuals will leave the immediate area, and the more likely it is that observers will make comments in relation to their own behaviour.

Stop and ask yourself...

- How/why did Piliavin *et al.*'s study benefit from the collection of qualitative as well as quantitative data?

Links to methodological issues
- Qualitative/quantitative data

Model of response to emergency situations

In an attempt to explain their findings, Piliavin *et al.* developed a model of response to emergency situations. This proposes the following:

- Observation of an emergency creates in the bystander an emotional arousal state which the observer finds unpleasant.
- The level of arousal will be higher (a) the more the observer can empathise with the victim, (b) the closer the observer is to the emergency, and (c) the longer the state of emergency continues without the intervention of a helper.
- The level of arousal can be reduced in a number of ways, namely, (a) helping directly, (b) going to get help, (c) leaving the scene of the emergency, and (d) rejecting the victim as undeserving of help.
- The response that is chosen will be a function of a cost–reward analysis based on Table 1.7.

Table 1.7 Cost–reward analysis of responses in emergency situations

	Helping	Not helping
Costs	For example, effort, embarrassment, possible physical harm, etc.	Mainly self-blame and perceived censure from others.
Rewards	Mainly praise from victim, self and others.	Continuation with other activities.

Figure 1.5 Would you assist someone who needed help on a train?

It is worth emphasising that this model is not seeing helping behaviour as arising from a positive 'altruistic' desire to help someone in need; rather, it is suggesting that it arises from a selfish desire to get rid of an emotional state that the onlooker finds unpleasant.

Evaluation of the study by Piliavin *et al.*

Links to methodological issues

Research method

- This study was a field experiment. It was an experiment because it had independent variables, dependent variables and controls. It was a field experiment because it was carried out in a real-life setting (i.e. a carriage on the New York subway).
- As an experiment, it had the benefits of a standardised procedure that made it replicable; as an experiment carried out in the field, it had the benefit of being more ecologically valid than are most experiments.
- Although it was a field experiment, it is also worth noting that it used observation as a means by which to collect data.
- It was also a snapshot study. Although it was carried out over the course of two months, it was not longitudinal because they did not keep going back to the same participants to see if anything had changed. As a snapshot study, we cannot be certain that the results weren't just reflecting behaviour at a particular moment in time; in other words, we can't be certain that we'd get the same results if the experiment was replicated today.

Data

- The study by Piliavin *et al.* collected both quantitative and qualitative data.
- The quantitative data consisted of the numbers of 'victims' who were helped, the percentage of first helpers who were male or female, the numbers of bystanders who left the critical area, etc. This was good as it meant that Piliavin *et al.* were able to compare results from one condition to another (e.g. from the 'ill victim' condition to the 'drunk victim' condition).
- The qualitative data collected by Piliavin *et al.* consisted of the quotes from passengers. These helped to explain some of the quantitative data they collected, especially the finding that 90 per cent of first helpers were male. The qualitative data

⊘ Stop and ask yourself…

- How/why is this study an example of inductive research?

Links to methodological issues
- Induction

probably also helped in the development of their model of response to emergency situations, which sought to explain why people might or might not help out in a situation like this.

Ethics

- If ethical guidelines had been in place at the time when this study was carried out, it would have broken most of them.
- In the first place, the participants (i.e. the passengers on the subway trains) were deceived as to why someone was collapsing in front of them as they didn't know that the 'victim' was only pretending to collapse as part of an experiment.
- Similarly, the passengers did not consent to take part in an experiment and, whilst they could withdraw themselves from what was going on (e.g. physically, by leaving either the critical area of the carriage or the carriage as a whole; or emotionally, by providing a reason for not intervening to help), what they could not do was withdraw what they did or said from the data recorded by the researchers.
- In terms of protection from harm, those participants who didn't help the victim could well have come away from the experiment with a reduced sense of their own self-worth, having discovered that they were the sort of person who, if faced with an emergency, probably wouldn't come to someone else's aid.
- Finally, there is no mention of participants being debriefed in any way even though this would have been quite feasible (e.g. via an announcement over the public announcement system, or through the giving out of leaflets).
- On the plus side, at least Piliavin et al. didn't record the names of any of the passengers or record any details about them that would have made them identifiable.

Validity

- One of the great difficulties of conducting field experiments is imposing controls on extraneous variables to be able to say that the only thing that is different from one condition to another is the one thing the researcher wants to be different – namely, their independent variable. Bearing this in mind, Piliavin et al.'s study is remarkably well controlled for a field experiment – something that was aided, no doubt, by the fact that it was carried out in a confined setting.
- A large number of controls were imposed on this study. For instance, the trials were always run on the same train line at the same times of day and

with the victim always collapsing in the same part of the carriage (the centre of the end section). On top of this, the victim always collapsed in the same way (looking upwards) at the same point into the journey, and he was always a male; the victims were always dressed the same, too.

- That said, results could still have been affected by extraneous variables. In particular, if a carriage had been particularly busy, the victim might not have been able to collapse in the place he was supposed to collapse. Also, it is quite possible that some of the passengers might have witnessed this happen more than once, and this could have affected how they responded to the 'emergency'.
- In terms of ecological validity, in many ways the scenario created in this study can be seen as fairly true-to-life. Thus, it took place in a setting (a subway train) which millions of people use every day, and it is not implausible for someone to collapse in such a location and be in need of help.
- However, in other ways, the ecological validity of this study can be questioned. In particular, the fairly dramatic way in which the victim collapsed (i.e. falling down in the centre of his particular part of the carriage, and then lying on the floor of the carriage looking up at the ceiling) might seem fairly unusual, and appearing to be drunk as early as 11 o'clock in the morning would be less common than would appearing to be drunk at 11 o'clock at night. Similarly, it might have seemed more true-to-life if the person who had collapsed was quite a bit older than 26–35 years of age.

Reliability

- The findings from this study can be seen as fairly reliable because of the large number of trials that Piliavin et al. ran. By running 103 trials, they can be fairly confident that they have established a consistent effect. That said, this is more true of some conditions than others. The fact that they ran 65 trials in the 'ill/cane' condition and the victim was helped spontaneously on 62 occasions suggests that it is a reliable (consistent) finding that someone collapsing because they appear to be ill is likely to be helped. Although they would have liked more trials to have been run in the 'drunk' condition, in practice a total of 38 trials is probably sufficient to establish that a victim collapsing under such circumstances is much less likely to receive help from their fellow passengers than if he appeared to be ill.
- However, Piliavin et al. probably don't have enough results in relation to the other independent variables to

establish consistent effects as the results they report could have been distorted by 'fluke' or anomalous occurrences. For instance, while there were 81 trials run with a white 'victim' (57 in the cane condition and 24 in the drunk condition), there were only 22 trials run with a black 'victim'. Furthermore, as these comprised eight conditions in the cane condition and 14 in the drunk condition, these are probably insufficient to establish unarguably consistent findings.

- This problem is even greater with regard to studying the impact of the model's behaviour on that of the genuine passengers. The plan was that half of the trials wouldn't have a model intervening, while for the other 50 per cent of trials the way the model intervened would be spread across the four model conditions. However, as spontaneous helping of the victim occurred so frequently (particularly in the ill/cane condition), there were too few instances of action by the model to establish any consistent patterns with regard to the impact his behaviour had on genuine passengers in general terms, let alone if trying to break the results down by the time when the model intervened (early or late) or which part of the carriage the model came from (the critical area or the adjacent area).

- In terms of why there weren't more trials run across the various conditions, one of the footnotes to the original article explains this and in so doing contains an insight into the practical difficulties of carrying out research in psychology. It has already been mentioned that one of the four teams of students (Team 2) ran cane trials when they should have been running drunk trials because the victim 'didn't like' playing the drunk. The other problem that Piliavin et al. had was that 'Then the Columbia [University] student strike occurred, the teams disbanded, and the study was of necessity over. At this point, Teams 1 and 3 had run on only 3 days each, while 2 and 4 had run on 4 days each' (page 291).

Sample

- In many ways, the sample of participants studied by Piliavin et al. is extremely impressive. Thus, the sample size of 4,450 can be seen as large enough to establish reliable findings, while the ethnic diversity of the sample (Piliavin reports that 'The racial composition of a typical train, which travels through Harlem to the Bronx, was about 45 per cent black and 55 per cent white') helps back up the claim that the findings from the study are generalisable to a wide cross-section of the city.

- That said, their sample can nevertheless be said to lack generalisability. There are many different types of people who are unlikely to be represented in their sample, such as children (who, presumably, would have been at school), people who work full-time, and

people with disabilities (who may have been more likely to use buses or taxis to get around the city). It is likely, as well, that the study is only telling us about the behaviour of urban-based people.

Ethnocentrism

- Although Piliavin et al.'s study was carried out within one city in one country, nonetheless it can be argued that it is not ethnocentric because New York is such a heterogeneous city. Furthermore, as they explicitly state that about 45 per cent of the people on the train were black and about 55 per cent were white, this confirms that the findings are not of relevance to people from one ethnic group alone.

- However, while the sample of participants may have had different racial origins, they nevertheless all lived within the same culture. For this reason, it could be argued to still only tell us about the behaviour of American people in response to people in need.

Links to debates

Free will/determinism debate

- The results from this study suggest that in a situation in which someone collapses because of illness it is highly likely that people will go to their aid. However, as the 'drunk' victim only received spontaneous help on 50 per cent of occasions, witnesses clearly have control over their behaviour and make their own decision as to whether to help or not.

- Insofar as it is determined that people will help out when someone appears to be ill, what is unclear is what the determining factor might be. Piliavin et al. suggest that it is determined by a combination of physiological and cognitive factors (arousal, followed by a cost–reward calculation) while it is possible that situational factors (principally the confined nature of the setting) could have played a part; however, as they didn't manipulate the setting of the experiment as an independent variable (e.g. have some of the emergencies in the subway train and some up on the street), this can only be speculation.

Reductionism/holism

- The model of response to emergency situations that Piliavin et al. developed to explain their results can be seen as holistic in the sense that it is taking account of a range of different factors (physiological and cognitive) rather than just explaining helping behaviour as the result of one factor alone.

- However, it can be argued that their model is reductionist as it misses out other reasons why people might help, such as kindness and a genuine (unselfish, altruistic) desire to help another person simply because they are in need.

Psychology as a science

- This is a really good example of inductive research as the theory that Piliavin *et al.* developed about how people behave when witnessing an emergency (their model of response to emergency situations) was developed from the data they had collected, and was very much an attempt to explain what they had seen.
- This is the opposite of deductive research, in which the theory is developed first and then research is carried out to see if the theory is confirmed (backed up) by the evidence.

Links to areas/perspectives

- Piliavin *et al.*'s study falls within the social area because they were investigating the impact that other people have on our behaviour and, in particular, whether the likelihood of someone helping out in an emergency situation is increased or decreased by the known (visible) presence of other witnesses to the event.
- However, it could also be argued to be slightly biological because of the suggestion that observation of an emergency will create in the bystander an emotional arousal state which the observer will find unpleasant – the suggestion is that this is something that will go on within our bodies, that we won't have any control over this, and that it will help to determine how we act.
- On top of that, it could also be seen as having a cognitive element because of the emphasis on cost–reward calculation as determining how witnesses to emergencies act to get rid of their arousal – although they don't say anything definitive about the degree to which this is consciously done, nonetheless the suggestion that actions are influenced by a mental calculation clearly implies a cognitive component to their model.

Links to the key theme

- In relation to the key theme of responses to people in need, Piliavin *et al.*'s study would suggest that (contrary to the theory of diffusion of responsibility) the likelihood of being helped in an emergency does not have to be reduced by there being many witnesses present, although this may be affected by bystanders being able to see how other witnesses are behaving. In addition, it suggests that people are more likely to be helped if they seem to need help due to factors beyond their control and that first helpers are most likely to be male.
- However, there are many questions that arise from Piliavin *et al.*'s study, such as:
  - Would the results have been different if the study had been carried out in somewhere other than New York? In particular, how might the results differ if the study were carried out in a comparable city in another country?
  - Would the results be different if the study were repeated now, or do they only reflect the behaviour of the time (i.e. the latter part of the 1960s)?
  - Were the levels of helping behaviour affected by the particular type of scenario with which the participants were presented (i.e. someone collapsing)? Would the levels of helping behaviour be different if the scenario was less dramatic?
  - Were the levels of helping behaviour affected by the fact that the experiment took place in a confined setting? Would the levels of helping behaviour be different if the scenario was enacted up on the street?
  - Would the levels of helping behaviour given to the victim have been different if the victim had been female and/or of a different age group? Would women have been more likely to help out if the victim was a woman?

Find out more

- Look up other studies carried out into how bystanders respond to people in need. A particularly interesting one was an experiment carried out by Darley and Batson (1973) in a theological seminary.
- Keep a watch on stories in the news of how people respond in real-life emergency situations. Which is more typical – the sort of response Kitty Genovese received when she cried out for help, or the sort of response Piliavin *et al.*'s 'victims' received?

Practice questions

1. From Piliavin *et al.*'s 'Subway Samaritan' study:
   (a) Explain what is meant by the term 'diffusion of responsibility'. [2 marks]
   (b) Outline one reason why diffusion of responsibility was not found in this study. [2 marks]
2. From Piliavin *et al.*'s 'Subway Samaritan' study:
   (a) Outline how qualitative data were collected in this study. [2 marks]
   (b) Identify one example of qualitative data collected in this study. [2 marks]
3. From Piliavin *et al.*'s 'Subway Samaritan' study, outline one way in which the procedure may be considered reliable. [3 marks]
4. From Piliavin *et al.*'s 'Subway Samaritan' study, outline one reason why the results may be considered to lack validity. [3 marks]

Levine *et al.* (2001)

Are strangers more likely to receive help in some cities than in others and, if so, why? To try to get answers to these questions, Levine *et al.* conducted a major cross-cultural study in 23 large cities around the world. In each of these different cities, measures were taken of three types of spontaneous, non-emergency helping – letting a pedestrian know that they had dropped a pen, offering help to a pedestrian with a hurt leg who was trying to reach a pile of dropped magazines, and helping a blind person cross the street. Results from these three measures of helping were then correlated against a series of different variables to try to identify what the most (and least) helpful cities had in common.

Aims

The study had three main goals:

1. To see if the tendency of people within a city to offer non-emergency help to strangers was stable across different situations in which people needed help.
2. To see if helping of strangers varies across cultures.
3. To identify the characteristics of those communities in which strangers are more (or less) likely to be helped.

Method

In most cities, one local individual – usually a student returning to their home country for summer vacation – collected all the data on helping behaviour. These people, who were confederates acting on behalf of the researchers, were college age and dressed neatly and casually. To control for gender effects and to avoid potential problems in some cities, all confederates were men.

The selection of countries was aimed at obtaining the widest possible sample of the regions and cultures of the world; however, for practical reasons, the selection was sometimes driven by convenience. The cities where the research was conducted were in most cases the largest city in each country, and all had populations of more than 230,000.

The confederates attempted to gain data in relation to five helping situations. However, two of these – asking for change, and seeing how many apparently mislaid letters would be picked up and posted on – ran into such difficulties that data for these could not be analysed. (For example, in the asking-for-change situation, it was found in Calcutta that there was a general shortage of small-value coins and notes, while the lost-letter technique ran into even more problems such as residents of Tel Aviv being afraid to touch the letters for fear that they might contain explosives and a simple absence of post boxes in many less developed countries.)

The three helping behaviours for which measures were taken were as follows:

1. **Dropped pen.** Walking at a carefully practised, moderate pace (15 paces/10 seconds), confederates walked toward a solitary pedestrian passing in the opposite direction. When 10 to 15 feet away, the confederate would reach into his pocket and accidentally, without appearing to notice, drop his pen behind him, in full view of the pedestrian whom he would continue walking past. A total of 214 men and 210 women were approached. Participants were recorded as having helped if they called back to the confederate that he had dropped his pen and/or picked up the pen and took it to him.
2. **Hurt leg.** Walking with a heavy limp and wearing a large and clearly visible leg brace, confederates would, seemingly by accident, drop and unsuccessfully struggle to reach down for a pile of magazines as they came within 20 feet of a passing pedestrian. A total of 253 men and 240 women were approached. Helping was defined as offering to help and/or beginning to help without offering.
3. **Helping a blind person across the street.** Confederates, dressed in dark glasses and carrying white canes, would locate city centre intersections which had pedestrian crossings, traffic signals and moderate, steady pedestrian flow. Just before the light turned green, they would step up to the corner, hold out their cane and wait until someone offered help. A total of 281 trials were conducted. Participants were recorded as having helped if, at a minimum, they informed the confederate that the light was green.

Each of the three helping measures (Figure 1.6) was administered in two or more locations, in main city centre districts, during main business hours, on clear days, during the summer months of one or more years between 1992 and 1997. For the first two measures, which required approaching pedestrians, only individuals walking alone were selected. Children (younger than 17 years old), and people who might not be capable of helping or be expected to help (e.g. those who were physically disabled, very old, or carrying heavy packages, etc.) were excluded. Participants were selected randomly, usually by approaching the second potential participant who crossed a predetermined line.

Results

Levels of helping behaviour in the 23 cities were as shown in Table 1.8.

Figure 1.6 Three helping measures

 Stop and ask yourself...

- To what extent is this study ecologically valid?
- What actions did Levine *et al*. take to try to ensure the reliability of their findings? Why, nevertheless, might the study still lack reliability?
- How can this study be *criticised* in relation to the ethical guidelines? How can it be *defended* in relation to the ethical guidelines?

Links to methodological issues

- Ecological validity
- Reliability

- Ethics

Table 1.8 Levels of helping behaviour

Rank	City, country	Overall helping index (% helped)	Dropped pen (% helped)	Hurt leg (% helped)	Blind person (% helped)
1	Rio de Janeiro, Brazil	93.33	100	80	100
2	San Jose, Costa Rica	91.33	79	95	100
3	Lilongwe, Malawi	86	93	65	100
4	Calcutta, India	82.67	63	93	92
5	Vienna, Austria	81	88	80	75
6	Madrid, Spain	79.33	75	63	100
7	Copenhagen, Denmark	77.67	89	77	67
8	Shanghai, China	76.67	75	92	63
9	Mexico City, Mexico	75.67	55	80	92
10	San Salvador, El Salvador	74.67	89	43	92
11	Prague, Czech Republic	75	55	70	100
12	Stockholm, Sweden	72	92	66	58
13	Budapest, Hungary	71	76	70	67
14	Bucharest, Romania	68.67	66	48	92
15	Tel Aviv, Israel	68	67	54	83
16	Rome, Italy	63.33	35	80	75
17	Bangkok, Thailand	61	75	66	42
18	Taipei, Taiwan	59	65	62	50
19	Sofia, Bulgaria	57	69	22	80
20	Amsterdam, Netherlands	53.67	54	49	58
21	Singapore, Singapore	48	45	49	50
22	New York, United States	44.67	31	28	75
23	Kuala Lumpur, Malaysia	40.33	26	41	54

- Levine *et al.* emphasise that their sample comprised the 23 cities in which they collected their data, with them' ...treating each city as a single subject in a correlational-type design' (page 544). To what extent can their selection of cities be regarded as representative of cities across the world? How far does this study succeed in avoiding being ethnocentric?
- Which sampling method would you say was used by Levine *et al.* when deciding which cities to collect data from?
- Look again at Table 1.8. Can you spot the error in it (made by Levine *et al.*)?

Links to methodological issues

- Sample/ethnocentrism

- Sampling method

- Nobody's perfect

Have a go yourself

Get a map of the world and plot on it the locations of all of these cities.

Analysis of results

In relation to the first goal of the study, statistical analysis of the results suggested a modest degree of consistency across the three measures of helping behaviour.

In relation to the second goal of the study, countries differed greatly in the amount of help offered to a stranger. The overall helping rate ranged from a high of 93 per cent in Rio de Janeiro, Brazil, to a low of 40 per cent in Kuala Lumpur, Malaysia.

In relation to the third goal of the study, a series of correlational analyses was carried out in which each of the different helping measures for the 23 countries were correlated against different features (community variables) of the country from which the data were collected. These community variables were as follows:

1. Population size of the city
2. Purchasing power parity (PPP) – an indicator of economic well-being measuring how much the average income earned in that country was capable of purchasing
3. Where the country could be placed on a scale from 1 (*the most collectivistic* – i.e. highest priority is given to the welfare of one or more collective

entities, such as a tribe) through to 10 (*the most individualistic* – i.e. there is an orientation to the individual and their nuclear family)
4. Pace of life – this was assessed by the confederates timing the speed at which 35 men and 35 women (pedestrians walking alone) covered a distance of 60 feet in the same city centre locations where the helping measures were taken.

Results of these correlation analyses confirmed that the only statistically significant relationship was between the measure for purchasing power and both overall levels of helping and helping of the blind person, suggesting that cities with lower levels of purchasing power tend to be more helpful (Table 1.9 and Figure 1.7). There was also a small relationship between walking speed and overall helping, with participants in cities with a faster pace of life being somewhat less likely to offer help; however, this relationship was not statistically significant.

Two other variables were also analysed, although not through correlations:

1. For the helping measures in relation to the hurt leg and the dropped pen, it was possible to analyse results to see if there was a gender difference in the proportion of individuals offering help. Treating gender as the independent variable and the two helping measures as dependent variables, no significant differences were found between males and females in levels of helping behaviour.

Table 1.9 Correlations between helping measures and other community characteristics

	Helping measures			
Community characteristic	Overall helping	Blind person	Hurt leg	Dropped pen
Population size (city)	−0.03 (23)	−0.06 (23)	0.22 (23)	−0.21 (23)
Purchasing power parity (PPP)	−0.43*** (22)	−0.42*** (22)	−0.21 (22)	−0.32* (22)
Individualism-collectivism	−0.17 (23)	−0.09 (23)	−0.21 (23)	−0.07 (23)
Walking speed	0.26 (20)	0.06 (20)	0.23 (20)	0.24 (20)

*$p < 0.15$. ***$p < 0.05$, two-tailed. Sample sizes in parentheses. Statistics for some community characteristics were not available for some countries, resulting in smaller sample sizes for those analyses.

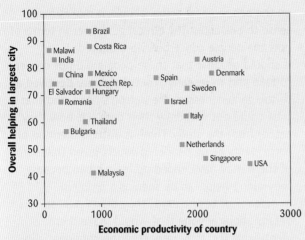

Figure 1.7 Scattergram representing the relationship between overall helping rates in cities and country-level economic productivity, measured in terms of per capita gross domestic product with purchasing power parity

2. The four Latin American countries (Brazil, Mexico, El Salvador and Costa Rica) and Spain were analysed in comparison to the other countries in terms of their average levels of helping behaviour. These countries share a culture of *simpatia* (in Spanish) or *simpatico* (in Portuguese), in which being friendly, nice, agreeable and good-natured (i.e. a person who is fun to be with and pleasant to deal with) is prioritised over achievement and productivity. As helping strangers is part of this culture, it was predicted that the simpatia countries would on average be more helpful toward strangers than non-simpatia cultures and, when results were analysed, the five simpatia cities were all above the mean in overall helping, and on average were more helpful than the other international cities (mean for simpatia countries = 82.87 per cent; mean for non-simpatia countries = 65.87 per cent).

Conclusions

Levine *et al.* conclude that overall levels of helping across cultures are inversely related to a country's economic productivity. They also conclude that countries with the cultural tradition of *simpatia* are on average more helpful than countries with no such tradition.

Discussion

The only variable that showed a significant correlation with helping behaviour was purchasing power, but it is unclear why there should be a negative relationship between these two variables. It may be that the lack of a strong economy is accompanied by a traditional value system that includes a requirement to help strangers, but this would need further investigation.

Another strong finding related to the relatively high levels of helping behaviour in the cities from Latin America and Spain. While the cultural script of simpatia might explain this, other explanations are also available. For example, the five simpatia cultures have primarily Roman Catholic populations, and they are also societies with cultures of honour. Future research could seek to disentangle these variables and study them separately.

It is also recognised that the findings in the present study could have been weakened by methodological problems, particularly experimenter effects, and that only a narrow range of helping behaviours have been examined. That said, it is hoped that the ranking of places may provide a basis for study of the quality of the helping environment in individual cities around the world and also enable comparison over time to mark trends in urban life throughout the world.

🚫 **Stop and ask yourself...**

- To what extent is it a problem that Levine *et al.* rely on correlational analysis in their attempt to identify the characteristics of those communities in which strangers are more (or less) likely to be helped?

Links to methodological issues
- Research method

🚫 **Stop and ask yourself...**

- In what way do Levine *et al.* themselves acknowledge that their data may lack validity? Are there any other ways in which their findings may not actually be a measure of the levels of helping behaviour in these cities?

Links to methodological issues
- Validity

Evaluation of the study by Levine *et al.*

Links to methodological issues

Research method

- Levine *et al.* are keen to emphasise that their study was, in essence, a correlation study, with the overall percentage of people helped in each city being treated as a co-variable and this then being analysed separately against four other co-variables (i.e. population size of the city; purchasing power parity; how collectivist/individualist the city's host country is; walking speed in the city).
- To some extent it is, of course, a problem that Levine *et al.* rely on correlational analysis in their attempt to identify the characteristics of those communities in which strangers are more (or less) likely to be helped as it means they cannot establish cause and effect. They are able, for example, to find that there is a (negative) relationship between the level of helping behaviour in a city and its level of economic well-being, but they don't know if the people in these cities lack purchasing power because they are too busy helping each other, if they help each other because they are under-employed (and therefore have the time to be helpful), or if there is some hidden third factor that sits behind both of these measures (e.g. a commitment to traditional values of good neighbourliness, which means they see it as important to look out for those people around them who are most in need and also means that they aren't prepared to work any harder than they have to).
- It is worth noting that the data for their correlational analyses were collected through observation of how people responded to the actions of a confederate of the researchers.

Data

- The data that Levine *et al.* collected in their study was all quantitative. It is arguable that they may have got a greater understanding of the motives behind people's behaviour (whether they helped or not) by recording comments made by bystanders.

Ethics

- Given that the 'sample' comprises those cities from which data were collected, technically we should consider the extent to which these cities consented to take part in the study, were deceived, etc. However, since the data from the 23 cities are based on the behaviour of actual people, it makes more sense to talk about the ethical guidelines in terms of how the people concerned were treated.
- It should be clear that these people did not consent to take part in research, that they were deceived as to the genuineness of the person's need, and that they could not withdraw their data (i.e. how they acted) from the study. There is also no mention of participants being debriefed which, given that some of them may have ended up feeling bad because they didn't help, can be seen as a problem.
- In defence of Levine *et al.*, they didn't publish details about anyone that would make them identifiable (i.e. they respected the confidentiality of those people who did or didn't help); moreover, for the two measures that involved actually approaching people (i.e. the dropped pen and hurt leg situations), restrictions were placed on the sorts of people their data collectors were permitted to approach. (That said, some of these seemed motivated more by practical considerations than by ethical ones – e.g. not approaching someone carrying heavy packages.)

Validity

- Levine *et al.* acknowledge that, for their one significant correlation (the negative correlation between levels of helping behaviour and the purchasing power of the average income earned in a given country), it is possible that the higher levels of helping seen in the countries with weaker economies could have been related to the traditional value systems often seen in such countries rather than to their (lower levels of) economic well-being as such.
- Also of relevance to validity is the possibility that members of the public might have seen what the data collectors were doing (i.e. repeatedly dropping pens while walking along, or dropping a pile of magazines while wearing a leg brace) and got suspicious about what was going on; this could then have affected how they behaved.
- To a very large extent, this study was high in ecological validity. In particular, data were collected in the field (rather than in a laboratory) and the scenarios in which someone might need help were entirely plausible. On top of this, Levine *et al.* even went so far as to get the Fresno Friendship Centre for the Blind to lend them white canes and to train their experimenters for the 'helping a blind person across the street' measure.

Reliability

- The procedures that Levine *et al.* developed were highly standardised, and they explain that '. . . all experimenters received both a detailed instruction sheet and on-site field training for acting their roles, learning the procedures for subject selection and scoring of subjects' (page 548). This was to help ensure that they were all measuring in a consistent manner.
- The fact that Levine *et al.* measured helping behaviour in three different ways (not just the one), and actually attempted to measure it in five different ways, also adds to the reliability of their findings as they were able to see the extent to which helping behaviour was consistent across a series of different measures, rather than just relying on one. (This was, of course, the first of their three research aims for the study as a whole.)
- In addition, the fact that Levine *et al.*'s data collectors ran large numbers of trials in relation to all three helping situations (424 for the dropped pen, 493 for the hurt leg, and 281 for the blind person needing help crossing the street) meant that they were able to obtain data suggesting a consistent, settled trend, rather than data that could be distorted by 'fluke' results.
- However, as a large number of people were used to collect data, Levine *et al.* themselves acknowledge that '. . . it is difficult to precisely assess standardisation between experimenters in acting their parts and scoring subjects' responses' (page 548), so it is possible that they weren't all measuring in precisely the same way.

Sample

- It is hugely impressive that Levine *et al.* managed to collect data from so many cities across the world, and their study genuinely is a cross-cultural study of differences in the helping of strangers (as they say in the title of their research paper).
- In terms of their sampling method, it seems as if, to a large extent, Levine *et al.* chose the cities that they did on an opportunity basis, in accordance with which cities they either had students visiting or knew people in. They write as follows: 'Data collection at the various international sites was conducted by interested, responsible students who were either travelling to foreign countries or returning to their home countries for the summer, or by cross-cultural psychologists and their students in other countries who volunteered to assist the authors' (page 547).

Ethnocentrism

- In spite of the impressively cross-cultural nature of this study, it is noticeable that there is an imbalance in the extent to which different continents are represented, with data being collected from only one city in Africa (Lilongwe, in Malawi) and one city in the Middle East (Tel Aviv, in Israel). Furthermore, no data are collected from any of the Arabic countries in the Middle East and North Africa, and nor are any data collected from any of the former Soviet Socialist Republics.
- Although, therefore, this study is impressively cross-cultural, nonetheless it remains centred on the Americas, Europe and Asia, and so is not quite as un-ethnocentric as it would ideally be. (In other words, it tells us about the helping behaviour of people from some cultural backgrounds, but not from all.)
- That said, a number of the cities from which data were collected can genuinely be regarded as 'world cities' in which people from a wide range of different cultural backgrounds will be living and working, so it can be expected that it won't just be life-long residents of these cities whose helping behaviour is being measured.

Nobody's perfect

- With an overall helping index (percentage helped) of 75, Prague should be ranked 10th; this city should be above San Salvador, in which the overall helping index was 74.67% helped.

Links to debates

Individual and situational explanations debate

- Given the extent to which levels of helping behaviour were found to vary in different cities around the world, the study by Levine *et al.* would appear to suggest that culture is one aspect of the situation that can influence the chances of people engaging in helping behaviour.
- Furthermore, as levels of helping behaviour were generally highest in the scenario involving the blind person, there is presumably something about this particular situation that makes people more likely to help.

Psychology as a science

- When people try defending the claim that psychology is a science, it is invariably the biological studies (e.g. Casey *et al.*) that they make reference to in support of their position. However, insofar as being scientific means such things as conducting research that is replicable, objective and falsifiable, it is arguable that the study by Levine *et al.* is scientific. They demonstrated that their methods were replicable by replicating them so many times in each different city; they trained their data collectors to follow clear guidance about what did or didn't count as an example of helping behaviour (to try to reduce the risk of it being their opinion as to whether someone had helped them or not); and it would be entirely possible to prove false their findings that Rio de Janeiro is a city where a person in need is likely to be helped and that Kuala Lumpur is a city where a person in need is relatively unlikely to be helped. (This last point would require a fairly generous research budget to cover the flights necessary to go to these cities to replicate Levine *et al.*'s study, but that would be the way to try to prove whether their findings were wrong.)

Usefulness of research

- As we can't choose where we are likely to need help, the study by Levine *et al.* would appear to have relatively few practical applications. That said, the information contained within it might be worth bearing in mind when planning locations to go on holiday to...

Links to areas/perspectives

- Levine *et al.*'s study has been located within the social area because, although they weren't explicitly investigating whether the likelihood of being helped is affected by the presence of other people, nonetheless all four of the variables against which they correlated levels of helping behaviour were social – namely, how many people live in the city, how well off the people in the city are, how individualistic (or collectivist) the people in the city are, and how quickly the people move around the city centre. As such, they can be seen as investigating the impact of other people on levels of helping behaviour, albeit perhaps more indirectly than did Darley and Latané or Piliavin *et al.*

Links to the key theme

- In relation to the key theme of responses to people in need, Levine *et al.*'s study suggests that levels of helping behaviour vary quite considerably around the world, with the highest levels being in the 'simpatia' cultures of Latin America and Spain.

- In terms of the extent to which Levine *et al.*'s study changes our understanding of the key theme of responses to people in need, it certainly helps to put the results from Piliavin *et al.*'s study in context, suggesting that New York is a city in which people are relatively unhelpful and, as such, results from there aren't necessarily ones that can be generalised from to elsewhere. Beyond that, the impression given in Piliavin's study of people being largely helpful is confirmed by Levine's study, although one difference between the two studies centres on the gender of those who help: whereas 90 per cent of first helpers in the study by Piliavin were male, in the study by Levine there was no significant difference between males and females in their levels of helping behaviour.

- In terms of the extent to which Levine *et al.*'s study changes our understanding of individual, social and cultural diversity, it is clear that this study shows significant cultural differences in levels of helping behaviour between different countries around the world. As such, it teaches us to expect cultural diversity in relation to people's preparedness to help those in need. With regard to social diversity, this study also changes the understanding that we were left with from the study by Piliavin. Thus, whereas that study suggested that first helpers were likely to be male, the study by Levine suggests that first helpers are as likely to be female as male.

Comparison with the classic study

- In what ways is the study by Levine *et al. similar to* the study by Piliavin *et al.*? In both studies:
  - Data were collected in the field.
  - Participants didn't know they were taking part in psychological research.
  - Data were collected in urban settings.
  - The person seemingly in need of help was a young male.
- In what ways is the study by Levine *et al. different from* the study by Piliavin *et al.*?
  - Whereas all the data for Piliavin *et al.*'s study were collected in one country, Levine *et al.* collected their data from 23 different countries.
  - Piliavin *et al.* were collecting their data in 1968, whereas Levine *et al.* collected theirs between 1992 and 1997.
  - Whereas Piliavin *et al.* collected their data in a confined subway setting, Levine *et al.* collected their data up on the street.

- Whereas Piliavin *et al.* collected all their data on helping behaviour in relation to just the one helping scenario, Levine *et al.* collected theirs in relation to three such scenarios (and, if it had been possible, would have collected data in relation to five helping scenarios).

Questions arising from Levine *et al.*

- What questions are we left with after studying the research by Levine *et al.*? Piliavin *et al.*'s study left many questions unanswered, many of which have been answered by Levine (e.g. about levels of helping behaviour above ground and in other cities apart from New York). Questions remain from this study, though, such as whether levels of helping behaviour would be different if the person in need of help was female.

- Can you think of any other questions left unanswered even after Levine *et al.*'s ambitious cross-cultural study?

Practice questions

1. From Levine *et al.*'s study into cross-cultural altruism:
   (a) Identify the two ways of measuring helping behaviour for which Levine *et al.* were unable to analyse data. [2 marks]
   (b) Outline why Levine *et al.* were unable to analyse the data for one of these measures of helping behaviour. [2 marks]

2. In relation to Levine *et al.*'s study into cross-cultural altruism:
   (a) Suggest one strength of the cross-cultural technique in this study. [2 marks]
   (b) Suggest one weakness of the cross-cultural technique in this study. [2 marks]

3. Suggest why Levine *et al.*'s study into cross-cultural altruism can be placed within the social area. [2 marks]

4. Suggest one way in which the study by Levine *et al.* into cross-cultural altruism changes our understanding of the key theme of **responses to people in need**. [3 marks]

Chapter 2

The cognitive area

Almost everything we do causes us to think. We think about what we are going to do, and then we think about what we have done. We plan, we discuss, we imagine, we remember, we try to make sense of both the concrete and the social world around us, and even when we are unable to do this, we try to work out the way it *should* be. Sometimes our working out produces the wrong answer, but the processes involved are all interlinked, and they all involve cognition.

Before the invention of computers, our understanding of how we processed information was limited. Much of the work in psychology involved simply looking at behaviour by observing the type of responses that were produced by different types of stimuli. There was little research on what happened between the stimulus and the response, not only because the techniques to investigate these processes were limited, but also because knowledge in this area was quite basic. However, the computer analogy opened up a whole new way of looking at the way the brain processes information. This information-processing approach works as follows:

1. Input – through one of the senses (e.g. eyes or ears)
2. Processing – this occurs using currently installed software (previous experience and knowledge)
3. Response – which may be action or chosen inaction.

Cognitive psychology is involved in understanding the middle process; that is, how the information is processed and what kind of choices are made. The information-processing model has opened up study in this area, allowing us to investigate cognitive processes using laboratory-based methods and experiment (Table 2.1).

Cognitive psychology covers a number of areas – memory, perception, language, thinking and attention – and all these processes are interconnected. You would

Table 2.1 Strengths and weaknesses of the cognitive area

Strengths of the cognitive area	Weaknesses of the cognitive area
Research within the cognitive area can help improve our understanding of human behaviour, particularly the extent to which it is affected by the way we think and how our brain processes incoming sensory information. In addition, understanding that often it is what we do not process can help us more fully understand our behaviour, as in studies of selective attention.	Findings from research within the cognitive area may not be true if studies lack ecological validity, and this is often a problem where laboratory experiments are used.
Research within the cognitive area can be extremely useful, having practical applications in the real world, such as developing effective interviewing techniques for police officers that avoid using leading questions.	At present, there are limitations to the way data are gathered in the cognitive area. Cognitive processes can only be studied by inference; that is, we cannot study them directly – we can only gather what is going on in someone's head by recording what they can or can't tell us (self-report) or can or can't do (observation), or at best by making and interpreting recordings of the active parts of their brain by, for example, using MRI scans.
A major strength of the cognitive area is that it favours the scientific method, using the laboratory experiment to investigate mental processes. This enables researchers to establish cause and effect between variables. This means that the cognitive area brings academic credibility to psychology as a discipline since it favours a scientific methodology. The cognitive area contributes heavily to the modern paradigm of cognitive neuroscience in psychology.	The use of laboratory experiments in the cognitive area also increases the chances of participants responding to demand characteristics in the study. An example of this from the core studies is the study by Loftus and Palmer. In this study, participants were shown film clips because of the practical and ethical problems with viewing real-life accidents, and were then asked questions about what they had seen, reducing ecological validity and introducing an opportunity for participants to work out the purpose of the study and behave accordingly. This means that there are a number of challenges to the validity of cognitive studies carried out in the laboratory.
The emphasis on controlled scientific study in the cognitive area makes it easier to test such studies for reliability. This means that the scientific value of studies in the cognitive area can be increased, since replication of findings is an important feature of scientific enquiry.	

find it very difficult to do one without involving another. However, research has often considered these processes separately, and the core studies do this, with two of them investigating the process of attention and two investigating memory.

The particular cognitive studies we will be examining are as outlined in Table 2.2.

Table 2.2 Cognitive studies discussed in this chapter

Key theme	Classic study	Contemporary study
Attention	Moray (1959)	Simons and Chabris (1999)
	Auditory attention	Visual inattention
Memory	Loftus and Palmer (1974)	Grant *et al.* (1998)
	Eyewitness testimony	Context-dependent memory

Further reading

Grant, H.M., Bredhal, L.C., Clay, J., Ferrie, J., Groves, J.E., Mcdorman, T.A. and Dark, V.J., 1998, 'Context-Dependent Memory for Meaningful Material: Information for Students'. *Applied Cognitive Psychology*, vol. 12, 617–623.

Loftus, E. and Palmer, J., 1974, 'Reconstruction of Automobile Destruction: An Example of the Interaction Between Language and Memory'. *Journal of Verbal Learning and Verbal Behaviour,* vol. 13, 585–589.

Moray, N., 1959, 'Attention in Dichotic Listening: Affective Cues and the Influence of Instructions'. *Quarterly Journal of Experimental Psychology*, vol. 11, no 1, 56–60.

Simons, D.J. and Chabris, C.F., 1999, 'Gorillas in Our Midst: Sustained Inattentional Blindness for Dynamic Events'. *Perception*, vol. 28, 1059–1074.

Memory

What is memory? It is difficult to find a precise definition of 'memory', but it is often referred to as the ability to retain information and demonstrate retention through behaviour. If we could not retain and use information that we have already discovered, it would mean that for every new experience we would have to process huge amounts of information, which could be very costly in terms of the time it might take.

Memory is a fundamental part of each of us. Our memories serve to tell us who we are and help us to make sense of the situations in which we find ourselves. Every day we carry out hundreds of tasks that use our memory and we often do so automatically with what appears to cost us very little effort. For example, when we get dressed we have to recall important information such as which drawer we keep our socks in, we also use our spatial memory to navigate our way to the bathroom, where our procedural memory tells us how to have a shower and clean our teeth, brush our hair, etc., and we are back to spatial memory to find our way to work or school. We use our memory for people and faces to recognise our workmates or classmates, and our memory for social behaviour so we say a cheery 'good morning' in the right places and at the right time. At both work and school, we will need to use our memory for information, so we can both recall what we have already learned and also assimilate new information.

Since memory seems to be essential for all our behaviour, it might be disconcerting for you to know that we cannot always rely upon our memory to be accurate. Although cognitive psychology uses a computer analogy to explain how we process information in our brains, when it comes to comparison between computer memory and human memory, we are woefully lacking. Information fed into a computer is saved, stored and returned to us by the machine in its original form, fully intact and unchanged. Our human memory is not at all like that, as you will know if you have ever forgotten someone's birthday, left your homework on the kitchen table, lost your mobile phone, or gone completely blank in a test. However, not only can information be forgotten or lost, it can also be changed, as once stored in our memory the human brain does not, unlike a computer, save the information in the same state in which it was originally stored. Our memory does not document everything we experience and recall it as necessary. In fact, many of the things we experience are not stored and other things are stored inaccurately.

How and why does this happen? It helps us to think of memory not just as 'storage', but also as a process, as a way we try to make sense of our environment. Schema theory is a way of explaining memory as such a process, and understanding schema theory will help you to understand how our memories become distorted – or positively inaccurate.

➡ Have a go yourself

Here's an exercise to test your memory!
Look at the 20 objects in Figure 2.5 for 2 minutes, then close the book and see how many you can write down in the right order.

Figure 2.5 Objects memory test

Did you do as well as you thought you would?

Endel Tulving (1972) suggested that we have two different types of memory: episodic memory, which is a memory of episodes (or events in our lives), and semantic memory, which is a memory of facts (e.g. trees lose their leaves in winter). Sometimes the experience of an episode leads us to learn new facts. Often (even when we do not have a damaged memory), we remember the facts rather than the actual episode. Why this happens can be explained in part by schema theory.

Each fact that we learn as a result of our experiences becomes part of a schema, which is a kind of packet of information about something. It may help you to think of schemata as files in the drawer of a filing cabinet. You have schemata about school, work, holidays, clubs, picnics, parties, and so on. You simply open the drawer of the filing cabinet in your head, take out the relevant file and look up the information, in a fraction of a second.

We have schemata for all different types of objects, events and situations, and they are put together from the experiences we have had and the information we have gathered. They seem to contain a kind of prototype which develops from this information, and the amount of detail they contain will vary accordingly.

Schema theory shows how we make use of our memory to enable us to repeat quickly and efficiently behaviours or experiences that occur regularly in our lives, or to manage experiences similar to those we have lived through before. Our knowledge of a typical (or perhaps stereotypical) trip to the supermarket means we are able to do the weekly shop efficiently, without having to keep learning how to do it. By putting schemata in order, we are able to produce a script, or template, for what to expect and how to behave.

As we have seen, schema theory emphasises the fact that what we remember is influenced by what we already know. It also helps to explain how the ideas, beliefs and attitudes we hold have an effect on what we will remember about an event. If you were asked to imagine going to a restaurant, and told to list 20 things that happened during the course of your time there, you would include many of the same things as other people, such as being seated, reading the menu, ordering food, having drinks and paying the bill. Such a study, conducted by Bower *et al.* (1979), involving 32 people, found that 73 per cent included the following six events on their list: sitting down, looking at a menu, ordering, eating, paying the bill and leaving the restaurant.

The participants in this piece of research named the same events, as they obviously had experience of restaurants and knew exactly what went on. Now imagine you are a small child and the only 'restaurant' you have been to is McDonald's. What sort of things would you describe if you were asked the same question? Then you visit a Harvester or Beefeater restaurant, and your knowledge of restaurants increases enormously, as you realise that restaurants involve sitting down at a table, reading the menu and having food brought to you rather than having to queue for it. Then you visit somewhere like the Savoy in London, and things would be different again.

With growing experience and knowledge, the packet of information contained in your brain which stores information about a certain event will increase in size as you get older. You will be able to use this stored knowledge to answer questions and interpret conversations without having to have all the details presented to you. You would understand what was meant by, 'We went to the Harvester last night and the service was excellent,' without wondering what on earth the person was talking about.

Schema theory was introduced by Frederick Bartlett in 1932, in order to explain why, when people remember stories, they regularly leave out some details and introduce what he called 'rationalisations', which they use to make the stories make sense. He investigated this using a story called *The War of the Ghosts*, asking people to recall a story which contained unfamiliar information. He found that they did not remember the story as it was told, but made errors in their recall, because they used their schemata to interpret the story and provide information which they believed was included, rather than what was actually there.

Bartlett asked people to recall the story at intervals over time, showing that distortions occurred. The story was made more westernised – for example, with 'fishing' substituted for 'hunting' seals. In addition, the amount recalled decreased over time, and there were further distortions.

Bartlett believed that when people remember stories, there is a tendency for them to sacrifice detailed recall in favour of 'making sense' of the information provided. He demonstrated that rather than being like computer memory, where input information is retrieved unaltered, human memory is reconstructive in nature. When we process information, we try to make it logical, sensible and coherent. As we have already seen, this means that we include what could or should have happened, according to our expectations, so our memory is likely to be an imperfect record of events, and can be a complete distortion, governed by our biases and prejudices. You may be unaware of ever doing this as it is not a conscious process, but if you want to see it in real life then just ask two squabbling siblings for their version of events and see how much they differ.

Loftus and Palmer (1974)

Bartlett's ideas are still widely accepted, as they explain how the information we take in is affected by already existing schemata representing previous knowledge. His work, however, has its critics. His findings were largely qualitative, as it is very difficult to establish objective measures of memory distortion. Later researchers, however, have undertaken laboratory studies to investigate scientifically the reconstructive nature of human memory, and to consider some of the factors which lead to these distortions. An eminent researcher in this field is Elizabeth Loftus, who, along with colleagues, has carried out a series of studies, particularly concerning the reliability of eyewitness testimony.

It is interesting that eyewitness testimony was once considered one of the most important factors in court cases. Many suspects were found guilty as a result of their identification by witnesses and witness reports of events. But if human memory is reconstructive, should we rely on this in a court of law?

Loftus was concerned not only with the fragility of memory, but also with the effects of stress on the ability of victims to recall facts. Loftus and Burns (1982) showed their participants a film of a hold-up and then tested their memory for details. The experimental group saw a violent version of the film, where one of the members of a group of young boys is shot and collapses on the floor, clutching his bleeding face. The control group saw the same film, but this scene was omitted. Instead, their film changed to a scene inside the bank, where the manager is explaining to staff and customers exactly what has happened.

Loftus and Burns found that participants who saw the violent version had significantly less memory for details of events before the shooting. Most participants failed to mention that one of the boys had a large number '17' on his jersey, which was very obvious from the film. There were actually 16 items that participants could have recalled, but those who had seen the violent version of the film recalled significantly less than the other group on 14 of those items.

The core study that we are concerned with here focuses on the effects of language on memory changes. Loftus suggested that there are two types of information that affect our memory of an event:

- information gained at the time of the event;
- information gained after the event (subsequent information).

Loftus was interested in how you can actually change a witness's recollection of an incident by subtly introducing new and subsequent information during questioning; that is, *after* the event. This depends on how language is used. For example, one study showed how changing the structure of a question could lead people to reconstruct an event and 'remember' false facts. In the study, film clips were shown and the independent variable was manipulated by asking one of two versions of the critical question:

- In one condition, participants were asked, 'Did you see a broken headlight?' This question suggests that there may or may not have been a broken headlight.
- In the second condition, participants were asked, 'Did you see the broken headlight?' The use of the definite article 'the' here suggests that there definitely was a broken headlight, so the participant should have seen it.

The results showed that more of those in the second condition reported seeing a broken headlight, even though there was no broken headlight in the film.

Aim

Loftus and Palmer carried out two experiments to investigate the effects of language on memory. Their expectation was that information received after the event in the form of leading questions would be integrated into a person's memory. It would form part of the memory and cause the event to be recalled in a way that was consistent with the subsequent information they were given.

Loftus and Palmer point out that it was already known that 'some questions are … more suggestive than others', and that a legal concept of 'leading questions' existed, along with rules for the use of such questions in the courtroom.

Their definition is as follows, 'A leading question is simply one that, by its form or content, suggests to the witness what answer is desired or leads him to the desired answer.'

Method

Two experiments were carried out to see whether leading questions could change a person's memory of an event. The first experiment also tested the established theory that witnesses are not very good at estimating the speed of vehicles.

Experiment 1

Method and design

This was a laboratory experiment, and the experimental design used was independent measures.

Participants

Forty-five student participants took part in this experiment. For test purposes, it was designed that overall there would be five conditions, with nine participants providing data for each condition.

Apparatus

Equipment was needed to screen seven film segments from the Evergreen Safety Council of the Seattle Police Department. Each segment lasted between 5 and 30 seconds. The films were safety promotion films, and four of the seven clips contained staged crashes. (There would have been serious ethical concerns about showing real crashes.) The staged crashes had the advantage that the speed at which the vehicles were travelling when they crashed was known: for two of the films it was 40 mph, for one, 20 mph, and for another, 30 mph. This meant the accuracy of speed estimates could be measured.

There were also sets of questionnaires corresponding to the film clips for each participant, to be completed after each clip.

Figure 2.6 The Loftus and Palmer study was testing their participants' memory of filmed car accidents

Procedure

All the participants were shown the seven film clips and were given a questionnaire to complete after each clip. There were two parts to each questionnaire. First, they were asked to give an account of the accident they had just seen, and second, to answer a set of questions relating to the accident. Of the questions asked, the one the researchers were interested in was about the speed of the vehicles at the time of the accident.

In order to counteract order effects, the groups were presented with a different order of films. The entire experiment lasted about an hour and a half.

The independent variable was manipulated by changing the wording of the critical question about the speed of vehicles at the time of the accident, using a different verb in the question. (In an experiment, the critical question is what is used to measure the dependent variable. It is common for these to be masked in a questionnaire by the use of distracter questions, so that participants cannot respond to the demand characteristics present when just one question is asked. The fewer questions that are asked, the more likely it is that participants will work out the purpose of the study and behave so as to support the hypothesis or scupper the study. This needs to be avoided, as it affects the internal validity of the study.)

The authors theorised that the stronger the verb, the higher the speed estimate would be. The standard format of the critical question was: 'About how fast were the cars going when they xxxxx each other?' There were five verb conditions: 'contacted', 'hit', 'bumped', 'collided' and 'smashed'.

Each subject received one of the five critical questions in their questionnaires. This means that the independent variable in this experiment was in which verb condition the participant was tested. The dependent variable was the mean speed estimate in miles per hour per condition, thus giving a quantitative measure.

Results

We will look at these in two parts.

1. How accurate are the witnesses' speed estimates?
   The accuracy of participants' speed estimates in miles per hour for the four staged crashes was as follows:

Film	Actual speed (mph)	Mean estimated speed (mph)
1	20	37.7
2	30	36.2
3	40	39.7
4	40	36.1

These results support previous studies in that they indicate that people are not very good at judging how fast a vehicle is actually travelling.

2. Does changing the verb in the critical question affect speed estimates?

Stop and ask yourself ...

- There are a number of different types of questions used in this study. Make sure you can explain what is meant by a leading question, a critical question and a distracter question, giving examples from this study.

Links to methodological issues
- Check your understanding

The mean speed estimates in miles per hour for each of the five verb conditions were as follows:

Verb	Mean estimated speed (mph)
Smashed	40.8
Collided	39.3
Bumped	38.1
Hit	34.0
Contacted	31.8

Inferential analysis of these results showed that they were significant, at the $p < 0.005$ level. This shows that the form of the question affected the witnesses' answers.

Discussion

Why does the wording affect the participant? Loftus and Palmer offer two interpretations. First, it may be due to response bias. This is the tendency to give a response in a certain direction according to the situation. If a participant cannot decide between 30 and 40, the word 'smashed' may cue the response of 40, as it suggests a higher speed. Second, it may be that the language used causes a change in the participant's memory representation of events. Loftus and Palmer say, 'The verb "smashed" may change a participant's memory such that he "sees" that accident as being more severe than it was' (page 586).

Loftus and Palmer carried out a second experiment to try to establish which of these interpretations was true. They theorised that if the person's memory had been changed, then they could be expected to 'remember' other details which did not occur, but which would fit in with their belief that the accident took place at a higher speed.

Experiment 2

Aim

The aim of the second experiment was to see if participants asked the 'smashed' question would be more likely than two other groups to report seeing broken glass in a filmed accident, when tested 1 week later. They were compared to a group asked the 'hit' question, and a control group not asked to make a speed estimate. Broken glass would be expected in an accident occurring at high speed, but no broken glass was actually shown in the film. A positive report of broken glass would suggest that the memory of the event was being reconstructed as a result of information (in the form of leading questions) received after the event.

Research method and design

This was also a laboratory experiment, using independent measures.

Participants

One hundred and fifty student participants were divided into three groups, with 50 participants in each condition.

Apparatus

Equipment was needed to screen a film showing a multiple car crash. The clip lasted less than 1 minute, with the accident itself lasting less than 4 seconds.

Each participant completed two questionnaires. The questionnaires completed immediately after viewing the film clip asked participants to describe the accident in their own words and to answer a series of questions (questionnaire 1). The critical question asked participants to estimate the speed of the vehicles.

 Stop and ask yourself ...

- Can you suggest three ways in which watching an accident on film is different from watching an accident in real life?
- What are the advantages that Loftus and Palmer gain by showing the events to be witnessed on film?

Links to methodological issues
- Ecological validity

- Design validity

 Stop and ask yourself ...

- What is an independent measure design? What are the strengths and weaknesses of using this design in this study?
- What do you think are the strengths and weaknesses of using a sample made up entirely of college/university students in this study?

Links to methodological issues
- Check your understanding

- Sample biases

There were three conditions, with two conditions being asked leading questions about the speed of the vehicles:

1. Fifty participants were asked, 'About how fast were the cars going when they smashed into each other?'
2. Fifty participants were asked, 'About how fast were the cars going when they hit each other?'
3. Fifty participants were not asked about the speed of vehicles, and thus acted as a control condition.

A second questionnaire (questionnaire 2) contained ten questions about the accident. The critical question was, 'Did you see any broken glass?' Participants responded to this by ticking Yes or No.

Procedure

This was a two-part procedure, with participants seeing the film and filling in one of the three versions of questionnaire 1 on one day, and returning a week later to complete questionnaire 2.

Results

Participants in the 'smashed' condition gave a significantly higher speed estimate than those in the 'hit' condition (10.46 mph and 8 mph, respectively), supporting the finding from the first experiment that the wording of the question can have a considerable effect on the estimate of speed.

Participants in the 'smashed' condition were also significantly more likely to answer 'Yes' to the question, 'Did you see any broken glass?' than those in the 'hit' and control conditions. The differences between the control and the 'hit' conditions were negligible.

The distribution of 'Yes' and 'No' responses to the question, 'Did you see any broken glass?', was as follows:

Response	'Smashed' condition	'Hit' condition	Control
Yes	16	7	6
No	34	43	44

Conclusions

The questions asked subsequent to an event can cause a reconstruction in one's memory of that event. The verb used in a question can affect the speed a witness estimates a vehicle to have been travelling at and also whether they recall having seen any broken glass.

Discussion

The conclusion of the second experiment was that the verb not only affected the estimate of speed, but also the likelihood of participants thinking they had seen

broken glass. Loftus and Palmer explain this by suggesting that participants took in information from the original scene and then merged this with information given after the event. This produced a memory of the event made up of some of the original information and subsequent information received when they were questioned about it. We are inclined to make our memory make sense, so those participants who believed the accident had taken place at a higher speed, and was therefore more severe (those in the 'smashed' condition), were more likely to think that broken glass was present.

Evaluation of the study by Loftus and Palmer

Links to methodological issues

Research method

- Loftus and Palmer carried out controlled laboratory experiments and these fulfil the scientific criteria of theory, control, evidence and replication; however, problems with ecological validity can arise with laboratory experiments (see Validity below).

Data

- This study collected and reported quantitative data and this enables results to be easily summarised. For example, Loftus and Palmer report the findings of study 1 as mean speed estimates for each verb condition and it can be easily seen that as the strength of the verb in the leading question increased so did the mean speed estimate. Comparison between conditions is also easier where quantitative rather than qualitative findings are presented and this can be seen in study 2 where the number who reported seeing broken glass in each condition was reported out of 50.

Ethics

- Although the participants knew that this was a test of memory, the hypothesis about leading questions was not revealed to them, and distracter questions were used to further conceal the exact hypothesis. However, this concealment was necessary in this study to ensure that demand characteristics did not affect the findings. The researchers chose to show clips of car crashes from safety films which did not contain gruesome images (not even any broken glass!), so they should not have upset the participants or caused them harm. The study was therefore conducted ethically.

Validity

- As a highly controlled laboratory experiment, this study has high design validity. The procedure – including film clips, tasks and questions asked – was standardised.
- However, as the participants knew they were in a study, they may have tried to affect the outcome of the study. For example, they may have thought they were 'supposed' to remember broken glass and so reported that they did when in fact they did not, so this may not be a valid demonstration of how leading questions affect memory.

Ecological validity

- As the study was carried out in the controlled conditions of the laboratory, it may be low in ecological validity. In the study, the participants were asked to watch the film clips and were prepared to recall what they had seen. Accidents happen spontaneously in the real world, and our memories of such events will obviously be different without the luxury of prior warning. We also have to question whether watching film clips of staged accidents leads to memories being laid down or recalled in the same way as they might be under the stressful and distressing circumstances of being a witness to a real car crash involving real people.

Reliability

- Loftus and Palmer's study uses highly controlled laboratory experiments. As such, it meets the important criteria for scientific research that it should be replicable in order for the reliability of its findings to be investigated. This study could be replicated and the findings of the original and subsequent study correlated to see if test–retest reliability could be established.
- In terms of the reliability of the findings, both the experiments carried out provided evidence that memory of an event can be distorted by information introduced afterwards. This supports the reliability of the theory that language – in this case, leading questions – can distort memory.

Sampling method and sample biases

- Where college students are used as participants in psychological research, generalisability beyond the sample, and to the wider population, is low. For both experiments, Loftus and Palmer drew their sample from a population of students. Since most psychologists undertake research while working at a university, the student body provides them with the perfect opportunity or volunteer sample. The researcher just needs to put up an advertisement on the noticeboard with the offer of money (or, for psychology students, the possibility of marks towards their course) and stand back to avoid being killed in the rush. Perhaps that is an exaggeration, but the fact is that students are plentiful on campus, and many researchers have benefited from using the time- and cost-effective sample that an undergraduate sample base can provide. The researcher is able to carry out the study from the comfort of their workplace, and students earn some money – so why are student samples a problem?
- In order for a sample to be generalisable to the wider population, you need a broader sample than that enticed out of the university library or the student bar. Sears (1986) reviewed the use of student samples in psychology and considered the problems presented in terms of biasing factors that reduce generalisability, and the consequences of basing our view of human psychology on such a narrow sample base.
- Biasing factors include the fact that students tend to represent only a narrow age range, and the upper levels of family income and educational background. This means that they present us with a biased sample, as no other age groups are represented. Moreover, students are not even typical of their own age group, as they are university students because they have displayed the cognitive skills required to gain entry, and in order to do this they tend to be more compliant to authority than their peers in general.
- Sears goes on to say that laboratory studies, such as that by Loftus and Palmer, compound the problems, since the students will be more willing to comply with researchers' requests, especially if studies they participate in form part of their course. So we should always be cautious when making generalisations from studies using student samples.

Ethnocentrism

- On the one hand, since cognitive processes, such as reconstructive memory, depend upon the physiognomy of our brain, we could argue that studies such as Loftus and Palmers' are not ethnocentric, since they are investigating a species-specific behaviour. On the other hand, it is possible that the findings only reflect how university educated people's cognitive processes work, since only students were studied. Student samples have ethnocentric biases, for example, most students come from the upper and middle social classes. Other groups may perform differently on these tests.

Links to debates

Psychology as a science

- Loftus and Palmer carried out controlled laboratory experiments and these fulfil the scientific criteria of theory, control, evidence and replication. As with many cognitive area studies, this supports the claim that psychology is a scientific discipline.

Usefulness

- Loftus and Palmer's study is one in a series of studies which showed that it is possible to distort the memories of eye witnesses to events. This has considerable repercussions for the police. Such studies have led to a great deal of research being carried out into the best way for police officers to question witnesses, suggesting that this study has real-life applications. However, look again at the responses of participants in the second experiment. Of 150 participants questioned, 121 answered correctly, 'No', including over two-thirds of the participants in the 'smashed' condition. So perhaps it is not so easy to change a memory for an important event, and we must be careful not to exaggerate the extent to which the recall of witnesses is affected by leading questions.

Ethical issues

- Given the findings of the study, we could describe it as ethically worthy, since it contributes to the debate about how witnesses to events should or should not be questioned in order to get a true picture of what happened.

Links to areas/perspectives

- Loftus and Palmer's study falls within the cognitive area because it is investigating the cognitive process of memory. Specifically, it aimed to investigate the reconstructive nature of memory, showing that information introduced after an event in the form of leading questions would have an effect on eye witnesses' memory of the event.

Links to the key theme

- In relation to the key theme of memory, Loftus and Palmer's study provides empirical evidence into the effects of information received after the event on a person's memory of an event. It is an experimental demonstration of the effects of leading questions on eyewitness testimony and shows how memory is reconstructive in nature.

Questions arising from Loftus and Palmer's study

- Can we ever trust our memory?
- What could the police or lawyers do to try to ensure that witnesses give an accurate account of events?
- How useful are studies that use students as a sample?

 Find out more

Elizabeth Loftus has done a great deal of subsequent research into memory, and is especially interested in 'recovered memories'. She and Katherine Ketcham have written an excellent book called *The Myth of Repressed Memory* which you could read to find out more about her work and about the fascinating subject of human memory.

Practice questions

1. Outline two quantitative findings from Loftus and Palmer's study into eyewitness testimony. [2 marks]
2. Identify four reasons why we should be cautious in generalising findings from the sample in Loftus and Palmer's study on eye witness testimony to people in general. [4 marks]
3. Loftus and Palmer (eyewitness testimony) suggested that our memory of an event is affected by information we take in at the time and information we receive after the event. How did they operationalise 'information received after the event' in this study? [3 marks]
4. Loftus and Palmer (eyewitness testimony) used a laboratory experiment to investigate eyewitness testimony:
   (a) Outline one strength of a laboratory experiment as used in this study. [2 marks]
   (b) Outline one weakness of a laboratory experiment as used in this study. [2 marks]

Grant *et al.* (1998)

Do people remember better if they are remembering information in the same context as when they learned the information? Imagine that someone asked you to make a list of all 25 of the children who were in your class in year 6 of primary school. You might not do very well. However, if you were taken to your year 6 classroom and allowed to make a list of classmates while in your seat, you may well do better. This is an example of context-dependent memory. The context-dependent memory effect occurs when the memory of the to-be-remembered information is better when tested in the same context in which the material was learned (the matching condition) than when tested in a different context or environment (the mismatching condition). An example of the context-dependency effect on recall is a study by Godden and Baddeley (1975) where they studied the effects of context on the memory of deep sea divers. They had some divers learn lists of words underwater and some learn on land, and then had half of each group recall the material underwater or on land. In the matching conditions (underwater study and underwater recall, land study and land recall), the divers recalled more than in the mismatching conditions. This is a classic demonstration of context-dependent memory.

Evidence for this effect has been shown to occur more in tests of recall than in tests of recognition. In other words, your recall of your year 6 classmates might be better in the classroom environment you were in with them in year 6, but if you were asked to circle names of your 25 classmates from a list of a hundred names, your performance might not be improved by being in the classroom you shared. Grant *et al.* suggest that the difference in context-dependency effects on recall and recognition shows that there are different processes involved in the two types of memory. The effect of context on recall shows that when the information is memorised, cues from the environment are subtly encoded and, when the material is to be recalled, the same environmental cues can prompt memory, which explains better recall in a matching context condition. However, in recognition tasks, the subtle environmental

cues are 'outshined' by the strength of the to-be-recognised items themselves, such that environmental or context cues fail to have an effect.

Aim

In their study, Grant *et al.* aimed to investigate context-dependent memory effects on both recall and recognition. They note that students often study in conditions that differ from test conditions. For example, students often study in environments that are noisy, such as using music as a background. In contrast, they are tested in silent conditions. Grant *et al.* suggest that if context-dependency effects indeed occur then students could be using study habits that do not work in their favour under test conditions.

Method

Because such a variety of music is preferred by different people, the researchers chose to manipulate 'background noise' as the independent variable rather than music. A second control was that both the test and study conditions were varied to ensure that it was not the case that 'noise' interferes with the encoding of material. The study used an independent measures design.

Task

Participants read a two-page article, so were reading for meaning. This was designed to be like learning in the classroom, testing comprehension of the text rather than learning verbatim. All participants were tested on their memory in both the recall and recognition conditions. Recall was operationalised by a short-answer recall test and recognition was operationalised by using a multiple choice test.

Participants

Eight psychology students from a psychology class acted as experimenters and each recruited five acquaintances as participants. Data from 39 participants were recorded. (Data for one male in the 'silent study–silent test' condition was omitted as his scores were atypically low.)

 Stop and ask yourself …

- What is the difference between a 'recall' memory task and a 'recognition' memory task?
- How do Grant *et al.* account for an effect of context on recall but not on recognition?

Links to methodological issues
- Check your understanding

Test conditions

Each experimenter randomly allocated one of their five participants to each of the following four conditions and tested the fifth of their participants in one of the conditions as instructed by the lead researcher:

Silent study	Silent test conditions
Silent study	Noisy test conditions
Noisy study	Silent test conditions
Noisy study	Noisy test conditions

 Stop and ask yourself...

- Can you explain why the 'silent study–noisy test' and the 'noisy study– silent test' conditions were included in the procedure?

Links to methodological issues
- Experimental controls

Figure 2.7 Many students listen to music while they are studying. Is this the best way for them to study?

Materials

- Each experimenter provided their own cassette tape player and headphones.

 Stop and ask yourself...

- Can you explain the purpose of getting all participants to wear headphones while they read?
- Can you identify four other controls in this study and explain how they help to establish design validity?

Links to methodological issues
- Experimental controls
- Design validity

- The 'noisy' condition was played at a moderately loud level. It was a recording of noise at lunchtime in a university cafeteria. Some words were audible, but not complete sentences.
- Participants read an article on psychoimmunology – two pages each with three columns of text per page. The experimenters judged the text to be both interesting and understandable for their participants.
- The Recognition Test was made up of 16 multiple-choice questions, each with four choices. Some questions used phrases word for word from the text, but most were close paraphrases of the information in the text. This was also true of the answers to this test.
- Recall Test – using items from the multiple-choice test that could be easily rephrased as a question, ten short-answer questions were created to test recall. Each question required a one-word or short phrase answer.
- The information in both tests followed the order in which the information occurred in the original text.
- As a control, the recall test was always taken first to ensure that any information being recalled was from the reading of the text and not recalled from the multiple-choice test.

Procedure

Participants were read aloud standardised instructions that described the tasks as part of a class project and which emphasised that they were voluntary.

 Stop and ask yourself...

- Why is it important that it was made clear to participants that the tasks were 'voluntary'?

Links to methodological issues
- Ethical considerations

Participants read the article once and were told that they could highlight/underline as they read. They had been told that they would have to complete a short-answer and multiple-choice task based on the article.

The procedure lasted approximately 30 minutes in total. Each participant was tested individually. There were 17 females and 23 males. Their ages ranged from 17–56 years, with a mean age of 23.4 years. As a control, all participants wore headphones while they read.

In the study phase of the experiment, the instructions given were:

- Silent Condition – told nothing would be heard through the headphones while they read
- Noisy Condition – told they would be played moderately loud background noise while they read, but that they should ignore it.

Between the test and study conditions, participants had a break of approximately 2 minutes during which they rested without headphones on.

In the test phase, again all participants wore headphones and the silent and noisy conditions were given similar instructions as in the study phase. The participants then did the short-answer (recall) test and the multiple-choice (recognition) test.

The participants were then debriefed as to the true purpose of the study.

Reading time was recorded and no difference in reading time was reported between the noisy and silent study conditions; most participants took approximately the same time to read the article.

Conclusions

There are context-dependency effects for newly learned meaningful material, with the best performance being achieved when studying and testing take place in environments that have the same levels of noise. Students are likely to perform better in exams if they study for them with a minimum of background noise because, although there was no overall effect of noise on performance, the fact that there was evidence for context-dependency suggests they are better off studying without background noise as it will not be present during actual testing.

Discussion

Whereas earlier studies had failed to show a context-dependent recognition effect, Grant et al.'s study did, and the authors suggest that the context-dependency effect in the recognition test may have occurred as a result of the nature of their task – learning meaningful prose – whereas earlier studies had had participants learning unrelated lists of words. They quote a study by Martin and Aggleton (1993) which also tested participants' context-dependency for new meaningful material. In this study, novice scuba students learned instructions on how to use decompression tables for 10 minutes. They were either underwater in a pool or on the side of the pool in full gear when in the study

phase. They were tested by using the tables they had learned in either the matching or mismatching context. This study agreed with Grant's finding that newly learned, meaningful material was remembered better in the same environment in which it was learned.

Grant et al. also refer to a study by Dalton (1993) where she tested the effects of context on recognition of unfamiliar and familiar faces and found an effect in the unfamiliar but not familiar face recognition condition. Grant et al. suggest that this may mean that, where recognition is concerned, context-dependency may be more important for newly learned material rather than familiar material.

The authors suggest that since there was no evidence of a negative effect of noise on performance that students' common claim that music does not interfere with their study may be true. However, since music, if ignored, is no different from background noise, students would, given the findings of this study, be best advised to study in silence given that tests and examinations are conducted in silence, in order to benefit from this context-dependent memory effect:

Because the testing conditions in academic settings are relatively quiet, a practical suggestion based on the current results is that students are likely to perform better on exams if they study for them with a minimum of background noise. (page 621)

Results

The results were recorded as mean number of correct answers out of 10 for the recall test (Table 2.6) and out of 16 for the recognition test (Table 2.7).

Table 2.6 Mean number of correct answers out of 10 on the recall task for each study and test condition

Recall (short-answer test)	Study condition	
	Silent study	Noisy study
Silent test condition	6.7	5.4
Noisy test condition	4.6	6.2

Table 2.7 Mean number of correct answers out of 16 on the recognition task for each study and test condition

Recognition (multiple choice test)	Study condition	
	Silent study	Noisy study
Silent test condition	14.3	12.7
Noisy test condition	12.7	14.3

In both the matching conditions ('silent study–silent test' and 'noisy study–noisy test') students' results showed a context-dependency advantage. This was true of both the recall and recognition tasks.

 Have a go yourself

Next time you are preparing for a test, see if you can benefit from Grant *et al.*'s advice to students and try studying in silence. Find out for yourself if the advice they give is useful!

Evaluation of the study by Grant *et al.*

Links to methodological issues

Research method

- Grant *et al.* carried out a controlled laboratory experiment and this method fulfils the scientific criteria of theory, control, evidence and replication. The study employed an independent measures design, and this could be a challenge to the design validity, since there could be individual differences between the groups. These could include their interest in the study, their general ability to focus their attention, or their usual preferred learning conditions (silent or noisy) which might have influenced the findings.

Data

- This study collected and reported quantitative data, which enables the data to be easily summarised and compared between conditions. For example, the test scores were reported as mean scores out of 10 for the recall task and out of 16 for the recognition task and this enabled the matching and mismatching study and test conditions to be compared and for the context-dependent memory effect in the matching conditions to be seen.

Ethics

- This study was conducted entirely within the ethical guidelines. Informed consent was obtained and participants were briefed about the task they were

to undertake and were told that involvement was voluntary. After they had taken part in the tasks, they were fully debriefed by the experimenters as to the true purpose of the study.

Validity

- As a highly controlled laboratory experiment, this study has high design validity. The procedure and apparatus were standardised and participants were tested individually. A number of experimental controls were used to ensure that the study was not confounded by extraneous variables (see above under Research method for a possible challenge to the study's design validity).

Ecological validity

- In this study, Grant *et al.* were aiming to test context-dependent memory using a more ecologically valid task than previous studies which had involved learning lists of unrelated words. The task in this study – reading an article for meaning and answering questions on it – was a more ecologically valid task, at least in terms of learning material in the classroom. However, that the task was conducted as part of a study not part of a lesson, and that participants wore headphones and some heard artificial background noise while reading the article, reduces the ecological validity of the task somewhat. Similarly, most test material for examinations is learnt more than just a few minutes ago, and so testing of the material may not truly represent assessment under typical examination conditions.

Reliability

- This study is a highly controlled laboratory experiment. As such, it meets the important criteria for scientific research that it should be replicable in order for the reliability of its findings to be investigated. This study could be replicated and the findings of the original and subsequent study correlated to see if test–retest reliability could be established.

 Stop and ask yourself...

- What type of data did Grant *et al.* collect? Can you give three strengths of using this type of data in this study?

Links to methodological issues
- Type of data

Sampling method and sampling biases

- Grant *et al.* obtained an opportunity sample, as each student experimenter recruited five acquaintances to take part in the study. While opportunity samples of this type are convenient for the researcher, especially if the study was to be done on students in the university, and make the study both cost- and time-effective, there is always the concern that biases in the sample may limit the generalisability of the findings. In other words, the participants may fail to represent the target population because they are atypical.

Ethnocentrism

- On the one hand, since cognitive processes such as reconstructive memory depend upon the physiognomy of our brain, we could argue that studies such as Grant *et al.*'s are not ethnocentric, since they are investigating a species-specific behaviour. On the other hand, this study was conducted in America and it may be that without cross-cultural research to confirm that this is a universal finding, the findings may be different if conducted on people who have not had a Western education.

Links to debates

Psychology as a science

- Grant *et al.* carried out controlled laboratory experiments and these fulfil the scientific criteria of theory, control, evidence and replication. As with many cognitive area studies, this supports the claim that psychology is a scientific discipline.

Usefulness

- On the basis of their findings, Grant *et al.* suggest that students are likely to perform better in exams if they study for them with a minimum of background noise in order to benefit from the context-dependency effect for newly learned material.

Individual-situational explanations

- This study suggests that the performance of students in exams may be affected by situational factors (e.g. the circumstances under which they revise) as opposed to just individual factors (e.g. a student's innate ability).

Links to areas/perspectives

- Grant *et al.*'s study falls within the cognitive area as it is investigating the cognitive process of memory. Specifically, it aimed to investigate context-dependent memory. This study demonstrated a context-dependency effect on both recall and recognition of newly learnt meaningful material.

Links to the key theme

- In relation to the key theme of memory, Grant *et al.*'s study demonstrates that, in the case of newly learned meaningful material, students' memory was improved by studying and being tested in matching environments. This context-dependent effect was true for both recall and recognition of the material they had learnt.
- In terms of the extent to which Grant *et al.*'s study changes our understanding of the key theme of 'memory', it can be seen as adding to our understanding of how memory works by investigating a different aspect of memory – namely, context-dependent memory, as opposed to reconstructive memory.
- As Loftus and Palmer had before them, Grant *et al.* studied the memory of a sample of students, and conducted their research from universities in America. As a result, Grant *et al.* do not change our understanding of social or cultural diversity, since they were studying students from a similar background and the same culture as the classic study by Loftus and Palmer.

Therefore, the study does not change but does confirm our understanding that there are individual differences in memory under different environmental conditions.

Comparison with the classic study

- In what ways is the study by Grant *et al. similar to* the study by Loftus and Palmer?
  - The two studies were highly controlled laboratory experiments carried out on university campuses.
  - Both studies used an independent measures design.
  - The samples in both studies were made up entirely of university students.
  - Both studies were conducted ethically.
  - Both studies gathered quantitative data.
- In what ways is the study by Grant *et al. different from* the study by Loftus and Palmer?
  - Whereas Loftus and Palmer were investigating reconstructive memory in eyewitness testimony, Grant *et al.* were investigating context-dependent memory.
  - Loftus and Palmer could not easily generalise their findings to the intended target population because of student bias in the sample. However, this was not such a problem for Grant *et al.* as their intended target population was students, so an all-student sample was entirely appropriate in their research.

Questions arising from Grant *et al.*

- What questions are we left with after studying the research by Grant *et al.*? As suggested in some of the previous evaluative comments, it would be worth knowing whether the effect they report would apply to content learned in other academic subjects apart from psychology and also in tests occurring some months after the original learning of the material.
- Can you think of any other questions to which this study leaves you wanting to know the answers?

 Find out more

1. Investigate a range of study skills or techniques that would be useful for you to acquire in order to study for psychology at AS or A Level. Use a variety of sources such as searching for study tips for psychology students from the internet, or general advice on how to study and prepare for exams from study skills guides in your library, or ask your teachers for advice, or ask students who have studied psychology before you for their words of wisdom!
2. Try out these study skills and see what works for you – make sure you try at least one technique you haven't used before.

Practice questions

1. From the study by Grant *et al.* (context-dependent memory):
   (a) Explain what is meant by the term 'context-dependent memory'. [2 marks]
   (b) Outline one conclusion from this study. [2 marks]
2. From the study by Grant *et al.* (context-dependent memory):
   (a) Suggest one way the study could be considered to be valid. [2 marks]
   (b) Suggest one way the study could be considered to not be valid. [2 marks]
3. Outline two ways in which the study by Loftus and Palmer (eyewitness testimony) and Grant *et al.* (context-dependent memory) are similar to each other. [4 marks]
4. Suggest why Grant *et al.*'s study on context-dependent memory can be placed in the cognitive area. [2 marks]

Attention Ⓐ

Our brains are bombarded with information from all our senses. Attention is the cognitive process that enables us to select some of this information to concentrate on while rejecting the other information. Psychological research into attention began in the 1950s and much of the research investigated how we are able to focus our attention to concentrate on one thing, while blocking all the other incoming sensory information. This is referred to as selective, or focused, attention. Research has been conducted into both auditory selective attention and visual selective attention.

Figure 2.1 The cocktail party effect

Colin Cherry was one of the first researchers in the area of auditory selective attention. He was interested in finding out how what he called the 'Cocktail Party Effect' works (Figure 2.1). A cocktail party is a type of party where people would stand around having conversations and drinking cocktails (all the rage in the 1950s!) and Cherry noted that people at cocktail parties were very skilled at tuning in to one voice or conversation, while tuning all the

other conversations out. He carried out a number of studies to investigate auditory selective attention by getting people to listen through headphones while two different messages were played, one in each ear. Participants were told to 'shadow' one of these messages, by which Cherry meant to repeat the message out loud as they were listening to it, and they were told to ignore the other message. In the shadowing tasks, Cherry found that very little could be remembered from the unattended message, with some participants not even noting if it was in a foreign language.

In the 1950s, aviation was, if you will pardon the pun, taking off. With more planes using airports the job of the air traffic controller to listen to the message from one pilot while ignoring the others was becoming more difficult. With increased cognitive load for the air traffic controllers, the likelihood of error and catastrophe also increased. Donald Broadbent's interest in selective attention arose from trying to address the practical problems faced by these air traffic controllers.

Broadbent's work made a great contribution to cognitive psychology, as he was among the first researchers to compare the processing of information by the human brain to the processing of information by a computer, and this computer analogy remains an important model for our understanding of cognitive processes in psychology.

Broadbent presented his Filter Model of selective attention in 1958 (Figure 2.2). In this model, he suggested that there was a sensory filter mechanism that, early on in our processing of information, selected only one channel of incoming sensory information and blocked all the others off, allowing attention to be focused. Broadbent argued that 'our mind can be conceived as a radio receiving many channels at once', where we tune in to one channel and as a result tune out all the rest.

Broadbent's Filter Model

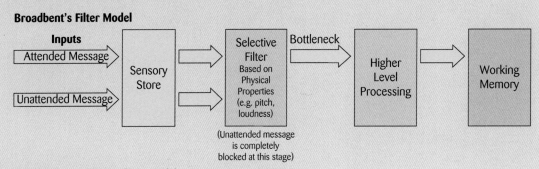

Figure 2.2 Broadbent's filter model

However, this theory did not stand up to empirical testing as it became apparent that unattended stimuli from other channels could often be well remembered.

Anne Treisman refined Broadbent's theory in 1964, presenting what she called the Attenuation Theory of Selective Attention. This theory suggested that, instead of being completely filtered out, the non-attended channels were instead 'turned down', or attenuated. This theory could account for the fact that some information in the unattended message would be well remembered.

However, Treisman failed to fully explain what the process of 'attenuation' means. We do not have a 'volume' button that can turn down incoming information, and she did not fully explain why some unattended messages were recalled and others were not.

In 1978, a further theory of selective attention was proposed by Johnson and Heinz. Unlike in Broadbent and Treisman's theories, they suggested that instead of selection of what to pay attention to happening at an early stage of processing incoming stimuli, selection could occur at a number of different stages in the processing of information. They would argue that the amount of time we might spend processing information that is 'unwanted' might be affected by how easy it is to discriminate between incoming stimuli – if they can easily be distinguished (a man's voice or a woman's voice) we may not process the unwanted message as much as if we were trying to distinguish between similar inputs, such as two women's voices.

This theory accounts best for the findings from listening experiments conducted into selective attention. The fact that selection can happen at any stage can explain why we might 'switch' attention if an unattended channel became meaningful to us.

It is this process of switching channels to attend to information you have been asked to ignore that is the basis of our classic core study by Moray. Once we have selected a channel to attend to and have put up cognitive 'blocks' or 'barriers', what, if anything, of the unattended channel would be recalled? Cherry had noted that however deep in conversation you might be at your cocktail party, if someone mentioned your name in another conversation, this would draw your attention. Moray wanted to test this empirically to see if hearing your name would indeed break through the 'barriers' put up in the process of focusing attention during a shadowing task.

The contemporary study by Simons and Chabris investigated visual selective attention, and investigated how much of a scene we might miss if we are told to focus on one aspect of it – could we fail to see something that happened right in the centre of our field of vision, right in front of our eyes?

Moray (1959)

As mentioned above, Colin Cherry had noted that however deep in conversation you might be at your cocktail party, if someone mentioned your name in another conversation, this would draw your attention. Moray wanted to empirically test this to see if hearing your name would indeed break through the 'barriers' put up in the process of focusing attention during a shadowing task.

Dichotic listening tasks present two different auditory stimuli into different ears through headphones (Figure 2.3). Moray points out that Cherry (1953) devised a method called 'shadowing' to study attention in listening. When shadowing a task, participants listen dichotically to two stimuli, usually spoken words or text and are instructed to listen to one of the stimuli and repeat it out loud as they listen. In this way they are focusing their attention on the task to be shadowed, the 'attended' task, while blocking out the other, 'rejected' task.

Figure 2.3 A dichotic listening task

Aims

Cherry had found that participants who shadowed one task could recall nothing of the content of the 'rejected' task, not even noting in which language the other message was being spoken. They could, however, distinguish between speech, noise and tones, could recognise clicks and obvious changes in pitch, e.g. changing from a male to a female voice.

The aim of Moray's study was to provide a 'rigorous', empirical test of Cherry's findings.

Sample

The sample was made up of undergraduate students and research workers of both sexes. Moray does not provide a sample size for his first experiment, but tells us that 12 participants took part in experiment two, and two groups of 14 participants were studied in experiment three.

Procedure

In this study, three laboratory experiments were conducted. All were dichotic listening tasks that required the participants to shadow one message while two messages were played to them, one in each ear.

When we pay attention to one message, we set up a 'block' on any other message and focus our attention on the selected message. Moray was interested in what types of message, if any, would penetrate this 'block' and be paid attention to by participants.

Common apparatus for the three experiments

- The apparatus used was a 'Brenell mark IV stereophonic tape recorder, modified with twin amplifiers to give two independent outputs through attenuators, one output going to each of the ear pieces in a set of headphones' (page 56).
- Loudness was matched to the earpieces by asking participants to say when the messages appeared to be of equivalent volume to them (to within ±1 db).

🚫 **Stop and ask yourself ...**

- Can you explain what is meant by both 'dichotic listening' tasks and 'shadowing' tasks in relation to studying auditory selective attention?

Links to methodological issues
- Check your understanding

🚫 **Stop and ask yourself ...**

- If this study was conducted today, we would expect to have more details of the sample, including sampling method, sample size, age and gender. Why?
- Can you give one strength and one weakness of the sample used in this study?

Links to methodological issues
- Sampling issues
- Population validity
- Reliability

- Participants all completed four trial-shadowing tasks on passages of prose for practice before the study.
- The loudness of each message was approximately 60 db above the participant's hearing threshold, and the speech rate approximately 150 words a minute.
- All passages were recorded by one male speaker.

Experiment 1

In this experiment, a short list of simple words was spoken 35 times as the 'rejected' or 'blocked' message.

At the end of the shadowing task, participants were asked to recall all they could remember of the rejected message. Then, approximately 30 seconds after the completion of the shadowing tasks, participants were given a recognition test of 21 words. Seven of these were from the shadowed passage, seven were from the list of words in the rejected message and seven were similar words but not present in either passage (these words acted as a control condition) (Table 2.3).

Table 2.3 Results of experiment 1

Word list	Mean number of recognised words
Seven words taken from the shadowed passage	4.9
Seven words taken from the list in the 'rejected' message	1.9
Seven similar words that appeared in neither message	2.6

Despite the fact that the short list of words was repeated many times during the inattended message, the participants still could not recall them.

Discussion

Moray concludes, 'In a situation where a subject directs his attention to the reception of a message from one ear and rejects a message from the other ear, almost none of the verbal content of the rejected message is able to penetrate the block set up' (page 60).

Experiment 2

Moray reports that there is anecdotal evidence that the 'block' built up while shadowing one message that enables the other message to be rejected can be broken down if the material in the rejected message is important enough to the listener:

Mothers hear children crying, and it is always said that a subject will respond to his own name ... as at a cocktail party (to give an everyday situation).

The second experiment aimed to test whether an affective cue – a cue that has a strong meaning for the participant – would penetrate the 'block' and be attended to. The affective cue was to be the participant's own name, given alongside instructions. So the participant might hear:

'John Smith, change to your other ear', or

'John Smith, you may stop now'.

These were compared with non-affective instructions which did not begin with the participant's name, such as 'Change to your other ear' or 'All right, you may stop now'.

The participants heard two passages of light fiction at once: one was presented to one ear and the other was presented to the other ear. Both passages that the participant heard contained an instruction at the start and an instruction within it (Table 2.4). In all cases, the passages began with an instruction to the participant to listen to their right ear, and in two cases (passage VIII and passage X) this initial instruction was immediately followed by a warning that the participant would receive instructions to change ears. The instructions that were contained *within* the passages took three forms:

- Three comprised affective instructions (participant's own name prefixed the instruction) – these were passages III, VII and X.
- Three comprised non-affective instructions (their name was not mentioned) – these were passages I, V and VIII.
- In four cases, there were no instructions within the passage – these were passages II, IV, VI and IX.

In total, participants had ten trials, each time listening to two passages of light fiction. They were required to do a shadowing task each time (which we can assume to have been of the passage heard in their right ear, in line with the instructions they heard at the start of each passage), and what Moray was interested in was whether participants were more likely to hear the instruction within the message they weren't paying attention to (i.e. the rejected message) if it was preceded by their name.

Table 2.4 The standard order of presentation of the rejected passages

Passage	Instructions at start of passage	Instructions within passage
I	Listen to your right ear.	All right, you may stop now.
II	Listen to your right ear.	No instructions.
III	Listen to your right ear.	John Smith, you may stop now.
IV	Listen to your right ear.	No instructions.
V	Listen to your right ear.	Change to your other ear.
VI	Listen to your right ear.	No instruction.
VII	Listen to your right ear.	John Smith, change to your other ear.
VIII	Listen to your right ear: you will receive instructions to change ears.	Change to your other ear.
IX	Listen to your right ear.	No instructions.
X	Listen to your right ear: you will receive instructions to change ears.	John Smith, change to your other ear.

The passages of light fiction were read in a steady monotone at about 130 words a minute by a single male voice and they were also checked to make sure there was no increase in intensity when the participant's voice was spoken. Participants were told that the aim was for them to make as few errors in their shadowing of the passages as possible.

There were 12 participants and they were all students or research workers. As they each shadowed ten passages of light fiction, this meant that Moray (focusing only on the participants' responses to the rejected messages, not the passages they were shadowing) anticipated having 36 affective and 36 non-affective instructions to analyse the responses of the participants. Their performances on the shadowing tasks were tape recorded and analysed (Table 2.5). This experiment used a repeated measures design.

Table 2.5 Results: relative frequencies of hearing affective and non-affective instructions when presented in the rejected message

	Affective instructions (preceded by name)	Non-affective instructions (not preceded by name)
Number of times presented	39*	36
Number of times heard	20	4

*This changeover by some participants – which, whenever it occurred, occurred in passage X – also accounts for the fact that there were 39 opportunities for the 'names' instruction to be heard rather than 36.

Participants were deemed to have heard a message if they reported hearing the instruction when asked about the experiment in between the fiction passages or if, when they received an instruction preceded by their name, they actually followed the instruction and changed messages (something that accounted for four out of the 20 occasions on which the 'names' instructions were deemed to have been heard).

T-test analysis of the results showed that there was a less than 1 per cent probability of the results being due to chance, so this was a highly significant effect: the participant's own name did indeed break through the 'block' on the rejected message and was heard. This supports the claim that a person will hear instructions if they are presented with their own name.

Moray noted that when the participants were given a warning at the start of the passage to expect instructions to change ears there was a slight increase in the mean frequency with which they heard instructions in the rejected message. This led Moray to think this might mean that being given a pre-warning (i.e. receiving instructions before a shadowing task) might mean a participant is more likely to hear material in the rejected message. Their third experiment tested this theory.

Experiment 3

Two groups of 14 participants were asked to shadow one of two simultaneous dichotic messages.

In some of the messages, digits (spoken numbers) were put into the message towards the end of the message. Sometimes numbers were in both messages, sometimes only in the shadowed message, and sometimes only in the rejected message. Control passages with no digits were also included.

The independent variable here was the manipulation of the instructions given to 'set' the two groups of participants:

1. One group was told they would be asked questions about the shadowed message at the end of each message.
2. The other group were specifically told to remember as many of the digits as possible.

This experiment used an independent measures design.

Results

The results showed no difference in the mean scores of digits recalled correctly between the two 'set' conditions.

The author concluded that this was because the numbers were, unlike the person's own name in experiment 2, not 'important' enough to break through the 'block' on the rejected message.

The author's overall conclusions

Having conducted these three experiments on dichotic listening, Moray drew four conclusions:

1. In a situation where a subject directs his attention to the reception of a message from one ear, and rejects a message from the other ear, almost none of the verbal content of the rejected message can penetrate the block set up.
2. A short list of simple words presented as the rejected message shows no trace of being remembered even when presented many times.
3. Subjectively 'important' messages, such as a person's own name, can penetrate the block: thus a person will hear instructions if presented with his own name as part of the rejected message.

4. While perhaps not impossible, it is very difficult to make 'neutral' material important enough to break through the block set up in dichotic shadowing. (page 60).

> ### ▶ Have a go yourself
>
> - Conduct your own dichotic listening study using a shadowing task. For example, record a text as a voice message on one smartphone, and record a list of seven words repeated over and over on another phone. Use five participants and get them to put one earphone from one phone in one ear and one earphone from the other phone in their other ear. Instruct them to shadow the text while you play them both messages. After the shadowing task, ask them to recall as much of the unattended message as they can. Do your findings agree with Moray's first experiment?
> - Make a list of five elements of the procedure that you would need to control in your study, and explain why you would need to control them.
> - Design and conduct an experiment that would test the reliability of Moray's claim that 'important' information can break through the attentional block put up in a shadowing task.

Evaluation of the study by Moray

Links to methodological issues

Research method

- Moray carried out controlled laboratory experiments and these fulfil the scientific criteria of theory, control, evidence and replication. For example, he was able to isolate the independent variables in his studies. Using a standard procedure to control for extraneous variables, he was able to manipulate the instructions given to the participants in experiment 3 to test his theory that participants would not recall 'unimportant' details of a message, such as a list of numbers. However, as this was a laboratory experiment it is possible that since participants were aware they were in a study, some of the results may have

> ### 🚫 Stop and ask yourself ...
>
> - Can you identify the independent and dependent variables in these three experiments?
> - Using Moray's study as an example, give one strength and one weakness of using laboratory experiments psychology.
>
> #### Links to methodological issues
> - Independent and dependent variables
> - Laboratory experiments

been affected by the participants responding to demand characteristics and giving answers they thought they were supposed to give.

Problems with ecological validity can also arise with laboratory experiments (see Validity below).

Data

- This study collected and reported quantitative data, for example the number of words from a list in an unattended message that participants could recall or recognise, and the number of times participants reported hearing instructions with or without their name in the unattended message.

  This type of data allows for easy comparison between conditions and for the results to be easily summarised, e.g. as mean averages of the number of words recognised. In addition, quantitative data also allow the reliability of the research to be tested. The study could be repeated and the results correlated with Moray's results to establish whether or not Moray's findings have test–retest reliability.

Ethics

- This study was conducted ethically as tasks were clearly explained to participants before the study and the procedure did not put the participants under undue stress or discomfort.

Validity

- As a highly controlled laboratory experiment, this study has high design validity. The procedure and apparatus were standardised.
- However, as the participants knew they were in a study, they may have tried to affect the outcome of the study. For example, they may have thought they were 'supposed' not to remember anything from the inattended message and so reported they did not when in fact they did.

Ecological validity

- As the study was highly controlled with information being fed to each ear through headphones, blocking out all background noise, and participants were 'shadowing' the message they were instructed to attend to, this means the study may lack ecological validity as participants would not experience these conditions in everyday life.

Reliability

- Moray's study uses highly controlled laboratory experiments. As such, it meets the important criteria

for scientific research that it should be replicable in order for the reliability of its findings to be investigated. This study could be replicated and the findings of the original and subsequent study correlated to see if test–retest reliability could be established.

Sample

- The sample was made up of students and research workers. An advantage is that such a sample enables research to be carried out relatively quickly and cheaply for a researcher carrying out research at a university. However, it may be the case that students and research workers, who are preselected for their high level of cognitive ability, may outperform the general population on tasks that require cognitive skills such as selective attention and fail to represent the general population on these cognitive tasks. In addition, the samples used in each study were quite small, and this may also limit generalisability to a broader population.

Ethnocentrism

- On one hand, since cognitive processes such as selective attention depend upon the physiognomy of our brain, we could argue that studies such as Moray's are not ethnocentric since they are investigating a species-specific behaviour. On the other hand, it is possible that the findings of the study only reflect how English-speaking westerners' attentional processes work and it may be that people whose brains have been shaped by a different language or culture might perform differently on the tests.

Links to debates

Psychology as a science

- Moray carried out controlled laboratory experiments and these fulfil the scientific criteria of theory, control, evidence and replication. As with many cognitive area studies, this supports the claim that psychology is a scientific discipline.

Usefulness

- Moray's study contributes to psychology as an academic discipline as it provided rigorous, empirical evidence for Cherry's cocktail party phenomenon and contributed to our understanding of auditory selective attention, feeding into theories such as those by Broadbent and Treisman.

Links to areas/perspectives

- Moray's study falls within the cognitive area because it is investigating the cognitive process of attention. Specifically it aimed to investigate selective attention by trying to find out whether (and what types of) 'unattended' material could break through the attentional barrier that is set up when a person focuses their listening on a specific task.

Links to the key theme

- In relation to the key theme of attention, Moray's study provides robust empirical evidence into auditory selective attention. For example, Moray's study confirms Cherry's 'cocktail party' effect whereby auditory information important to the individual, such as their name being said, can break through the attentional barrier or block that is put up when focusing our attention. The study also provided evidence that information that is either neutral or not important does not penetrate the block and that we have little or no memory of this information when our attention has been focused on a different auditory task.

Questions arising from Moray's study

- Is this effect specific to our auditory sense, or is it generalisable to our other senses, such as vision or touch?
- Since we can miss information to which we are not selectively listening, is it possible that if we selectively look at something and focus our attention on one element of a scene we could miss information that is right in front of our eyes? The contemporary study by Simons and Chabris investigates this very question.

Practice questions

1. From Moray's study into auditory attention describe how a dichotic listening task was used in any one of the experiments in this study. [3 marks]
2. Explain why Moray's study into auditory attention can be placed in the cognitive area. [2 marks]
3. Outline two conclusions that Moray drew from his study into auditory attention. [4 marks]

Simons and Chabris (1999)

Simons and Chabris ask you to imagine that you are in a crowded cinema, focused on finding a place to sit. So intent are you on the task of finding a seat that you fail to see your friends waving at you, even though you were looking straight at them. This is known as inattentional blindness; that is, the failure to see an event or object in your field of vision because you are so focused on other elements of what you can see. The event that you 'miss' is unrelated to the task at hand so does not draw your attention.

The information that is 'missed' reaches our brain but is nonetheless missed by the viewer, which suggests that perception does not happen without attention first being paid.

Simons and Chabris refer to two types of research done into this area:

1. Computer-based dynamic (moving) displays. An example of this is the 'Cross' study by Mack and Rock (1998) where participants are instructed to judge which of the two 'arms' of crosses displayed on a screen is the longer, and on the fourth trial of this an object (such as a smiley face) appears. Often the observers failed to see the unexpected object. This method was designed to be the visual equivalent of the dichotic listening tasks used, among others, by Moray (1959), the classic core study in this key theme. In line with Moray's findings, the computer-based tests of inattentional blindness showed that more meaningful material does draw attention to the object — more people noticed their name if it appeared in a smiley face, for example.

   The findings of both the computer-based tests and dichotic listening tests are themselves in line with real-life experiences such as not seeing your friends in a crowded cinema or of hearing your name over a noisy party (the 'Cocktail Party Effect' – see Moray's study).

2. Video-based dynamic events – known as 'selective looking'. Simons and Chabris describe studies by Neisser *et al.* where a method was created that would test inattentional blindness using a more realistic event that was video recorded. In the recording, two teams of basketball players appeared. Each team passed a ball from one player to the next. The participants would be instructed to watch either the team with white shirts or the team with black shirts, and to press a key every time a pass was seen. This focused their attention. Approximately 30 seconds into the film, the 'unexpected event' happened, in the form of a woman carrying an open umbrella walking across the screen. The findings from 28 naive observer-participants were as follows:

Reported seeing the umbrella woman	Did not report seeing the umbrella woman
6	22

That 22/28 failed to spot the umbrella woman is evidence for inattentional blindness and, since she was in full view for 4 seconds, this was *sustained* inattentional blindness; they didn't just miss a glimpse of her, they missed a whole 4 seconds' worth of her! In comparison, a group of participants who just watched the video spotted the umbrella woman 100 per cent of the time.

Both of these methods showed that the phenomenon of inattentional blindness could be created in the laboratory, and that levels of inattentional blindness were high. However, some researchers remained sceptical about whether the rates of inattentional blindness recorded were generalisable to real-life, everyday experiences. The 'cross' paradigm is not closely related to a real-life experience and the video method used by Neisser was also unrealistic. This was because of the way it had been created. The two basketball teams had been separately video recorded and transposed onto each other, and the umbrella woman had also been separately recorded and superimposed. This meant that the people in the video were 'transparent' and could at times be seen through one another, and some researchers argued that this made the unexpected event more difficult to see, which they suggested would not be the case in a realistic setting. It might therefore be that the findings from laboratory studies of inattentional blindness lack ecological validity.

Aims

Using Neisser's video-based method as a model, Simons and Chabris aimed to confirm that inattentional blindness occurs in a realistic, complex situation, a video recording of events, and that this is sustained; that is, the unexpected event lasts for 5 seconds or more but is nonetheless unnoticed by observers (participants).

In addition, the study sought to identify the effect of a number of variables on the rate of inattentional blindness:

● Neisser's work had included versions of the video where the umbrella woman wore either a white shirt or a black shirt, but the findings suggested that similarity of the unexpected event to the event being focused on did not mean she was noticed more. In their study, Simons and Chabris wanted to investigate this further and aimed to see if similarity of the unexpected event to the attended event would have an effect on inattentional blindness.

- The study aimed to find out whether events that are particularly unusual are more likely to be detected.
- The level of difficulty of the focused task was also to be tested – would a more difficult task increase the rate of inattentional blindness?
- Finally, the study aimed to investigate the effect of the unusual superimposition and 'transparency' of characters in the video used by Neisser: would a more realistic video recording give similar or different findings?

Method

Sample

There were 228 'observers' (participants), almost all of whom were undergraduate students (the researchers were based at Harvard University). Some volunteered without payment, some were given a large candy bar for taking part, and others had received a single payment for taking part in this and another unrelated study.

Materials

Four videotapes were created:

- They were recordings of the same actors and were recorded on the same day in the same location.
- Each video lasted 75 seconds.
- Each video showed two teams, each made up of three players, one team wearing white shirts (the white team) and one team wearing black shirts (the black team).
- The teams each passed a standard basketball between them, using both aerial (thrown) passes and bounced passes. The team members also dribbled the ball, moved around and waved their arms – behaviour consistent with playing basketball.
- Players passed the ball in a standard order: player 1 passed to player 2, then player 2 passed to player 3, then player 3 passed to player 1, and so on.

- The location for the video was the area in front of three elevator (lift) doors, in an area approximately 3 × 5 metres.
- Between 44 and 48 seconds into each video, the unexpected event occurred. There were two types of unexpected event, but only one was shown in each clip:
  - Umbrella-woman condition – a tall woman holding an open umbrella crossed the scene from left to right (as in Neisser's earlier study).
  - Gorilla condition – a shorter woman, in full gorilla costume, crossed the scene from left to right. Each event lasted for 5 seconds.
- During the unusual event, the teams continued their actions.
- There were two video conditions:
  - Transparent (similar to Neisser's earlier study): Here the black team, white team and unexpected event were filmed separately and then the three separate video streams were superimposed on each other in such a way that each character was transparent.
  - Opaque (a more realistic-looking video): After rehearsal to avoid collisions and to make sure the events looked natural, all seven actors (the two teams of three players and either the umbrella woman or the gorilla) were recorded at the same time.

Procedure

The procedure was scripted and standardised and a team of 21 experimenters gathered data from the 228 participants.

Participants were always tested individually.

Participants were informed that the task would involve watching a clip of basketball players and that they should pay attention to either the white team or the black team and count the number of passes of the ball between the players of the team on which they were to focus.

The task given was varied to give two types of task: 'easy' (the participant kept a mental note of all the passes their team made), and 'hard' (the participant kept separate mental notes of the number of aerial passes and the number of bounced passes that their team made).

Stop and ask yourself ...

- What experimental design is being used here? Can you give one strength and one weakness of using this experimental design in this study?
- Test your understanding: can you create a list of the 16 conditions created for this study?

Links to methodological issues

- Experimental designs
- Experimental conditions

Transparent Umbrella-Woman

Transparent Gorilla

Opaque Umbrella-Woman

Opaque Gorilla

Figure 2.4 These single frames show the transparent and opaque conditions and show the two unusual events: the umbrella woman and gorilla (Simons and Chabris, 1999). Figures provided by Daniel Simons.

This procedure enabled the manipulation of the following variables:

- The type of video: transparent or opaque
- The type of event: umbrella woman or gorilla
- The difficulty of the focused task: easy or hard.

This gave 16 test conditions in total, and each participant was tested in only one of these conditions after giving their informed consent to take part. After viewing the tape, participants were asked to immediately record the number of passes on paper and were then asked a number of surprise questions:

(i) While you were doing the counting, did you notice anything unusual on the video?

(ii) Did you notice anything other than the 6 players?

(iii) Did you see a gorilla [woman carrying an umbrella] walk across the screen? (page 1067)

If they said 'yes', they were asked to provide details. If they mentioned the unexpected event at any point, the rest of the questions were not asked.

Participants were also asked if they had seen anything similar before, and if they said 'yes' then their data was not used in the results.

At the end of the procedure, the observer participants were fully debriefed, which included a repeat showing of the video if necessary.

🚫 **Stop and ask yourself...**

- What exactly would the participants be told in the 'debriefing'? Why is it important to debrief participants in psychological studies?

Links to methodological issues

- Ethical considerations

Results

Thirty-six observer-participants' data were not included for a variety of reasons, including having seen a similar video before, losing count, and having made an inaccurate count of passes. This left a total of 192 observer-participants' data to analyse.

- The overall level of inattentional blindness recorded was 46 per cent, with 54 per cent noticing the unexpected event. Simons and Chabris describe this as 'a substantial level of sustained inattentional blindness' (page 1068).
- The type of video had an effect on the level of inattentional blindness, confirming the researchers' suspicions that the transparency of the unexpected object/event did lead to a higher level of inattentional blindness. In the transparent video condition, only 42 per cent noticed the unexpected event compared with 67 per cent in the opaque video condition. However, this means that, even in the more realistic opaque version, 33 per cent (one in three) of the observer-participants failed to see an object that was in their line of vision for 5 seconds and about which they were specifically asked questions immediately after viewing the video.
- As the difficulty of the task increased, the likelihood of inattentional blindness also increased, with 64 per cent of observer-participants seeing the unexpected event in the 'easy' condition compared with 45 per cent in the 'hard' condition. It was also shown that an interaction of the 'hard' task and the transparent condition further increased the likelihood of inattentional blindness occurring, as in the transparent video condition 27 per cent of those in the 'hard' task condition saw the unexpected event compared to 56 per cent in the 'easy' task condition.
- Finally, the authors consider whether the similarity of the event to the attended task had an effect. The umbrella woman was seen more times (65 per cent) than the gorilla (44 per cent), and the authors suggest that this is because she was more closely related to the attended task in that in a basketball match we may expect to see a woman, but not expect to see a gorilla. However, they also point out that she may have been spotted as her umbrella made her taller than the players. There was an interaction between the attended team (black or white) in spotting the gorilla. The gorilla was seen more in the black condition (58 per cent) than the white condition (27 per cent). Simons and Chabris suggest that this contradicts Neisser's claim that similarity has

no effect, as the fact that those tracking the black team saw the black gorilla more suggested that similarity, in this case in terms of colour, makes the unexpected object more likely to be spotted.

Conclusion

The authors conclude that inattentional blindness occurs in dynamic events that are sustained, lasting more than 5 seconds.

As even in the opaque video, many participants missed the unusual event, they conclude that the phenomenon of attentional bias cannot be accounted for as simply a response to the transparent video. Also, the findings of this study are consistent with the earlier computer-based studies and this suggests that the findings of the computer-based studies do generalise to situations close to real-life experiences, as in the opaque video condition.

The study showed that objects can pass through our central field of vision and still not be seen if they are not specifically attended to. This is, according to Simons and Chabris, 'consistent with the claim that there is no conscious perception without attention' (page 1070).

▶ Have a go yourself

- Visit Daniel Simons' excellent webpage and go to the 'videos' section. You should find a version of the gorilla condition video there. Test ten people by showing them an excerpt from the video and record how many report seeing the gorilla. Do your findings support Simons and Chabris?
- Why will it be important for you to find out afterwards if your participant has seen this type of video before and discount them from your study if they say they have?
- How will you ensure that your study is carried out ethically?

Evaluation of the study by Simons and Chabris

Links to methodological issues

Research method

- Simons and Chabris carried out controlled laboratory experiments and these fulfil the scientific criteria of theory, control, evidence and replication. As a highly controlled laboratory experiment, Simons and Chabris' study has high-design validity, since extraneous variables could be strictly controlled.

However, one challenge to the design validity of this laboratory study is that demand characteristics could have influenced the participants (see second bullet point on Validity below).

Data

- This study collected and reported quantitative data, which enables the data to be easily summarised and compared between conditions. For example, Simons and Chabris report that the umbrella woman was noticed by 65 per cent of participants, whereas in the gorilla condition the rate of noticing was lower at 44 per cent. In addition, they quantify the overall level of inattentional blindness in their study at 46 per cent, so the general strength of this phenomenon is easy to see. Quantitative data also have the advantage that they can be statistically analysed, and also means that the study can be easily repeated in order to establish its reliability.

Ethics

- This study was conducted entirely within the ethical guidelines. Informed consent was obtained and participants were briefed about the task they were to undertake. After they had taken part in the study, they were debriefed and, where necessary and sometimes to their amazement, shown the video again to confirm there was indeed a gorilla-suited person or a woman with an umbrella in the scene.

Validity

- As a highly controlled laboratory experiment, this study has high design validity. The procedure and apparatus were standardised.
- However, as the participants knew they were in a study, they may have tried to affect the outcome of the study. For example, if they had seen a video like the one shown in the study before but failed to report this to the experimenter when asked because they hoped to 'look clever' in spotting the gorilla, or hoped to give the message 'you can't fool me', this might mean that that inattentional blindness was not accurately measured in the study.
- The findings of this study are concurrently valid with both the computer-based studies and Neisser's earlier umbrella-woman video, and this suggests that it is valid to conclude that participants can entirely miss an unexpected event in a dynamic scene when focusing their attention elsewhere.

Ecological validity

- In this study, Simons and Chabris were aiming to increase the ecological validity of a method for testing for inattentional blindness. The earlier computer-based tasks and Neisser's transparent umbrella-woman video task were both low in ecological validity, and critics claimed that this may mean their results would only occur in a laboratory test and that in real life inattentional blindness would not occur as often or as readily. The design of the 'opaque' version of the basketball video was more realistic, and since both the umbrella-woman and gorilla versions of this gave rise to significant levels of inattentional blindness, Simons and Chabris concluded that these more realistic, and more ecologically valid, tasks suggested that findings from the earlier studies could in fact generalise beyond the laboratory to real-life experience. On the other hand, it could be argued that responding to a filmed task is not entirely the same as focusing attention in a real setting, so even the more realistic 'opaque' video is not wholly ecologically valid.

Reliability

- This study is a highly controlled laboratory experiment. As such, it meets the important criteria for scientific research that it should be replicable in order for the reliability of its findings to be investigated. This study could be replicated and the findings of the original and subsequent study correlated to see if test–retest reliability could be established.
- The fact that the computer-based studies, Neisser's umbrella-woman study and Simons and Chabris' investigation all show evidence of information in plain sight being missed by many participants suggests that inattentional blindness is a reliable phenomenon supported by a range of evidence.

Sample

- A sample size of 228 was selected, with data from a final sample of 192 participants being reported. This is a large sample and enables the researchers to establish a trend in their findings, and for this to be unaffected by atypical or 'fluke' results. The sample was made up of undergraduate students. A student sample has the advantage of homogeneity so that, when allocated to conditions in an independent measures design, participant variables can be controlled. Another advantage is that such a sample enables research to be carried out relatively quickly and cheaply, especially if it is to be conducted at a university. However, student samples can present problems as coming from a narrow age range and narrow socio-economic background means students can fail to fully represent the general population. In a cognitive study such as this one, it may also be the case that students, who are preselected for their high level of cognitive ability, may outperform the general population on tasks that require cognitive skills such as selective attention.

Sampling method and sampling biases

- Simons and Chabris recruited a volunteer sample, some receiving no payment, some a candy bar and some being paid for taking part in this and another larger study. While self-selected samples of this type are convenient for the researcher, especially as the study was to be done on students in a university, and make the study both cost- and time-effective, there is always the concern that volunteer bias may limit the generalisability of the findings. In other words, the participants may fail to represent the general population because they are especially interested in research, or may be biased towards responding to demand characteristics to make the study 'work' for the researcher.

Ethnocentrism

- On the one hand, since cognitive processes such as inattentional bias depend upon the physiognomy of our brain, we could argue that studies such as Simons and Chabris' are not ethnocentric, since they are investigating a species-specific behaviour. On the other hand, it is possible that the findings only reflect how university educated people's cognitive processes work, since only students were studied. Student samples have ethnocentric biases, for example, most students come from the upper and middle social classes, and other groups may perform differently on these tests.

Links to debates

Individual and situational explanations debate
- The overall level of inattentional blindness recorded in Simons and Chabris' study was 46 per cent. This means that more than half of participants actually saw the unexpected event and did not experience inattentional blindness in this study. This perhaps suggests that there are individual differences in attention.

The study showed that the situation could affect inattentional blindness. Colour, in the case of the black gorilla in the black team condition, created similarity between the unexpected event and the attended event and this seemed to have made the gorilla more noticeable. This suggests that context has an impact on attentional processes.

Free will/determinism debate

- We make the assumption that we act according to our own free will on the evidence of our own eyes, yet this study demonstrates that our attentional processes can influence us such that we fail to see an object that was in our centre of vision for 5 seconds. Our cognitive processes clearly have an influence on our behaviour and are an influence over which we have no conscious control, suggesting that this is not freely chosen behaviour.

Psychology as a science

- Simons and Chabris carried out controlled laboratory experiments and these fulfil the scientific criteria of theory, control, evidence and replication. As with many cognitive area studies, this supports the claim that psychology is a scientific discipline.

Links to areas/perspectives

- Simons and Chabris' study falls within the cognitive area as it is investigating the cognitive process of attention. Specifically, it aimed to investigate selective attention by trying to find out if an unexpected event that is in our central field of vision might be entirely missed if a person focuses their visual attention on a different feature of a visual event. This is a phenomenon called 'inattentional blindness'.

Links to the key theme

- In relation to the key theme of attention, Simons and Chabris' study is a rigorous and empirical demonstration of visual selective attention. The study confirms the phenomenon of inattentional blindness in dynamic events. This study showed that not all information available to us in our visual field is processed, and that selective attention paid to one element of a scene may mean that other elements, especially ones that do not fit in with the attended task, may not be paid attention to and people will therefore have no memory of these. Simons and Chabris suggest that their findings show attention to be an essential early cognitive process since without attention being paid it seems we do not consciously perceive information received by our senses.

In terms of the extent to which Simons and Chabris' study changes our understanding of the key theme of 'attention', in many ways the main thing it does is extend the broad principle that we can miss events that we are not paying attention to from the realm of hearing ('inattentional deafness') to sight ('inattentional blindness').

- How does the contemporary study by Simons and Chabris change our understanding of individual social and cultural diversity?
- Following on from Moray's work into auditory selective attention, Simons and Chabris studied visual inattention. In terms of individual diversity, their work showed that some individuals are more likely than others to be affected by the phenomenon of inattentional bias, even when the unattended event happens over time in the centre of their visual field. For example, 46 per cent of the participants overall failed to see the unattended event, whereas 54 per cent noticed it, showing a clear individual difference in susceptibility.

Comparison with the classic study

- In what ways is the study by Simons and Chabris *similar to* the study by Moray?
  - Both studies were highly controlled laboratory experiments.
  - The samples in both studies included university students.
  - The studies were both investigating the process of selective attention.
  - Both studies were conducted ethically.
  - Both studies gathered quantitative data.
  - Both studies conclude that, in order to be consciously perceived, attention must first be given to sensory information.
  - Both studies agree that important information such as a person's name will break through an attentional barrier. This happened in Moray's dichotic listening tasks, and Simons and Chabris report that in the computer-based 'Cross' studies if a person's own name appeared they would report noticing it.

- In what ways is the study by Simons and Chabris *different from* the study by Moray?
  - Whereas Moray was investigating auditory inattention, Simons and Chabris were investigating visual inattention.
  - Simons and Chabris had a relatively large sample, whereas Moray's was quite small.
  - Simons and Chabris used sophisticated video technology to create simultaneous visual dynamic visual events for their study, whereas Moray adapted a tape recorder to deliver simultaneous audio recordings.

Questions arising from Simons and Chabris

- What questions are we left with after studying the research by Simons and Chabris? It would be reasonable to wonder whether the effect that they report would apply to the same extent if the event occurred in person in front of any observer-participants, as opposed to it being shown in a video recording. Also, what factors (either to do with the event being witnessed or to do with the person doing the witnessing) might weaken or strengthen the effect of inattentional blindness? This study raises as many questions as it answers.

Find out more

- Use the internet to find out about the phenomenon of 'change blindness'.
- Visit Daniel Simons' website to find out more about his work into inattentional blindness.

Practice questions

1. From the study by Simons and Chabris (visual inattention) outline two ways in which the procedure was standardised. [4 marks]
2. From the study by Simons and Chabris (visual inattention) identify one of the researchers' aims and state the conclusion they drew in relation to this aim. [4 marks]
3. Outline two ways in which the study by Moray (auditory attention) and Simons and Chabris (visual inattention) are different from each other. [4 marks]

Chapter 3

The developmental area

The developmental area of psychology is also known as 'lifespan psychology' as it is now understood that our behaviour develops over time throughout our life. However, there is no getting away from the fact that much of our behaviour develops in childhood and adolescence, and as such the developmental area often refers to the psychology of development in young children. The core studies in this section all reflect this emphasis on early experiences and maturation as a major factor in the development of behaviour.

Because the developmental area does not focus on one particular explanation, unlike the biological or cognitive areas, the theories and methods found in the developmental area can encompass everything from Freud's psychodynamic theory of development through psychosexual stages, to the behavioural psychologists' view of behaviour being learned, such as in Bandura *et al.*'s study. This means that the methods can vary from case studies, to observations, biological methods such as MRI scans and cognitive experiments.

There is no single explanation of behaviour in developmental psychology; it is more a focus on how behaviour develops, and the extent to which it is a result of the environment interacting with innate behaviours. One of the key questions about development which psychologists from all areas set out to answer is how much is behaviour innate (i.e. we are born with it or it develops with maturation) and how much is learned. This has impacts on our education system, our parenting styles, and even genetic testing. If behaviour is all learned, then the environment we provide is of maximum importance. If behaviour is totally down to inheritance then the environment becomes less important: as long as the basic physical requirements are met, maturation will occur and the behaviour will develop (Table 3.1).

Table 3.1 Strengths and ethical issues in developmental area research

Strengths of the developmental area	Weaknesses of the developmental area
Many useful applications to child care, education, etc.	Research with children may raise ethical issues, such as consent and protection.
Attempts to answer the nature/nurture debate.	Using children as participants can highlight practical issues, such as making inferences from observed behaviour as they can't tell us.
Uses a variety of qualitative and quantitative methods so will gain useful data.	Research may be constrained by time or culture due to changes in early years environments and cultural differences in child rearing.
Can study participants over time to reduce participant variables.	Samples are often small and may be unrepresentative.

The particular developmental studies we will be examining are as outlined in Table 3.2.

Table 3.2 Developmental studies discussed in this chapter

Key theme	Classic study	Contemporary study
External influences on children's behaviour	Bandura *et al.* (1961) Transmission of aggression	Chaney *et al.* (2004) Funhaler study
Moral development	Kohlberg (1968) Stages of moral development	Lee *et al.* (1997) Evaluations of lying and truth-telling

Further reading

Bandura, A., Ross, D. and Ross, S.A., 1961, 'Transmission of Aggression Through Imitation of Aggressive Models'. *Journal of Abnormal and Social Psychology*, vol. 63, no 3, 575–582.

Chaney, G., Clements, B., Landau, L., Bulsara, M. and Watt, P., 2004, 'A New Asthma Spacer Device to Improve Compliance in Children: A Pilot Study'. *Respirology*, vol. 9, 499–506.

Kohlberg, L., 1968, 'The Child as a Moral Philosopher'. *Psychology Today*, vol. 2, no 4, 25–30.

Lee, K., Cameron, C.A., Xu, F., Fu, G. and Board, J., 1997, 'Chinese and Canadian Children's Evaluations of Lying and Truth-Telling'. *Child Development*, vol. 68, no 5, 924–934.

External influences on children's behaviour

The environment in which a child is brought up can vary within and between cultures. Imagine one child in a western culture, born in a hospital environment with an environment consisting of brightly coloured toys, stimulation through a variety of media such as television, in childcare for some or all of the working week, without an extended family. However, in that same culture, the child could be born at home in a birthing pool, have little in the way of toys or television, stay with parents throughout the week, with an extended network of relations. Then compare that with a different culture, where perhaps fathers are the main child carers, or the home is not built of brick, where children are reared completely by other adults and have very little parental contact. All of these, and any combination of them, can be found throughout the world. It is now easy to see that there are many external influences in a child's early years, all of which can have an impact on their behaviour.

However, in all of these varying environments there will be some consistencies. Children are not capable of looking after themselves, so there is going to be someone to care for the child's physical and safety needs, whether that is one person or many. Also, there is going to be some interaction with the environment, and the consequences of behaviour in any given situation will be pleasant or unpleasant. Developmental psychologists will try to isolate each of these factors to see its impact on a child's behaviour.

'Give me a child until he is seven, and I will give you the man' is a quote attributed to St Francis Xavier of the Jesuit religious order, and this reflects the World Health Organization's belief that early childhood (from pre-natal to eight years) is the most important developmental period for any person, and the effects of the external influences during this period can be seen throughout life in terms of physical, emotional, social, linguistic and cognitive development.

Developmental psychology can look at each of these areas and focus on one or more aspects of development. The social relationships a child develops with parents, siblings and peers is one that will depend heavily on the type of parenting a child has and the bonding with their caregiver. This attachment figure may or may not be the mother, as we have come a long way from Bowlby's belief (1953) that 'mother-love in infancy and childhood is as important for mental health as are vitamins and proteins for physical health.' This mother–child bond is also influenced by such things as the mother's temperament and the type of parenting the child experiences. Diana Baumrind (1967) identified three types of parents – permissive, authoritarian and authoritative – and she identified the effects each style would have on the child's emotional and social behaviour and disposition.

Then there are the biological influences, such as nutrition, which will enable healthy brain development and allow for full maturation. However, Bowlby may have been right and the social interactions children experience are more important than healthy diets. Social isolation case studies such as Genie, who was locked away by a stepmother at the age of twenty months, but who was fed enough to grow, showed at the age of thirteen when she was found, to have insurmountable problems with such behaviours as speech, brain development due to lack of stimulation of the left hemisphere and social interaction, such as maintaining a conversation. The whole area of early years' experiences has also been studied intensively to look at the impact of day care on a child's social and cognitive skills. Conflicting studies have shown some increase in cognitive skills and some decrease, and some more developed social skills, such as peer relationships, and some more negative skills such as bullying. However, all this confirms the idea that for every child their early years' experience is unique and the individual differences of each child will also mediate the impact of those experiences.

The idea of children *learning* from their interaction with the environment is firmly seated in the behaviourist perspective, which believes children are born a blank slate and all their behaviours, characteristics and skills are learned through interaction. If this is the case then it would explain why behaviour is so different in young children from within a culture and in different cultures. However, there is some evidence that innate behaviours will occur whatever the input. Children tend to learn to speak in the same stages and at about the same age, whatever their early years' environment, providing it is sufficient. Children watching children's television from an early age and children who are kept with adults throughout their early years will develop language skills which are similar by the time they reach about five years. However, there is no doubt that children will also learn readily when they are rewarded with positive and negative consequences. Also, as a result of watching others, both animals and humans will imitate the behaviour of their role models.

Bandura et al. (1961)

Bandura et al.'s study on the transmission of aggression was one of the first studies to look at learning via observation and imitation, leading on from other behaviourist theories of learning, such as operant and classical conditioning. He also was one of the first to highlight that behaviour was not simply displayed once it had been observed, but that some cognitive processing was allowing children to decide if it was appropriate to display that behaviour. Bandura found that previous research had indicated that children would imitate behaviours shown by an adult model, but this was restricted to children imitating while the adult was still present. Bandura wanted to investigate in a more controlled way if the observed behaviour would be shown when the model had left and would be generalised to different settings. Also, the features of the role model were important in terms of whether a child's later aggression would be affected by whether the model was the same sex as the child and also if they were showing gender stereotypical behaviour, such as aggression. Bandura felt all of these variables could influence the child's behaviour and he formulated four hypotheses for his study:

- Children exposed to an aggressive model would reproduce aggressive acts resembling those of their models.
- Observing non-aggressive adults would inhibit the children's behaviour and they would display less aggression than control groups who did not witness any model.
- Children would imitate behaviour from same-sex models more than opposite-sex models.
- Boys would show more aggression than girls, particularly in the male aggressive role model condition.

Participants

The participants were 72 children enrolled at Stanford University nursery. They ranged in age from 37 to 69 months (3 years 1 month to 5 years 9 months). Their mean age was 52 months (4 years 4 months). There was an equal number of boys and girls.

Experimental design

Bandura et al. set up groups of children to experience different conditions. No child experienced more than one condition. To control for participant variables,

Bandura matched each of the eight experimental groups of six children on their mean age, gender split (50/50) and mean aggression rating. The remaining 24 children were in a control group which didn't experience any role model behaviour.

Bandura et al. obtained the aggression rating of each child by having two observers (the teacher and the experimenter) observe each child in their social interactions at the nursery. There were five-point rating scales for:

- Physical aggression
- Verbal aggression
- Aggression towards inanimate objects
- Aggression inhibition (the tendency not to show aggression when provoked)

Each child was given an overall rating score and children were then put into groups of three with the same aggression rating. They were then randomly allocated with one child from each group of three put into the aggressive role model condition, one into the non-aggressive role model condition and one into the (no role model) control group.

To ensure that the observations were valid, two observers' scores for 51 of the children were correlated, and found to have a correlation co-efficient of 0.89 (remember a perfect correlation is only 1.00) to check the inter-rater reliability.

Experimental conditions and procedure

Stage 1

Each child in the experimental conditions was taken individually to a room and the model was invited in to join the game. The child was taken to a table and shown high-interest activities, such as potato printing and stickers. The model then sat at another table with tinker toys (small construction toys with figures, cars, etc.), a Bobo doll and a mallet. The child was told these were the model's toys. The experimenter then left the child with the model.

In the *non-aggressive* condition, the model played with the tinker toys and ignored the Bobo doll.

In the *aggressive* condition, the model began playing with the tinker toys but then after 1 minute turned to the Bobo doll and was aggressive towards it for the rest of the time.

The total time in that room was 10 minutes.

⊘ Stop and ask yourself ...

- What do you think are the problems with using this sample?
- How do you think Bandura et al.'s sampling method could have resulted in an unrepresentative sample?

Links to methodological issues

- Sample
- Sampling method

Figure 3.1 Original photos from the Bandura *et al.* Bobo doll study

Aggression arousal

Previous research had shown that witnessing aggression tends to reduce immediate aggression and so it was decided that all subjects (experimental and control) would be aroused so that any aggression learned from the model would be shown. If, even in the light of this arousal, the children in the non-aggressive condition still didn't show aggression the research could confirm the inhibitory influence of the non-aggressive model.

Stage 2

To achieve this arousal, the children were taken to a smaller room by the experimenter and in this room were some attractive toys – a toy fire engine, train and jet plane, a cable car, a spinning top, and a doll set with doll, clothes, pram and cot (remember, this is 1961).

The child was told he or she could play with these toys, but once the child had settled in to playing (about 2 minutes), the experimenter told the child that these were her very best toys, and not just

anyone could play with them and she had decided to keep them for the other children. However, there were some other toys in another room the child could play with.

Test for delayed imitation

Stage 3

In the third room was a range of toys, always set up in the same place for each child. These included all the toys in the first room – a Bobo doll (smaller than the one the adult had used) plus some other aggressive toys, for example two dart guns, and a ball hanging from the ceiling. The non-aggressive toys included a tea set, crayons, cars and trucks, and farm animals.

For 20 minutes, the child was allowed to play in this room while being observed through a one-way mirror. A time point sample was used where every 5 seconds a note was made of the behaviour shown on one of the behavioural categories.

 Stop and ask yourself…

- How do you think the child felt on being told they couldn't play with the toys?

Links to methodological issues

- Ethics

Measures of imitation

- Imitation of physical aggression – e.g. hitting Bobo with a mallet, kicking Bobo
- Imitation of verbal aggression – e.g. repeating phrases, such as, 'Sock him', 'Hit him down'
  - Imitative non-aggressive verbal – e.g. repeating 'He keeps on coming back for more', 'He sure is a tough fella'
- Measures of partial imitation
  - Mallet aggression – e.g. hitting other objects with mallet
  - Sitting on Bobo – sitting on but not hitting Bobo
- Non-imitative aggression
  - Non-imitative verbal and physical aggression – e.g. aggressive acts directed at other objects and hostile remarks, such as, 'Shoot the Bobo', which the model hadn't said
  - Aggressive gun play – shooting or aiming gun in the room (which the model hadn't done)
- Non-aggressive measures
  - Non-aggressive measures – e.g. sitting quietly, playing non-aggressively, not playing at all.

Again, to ensure objectivity, there was a second observer for half of the subjects and the observers didn't know which category the child had been in except for the male aggressive model (who was also the experimenter who was observing) and the fact that the imitation was so obvious it was clear from the start which children had seen the aggressive role model.

 **Have a go yourself**

Try observing the pro-social behaviour in a children's television programme. Watch one episode (for example *In the Night Garden*) to see what pro-social behaviours are shown, then make a list of behavioural categories and observe another episode to see how often they occur and which ones occur most frequently. Try comparing a programme aimed at older children and then teenagers – is there a difference? Does a time point observation give different results to an event sample?

Results

Bandura *et al.* had four hypotheses and the data table (Table 3.3) shows support for each one of them.

Table 3.3 Bandura *et al.*'s results table

Response category	Experimental groups				Control groups
	Aggressive		Non-aggressive		
	F Model	M Model	F Model	M Model	
Imitative physical aggression					
Female subjects	5.5	7.2	2.5	0.0	1.2
Male subjects	12.4	25.8	0.2	1.5	2.0
Imitative verbal aggression					
Female subjects	13.7	2.0	0.3	0.0	0.7
Male subjects	4.3	12.7	1.1	0.0	1.7
Mallet aggression					
Female subjects	17.2	18.7	0.5	0.5	13.1
Male subjects	15.5	28.8	18.7	6.7	13.5
Punches Bobo doll					
Female subjects	6.3	16.5	5.8	4.3	11.7
Male subjects	18.9	11.9	15.6	14.8	15.7
Non-imitative aggression					
Female subjects	21.3	8.4	7.2	1.4	6.1
Male subjects	16.2	36.7	26.1	22.3	24.6
Aggressive gun play					
Female subjects	1.8	4.5	2.6	2.5	3.7
Male subjects	7.3	15.9	8.9	16.7	14.3

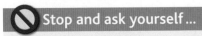 **Stop and ask yourself ...**

- How do you think Bandura *et al.*'s study shows standardisation?

Links to methodological issues
- Psychology as a science

The suggestion that children seeing the aggressive model would show more aggressive acts copied from the models was supported by the significant differences shown between the aggressive condition and the non-aggressive and control groups. The comparison between the groups on non-imitative physical and verbal aggression is significant ($p < 0.02$). The reason is because children exposed to the aggressive model became more aggressive in general, with means of 21.3, 8.4, 16.2, 36.7 compared to the non-aggressive model means of 7.2, 1.4, 26.1, 22.3.

The hypothesis that boys are more likely to show aggression than girls was partially supported. There was a significant difference in the amount of imitative physical aggression (boys showed a mean of 38.2 imitative physical aggressive acts, but girls only showed a mean of 12.7 acts; $p < 0.01$), but there was no significant difference in their imitation of verbal aggression. (Boys in the aggressive condition showed a mean of 17 imitative verbal acts and girls showed a mean of 15.7.)

The influence of the sex of the model was less clear cut. The boys showed more physical and verbal imitative aggression and more non-imitative aggression and aggressive gun play than the girls when shown the male model. However, the small group sizes didn't allow a significant difference to be calculated when the girls showed more imitative verbal agression (mean 13.7 acts with female model to 2.0 with male model) and non-imitative aggression (mean 21.3 acts with female model to 8.4 with male model) than the boys, when exposed to the female model. However, because the girls tended to show the same amount of behaviour as the control, if we look at the boys' behaviour we can see that the boys showed significantly less aggression in the non-aggressive model conditions than in the aggressive model conditions for imitative physical aggression, imitative verbal aggression, mallet aggression, non-imitative physical and verbal aggression and punching Bobo.

The mallet aggression showed some large discrepancies. This was a measure of partial imitation, which was the use of the mallet on objects other than Bobo. The girls in the non-aggressive model conditions showed a mean number of 0.5 mallet aggressive acts which was fewer than the girls in the aggressive group who showed a mean of 18 acts, but interestingly also many fewer acts than the control group girls who showed a mean of 13.1 mallet aggressive acts. This would support the hypothesis that the non-aggressive model would indeed reduce the 'normal' amount of aggression shown by the control group, at least among the girls. This is also reflected in the fact that children in the non-aggressive condition spent significantly more time in non-aggressive play with dolls than the control group.

These differences between the groups showed the following levels of significance (Table 3.4).

Table 3.4 Significance of the difference between experimental and control groups in the expression of aggression

Response category	Comparison of pairs of treatment conditions		
	Aggressive vs non-aggressive p	Aggressive vs control p	Non-aggressive vs control p
Imitative responses			
Physical aggression	<0.001	<0.001	0.09
Verbal aggression	0.004	0.048	0.09
Non-aggressive verbal responses	0.004	0.004	NS
Partial imitation			
Mallet aggression	0.026	NS	0.005
Sits on Bobo	0.018	0.059	NS
Non-imitative aggression			
Punches Bobo doll			
Physical and verbal	0.026	NS	NS
Aggressive gun play			

NS, not significant.

 Stop and ask yourself ...

- Which groups had the most significant difference in behaviour?
- Some differences were not significant, but of those which were the least? Can you think why this might be?

Links to methodological issues
- Probability

Conclusions

This study supported the claim that simply observing behaviour would produce imitative behaviour which would not be expected if that behaviour had not been observed. This moved on from Skinner's view that behaviour would only be shown if it was rewarded. There were no rewards for the children in this study.

Discussion

It could be that simply watching aggression could make us more aggressive if we then become aroused, but what was striking in this research is the amount of imitative aggression. Children weren't just more aggressive, they imitated aggression. However, their behaviour went beyond this in that they also showed more non-imitative aggression, concluding that witnessing aggression would, with subsequent arousal, make children more aggressive, and they would think of new ways to be aggressive alongside the behaviours they had seen.

It had previously been thought (Rosenbith, 1959) that the lack of male role models in the school made them more likely to be valued and therefore imitated. Bandura *et al.* proposed, however, that it was actually because physical aggression is a stereotypically male behaviour. Both males and females imitated the male model more, although with verbal aggression, which is less stereotypically male, the same-sex model was imitated more. So the sex of the model is important if the behaviour is seen as more acceptable by one sex or the other.

The qualitative data, in terms of the utterances made by the children, supported the view that they saw aggression as a male behaviour. They said things like, 'That ain't no way for a lady to behave', and 'That girl ... was just acting like a man'. However, both boys and girls said things which suggested males behaving aggressively was acceptable, 'He's a good fighter like Daddy', 'Al's a good socker, he beat up Bobo. I want to sock like Al'.

A final point is that the role model was not known to the child, they were not seen as authority figures such as parents, and neither kind nor punitive, so it doesn't appear to matter what the relationship or status of the role model, there is still evidence that imitation is one way in which behaviour is learned.

> 🚫 **Stop and ask yourself ...**
>
> - How might this study be seen to have been used in society?
>
> Links to methodological issues
> - Usefulness

Evaluation of the study by Bandura *et al.*

Links to methodological issues

Research method

- This study used a laboratory experiment method as it had independent variables, dependent variables and controls. It is also an example of a controlled experiment. This control enhanced the validity of the study by controlling extraneous variables, for example, putting the toys being set out in the same order for every child meant that the child wouldn't confound the results by playing with the first toy he or she saw in the room. However, the set up was not really natural for the child and so to some extent lacked ecological validity.
- It used a matched participants design as the children were matched on the basis of their prior levels of aggression – this would control participant variables and increase the validity of the research.

Data

- Bandura *et al.* collected both quantitative and qualitative data, and his analysis of the probability of the results being due to chance showed that there was a significant difference between many of the conditions. The probability of $p < 0.09$ in the comparison between control and non-aggressive conditions seems to be less of a significant difference, but this is because no child in either condition saw the model hitting the Bobo doll, so probably both groups showed very little of this behaviour rather than similar high levels of such behaviour. This is reflected in several of the comparisons between these two groups where there is no significant difference. This is what we would expect in terms of imitation. Perhaps the most interesting non-significant comparison is the amount of non-imitative physical and verbal behaviour between the control group and both the aggressive and non-aggressive conditions. This might be explained by the fact that the boys' aggression was high in all conditions except the female aggressive model condition, but this is counteracted by the higher level of aggression shown by the girls in this condition. So although there is no significant difference shown, if you look at the data you can see the reasons why. Probability shows us that there are trends in behaviour, but no certainties, for example not every boy who saw an aggressive role model showed aggressive behaviour. The strength of collecting quantitative data is the ability to analyse the results to test for significance and make clear comparisons between the variables. However, it didn't show us why children might have displayed such behaviour.

- The qualitative data comprised the quotes of things the children said which did illustrate their reasons for some behaviour, and so enhanced our understanding. For example, when the children suggested that being aggressive was 'no way for a lady to behave', this showed the impact of cultural norms on observed behaviour.

Ethics

- There is often a debate about how ethical Bandura *et al.*'s research was. Teachers can give consent *in loco parentis* (in place of parents) and are expected to adopt the view of the parent in terms of what is likely to be the consequences for the children. The parents of children attending Stanford University day nursery knew it was linked to the university, and although it is not mentioned in the original article it is likely that then, as now, the parents agreed to their children taking part in research when they signed them up for the nursery. The children were not aware of the right to withdraw and so they had no choice as to whether they took part. The question is how much would children of that age understand if you did ask them if they wanted to play a game of Watch the Bobo?
- Of course, the nature of this research may be considered to harm the children. The fact that the children saw an aggressive role model and then behaved in an imitative and non-imitative aggressive way would suggest that their behaviour was changed, and it would be difficult to debrief young children as telling them not to be aggressive in the future is not going to work.
- The second stage of the experiment (the 'mild aggression arousal' stage, in which the children were told that they couldn't play with the toys for the 'good' children) would also be harmful to a child's self-esteem, and causing anxiety in such young children considered unacceptable.
- Bandura *et al.*'s research was carried out in the 1960s when ethical guidelines for research and society's view of the development of children were very different.
- It is also arguable that the research was of such value to society (in terms of telling us how children can learn to be aggressive, and suggesting the kinds of application outlined above) that perhaps 'the end justifies the means', and the harm that was arguably caused to the children in the study was outweighed by the benefits it brought.

Validity

- Bandura *et al.* worked in a controlled manner to ensure that there was little in the way of extraneous variables which would reduce the validity of his research. By putting the toys in the same place in the observation room, the children would not behave differently if they went for the first toy they came across. The model also had a certain number of actions to be repeated an exact number of times, so that again the child wasn't exposed to different aggressive acts.
- The pre-testing of the children (for their prior levels of aggression) and the way in which they were placed in different conditions on a matched basis meant that the results could not have been affected by all the 'naturally' aggressive children accidentally ending up in the same condition.
- The highly stylised way in which the models aggressed against the Bobo doll (hitting it in particular places, saying particular phrases) enabled Bandura *et al.* to know whether behaviour shown by the children in the third room had been learned during the experiment, or not, as some of these behaviours were so particular that they could only have been learned during the experiment.
- However, whether the children were still behaving in the same ways several weeks, months or years after the experiment was not tested, so it is questionable how 'long-term' the learning lasted.

Reliability

- The procedure was highly replicable, as was shown by the fact that it was replicated with so many children during the experiment.
- However, it is arguable that the sample was not large enough to establish reliable effects, as there were only six children in each condition.

Sample

- Bandura *et al.*'s sample of children will immediately raise concerns of representativeness. The fact that young children will imitate adults does not tell us anything about how likely adults are to imitate behaviour. (If you consider all the adults who watch violent films, or who play violent games, if behaviour was learned simply through observation and reinforcement then there would be a lot more violence in society.) The young children may simply have been doing what adults do in a new situation. They had not seen a Bobo doll before and when given something unfamiliar then they just copied.

- Bandura *et al.*'s technique of using a restricted sample, also limits some of the generalisability of the results. The parents who used the Stanford University nursery probably had similar characteristics such as socio-economic status, and therefore the children were limited in their representativeness of all children.

Ethnocentrism

- The fact that the study was carried out in America (presumably on American children) is also of relevance here, given that America is different from many other countries in its high levels of gun ownership. This may have affected the likelihood of the children learning aggressive behaviour. So the research is ethnocentric if we assume the same imitative nature of learning behaviour happens in every culture as it does in America.
- Perhaps the influence of culture is really what makes this study ethnocentric, for example not imitating a female model being aggressive, but if the implication is that whatever the cultural norms are they will always influence a child, then this is not ethnocentric.

Links to debates

Nature/nurture debate

- On the face of it, Bandura *et al.*'s study might be seen as a clear indication of the nurture side of this debate as the influence of the environment can be seen quite obviously in all of the hypotheses.
- Why, though, did the boys show more aggression than the girls? It could be that boys are naturally more aggressive than girls; a biological area explanation would be the presence of testosterone in boys, which from when they were in the womb is a higher exposure than girls. And research has linked high levels of testosterone to higher levels of aggression in animals and humans. But is that the only answer? What about the effect of society on those boys before they took part in Bandura *et al.*'s research? Could society have unwittingly shown acceptance of aggression in boys as young as three years? The fact that the qualitative data included comments such as, 'That ain't no way for a lady to behaviour' would indicate this might be the case. Research shows that parents reinforce stereotypical behaviour, playing with a boy who picks up a tractor, and not playing with a boy who picks up a doll. Also, the words parents use when talking to babies, strong masculine words of big boy, strong little man, etc., compared with beautiful little girl, can from the first interactions mould a child to fit in with society's stereotypical view. This is more

evidence of the nurture side of the debate, but we need to consider the nature side of testosterone levels alongside this. Cross-cultural research is a good way of assessing what are universal human behaviours and what are culturally specific behaviours.

Free will/determinism debate

- If children are exposed to aggressive role models, how much is their behaviour determined, and therefore out of their control, and how much free will do they have over whether they behave in a certain way? This can probably be seen best in data which shows that physical aggression shown by female role models was not imitated to the extent that aggression shown by male role models was. This indicates some choices being made by the children as to what was an acceptable way to behave. Also the verbal aggression (more acceptable when the model was the same sex as the child) was imitated more by the children. This cognitive aspect of the children's behaviour, thinking about what they should or shouldn't do, would indicate that humans have some free will, even in what seems to be an environmentally deterministic situation. There is also the concept of biological determinism, which if we accept that testosterone levels are linked to aggression, means that the boys would be more likely to show aggression than girls. An interactionist view of nature having some impact on behaviour but the environment encouraging or discouraging such behaviour being shown is perhaps a better way of trying to answer the free will/determinism debate.

Usefulness

- Many later studies supported Bandura *et al.*'s findings on learning through observation and imitation, and eventually society took note of the impact television and films could have on impressionable young people. The 9 p.m. watershed was introduced by the BBC as part of their Family Viewing Policy in the 1970s. Watershed is a geographical term meaning divide and this is the time when the television divides between programmes that are suitable for children and programmes that are unsuitable for children.
- Social learning theory is used a lot in society. Role models (for example, in sport or fashion) are often castigated (complained about) for displaying behaviour which we don't want children to imitate. It's a good job not every child imitates every behaviour, or how many young footballers would be biting their opponents after observing Luis Suarez in the 2014 World Cup?

Links to areas/perspectives

- Bandura *et al.*'s study falls within the developmental area because it is investigating how the environment around a child (particularly in terms of the adult behaviours they see and hear) can affect the behaviours they end up adopting themselves.
- Bandura *et al.*'s study also illustrates the behaviourist perspective because he believed that all behaviour was learned and Social Learning Theory, which he developed alongside his research, suggested a new way in which this can happen (beyond the ways suggested by classical conditioning and operant conditioning).
- Bandura *et al.*'s study can also be seen as cognitive because he believed that children could choose whether to imitate behaviour, depending on the circumstances, and social learning theory has many cognitive components, such as attention and memory. The first stage is attention, as children have to actually notice a behaviour, which was easy to do in the controlled observation of Bandura's Bobo doll experiment, but also happens all the time for children in everyday life. Children then have to observe the behaviour. Then they have to retain in their memory what the adult does, which may be more likely to happen if there is some reward/punishment involved, or again if the behaviour is particularly striking. Then the child will imitate the behaviour. The cognitive element is shown that not all behaviours are imitated (e.g. in this experiment, the boys did not imitate much of the female model's verbal aggression), but in later research Bandura did note that children would know what a model had done but, as a result of seeing that behaviour punished, would choose not to reproduce it. Their thought processes would allow them to select whether to show the behaviour or not.

Links to the key theme

- With reference to the key theme of external influences on children's behaviour, Bandura *et al.*'s study demonstrates the importance of the environment in which the child is brought up, as these external factors will shape a person's behaviour. There is much evidence that children with aggressive role models, such as siblings or parents, will become more aggressive, but whether

that is due to social learning theory or some other aspect of their environment is difficult to isolate as it obviously wouldn't be ethical to bring up children in situations where they have little or no contact with family or society, to isolate the effect of certain variables, which is why research in this area is quasi experimental in many cases. While acknowledging the part external influences play in the development of children, there is no escaping the biological factors such as genetic transference or biochemical composition.

- However, there are many questions that arise from Bandura *et al.*'s study, such as:
  - Would the effects observed in this study apply to other behaviours apart from those connected to aggression?
  - Would the effects apply to older children?
  - Would the effects apply to children in other cultures?
  - For how long would the effects observed in this study last?
  - Are there other ways in which children learn?

Find out more

- Use the internet to locate video footage of Bandura *et al.*'s experiment.
- Find out more about the other research Bandura *et al.*'s carried out using reinforcement and punishment for the models.
- Look at how television and films use parental guidance to avoid children imitating violence. Look at some of the programmes before the 9 p.m. watershed. Do you think the violence is acceptable for young children to see?

Practice questions

1. In Bandura *et al.*'s study into transmission of aggression, give two of the characteristics on which the participants were matched in their groups. **[2 marks]**
2. Why was it necessary for Bandura *et al.* to use the matched participants design? **[2 marks]**
3. Identify one of the hypotheses in Bandura *et al.*'s study into transmission of aggression. **[2 marks]**
4. Give one piece of evidence to show support for this hypothesis. **[2 marks]**

Chaney et al. (2004)

If we accept the behaviourist principle that behaviour will be repeated if it is rewarded (operant conditioning) then the environment that a child is brought up in will have a major impact on its behaviour. We may unwittingly reinforce unwanted behaviour, for example by giving attention to children who have been disobedient, or we may ignore wanted behaviour and find that it is not repeated. Chaney *et al.* wanted to find out if the principle of reinforcement could be applied in a health setting. There is some evidence that parents can reinforce pain behaviour through giving lots of cuddles and treats if a child is in pain, but Chaney wanted to see if the rewards could be used to increase health behaviours rather than illness behaviours.

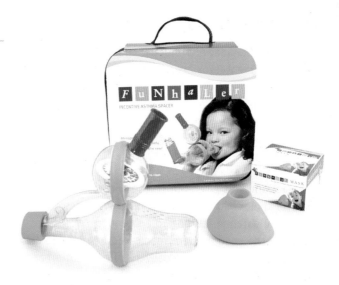

Figure 3.2 The Funhaler

Procedure

Parents of children who had asthma and who were using the standard AeroChamber or Breath-a-Tech inhalers were recruited via their GP or paediatrician. The parents were contacted by phone and then were visited at home. They were given a questionnaire to answer about their current inhaler which included a consent form for them to sign. They had no idea about the Funhaler (Figure 3.2) at this point. They were then given the Funhaler to use for 2 weeks with the instructions that parents had to use it with the child. At various times on an *ad hoc* (random) basis, the parents were contacted and asked if they had used the Funhaler the previous day. At the end of the 2 weeks, the parents were again visited and they were given another questionnaire to complete.

The Funhaler was designed to incentivise the children to use their inhaler more frequently to manage their asthma. It had a toy – which included a spinning disk and whistle – which was activated (when the child exhaled, to avoid compromising any inhalation). A good steady breath out (ideal) would result in the best toy performance – if the breath was not deep enough, the toy wouldn't be activated. For preschool children there was a face mask, which is usual in inhalers for young children.

The Funhaler was tested to ensure that it delivered the appropriately sized dose compared to a standard instrument. There is no point in using something more if it is not doing the job!

Participants

The sample of participants who took part in this research comprised 32 children from Australia, aged between 1.5 and 6 years. The mean and median age was 3.2 years, but 75 per cent of the children were older than 3. There were 22 boys and 10 girls, with an average duration of having asthma of 2.2 years. They were being treated for asthma using a variety of regular spacer devices and inhalers. The children were in a repeated measures field experiment.

 Stop and ask yourself ...

- How do you think the issue of social desirability might be shown by parents?
- What effect would this have on the validity of the data?

Links to methodological issues
- Validity

 Stop and ask yourself ...

- What do you think are the issues with carrying out research in the uncontrolled conditions of the children's home?
- What aspects of the study could be controlled?

Links to methodological issues
- Validity

- Psychology as a science

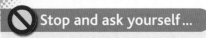
Stop and ask yourself...

- Why could Chaney *et al.* not use counterbalancing in this research?
- What are the weaknesses and strengths of using a repeated measures design?

Links to methodological issues
- Experimental design

The questionnaire

Measures

The questionnaires given out to the parents both before and after their child used the Funhaler were designed to measure parents' attitude to adherence, and how frequently the children were medicated. There were also questions on problems with delivery of medication and the child's attitude. Due to the way the research was conducted, there was a 100 per cent response rate to the questionnaires. The results are detailed in Table 3.5.

Have a go yourself

Try constructing a questionnaire which would find out about the information Chaney *et al.* needed. Would you use open or closed questions, or rating scales?

Table 3.5 Percentage results of children using Funhaler

	Normal device	Funhaler
Percentage of children who had used their inhaler the day before a question to parents (asked at random intervals)	59	81
Percentage of children who achieved four or more breath cycles per delivery	50	80
Percentage of parents successfully medicating child always	10	73

The quantitative data also showed that the problems experienced when using the normal inhaler were lessened with the Funhaler (Table 3.6).

The attitude of the children towards their medication was also more positive when they were using the Funhaler. While there was more suspicion (after all, they were used to their normal device), there was much more pleasure in using the Funhaler, and much less dislike or phobia (Table 3.7).

Because the attitude of parents is so important on how much the child uses the device, it was important to look at their attitudes (Table 3.8).

Again, some parents, as well as children, seemed wary of the Funhaler, but there was no strong concern or dislike, and many more happy parents. This probably meant that they would be more likely to use the Funhaler with their child.

Table 3.6 Quantitative results of percentage of children using inhaler

Problem identified	Percentage of children having problem with existing inhaler	Percentage of children having problem with Funhaler
Unwilling to use the mask	58	3
Unwilling to breathe through the device at all	61	7
Breathes through the device, but not deeply	68	19
Unwilling to breathe for very long through the device (e.g. for a period to the count of 1 s)	61	13
Struggles a little	32	10
Struggles a lot	35	3
Screams when device is brought close to face	48	3

Table 3.7 Children's attitude towards medication

Child's attitude to using their device	Percentage of children with attitude to existing inhaler	Percentage of children with attitude to Funhaler
Pleasure	10	68
Acceptance	58	19
No interest in device	3	3
Suspicion	0	10
Mild fear or dislike	13	0
Strong fear or dislike	19	0
Panic or phobia	6	0

Stop and ask yourself...

- Can you think of any extraneous variables which might have affected the attitude of the children towards the Funhaler?

Links to methodological issues
- Validity

Table 3.8 Parents' attitude to medication

Parent's approach to medicating their child	Percentage of parents with attitude to existing inhaler	Percentage of parents with attitude to Funhaler
Completely happy	10	61
Confident	32	16
Acceptance	39	19
Mild concern	7	3
Strong concern	13	0
Dislike	16	0

Conclusions

From the questionnaires, it would appear that the Funhaler led to an increase in use, and correct use at that (four or more breaths per cycle). Parents also tended to be less likely to give up and resort to a nebuliser if they were using the Funhaler.

Discussion

Of course, there is the idea that these results could just be due to the novelty factor of using a different inhaler. However, Chaney et al. argue that this was not the case, as anecdotally the parents reported continued pleasure and use of the Funhaler after months of use. The idea that parents and children just behaved differently due to the fact that they were in a study (Chaney calls this the 'recruitment effect') is dismissed as this alone wouldn't have been enough to show the large increases in positive outcomes and attitudes in such a short space of time.

Chaney et al. suggest that follow up research (which has now been published) would need to focus on longevity of positive results, whether there was a need to have changeable toys to stop boredom with one toy and whether the Funhaler could be used to reintroduce children to inhalers, if they had developed a phobia of normal inhalers.

There were a number of features which made the use of the Funhaler rewarding and so, according to operant conditioning theory, more likely to be repeated. These were the toy and whistle, the link between outcome of the toy and the breathing technique, the ability to increase the rewards as the breathing technique became more acceptable, and the use of colour to detract from the idea that it was an inhaler and to emphasise it as a toy. Further research would be needed to see if all of

these are needed to increase compliance or which ones are the most likely to do so.

The application of the Funhaler should be to increase the medication a child receives and therefore produce better health outcomes; this wasn't studied here, but could be an idea for future research. If the health outcomes are better, then this would have an impact on child morbidity, hospitalisation and health costs.

Evaluation of the study by Chaney et al.

Links to methodological issues

Research method

- This study was a field experiment as it was conducted in the participants' regular settings and it had independent variables, dependent variables and some controls.
- The design of this experiment was, in effect, repeated measures as the researchers assessed the children's use of their regular inhaler and compared this against their use of the Funhaler. The good thing about this design is that participant variables were controlled: if a parent didn't always remember to use the inhaler or a child didn't like the inhaler, this would be the same at the start of each condition. However, using a repeated measures design also meant that the parents could probably work out what the research was about. 'How much do you use the inhaler, and what are the problems? Here's a whizzy Funhaler, now how much did you use this, and what were the problems?' It doesn't take much working out! So demand characteristics could have been a problem where the parents worked out that the Funhaler was meant to make things better, and so they made sure

it did (or gave answers that indicated it did). Using an independent measures design might have been possible (half of parents being given the Funhaler and half keeping their standard inhaler), but then we have even more reason to be wary of extraneous variables.

- Importantly, the use of the repeated measures design in this situation was undermined by the fact that there could not be counterbalancing in this research. Ideally, to avoid order effects, half of the children would have had the Funhaler then their standard inhaler, and half their standard inhaler and then their Funhaler. In this research, however, the possibility that the effect of the Funhaler being given as the first condition could, increase adherence in the second condition (standard inhaler) simply due to using the Funhaler the week before. This means that counterbalancing was not appropriate. Alternatively, the child might have not wanted to go back to their standard inhaler and so decreased their amount of inhaler use after the Funhaler and so shown an even greater difference, which would have confounded the data.
- Data were collected through self-report, both through the questionnaires and the telephone interviews.

Data

- The data collected were quantitative. The answers to the Yes/No questions as to whether the parents had used the inhaler the day before made for direct comparisons, and easy statistical analysis of difference. However, what these data don't tell us is why there was a difference in attitude and behaviour. Chaney et al. assumed it was the reinforcement, but it could have been something else that no one considered. Questions which asked for qualitative data might have supported their conclusions.

Ethics

- Although the participants were not told about the Funhaler at the start of the experiment, nonetheless it can be assumed that all ethical guidelines were adhered to. Importantly, by using a repeated measures design (as opposed to an independent measures design), no participants missed out on the beneficial effects of the Funhaler intervention.

Validity

- This raises the question of how sure we are that the research was actually measuring how different space devices might influence behaviour, in terms of use and attitude, of children with asthma and their parents.

- A problem with using self-report, which will affect the validity of the research, is the problem of social desirability. Parents were asked about their use of the inhaler when they were phoned up at random intervals and in the questionnaire. What parent is going to admit to forgetting to use the inhaler on their child or say that they found it too much of a problem to use it frequently? Society demands parents to take care of their children, and to admit a failure to do so is unthinkable, therefore parents might lie to do as society wishes (social desirability). If this happens then the research is actually measuring what the parent thinks is the right behaviour, not the behaviour that the parent actually shows.
- By using a field experiment, Chaney et al. had to contend with extraneous variables which might also reduce the validity of the research. How can we accurately measure the impact of the inhaler if there are other factors which might have a stronger impact on the use of the inhaler? We don't know how efficient parents were in using the inhaler, or how much they persevered if the child didn't want to take it. Did the parent adhere strictly to the guidelines of how much to use the inhaler? Then, within each family, there will be situations when the level of perseverance might change. The parent might be too tired to insist, or there might be a family gathering during the first condition and the whole inhaler use goes right out of their head. Without bringing the children in to a lab and giving inhalers, we have no way of knowing what went on during this research which might have also influenced the use of the inhaler. This is where we would reduce the ecological validity of the research and we would no longer see natural behaviour.

Ecological validity

- The natural setting of the research, taking place in the child's home where they would normally use their inhaler, means ecological validity is high. The children are not taken anywhere different, it can be the same as it has always been, and so the child would show natural behaviour when using their inhaler. It is not every day, though, that a parent of a child has to complete a questionnaire, and therefore this aspect of the research would reduce the ecological validity. There were some interviews, which might make it a bit more normal as parents will often chat to other people about their child and this would include their inhaler use and the problems associated with it, so chatting to an interviewer might be more natural than a questionnaire.

Reliability

- Although this was conducted in the field, there were many aspects that were standardised, aiding replicability. The questionnaire was the same for each participant, and the length of time using the Funhaler was the same. The Funhaler was the same for all the children – same design, same instructions and so the action of the Funhaler would have been the same for each child, with weak spins for poor breath exhalation and faster spins for good breath exhalation.
- However, the fact that the study was conducted with only 32 children raises the question of whether the sample was large enough to establish a consistent effect.

Sample

- The narrow age range of the children restricts the study's generalisability, but given that the Funhaler wouldn't be expected to appeal to people much beyond this age range, it is appropriate to their target population.

Ethnocentrism

- The sample were all from Australia which, arguably, makes the study ethnocentric as it is not obvious that the toys built into the design of the Funhaler would appeal equally to children from all cultures.

Links to debates

Individual/situational explanations

- Although there might be individual differences in the amount of inhaler use and the effectiveness of the way it was used, this study is looking clearly at the role of the situation in determining behaviour. It is the features of the inhaler, where a child has to use an inhaler, which influence the frequency and success of its use. Also these features will, according to Chaney et al.'s data, also influence the attitude (psychologists acknowledge attitudes as behaviour) of the child and parent. If the only thing changing within the research is the type of inhaler, and the resultant behaviour is significantly different, the situation must be inferred to have an impact on the behaviour.
- However, the differences in attitude between the children and the parents both prior to and after the use of the Funhaler show how individual differences can influence behaviour, with some children having a phobia of their inhaler and other children taking pleasure in using their inhaler.

Usefulness

- The usefulness of this study can be considered in several ways. First, there is its usefulness in helping us understand how children develop and acquire behaviours, and how the principles of the behaviourist perspective can be used to facilitate this.
- Second, the practical application of incorporating rewards into behaviours which we want to be repeated can be used in health settings to improve adherence or reduce unwanted illness behaviours, but also can be used in education and parenting.
- That said, there are limitations to its usefulness. The research was carried out on a limited age range, and so this limits the usefulness of the research due to the lack of generalisability of the results. How would this impact on teenagers having to use an inhaler? Would they be impressed enough by a spinner and whistle to see the inhaler more positively and continue using the inhaler effectively? This was a sample of Australian children, and while we may not think that there is any difference between children in Australia and children elsewhere, the reinforcer might need to be different and cross-cultural research needed to see how universal the application of the Funhaler might be. Also, the children all had asthma: how would this work on, say, the application of wraps in children with eczema? Again, it is probable that some kind of reward would be useful, but we can't just assume this from one piece of research limited to one illness. The lack of control of extraneous variables and inherent reduction in validity will also reduce the usefulness of this research, and some more research to give the study concurrent validity would help us to know the usefulness of the research.

Links to areas/perspectives

- This study falls within the developmental area as it is illustrating a way in which children learn and how parents can help their children to acquire desired behaviours – namely, through both positive and negative reinforcement.
- As such it also clearly links in with the behaviourist perspective. Chaney et al.'s research is set firmly in the area of operant conditioning as a means of explaining the development of behaviour in children. Operant conditioning is a behaviourist theory devised by Skinner to explain how behaviour is learned as a result of consequences. If behaviour is positively reinforced – i.e. something pleasant happens after

the behaviour (a spinner going round or whistle blowing) – then the behaviour will be repeated. Similarly, if the child is negatively reinforced – i.e. something unpleasant is taken away (feeling breathless is stopped) – then the behaviour again is rewarded and so repeated.

- Arguably, the study also illustrates the classical conditioning theory of behaviourism, which states that people learn to associate two stimuli. In this case, the child could come to associate the inhaler with an unpleasant experience (mother getting cross, stopping being able to play) and so the response to the latter (getting upset as can't continue playing) is linked to the first (the inhaler) so the minute the inhaler is shown, the response of the child is a negative association (and consequential crying or avoidance of the inhaler).

Links to the key theme

- In relation to the key theme of external influences on children's behaviour, Chaney *et al.* have shown how the external influences favoured by the behaviourist perspective have a great impact on children's behaviour. The Funhaler changed not only the use of the inhaler, to increase adherence, but also the attitude towards the inhaler in both parents and children, which would be linked to increased adherence.

- In terms of the extent to which Chaney *et al.*'s study changes our understanding of the key theme of 'external influences on children's behaviour', it can be seen as adding to our understanding of how this can happen. Whereas, then, Bandura's study showed how children can learn through imitation in a process of social learning, Chaney *et al.*'s study shows another way in which children can learn – namely, through a process of reinforcement.

- In terms of the extent to which Chaney *et al.*'s study changes our understanding of individual, social and cultural diversity, the fact that it was carried out in Australia compared to Bandura's older study of children in America, seems to imply that learning occurs whatever the culture. Both studies used male and female children and seem to suggest that learning certainly occurs in childhood, through both imitation and reinforcement. However, neither of these studies shows any insight into how adult individuals might learn behaviour. Bandura's study shows the impact of cultural norms on behaviour acquisition, but this is not seen in Chaney's study.

 **Find out more**

- Look on the internet at how operant conditioning has been used in health care settings. Work out if the suggestions use positive reinforcement, negative reinforcement or punishment. Check out these terms if you are not sure of the difference between them. You could then take a health behaviour in children you would want to see (eating five portions of fruit, taking exercise, testing their insulin levels regularly) and work out a reinforcement schedule (for example, a star chart), deciding when the rewards will be given. Look at schedules of reinforcement in operant conditioning to decide on the schedule most likely to first of all start and then maintain the behaviours.

Comparison with the classic study

- In what ways are Bandura *et al.*'s and Chaney *et al.*'s studies *similar*?
  - Both studies used young children as their participants.
  - Both studies were basing their research in behaviourist principles of learning.
  - Both studies gained quantitative data for analysis.
  - Both studies showed the importance of external influences on children's' behaviour.
- In what ways are Bandura *et al.*'s and Chaney *et al.*'s studies *different*?
  - Bandura used observation and Chaney used self-report to collect their data.
  - Bandura used a controlled setting, whereas Chaney used a natural setting.
  - The behaviourist theories of learning they were investigating were different.
  - Bandura's study was carried out in America, whereas Chaney's study was carried out in Australia.
  - Bandura had a fairly large sample, whereas Chaney had a sample half the size of Bandura's.
  - There was an equal gender split in Bandura's sample and not in Chaney's sample.
  - Chaney had to use participants with asthma, making his sample biased.

Questions arising from Chaney *et al.*

- What questions are we left with after studying the research by Chaney *et al.*? It certainly suggests the potential for applying operant conditioning principles in health settings, but could these principles work equally well with older age groups, with other illnesses, or even in other applied areas apart from health? Are there other questions to which the study leaves you wanting answers?
- Over to you ...

Practice questions

1. From Chaney *et al.*'s study of adherence:
   (a) Describe the difference between the Funhaler and a normal inhaler. [2 marks]
   (b) With reference to Chaney's study of adherence, outline the theory of operant conditioning. [2 marks]
2. From Chaney *et al.*'s study on children with asthma, outline one result which shows the positive impact of the Funhaler on adherence. [2 marks]
3. Describe the key features of Chaney *et al.*'s sample. [2 marks]
4. Outline two ways in which the study by Bandura *et al.* is different from the study by Chaney *et al.* [4 marks]

Moral development Ⓐ

Morality relates to how we interact with others, and moral development refers to the way children begin to construct, cognitively, a system of beliefs about this. This is done as an interaction with their environment, adopting moral rules and attitudes which reflect the society in which they live. Jean Piaget, a Swiss psychologist, suggested that this moral development was linked to how the child thought about themselves and their surroundings. His theory was that they would start off with a rigid view of the world which reflected their moral stance of obedience to authority and the outcomes of actions. He called this the 'heteronomous stage of moral reasoning'. A child at this stage might be more likely to judge the outcome, e.g. breaking something, without taking into account intention (it was an accident or it was deliberate). This is because they don't see anything from another person's perspective. However, Piaget felt that as children reach the age of 8 they begin to understand that there are rules, but these may be modified in certain situations. This develops from social interactions with peers, and the child begins to develop the idea of morality being fluid and subject to negotiation rather than adult authority.

Kohlberg based his theory of stages of development on Piaget's suggestion. He was interested to see how moral development occurred, and how this impacted on the beliefs of individuals. His theory that moral thinking developed through stages and was a developmental process was the first to have clear evidence to support it. Kohlberg's theory contradicted the behaviourist view that morality was learned from interaction with others, through operant or classical conditioning, or through the Social Learning Theory. The empirical part of Kohlberg's research (where he gathered evidence to back up his theory) would involve him presenting participants with moral dilemmas and asking them what they would do.

Of course, it is part of their nature that moral dilemmas are not always a clear-cut decision. Have you ever been given a present which wasn't what you wanted, or even liked? What did you do? Lie and say, 'I love it – it's just what I wanted!', or hurt the giver's feelings by being truthful and saying, 'Never in a million years would I wear this!'? The philosopher Immanuel Kant believed that certain acts are always right or wrong and we should always act the right way even if the outcome is bad. This is based on his argument that morality comes from duty to do right rather than from a weighing-up of the likely consequences of action (as utilitarians would argue). As a deontologist (*Deon* is from the Greek for duty), Kant had some universal moral rules such as:

- It is wrong to kill innocent people.
- It is wrong to steal.
- It is wrong to tell lies.
- It is right to keep promises.

These universal moral rules emerged from his 'categorical imperative' by which Kant argued that we can work out the right thing to do in a given situation by reflecting on whether we can honestly wish that something becomes a universal (moral) law or not (e.g. it's unlikely that we would wish that it become a universal law that it's alright to break promises because, although on occasions I might want to break the odd promise to other people, I don't want them breaking their promises to me – hence it is everyone's duty to keep our promises).

However, Kant was a moral philosopher, and his job was to try and work out a means by which to discover the right thing to do in a given situation. Psychologists are more likely to investigate such questions as the age at which people develop their ability to think morally, the factors that influence the development of this ability (e.g. is it as a result of external or internal influences?), why there are individual differences in who does or doesn't develop moral thinking, whether there are cultural differences in moral thinking, and the nature of how people think morally. For example, in the previous present-giving example, I might decide that if I lie it isn't going to do anyone any harm and it will leave the other person feeling good; yes, I might get another unsuitable gift next time, but it's hardly the end of the world and if I give it to a charity shop then it may end up making someone genuinely happy.

🚫 Stop and ask yourself...

- Are there any times when it is acceptable to break the four rules identified?
  Are some easier to break than others?

Keep in mind that the concept of moral development is a construct – it can't be seen, but its existence is inferred from what people do. This applies particularly to Kohlberg's paper, in which he infers the existence of six distinct stages to people's moral thinking from the responses he receives when presenting people with different moral dilemmas. A final point worth noting, before we start looking at the two core studies, is that the title Kohlberg gave to his research paper was 'The child as a moral philosopher'. He is suggesting that, when we reflect on how we should behave in given circumstances, we are all, to some extent, behaving a bit like Immanuel Kant.

Kohlberg (1968)

Kohlberg puts forward his theory of moral development and explores the cognitive background of this area of development. He then uses the research he has carried out to explain and support his stage theory, with examples showing how moral thinking changes as the child gets older. He looks at some data from cross-cultural research (although he doesn't go into much detail about this research) which suggests a universality in moral development across cultures.

Aims

Kohlberg writes about his research in relation to Piaget's theory, which he claims was his inspiration, as well as behaviourism (which believes that all behaviour is learned, including moral behaviour), and Freudian psychology, which supports the idea of morality as being linked to the development of the superego. Kohlberg's aim is to show how his research supports his stage theory of moral development.

Procedure

Over the course of twelve years, Kohlberg studied 75 American boys aged at the start from 10 to 16 years, through to when they were 22–28 years. Each one of the boys was, at three-yearly intervals, presented with hypothetical moral dilemmas, all deliberately philosophical. Their answers and the reasoning behind their answers were linked to 25 basic moral concepts or aspects.

Background

Kohlberg believed that the stages of moral development in his theory were invariant – that they did not change order at all and that they came one at a time, with someone moving onto the next stage in order. No stages were missed, but the speed at which a child passed through the stages could vary. He also felt that not all people would achieve the highest level of moral development. Some people would remain at a lower level. There is some evidence, for example, that criminals tend to have a lower level of moral reasoning than non-criminals.

One such moral aspect is the motivation to obey rules. Kohlberg identified six reasons that might be given for this, which he placed in ascending order as follows:

- to avoid punishment
- to obtain rewards
- to avoid dislike by others
- to avoid punishment by authority
- to be respected by others
- to avoid self-condemnation.

Another aspect is the value of human life. Again, Kohlberg saw this as progressing upwards through six stages as follows:

- The value of a human life is based on the social status or physical attributes of its possessor.
- The value of a human life is linked to satisfying the needs of its possessor or other people.
- The value of a human life is based on the affection of family members for its possessor.
- Life is valued because of its place in a defined order (e.g. 'because God created it').
- Life is valued both in terms of the welfare of society and because the right to live is a universal human right.
- Life is valued because of universal respect for the individual.

These show the kind of moral stages that Kohlberg was using as a basis for his research. He wanted to judge the boys' responses to see how developed their moral reasoning was. He identified the type of thinking which would be shown by someone at each stage of development and matched the boys' responses to these (Table 3.9).

 Stop and ask yourself ...

- Kohlberg only asked American boys – how does this limit the representativeness of the sample?
- What are the strengths and weaknesses of carrying out longitudinal research?

Links to methodological issues

- Sample, ethnocentric bias

- Longitudinal research

97

Figure 3.3 Moral development: weighing up self versus humanity

Kohlberg uses the responses of the boys to show how they are moving from stage to stage. Table 3.10 shows some of the responses which illustrate each stage of development:

Kohlberg reports that he decided to explore moral development in other cultures aside from just the USA. In the first instance, he went to Malaysia and Taiwan, although he also reports collecting data in Mexico, Turkey, Canada and United Kingdom. There were some cultural differences in the reasoning behind the same decision. Taiwanese boys at stage 2 regarding the theft of food suggested that it would be acceptable for a man to steal to feed his wife otherwise she would die and he would have to pay for the funeral. However, in an Atayal (Malaysian aboriginal) village, the same decision was based not on the cost of a

Table 3.9 Kohlberg's stage theory of moral development

Level	Motivation and behaviour	Child's thinking
Level 1: (Pre-conventional) Approximate age 4–10 years	Stage 1 – Obedience and punishment orientation: Child is well behaved and responsive to cultural norms but able to behave in an immoral way if authority structure is missing.	How can I avoid punishment? Unquestioning obedience to superior power ('might is right'). The physical consequences (e.g. punishment) determine whether an act is seen as good or bad.
	Stage 2 – Self-interest orientation: Child behaves in a self-centred way, doing what brings benefit to self.	What's in it for me? Occasionally, 'what's in it for them?' What will I get in return?
Level 2: (Conventional)	Stage 3 – Conformity to expectations and rules: Child now seeking approval from others and begins to consider the intention of the act.	What does everyone in my world say is right and wrong? I am a good girl/boy. Why did the person do that?
	Stage 4 – Authority and social order orientation: Child now sees right behaviour as duty to show respect and maintain social order. Laws are set in stone.	I must do what is right and make sure everyone else does, too. I must respect others by doing the right thing.
Level 3: (Post-conventional)	Stage 5 – Social contract orientation: Child now does what is right based on law plus personal values and opinions. Sees laws as changeable.	There is a difference between law and morality. What makes a law right is whether it promotes social utility (the greatest happiness of the greatest number). Laws can be questioned.
	Stage 6 – Universal ethical principles: Child now bases judgement on universal human rights of justice, equality, reciprocity and respect for the individual.	All individuals have value, even those who don't value themselves. We should be wary of ethical positions that could potentially involve sacrificing the well-being of an individual for the well-being of the majority.

Table 3.10 Results showing evidence to support Kohlberg's theory

Level	Motivation and behaviour	Dilemma and response	Kohlberg's explanation
Level 1: (Pre-conventional)	Stage 1 – Obedience and punishment orientation: Child is well behaved and responsive to cultural norms but able to behave in an immoral way if authority structure missing.	*Is it better to save the life of one important person than a lot of unimportant people?* 'All the people that aren't important because one man has one house, maybe a lot of furniture, but a whole bunch of people have an awful lot of furniture and some of these poor people might have a lot of money and it doesn't look it.' (Tommy, aged 10)	Stage 1 – confusing the value of a human being with the value of the property he possesses.
	Stage 2 – Self-interest orientation: Child behaves in a self-centred way, doing what brings benefit to self.	*Should the doctor 'mercy kill' a fatally ill woman requesting death because of her pain?* 'Maybe it would be good, to put her out of her pain, she'd be better off that way. But the husband wouldn't want it. It's not like an animal. If a pet dies you can get along without it – it isn't something you really need. Well, you can get a new wife, but it's not really the same.' (Tommy, aged 13)	Stage 2 – the value of the woman's life partly rests on its value to the wife herself but even more on its instrumental value to her husband, who can't replace her as easily as he can a pet.
Level 2: (Conventional)	Stage 3 – Conformity to expectations and rules: Child now seeking approval from others and begins to consider the intention of the act.	*Should the doctor 'mercy kill' a fatally ill woman requesting death because of her pain?* 'It might be best for her, but her husband – it's a human life – not like an animal; it just doesn't have the same relationship that a human being does to a family. You can become attached to a dog, but nothing like a human you know.' (Tommy, aged 16)	Stage 3 – based on the husband's distinctively human empathy and love for someone in his family. Equally clearly, it lacks any basis for a universal human value of the woman's life, which would hold if she had no husband or if her husband didn't love her.
	Stage 4 – Authority and social order orientation: Child now sees right behaviour as duty to show respect and maintain social order. Laws are set in stone.	*Should the doctor 'mercy kill' a fatally ill woman requesting death because of her pain?* 'I don't know. In one way, it's murder, it's not a right or privilege of man to decide who shall live and who should die. God put life into everybody on earth and you're taking away something from that person that came directly from God, and you're destroying something that is very sacred, it's in a way part of God and it's almost destroying a part of God when you kill a person. There's something of God in everyone.' (Richard, aged 16)	Stage 4 – life is sacred in terms of its place in a categorical moral or religious order. The value of human life is universal, it is true for all humans. It is still, however, dependent on something else, upon respect for God and God's authority; it is not an autonomous human value.
Level 3: (Post-conventional)	Stage 5 – Social contract orientation: Child now does what is right based on law plus personal values and opinions. Sees laws as changeable.	*Should the doctor 'mercy kill' a fatally ill woman requesting death because of her pain?* 'There are more and more people in the medical profession who think it is a hardship on everyone, the person, the family, when you know they are going to die. When a person is kept alive by an artificial lung or kidney it's more like being a vegetable than being a human. If it's her own choice, I think there are certain rights and privileges that go along with being a human being. I am a human being and have certain desires for life and I think everybody else does too. You have a world of which you are the centre, and everybody else does too and in that sense we're all equal.' (Richard, aged 20)	Stage 5 – the value of life is defined in terms of equal and universal human rights in a context of relativity ('You have a world of which you are the centre and in that sense we're all equal'), and of concern for utility or welfare consequences.
	Stage 6 – Universal ethical principles: Child now bases judgement on universal human rights of justice, equality, reciprocity and respect for the individual.	*Should the doctor 'mercy kill' a fatally ill woman requesting death because of her pain?* 'A human life takes precedence over any other moral or legal value, whoever it is. A human life has inherent value whether or not it is valued by a particular individual. The worth of the individual human being is central where the principles of justice and love are normative for all human relationships.' (Richard, aged 24)	Stage 6 – seeing the value of human life as absolute in representing a universal and equal respect for the human as an individual. He has moved step by step through a sequence culminating in a definition of human life as centrally valuable rather than derived from or dependent on social or divine authority.

Stop and ask yourself ...

● How do you think the data might have been different if the children had been observed rather than asked about what they would do?

Links to methodological issues
● Self-report
● Validity

 Stop and ask yourself ...

● What are the strengths and weaknesses of carrying out research in different countries?

Links to methodological issues
● Cross-cultural research

funeral (something the Atayal village wouldn't have) but because otherwise the wife would die and the man would have no one to cook for him. Both were showing fundamental stage 2 'what's in it for them?' thinking, but set within cultural contexts. Some other cultural differences were also found, such as stage 5 being more common in American teenagers than Mexican or Taiwanese adolescents, but enough cultures showed stage 5 thinking to be sure it was not simply an American phenomenon.

Another difference Kohlberg found was that the rate at which children moved through the stages differed depending on social class and setting. Development was quickest for middle class children, then lower class urban children and village boys were the slowest to pass through the stages, although the sequence of the stages in all of the research did not vary. Kohlberg, however, found no differences between religions; whatever religious values a person had, they appeared to go through the same stages.

 Have a go yourself

Kohlberg suggested the ages of up to nine years for pre-conventional, nine years to adolescence for conventional, and adulthood for post-conventional thinking. Make a poster with three pictures of people to represent the three levels, then put speech bubbles around each figure with typical reasons people at that level might give. You could use two different colours to represent the two stages in each level.

Conclusions

Moral development occurs in the same sequence regardless of where a child grows up. The nature of this sequence is not significantly affected by social, cultural or religious conditions. Furthermore, moral thought develops like all other kinds of thought, with each successive stage being a better cognitive organisation than the one before it.

Discussion

The evidence shows a universal development of morality, from the egocentric view of the self being the centre of the world, to the final impersonal stage where dilemmas can be seen with a reference to humanity rather than self. The actions to be taken at stage 6 were spoken of with phrases such as 'regardless of who it was' or 'I would do it in spite of punishment'. Such people as Socrates and Martin Luther King spoke with a post-conventional level of moral thinking, expressing ideal principles of justice which reflected their actions. There was coherence between their thought and actions, whereas the behaviourist and psychodynamic perspectives have differentiated between moral behaviour and moral thinking, one not necessarily linked to the other.

Kohlberg at first thought he would have to develop culturally specific dilemmas to enable cross-cultural research to take place. However, he found that this was not necessary and the dilemmas could be used in different cultures and appeared to find the same stages of development albeit with different reasoning.

There is a clear link between the development of moral thinking and the development of cognition. At each stage, the child uses what he has learned from the previous stage and brings new thinking skills, such as consideration of other people's points of view, to their moral thinking in the new stage. Interestingly, children can understand the previous stages before where they are now but are unable to comprehend the stage after their next one. There appears to be an ability to move from stage 3, for example, to stage 4 in a discussion, and a child at stage 3 will comprehend the stage 4 arguments and accept them. They cannot comprehend the stage 5 arguments. However, a child at stage 4 will understand, but not accept the stage 3 arguments they have already left behind.

Kohlberg argues that his theory is scientific in that each stage a child progresses through generates its own data (thinking) and this expands to take in new information to keep the balance (equilibrium) between experience and thought.

Evaluation of the study by Kohlberg

Links to methodological issues

Research method

- Kohlberg's study was longitudinal as he studied the same boys over a period of twelve years, collecting data from them every three years. This longitudinal approach is excellent when it comes to controlling participant variables, but there are the extraneous variables of upbringing which might influence the behaviour. In this case, Kohlberg found consistent developmental changes in line with his theory. One of the problems with this type of research is that over the course of time there will be participant attrition, where for some reason or another a number of the participants will drop out. This can often be a problem when there is something in the research which might stop a person continuing, such as testing a stop smoking device, if a participant goes back to smoking they may drop out, not wanting to look a failure. This wouldn't have been the case with Kohlberg, but for reasons of illness, death, moving away or just disinterest, the number at the end would be smaller than the number at the beginning, and this could give a skewed sample. If only the interested participants remained, they may have similar characteristics which could impact on their moral development. Often the issues of longitudinal research being time-consuming and expensive are used as limitations of longitudinal studies, but as the researcher starts the research expecting as it is longitudinal that it will take a long time, then it is not time-consuming. If you plan to spend twelve years doing research it is not time-consuming any more than is spending one week on a snapshot study. Also the cost is not necessarily an issue, as sending a questionnaire or interviewing a participant once a year for twelve years would not be any more costly than setting up a whole shock generator simulator in a university.
- Kohlberg's study was also cross-cultural as he followed up his work collecting data from American boys with work collecting data in other cultures around the world. This is a major strength of his research as it enables him to demonstrate that his theory of moral development doesn't just apply to Americans (i.e. it isn't ethnocentric). Inevitably, there are cost implications to this kind of research and also language barriers to overcome; on top of this, a concern that Kohlberg had before he began this side to his research was that the moral dilemmas with which he presented his participants might be too culture-bound to the USA.

Data

- The data that Kohlberg collected were qualitative as what he was interested in was listening to the ways in which his participants justified how they would behave in the various moral dilemmas. However, a major problem with using qualitative data is the subjective analysis which researchers could use to ensure that their data supports their theory. There is no quantitative difference between the different age groups, but Kohlberg infers from their responses the level of their moral development. It is difficult to argue with this, but it could be that these examples are unusual or atypical of those age groups, but Kohlberg uses them as support that this level of thinking can be seen. More quantitative methods might enable us to see if these differences were frequent enough to show significance.

Ethics

- It can be assumed that Kohlberg's participants consented to take part in his research, and they could certainly have withdrawn by just not co-operating when he returned three years later to collect further data from them.

Validity

- Giving participants hypothetical moral dilemmas could lack ecological validity as how people say they would act in a given situation may be very different from how they actually would act if they found themselves in that situation.
- Asking any participant to report on their thoughts or behaviour is leaving the data open to reduced validity, as there is the chance of demand characteristics or social desirability. However, it is difficult to see how a person could show a higher level of moral reasoning than they have, just to support a researcher's aim. It could be argued that everyone has post-conventional levels of moral development and chooses to show pre-conventional levels when they are younger, to appear socially desirable or help the researcher, but this is unlikely.
- There are some other factors which might affect the validity, such as extraneous variables, and it could be factors such as upbringing, socio-economic status or education which actually influence moral development, not the invariant nature of the stages themselves.
- It could be that the dilemmas which Kohlberg used are not testing moral development, but maybe linguistic understanding, or intelligence. This would reduce the validity.

101

Anti-social Behaviour/Truth-telling Physical Story	Pro-social Behaviour/Truth-telling Physical Story
Here is Ryan. Ryan wanted to make paper airplanes so he tore some pages out of a storybook from the library. **(Question 1: Is what Ryan did good or naughty?)** **So Ryan tore the pages from a storybook, and when the teacher noticed the missing pages in the book, she said to the class, 'I see that someone has torn some pages from this book.' The teacher then asked Ryan, 'Do you know who tore out the pages?' Ryan said to his teacher, 'I did it.'** **(Question 2: Is what Ryan said to his teacher good or naughty?)**	**Here is Jenny. When Jenny was out at recess, she saw that the school yard was littered with garbage, so she picked up all the pieces she could find and threw them in the litter bin.** **(Question 1: Is what Jenny did good or naughty?)** **So Jenny cleaned the school yard, and at the end of recess, the teacher said to her students, 'I notice that the school yard is now nice and clean.' The teacher then asked Jenny, 'Do you know who cleaned the yard?' Jenny said to her teacher, 'I did it.'** **(Question 2: Is what Jenny said to her teacher good or naughty?)**
Anti-social Behaviour/Lie-telling Social Story	Pro-social Behaviour/Lie-telling Social Story
Here is Paul. A new boy, named Jimmy, had just joined Paul's class, and Paul decided that he did not like him. Paul went over to Jimmy, and when the teacher was not looking, Paul pushed Jimmy to the ground and made him cry. **(Question 1: Is what Paul did good or naughty?)** **So Paul pushed Jimmy and made him cry, and when the teacher came over to see if Jimmy was all right, she said, 'Oh dear, Jimmy's been hurt.' The teacher then asked, Paul, 'Do you know who just hurt Jimmy?' Paul said to his teacher, 'I did not do it.'** **(Question 2: Is what Paul said to his teacher good or naughty?)**	**Here is Kelly. Kelly knew that her friend, Anne, had lost her money for the class trip and now could not go on the trip with the rest of her class. When Anne hung up her coat, Kelly secretly put some of her own money in Anne's pocket so Anne could go on the trip.** **(Question 1: Is what Kelly did good or naughty?)** **So Kelly left the money for Anne, and when Anne found the money and told her teacher, the teacher said to the class, 'Anne just told me that someone has given her money so she can now go on the trip.' The teacher then asked Kelly, 'Do you know who left the money for Anne?' Kelly said to her teacher, 'I did not do it.'** **(Question 2: Is what Kelly said to her teacher good or naughty?)**

Figure 3.5 Lee *et al.*'s four types of stories (*Source*: Lee *et al.*, 1997)

Stop and ask yourself...

- What could be the problems in carrying out this particular cross-cultural study?

Links to methodological issues
- Cross-cultural research

Stop and ask yourself...

- What are the independent variables and dependent variables in this study?

Links to methodological issues
- Operationalised variables

| Very very good | Very good | Good | Neither | Naughty | Very naughty | Very very naughty |

Figure 3.6 Seven-point rating chart

Method

The children were randomly allocated to either the social story condition or the physical story condition (Figure 3.5). They were seen individually, and first of all the rating chart was explained. When the children had to answer the questions, they could use the words, symbols, or sometimes both (Figure 3.6).

Each child listened to all four social or all four physical stories. The meaning of the symbols on the chart was repeated each time the question was asked. The good and naughty meanings were alternated so that the researchers knew the child wasn't just saying the first option each time. The researchers also used counterbalancing by randomly allocating stories to one of two orders and then giving about half of the children one order and the rest of the children the second order.

Results

Having established that there was no significant difference between the order in which the stories were given and the gender of the child, these variables were ignored and the data could be analysed just in terms of the difference between cultures and type of story.

The scale was converted to quantitative data as shown in Figure 3.7. The higher the score, the more the

🚫 **Stop and ask yourself...**

- How could you randomly allocate the stories to get two different orders?
- Why was it important to counterbalance in this study?

Links to methodological issues
- Standardisation and control

child approved of the action, and the lower the score, the more the child disapproved of the action.

For the first question, every good deed had a positive score and every bad deed had a negative score, whatever the type of story and whatever the age of the child, and whatever the ethnicity of the child (Table 3.11).

However, the ratings of the truth-telling and lie-telling as good or bad showed differences between the cultures (Table 3.12).

From this, you can see that generally as they got older the Chinese children began to see lie-telling in a positive light, and gave it a higher rating than truth-telling in good deed situations. This was only shown in the oldest children in the social story, but by the 9- and 11-year-olds in the physical story. However, they didn't just approve of any lie-telling as shown by the negative ratings given by all of the Chinese children in the bad deed situation.

🚫 **Stop and ask yourself...**

- Why was it important to ensure the extraneous variables of gender and order did not impact on the results?
- How could the researchers do this?

Links to methodological issues
- Validity

Rating scale	Very very good	Very good	Good	Neither	Naughty	Very naughty	Very very naughty
Number given to rating	3	2	1	0	–1	–2	–3

Figure 3.7 Lee *et al.*'s rating scale of quantitative data

Table 3.11 Mean ratings of good and bad deeds

	China			Canada		
	Social	Physical	Combined	Social	Physical	Combined
Story 1: good deed situation						
7 years	2.45	1.60	2.03	1.90	2.35	2.13
9 years	1.25	2.50	1.88	1.80	2.35	2.08
11 years	1.20	2.15	1.68	2.29	2.33	2.31
Story 2: good deed situation						
7 years	2.45	1.65	2.05	2.00	2.35	2.18
9 years	1.25	2.55	1.90	1.75	2.10	1.93
11 years	1.65	1.85	1.75	2.06	1.93	2.00
Story 3: bad deed situation						
7 years	−2.15	−1.65	−1.90	−1.95	−2.35	−2.15
9 years	−2.35	−2.80	−2.58	−1.85	−2.50	−2.18
11 years	−2.30	−2.40	−2.35	−2.53	−2.67	−2.60
Story 4: bad deed situation						
7 years	−2.40	−1.35	−1.88	−1.63	−2.12	−1.88
9 years	−2.60	−2.25	−2.43	−1.60	−2.30	−1.95
11 years	−2.65	−2.25	−2.45	−2.47	−2.27	−2.37

Table 3.12 Mean ratings of lie-telling and truth-telling in good and bad deed situations

	China			Canada		
	Social	Physical	Combined	Social	Physical	Combined
Story 1: truth-telling (good deed situation)						
7 years	1.75	1.90	1.83	2.11	2.35	2.23
9 years	1.65	0.85	1.25	1.45	1.70	1.58
11 years	0.55	0.10	0.33	2.06	1.80	1.93
Story 2: lie-telling (good deed situation)			*1.14*			*1.91*
7 years	−0.50	−0.70	−0.60	−1.26	−1.47	−1.37
9 years	−1.00	1.05	0.03	−0.95	−0.95	−0.95
11 years	0.85	1.10	0.98	−1.12	−0.87	−1.00
Story 3: truth-telling (bad deed situation)			*0.14*			*−1.12*
7 years	1.95	1.90	1.93	1.79	1.77	1.78
9 years	2.00	2.10	2.05	1.90	1.90	1.90
11 years	1.75	1.90	1.83	2.18	2.13	2.16
Story 4: lie-telling (bad deed situation)			*1.94*			*1.95*
7 years	−2.40	−1.80	−2.10	−1.84	−2.59	−2.22
9 years	−2.60	−2.65	−2.63	−2.35	−2.25	−2.30
11 years	−2.90	−2.35	−2.63	−2.53	−2.67	−2.60

−2.45   *−2.37*

The Canadian children showed the Western moral thinking of disapproving of all lie-telling in every situation, every story type and across all ages. However, they consistently approved of truth-telling, as did the Chinese children.

The statistical analysis was an analysis of covariance. (This is a sophisticated analysis beyond A Level requirements.) It was a 2 × 2 × 3 analysis. (Two cultures × 2 stories × 3 age groups.)

In terms of significance, the findings were:

- Pro-social/Truth-telling
  The two cultures showed no significant difference in their rating of pro-social behaviours. However, there was a significant interaction between age and culture as Canadian children gave similar ratings to truth-telling at each age, whereas Chinese children rated truth-telling less positively as age increased.
- Pro-social/Lie-telling
  The children in each culture and of each age rated the lie-telling behaviour differently in the pro-social situation. Canadian children rated the lie-telling negatively, although this became less negative as age increased. For the Chinese children, they changed from rating the lie-telling negatively at age seven to rating it positively at age eleven.
- Anti-social/Truth-telling
  There was no significant difference between the children from Canada and China, with children from each culture rating truth-telling very positively in the anti-social situations.
- Anti-social/Lie-telling
  This time the significant difference was shown between age groups, with the negative ratings increasing with age irrespective of culture.

Have a go yourself

Make up a chart with the conditions in four columns and the independent variable of culture in the first column.

	Pro-social truth	Pro-social lie	Anti-social truth	Anti-social lie
Chinese	1.14	0.14	1.94	−2.45
Canadian	1.91	−1.12	1.95	−2.37

Now summarise the quantitative data in each box to show the differences and similarities between the two cultures.

To gain qualitative data, the children were asked why they had given the ratings that they had. In relation to their negative ratings for truth-telling in the pro-social situations, nearly half of the Chinese children said they had done so because the child in the story had been 'begging for' or 'wanting' praise. A third of the Chinese children said you shouldn't leave your name after doing a good deed or you shouldn't tell the teacher, and this was repeated as the reason for rating the lie-telling positively in the pro-social situations. The children didn't explain why these rules existed, but they may not have felt they needed to; after all, if it is the cultural norm, why would they need to explain it?

🚫 Stop and ask yourself...

- What are the benefits of converting to quantitative data?
- What might be missing if Lee *et al.* only had quantitative data?

Links to methodological issues
- Qualitative and quantitative data

Conclusions

The conclusion is that moral development is different in different cultures as a result of socio-cultural norms and practices, and not only as a result of cognitive development as proposed by earlier research.

Discussion

Comparing the moral evaluations of truth- and lie-telling in two different cultures showed the expected outcome of Chinese children rating truth-telling in pro-social settings less positively than Canadian children, and this corresponded with an increasingly positive rating of lie-telling in pro-social situations as the Chinese children got older. This can be explained that children become more socialised into cultural norms (of self-effacement and modesty) as they get older.

We cannot assume that the reason for both cultures rating truth-telling in a misdeed situation as positive is the same for both cultures. In a collectivist culture such as China, the emphasis is on telling the truth for the good of the group. However, in an individualist culture such as Canada, the emphasis on truth-telling may be due to the belief that individuals have a duty to other individuals to be truthful.

Evaluation of the study by Lee *et al.*

Links to methodological issues

Research method

- Lee *et al.*'s study can be seen as a quasi-experiment as the main independent variable (i.e. the ethnicity of the children – Canadian or Chinese) was naturally occurring.
- It can also be seen as a cross-cultural study as Lee *et al.*'s research was carried out on samples from two very different cultures. This is a good way of increasing the representativeness of the sample, and for identifying whether a behaviour is something seen in all people, regardless of culture, or whether it is culture-dependent and therefore learned through interaction with society. The problems of such research can be in the assumption of the researcher that their materials will be interpreted in the same way by all cultures being researched, and that the set-up of the research is seen in the same way by all participants. In some cultures, children may not be used to one-to-one interviews with adults and this could cause them to try and answer the way they think they should rather than tell the truth. Another problem which can happen is ethnocentric bias when the assumption is that one culture is the 'normal' culture and any other behaviour is seen as inferior because it is different from the 'norm'. Western children might think Chinese children are wrong to think telling lies can be a good thing.
- Lee *et al.*'s study can also be seen as a snapshot study as (unlike Kohlberg's longitudinal study) data were collected from all participants in one go. They were able to see if children of different ages gave different responses by making the study cross-sectional (i.e. by having children of various different ages in their study).

Data

- Often research does not simply have one independent variable, and the dependent variable can be measured in a number of ways. In Lee's research, he has independent variables of culture (Chinese or Canadian), age (7, 9 or 11 years old), the type of story (physical or social), and the behaviour in the story (pro-social or anti-social). He also looked at the gender of the children, but lack of difference between the genders meant he could dismiss this as an independent variable in his discussion.

- The dependent variable was measured in two ways. First, it was measured *quantitatively* by giving the children a seven-point semantic rating scale which was converted into quantitative data to give numerical raw data which could be analysed. Then he also asked for *qualitative* data in the form of reasons why the participants chose the option they did. This was to see if there was any difference in the actual moral thinking between the cultures, so if the Chinese children did see lie-telling in a pro-social situation as more positive than Canadian children their reasons would tell the researchers if it was due to cultural upbringing.

- Lee *et al.* used the semantic rating scale with images of stars and crosses to gather the data for his research. They then allocated each point on the scale with a numerical value from +3 to −3. This way they could give each participant a rating for how good or naughty the characters in the story were. This allowed for comparisons to be made between the mean rating for each condition, and statistical analysis to see if any differences were significant (i.e. probability of them being due to chance was less than 5 per cent). Their data show there is a significant difference in the ratings of each condition, with some significance levels much less than 5 per cent. For example, the age and culture differences were significant in ratings of pro-social truth-telling at a significance level of $p < 0.001$ (99.9 per cent certain it was due to independent variables, not chance). However, this would have shown us a difference but not why, if Lee *et al.* hadn't also asked the children to explain their choice. The qualitative data, which were phrases such as the children saying, 'You shouldn't leave your name after doing a good deed', shows that it is indeed the cultural stigma of bragging about heroic deeds being not the 'done thing' which causes this fundamental change in moral thinking.

Ethics

- It can be assumed that ethical guidelines were adhered to. As Lee *et al.* explicitly thanks '... the participating children, their parents, and their schools for their cooperation and support' (page 932), it can be assumed that consent for the children to take part was given by their parents. Presumably, the unequal numbers of children from the two cultures (120 from China and 108 from Canada) could reflect at least some Canadian parents exercising their right to withdraw.

- The stories that were read out to the children were accompanied by illustrations and ought not to have caused upset to the children, although in the case of two of them they did involve children being pushed to the ground and made to cry. In the study, children were seen individually – is it possible that some of them may have found this uncomfortable?

Validity

- When you carry out an experiment, the problem with extraneous variables is that they can confound the data so what looks like an effect of the independent variables is actually more likely caused by the extraneous variables. Lee et al. tried to control as many variables as possible e.g. the same age and gender mix as far as possible in the two groups. They also reduced the participant variables in the choice of target population, i.e. from non-heavy industry cities. However, there are still some factors which might have affected the results. For example, the contact with the researchers could be seen differently in different cultures, as could the familiarity with rating scales. No piece of research is going to be entirely valid: there are always going to be variables which can't be controlled; it's the nature of psychology and its research on people. The stories were the same for each participant, but there is an assumption that a story in the Western format is going to be seen the same in an Eastern culture, and that linguistic translations will have the same meaning in each culture.
- Lee et al. used a standardised procedure, with several controls. The stories were very similar, and equal in terms of gender. They were randomly allocated to each of the two orders so that there was no bias in which students had which stories. The children themselves were randomly allocated to either the pro-social or anti-social conditions, so again no bias. The use of counterbalancing also controlled for order effects, so that there was no response bias, or children getting bored and just saying the same thing in the last stories as the first ones. Lee et al. also controlled for culture within the country, by using students from cities without heavy industry, which will reduce participant variables, but will therefore limit the generalisability of the results.

Reliability

- The study followed a standardised procedure, and the inclusion of the eight stories that the researchers used during their investigation would make it possible for their study to be replicated.
- With a reasonably large number of children in each condition, it can be assumed that the sample was large enough to establish consistent effect.
- Each child had either four social or four physical stories read to them. This helped make the results more reliable than if just one story had been read to each child as it meant that the data obtained from each child would have reflected a consistent, settled viewpoint as seen across a number of scenarios.

Sample

- The samples were carefully assembled to ensure that the children were from similar kinds of background (e.g. the cities they were from were both provincial capitals) as well as large enough numbers of children of each age group to establish reliable effects, and an even gender split. However, there were fewer children in the Canadian sample than there were in the Chinese sample, and the city of Fredericton was much smaller than the city of Hangzhou. More importantly, all of the children were from urban centres, rather than rural ones, which could be important as it is possible that attitudes to truth- and lie-telling might be different among children growing up in villages (where it may be harder to be anonymous). The sample also misses out children from Europe, South America, Africa and Australasia.

Ethnocentrism

- As a cross-cultural study, Lee et al.'s investigation was clearly trying hard to avoid being ethnocentric. However, there are questions to be asked about whether their procedure would have been perceived in the same way by children from both cultures (see above). Also, it is questionable whether Canada can be taken to illustrate all 'Western' cultures any more than China can be taken to represent all 'Eastern' cultures.

Links to debates
Individual/situational explanations

- The debate concerning the individual or situational explanation reflects to some extent the nature/nurture debate. Is it something about the person or about the situation in which they find themselves? Kohlberg had suggested that moral development is something innate within the person, but Lee et al.'s research shows that the situation or culture that a child is brought up in will significantly change their moral thinking. This suggests that levels of pre-conventional, conventional and post-conventional moral thinking, reflecting the moral values of honesty and integrity, are not universal across all cultures.

Free will/determinism

- Lee *et al.*'s research challenges Kohlberg's theory that the moral positions we adopt are determined by the stage of moral development we are at and that this follows an invariant universal pattern.
- However, arguably, it is just as determinist but in a different way, suggesting that what determines our moral thinking is the culture in which we grow up.
- This may be true, but it is worth noting that while we may not be able to change our moral development we do have the free will to over-ride our morality and do things which are immoral or amoral.

Reductionism/holism

- Lee *et al.*'s research suggests that our moral development is not simply a series of predetermined cognitive stages which we will pass through, all at the same time, with the same outcome.
- Instead, it takes on a more holistic approach by acknowledging the influence of society on our behaviour and the social cognitions which develop as a result of this.

Links to areas/perspectives

- Lee *et al.*'s research can be seen as falling within the developmental area because it is looking at changes in children's moral development not only by age but also by culture – it is looking at the influence of both of these factors on a child's moral thinking.
- The fact that it is changes in an aspect of children's *thinking* that Lee *et al.*'s research looks at means that it can also be placed within the cognitive area.
- However, there is also evidence of the impact of society on a child, which would allow this to sit in the social area of psychology which assumes that the people around us (or the implied presence of others) will influence our behaviour.
- The area of social cognition is a wide one and cross-cultural research, such as Lee *et al.*'s, can enable us to see the impact of social settings on the development of our thought processes.

Links to the key theme

- In relation to the key theme of moral development, this study shows that moral development still occurs, as there are age-related changes in moral thinking within cultures.
- In terms of the extent to which Lee *et al.*'s study changes our understanding of the key theme of 'moral development', this study disagrees with Kohlberg's theory of universal stages of moral thinking, and suggests that cultural differences not only change the context of the thinking, but also the fundamental moral rules, so that the rule 'you must not tell lies' becomes in some cultures 'you should tell lies in certain circumstances'.
- In relation to the extent in which Lee *et al.*'s study changes our understanding of individual, social and cultural diversity, there are clear cultural differences between children's answers to the stories. It suggests (in contradiction to Kohlberg) that culture can play a significant role in a child's moral development, and it did this by looking at both boys and girls from the ages 7 to 11 years. However, it doesn't show the influence of culture on individuals when they reach adulthood, and it could be that adults are more likely to reject their cultural norms, once they are exposed to other cultures. Also, these were two very different cultures, but it would be interesting to see how the rest of the world reflected either of these two stances regarding lie-telling.

Comparison with the classic study

The focus of Kohlberg's article is not the research, but more the application of the research to his theory. However, there are some details about his research which we can use to compare the two articles.

- In what ways are Kohlberg's and Lee *et al.*'s articles *similar*?
  - Both studies used children as their participants.
  - Both studies were looking at stages of moral development.
  - Both studies gained qualitative data.
  - Both studies had cross-cultural aspects to them.
  - Both studies collected data through self-report.
  - Both studies involved participants being presented with scenarios on which to comment.

- In what ways are Kohlberg's and Lee *et al.*'s studies *different*?
  - Kohlberg's article explains how his research supports his theory, whereas Lee *et al.*'s is more research-focused.
  - Kohlberg explains the universality of moral reasoning, whereas Lee *et al.* shows cultural differences in moral rules.
  - Kohlberg focuses on male participants, whereas Lee *et al.* has mixed gender samples.
  - Kohlberg's research is longitudinal, whereas Lee *et al.* uses a snapshot study.
  - Lee *et al.* gained quantitative data which provided statistical analysis.

Questions arising from Lee *et al.*

- What questions are we left with after studying the research by Lee *et al.*? It suggested (in contradiction to Kohlberg) that culture can play a significant role in a child's moral development, and it did this by looking at both boys and girls from the ages of 7 to 11 years. However, does the effect of culture decline as people get older, and would this effect be seen in other cultures apart from Canada or China? Moreover, China has changed a lot even since 1997, so it is reasonable to ask whether the value placed on self-effacement and modesty would still be seen today and/or whether it would be seen equally in urban and rural parts of China.
- These are some questions that can be seen as arising from the study by Lee *et al.* Can you think of any others?

 Find out more

- Our body language can often give away the fact that we are lying. It is not something that we do consciously, and we often subconsciously pick up on mannerisms that suggest a person is lying and it can make us distrustful. While we may say 'we can't put a finger on why we don't trust that person', it is usually their body language that makes us uneasy. Have a look at books or on the internet about body language when people are lying. There is big business in training people such as politicians to hide their body language when lying. Using what you have found out about body language, what advice would you give to people who wanted to hide the truth when they are giving a speech? Watch politicians when they are talking to groups of people and see if you can spot any give-away signs that they are lying – or that they are emphasising 'truth-telling' body language.

Practice questions

1. From Lee *et al.*'s study into cross-cultural attitudes to lying:
   (a) Identify one of the experimental conditions in this study. [2 marks]
   (b) Outline one of the stories used in this condition. [2 marks]
2. In Lee *et al.*'s study of cross cultural attitudes to lying, what effect did age have on attitude to lie-telling in one of the cultures? [4 marks]
3. Explain why Lee *et al.*'s research could be considered a developmental study [3 marks]

Chapter 4

The biological area

The biological area assumes that behaviour can be largely explained in terms of biology (e.g. genes/hormones): what is psychological is first biological. The biological area assumes that psychology should study the brain, nervous system and various biological systems in an attempt to explain behaviour. According to the biological area, psychology should be seen as a science, to be studied in a scientific manner (usually in a laboratory), measuring variables objectively, for example using physiological measures, such as MRI scans. The amalgamation of the cognitive area with the biological areas is at the cutting edge of modern psychology as 'cognitive neuroscience'. In this introduction we can give just a brief introduction to the underpinning biology that affects our behaviour. It includes what it would be helpful for you to know in relation to the biological area core studies.

What are neurones?

Neurones are the cells of the nervous system and are responsible for carrying messages from one part of the body to another. We have three types of neurone:

- sensory neurones;
- motor neurones;
- inter-neurones.

There are between 10 and 12 billion neurones in the nervous system, which will give you an idea of how tiny they are. A nerve is actually a bundle of neurones (like a telephone cable), which are held together by glial cells. Glial cells are smaller cells than neurones and provide the neurones with nutrients and structural support.

The three different types of neurones all have different functions:

1. Sensory neurones transmit impulses received by receptors to the central nervous system.
2. Inter-neurones receive the signals from the sensory neurones and send impulses to other inter-neurones or to motor neurones. They are found only in the brain or the spinal cord.
3. Motor neurones carry outgoing signals from the brain or spinal cord to the effector organs, such as the muscles or the heart and lungs.

All these neurones form connections with each other in order to carry information around the body by way of impulses or electric messages. The messages or impulses that travel along our neurones can be thought of as bursts of electrical energy. We talk about these bursts of electricity as bursts of fire. A single neurone 'fires' when the stimulation reaching it from other neurones exceeds a certain threshold. Imagine a number of drips falling from various branches of a tree into a large bath underneath – when the bath is full, a final drip will make it overflow. The firing of a neurone is just like this – the sum of lots of stimulation makes it reach a certain level, causing it to fire.

Some of these impulses are messages to do something (excitatory messages), and some are messages to remain inactive (inhibitory messages). The messages are passed from one neurone to another across what is known as a synaptic gap (a synapse is the junction between two nerve cells) by neurotransmitters which are actually chemical messengers. The whole process is extremely complex and it is not necessary for our purposes to go into the way synapses work. Sufficient to say, increases or decreases in the levels of neurotransmitters can affect the speed of message transmission which, in turn, will affect the way a person thinks, reacts or responds physically to different situations. Many of the drugs that are used to change mood, such as antidepressants, affect the quantity or actions of neurotransmitters in the brain.

If you imagine a set of roads converging, with roundabouts and junctions and flyovers, giving you unlimited choices as to where you can go, this should give you an idea of the range of connections that can be made with the increasing number of junctions between neurones. No single neurone creates thoughts or behaviours; it is the different patterns of activity that arise from the firing of millions of different neurones which result in different activities. In fact, even when a person thinks they are at rest (and neurones should be relatively quiet), if we were to scan the activity of the brain we would see that the neurones still seem to be alive, with constantly changing interconnections. If you think how these patterns must increase and interconnect when we are engaged in any sort of task, from complex mental thought to physical activities, it will give you some idea of how active our brains must be. Every time we experience a sensation this will result in new neuronal connections being made, and this pattern will fade away unless the information relating to this experience is stored in our brains for a particular reason.

The brain

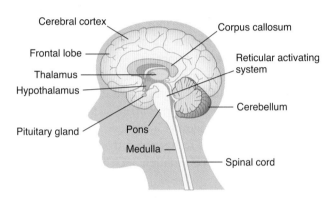

Figure 4.1 The main structure of the brain

The area of the body where most of our neurones are located is the brain (Figure 4.1). In fact, the brain consists of nothing but millions of neurones. It is the most amazing wiring network, and different areas seem to be responsible for different things. It looks rather like a walnut, with lots of furrows or crevices, which are known as sulci. Just like a walnut, it is divided into two halves, called hemispheres. The left hemisphere controls most of the right-hand side of the body, and the right hemisphere controls the left-hand side.

Much of the evidence we have about which part of the brain is responsible for particular responses or activities – commonly known as 'localisation of function' – comes from the investigation of individuals who have suffered some form of brain damage. If a certain area is damaged and results in a person being unable to perform a certain action, this would suggest that the damaged area is responsible for the non-function.

Each hemisphere has the equivalent of three layers: the hindbrain at the core, the midbrain and the forebrain (which contains the cerebral cortex) (Figure 4.2). Although the cerebral cortex is the area most relevant to us, it is useful to have an overview of how the other structures of the brain assist in our day-to-day activities.

The hindbrain

The hindbrain consists of the cerebellum, the pons and the medulla. The cerebellum plays an important part in movement. It is where memories for automatic sequences of actions are stored and any damage to it will cause problems in movement, such as walking or the coordination of fine movements. The pons is a kind of bridge or connection, between the two halves of the cerebellum. The medulla oblongata is the crossover point between the fibres from the brain and the spinal cord. The medulla also contains lots of vital reflex centres that control and regulate many of our basic bodily functions, such as the cardiovascular system and respiration.

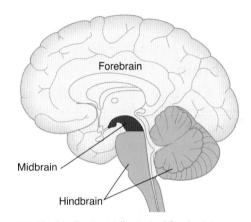

Figure 4.2 The hindbrain, midbrain and forebrain

The midbrain

The midbrain is smaller in humans and other mammals than in birds and reptiles. It is the top of the brainstem and connects the cerebral cortex (or forebrain) to the spinal cord and hindbrain. At its core is the reticular activating system (RAS), which brings sensory information from the spinal cord to the cerebral cortex and takes back motor information. It plays a very important part in maintaining or controlling levels of arousal and may even have an influence on personality. According to Eysenck (1970), people who fit the category of introverts have a high level of arousal in their RAS and therefore seek to reduce it, whereas extroverts have a low level of arousal and constantly seek to raise it, by choosing external situations which are 'busier' than their introvert counterparts. It is the RAS which influences our ability to pay attention selectively to different stimuli, as well as the way we become used to stimuli which are continuous and therefore not necessarily important. It also has a role in sleeping and waking, because it is when the level of activity in the RAS falls below a certain level that we fall asleep.

The brainstem

The brainstem, made up of the midbrain, pons and medulla, is the most primitive part of the brain and is estimated to have evolved more than 500 million years ago. It is often referred to as the reptilian brain because it controls the basic elements of life, with no higher-order thought processes. You cannot form a close, loving relationship with a reptile because it is incapable of thinking and feeling in the same way as even lower-order mammals, such as rats and mice. It simply functions from day to day, with a heart that beats, lungs that inflate and deflate, and a maintained blood pressure level; it can move, fight, mate and produce other stereotypical behaviours which give it the ability to survive. Beyond that, none of the characteristics we associate with intelligent life exists, simply instinctive behaviours.

The forebrain

The forebrain is the largest and most obvious part of a mammal's brain. The outer layer is called the cerebral cortex and is made up of the cerebral hemispheres. Under the cortex are a number of other structures, including the thalamus, the hypothalamus, the pituitary gland, the basal ganglia, hippocampus and amygdala, some of which form what is known as the limbic system (involved in emotional behaviour, motivation and learning). The limbic system is a kind of centre where the more primitive parts of the brain join with the 'newer' cortex and integrate information from the outside world and the internal functioning of the body.

Although only some of these individual structures are referred to in our core studies, they all have an influence on our behaviour and, for that reason, they are briefly described below:

- The thalamus works as a kind of relay station, linking sensory signals between the cerebral cortex and the sense organs.
- The hypothalamus helps to control the body's internal environment, such as temperature regulation, appetite and thirst. It also influences other motivated behaviours, such as sexual behaviour and emotional arousal levels. Eating disorders can be triggered by a disorder of the hypothalamus; if it is damaged, a person's internal temperature regulation may well be affected, making them overheat or feel extremely cold. The hypothalamus is also involved in the regulation of levels of hormones in the body and controls pituitary gland activity.
- The pituitary gland is actually an endocrine gland (producing hormones). It is attached to the base of

the hypothalamus and responds to information from the hypothalamus to release hormones into the bloodstream. The secretions of the pituitary gland control the timing and amount of secretion by other endocrine glands.

- The basal ganglia play a part in voluntary movements.
- The hippocampus plays an important role in the laying down of new memories, so any damage seems to result in a lack of ability to store new information. According to Colin Blakemore (1988), it is the 'printing press' for our stored memories. The hippocampus is also linked to spatial memory, and recent research has indicated that lesions to the hippocampus affect our ability to remember the location of different things.
- The amygdala is important for feeding, drinking, sexual behaviour and aggression. If it is electrically stimulated in non-human animals, such as cats, they will either attack another individual or become very placid. What seems to happen is that it changes how animals interpret information and therefore affects their responses.

The cerebral cortex

The cerebral cortex itself, as we have seen, consists of two hemispheres, each receiving information from the opposite side of the body. The two sides, which are almost mirror images of each other, communicate via a tract of fibres called the corpus callosum. Each hemisphere is divided into four lobes (Figure 4.3), which are defined by major sulci.

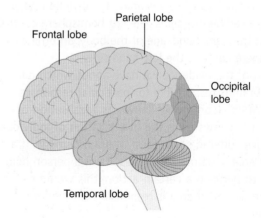

Figure 4.3 Lobes of the cerebral cortex

- The occipital lobes, located at the back of the head, are the areas which receive the main input from the visual pathways. The rear of the lobe contains the primary visual cortex; if this is destroyed the person loses their sight.

- The parietal lobes are located between the occipital lobe and the central sulcus (which divides the parietal lobe from the frontal lobe). They are specialised to deal with information from the body such as touch and temperature, and help to interpret body position. They also play a part in vision; it has been found that damage in this area does not result in a failure of vision or touch, but produces disturbances in the integration and analysis of sensory information. A good example of this is the case of a man who had a tumour in his parietal lobe – he could recognise a clock as a clock but could not tell the time from the position of the hands on the clock face.
- The temporal lobes, located on either side of the head, near the ears, receive information from the ears about sounds and balance. They also contribute to the more complex aspects of vision, such as face recognition. They play a part in emotion and motivation, and if they are damaged this may lead to extremes of emotional response. Wernicke's area is located in the temporal lobe on the left-hand side, and plays a critical role in language comprehension.
- Finally, the frontal lobes seem to be responsible for all the higher-order and more complicated functions, such as thinking, planning and forming ideas. They also play a part in memory formation and retention. Frontal lobes are said to contain our personalities; they contribute to our emotional responses and control our social inhibitions. This area is the last part of the brain to stop growing, and it continues to change even after birth, since the neuronal connections that are located here seem to continue forming. Broca's area is found in the left frontal lobe in humans and is critical for the production of language. People who have left-sided strokes (burst blood vessels in the left-hand side of the brain) often lose their ability to speak, and this would indicate that Broca's area has been affected.

The area directly to the rear of the central sulcus is known as the sensory cortex and is responsible for receiving any sensory information, such as touch, pressure, pain, smell and temperature. The area at the back of the frontal cortex, directly in front of the central sulcus, is the primary motor cortex. This area is responsible for movement, especially fine movement.

Finally, it will be useful for you to be familiar with the term 'grey matter', which you may have heard used when referring to the brain. Grey matter really does exist in the brain. It is a general term given to the regions of the brain and spinal cord that are made up mainly of cell bodies and dendrites of nerve cells, rather than myelinated axons, which look white. Grey matter includes the cerebral cortex, the central part of the spinal cord and the cerebellum and hippocampus (Figure 4.4).

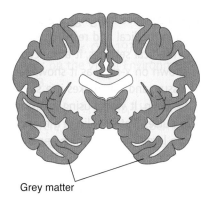

Grey matter

Figure 4.4 This coronal section through the brain illustrates the areas of grey matter and white matter (appears as light grey). Coronal sections are sections that are made through the brain from top to bottom, just like looking face-on at another person. The white areas in the middle are the ventricles of the brain.

Methods of investigating brain function

Much of what was learned about brain function in the early exploration of the brain was discovered either through anatomy (e.g. postmortem dissection of the brain), comparative studies with animal brains, or through the study of people who had suffered brain damage through disease, stroke or accident and inferring about the function of the normal brain from the activities that people with brain damage could and could not do. Technology has advanced, however, and there are today a number of ways of recording and observing the activity of the live human brain. It is possible to use a number of brain-imaging techniques, or brain scans, in order to assess the functioning of our brains, and both the normal and abnormal brain can be investigated using these techniques.

MRI scanners

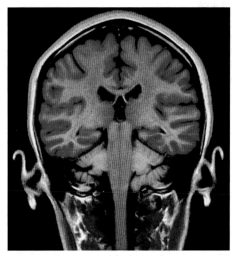

Figure 4.5 An MRI scan of the brain. Which of the brain structures you have read about so far can you identify in this scan?

Regions of the brain

The brain is divided into two relatively symmetrical halves, known as the left and right hemispheres. We also know that in right-handed people the left-hand side of the brain largely controls the right-hand side of the body, and vice versa, but it is not known why this crossover occurs. The two hemispheres are joined by what are known as commissural fibres, and the corpus callosum (Figure 4.7) is by far the largest commissure (cross-hemisphere connection), responsible for carrying the majority of information between the two hemispheres.

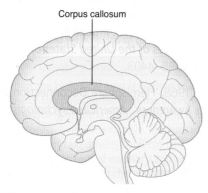

Corpus callosum

Figure 4.7 The corpus callosum

It is often misconstrued that the two hemispheres are totally different and have entirely different functions. It is true that they do differ in some ways, but they are nowhere near as different as we are led to believe by some books, which seem to suggest that the function of the left-hand side of the brain is to be clever, rational and reasoning, and that the right-hand side is purely the spiritual, artistic part.

Lateralisation of function

In most people, there is some 'lateralisation of function', which means that one side has a different role from the other. In the majority of people, the language centres are on the left-hand side – Broca's area is responsible for speech production and Wernicke's area is responsible for speech comprehension. This is the case for the majority of right-handed people, although people who are left-handed may well have their language centres on the right-hand side of their brain. However, it is virtually impossible to give exact percentages, so it is best to accept the fact that the majority of people, left- and right-handed, have their speech centres located in the left hemisphere. This would mean that any damage to the left side of your head would probably leave you either unable to speak or understand, or neither speak nor understand.

Much of the evidence that has been gathered about hemisphere function has come from people who have suffered strokes (or cerebrovascular accidents, to give them their correct name). This is the most common source of brain damage in old age and is caused by a blood clot or other obstruction closing off an artery, or by an artery rupturing. This will result in the area around the site being deprived of oxygen or nutrients and the relevant neurones dying. Because the left-hand side of the brain controls the right-hand side of the body, a left-sided stroke will result in right-sided lack of function. This can be quite mild, such as a non-mobile side of the face, or more severe, as with hemiplegia, where the whole of the right side of the body ceases to function. What makes it worse is the fact that the person often loses the ability to either comprehend or produce words, so not only are they non-mobile, but they are also isolated in their own little world. It is often very frustrating for a stroke victim who is recovering from damage that has affected Broca's area, as they know exactly what they want to say, but just cannot say it.

Severing the connection

The two symmetrical hemispheres are only slightly different in the tasks they carry out. In order for us to function adequately, these two parts need to communicate with each other, which they do by means of the corpus callosum. This gives the side of the brain without speech centres access to words and descriptions which it would be without if there was no bridge between the two. It is easy to imagine what would happen if that bridge was not there. Such a thought gives new meaning to the phrase, 'the left hand does not know what the right hand is doing'!

There are rare instances of people having the connections between their two hemispheres severed, either as a result of an accident or, more likely, as one of the surgical treatments for epilepsy. Epileptic seizures are a result of abnormal electrical discharges of groups of brain neurones, described by Carlson (1986) as the 'wild sustained firing of cerebral neurons'. The source of the hyperactivity is usually in the temporal lobe and results in the person briefly losing contact with reality, and even experiencing hallucinations. Sometimes the seizures can be more sustained, and these are known as grand mal seizures. During one of these, the person becomes unconscious for a few minutes and experiences muscle spasms which may result in them breaking their bones or damaging themselves; they may also lose bowel and bladder control. When the seizure is over, the muscles relax and the person will wake up, but they are often extremely disorientated and embarrassed. A seizure like this would obviously be quite debilitating and would put the person in some danger, so any attempt to reduce the severity or frequency of such seizures would clearly be of great benefit.

One surgical way of preventing the spread of the wildly excited neuronal firings was to sever the corpus callosum, preventing the other side of the brain from becoming involved and thus reducing the severity of the effects. This method was very successful and it was found that not only did it stop the discharges from spreading, but it also reduced the epileptic seizures to negligible proportions. This surgical procedure is known as a commissurotomy and was used in life-threatening and severe cases of epilepsy, known as status epilepticus, to treat patients and end the threat to their life of them experiencing a seizure which would not stop but would lead to heart failure and death.

You would think that an operation of this severity would result in many side effects, but, extraordinarily, most of the people who underwent the surgery suffered very few side effects that were noticeable in their everyday lives. In effect, they were living with two brains in a single head, each one functioning adequately. There *were* side effects, however, and it is these effects that form the focus of the core study undertaken by Roger Sperry in 1968. It also gave Sperry a unique opportunity to map lateralisation of brain function.

Sperry (1968)

Before we look at the study itself, you need to know a little about Sperry and his work. Sperry was a neuropsychologist who conducted a number of studies on split-brain patients while working at the California Institute of Technology. In the early 1950s, he undertook research which involved splitting the brains of cats and monkeys. By training the animals, he discovered that you could teach one hemisphere a task, while the other hemisphere remained unaware of the information learned. This supported his idea that the brain consisted of two separate modules rather than one unified whole. The importance of his work was recognised when he shared the Nobel Prize for physiology and medicine with David Hubel and Torsten Wiesel in 1981. (Hubel and Wiesel pioneered a method of studying the physiology of vision by inserting very thin wire electrodes into the columns of neurones in the optic cortex and recording their response to different stimuli.)

Many of the effects of splitting brains were investigated in the laboratory with relatively simplistic tasks. Sperry's work on cats and other animals had shown him that information which is in about 20 per cent of the centre of our visual field can be sent to both sides of the brain. However, information sent to the right or left of the visual field goes only to one hemisphere. For example, an image of a toad sent to the left visual field would only go to the right hemisphere. If the information was presented to the right visual field, it would go to the left-hand side of the brain, which contains the speech centres. Therefore the person would be able to say what they had just seen. If the information was presented to the left visual field, it would go to the right-hand side of the brain, which has no speech production centre. Therefore the person would know what it was, but would not be able to say what they had just seen. However, if this person was then asked to draw the object with their left hand (with their eyes closed), they could do so.

The participants were asked to fixate on a spot in the centre of a screen. The image was projected for one-tenth of a second, which was insufficient time for them to move their eyes enough to send information to the opposite side of the brain. Therefore, for any of the split-brain studies which involve projecting objects for someone to look at, we accept the fact that the information projected on one side of the fixation point (that is, in the left or right visual field) only goes to the opposite side of the brain.

Aim

The aim was to investigate the effects of this de-connection and show that each hemisphere has different functions; in other words, to map lateralisation of brain function and show that information in one side of the brain is not accessible to the other side.

Method

Method and design

The design was a quasi-experiment which compared split-brain subjects with 'normal' subjects in laboratory tests, and compared case studies of all the individual patients.

Participants

The split-brain participants were 11 patients who had already experienced a commissurotomy prior to the study. The sample type is therefore an opportunity sample. All subjects had a history of severe epilepsy which had not responded to drug therapy. Two of the patients had been operated on successfully to sever their corpus callosum some time before the experiments took place. The remaining nine had only recently undergone surgery.

Procedure

The equipment used allowed for various types of sensory information to be presented to one or other hemisphere, in different combinations. Visual information was presented by projecting images on a screen in front of the subject. The subject would sit at a table with their hands hidden from their view behind the projections screen (Figure 4.8). Tactile information would be presented to either the left or the right hand, or to both hands, without the patients being able to see what the object was. A representation of the apparatus is given in the figure below.

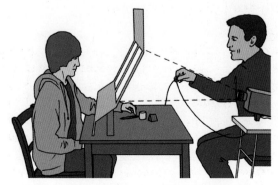

Figure 4.8 Apparatus used for study (*Source*: adapted from Sperry, 1968)

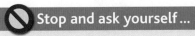

Stop and ask yourself...

- Sperry hoped to find out about brain lateralisation in normal brains. Why might his sample make it difficult to draw conclusions from about how normal brains work?

Links to methodological issues
- Sampling issues
- Population validity

Participants had to remain in silence during the studies unless they were asked questions by the experimenter. This was to prevent them passing information from the left side of the brain to the right side, as sound can be taken in by both ears simultaneously. For example, if the subject identified an object and then said what it was, this information would be available to both hemispheres.

Visual investigations

Visual investigations involved showing one stimulus at a time to one visual field, or showing two stimuli simultaneously to the two different visual fields.

One visual field (targeting only one side of the brain at once)

These tests required the subject to cover one eye. They were told to look at a fixation point in the centre of the screen. The image was projected for one-tenth of a second or less on either the left or the right of the fixation point, which would send the image to either the right or left visual field, respectively. It was projected for that short space of time to prevent the information going to the wrong half of the visual field if the subject moved their eye, which would send the information to both sides of the brain. This is because there is an overlap in the centre of the visual field (at the fixation point), which means that the right and left brain both get information about objects viewed at that point. For example, the first screen shown in Figure 4.9 would send the image of a key to the right side of the brain as it is projected in the left visual field. The next screen would send the image of the key to the left side of the brain as it is projected in the right visual field.

Both visual fields

The subject would look at the fixation point on the screen while two images were flashed simultaneously either side of the fixation point. This screen would send the image of a key to the left side of the brain (because it would be seen in the right visual field) and the image of an apple to the right side of the brain (because it would be seen in the left visual field). The participants would then be asked to say what they had seen. Typically, they would say 'key', although they would have no conscious awareness of having seen anything else. They would then be given a pen in their left hand and be asked to draw

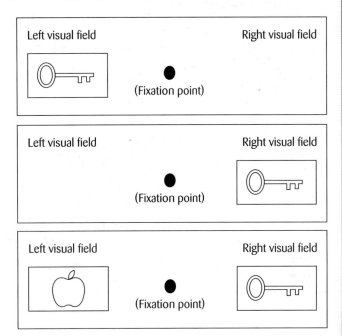

Figure 4.9 Testing both hemispheres at once

what they had just seen (although they would have to do this with their eyes closed or with their hand out of sight, because if they could see what they were doing, the dominant hemisphere would interfere with their recall). Typically, they would draw an apple. If asked what they had drawn, they would say without hesitation that the figure they drew was a key (the object that had appeared in the right visual field). If they were then shown the picture, they would not know why they had drawn it, as the information about the apple had *not* gone into the dominant left hemisphere, which is the hemisphere containing language (speech).

Tactile investigations
One hand

- The subject's hands are hidden from their view behind the screen. The subject is then asked to find an object corresponding to what they have seen on the screen.
- The object is placed in one hand, without the subject being able to see what they are holding, and they are then asked to say what they have been given.
- The object is placed in one hand, without the subject being able to see what they are holding, and they are then asked to point to what they have been given.

Stop and ask yourself ...

- From Sperry's visual tasks, what do the findings suggest about lateralisation of brain function in normal brains?

Links to methodological issues
- Check your understanding

Both hands at the same time

- The subject works with their hands out of sight. The subject is given two different objects, one in each hand, and then the objects are taken away. The subject is asked to find the objects by touch from a pile of items. The subject is asked to say what they have just held.

Tests of the right hemisphere

Because the right hemisphere does not produce language, in order to test if it has any ability to make mental associations, work logically or experience separate emotions from the left hemisphere, the following tests were undertaken:

- The left visual field (therefore right hemisphere) is presented with an object on the screen. The subject is asked to pick out similar objects by touch from an array of objects.
- Simple mathematical problems are presented in the left visual field. The subject is asked to sort objects by shape, size or texture, using their left hand.
- An array of geometric shapes is projected to both visual fields on the screen. In the middle of this selection is the picture of a nude, which is presented to the left visual field only. The subject is later asked if they saw anything other than the geometric shapes. The right hemisphere may respond non-verbally and this may reveal what has been seen.

Results

Visual investigations

Visual stimuli presented to one visual field

- When participants were shown an image in one visual field, they would only recognise the image

as one they had already seen if it was shown again to the same visual field. The reason for this is that information would have gone only to one side of the brain and not the other.

- If an image was shown in the right visual field (left hemisphere), the subject was able to say what they had seen, could identify what it was from an array of pictures shown to the right visual field by pointing to it, and could find it with their right hand from an array of objects.
- If it was shown in the left visual field (right hemisphere), the subject was unable to name it, but could draw it (with eyes closed) with their left hand, could identify what it was from an array of pictures shown to the left visual field by pointing to it, and could find it with the left hand from an array of objects.

Visual stimuli presented to both visual fields

The subject would be able to say what they had seen presented in the right visual field, but would be unaware that they had seen anything else. If they were given a pen in the left hand and asked to draw with their eyes closed, they would be able to draw what they had seen in the left visual field, although they would seemingly have no conscious knowledge of having seen anything else and would be very surprised when they discovered what they had drawn. They would be able to name the object once they had seen the drawing in the right visual field.

Tactile investigations

The results of the tactile investigations were the same, irrespective of whether the object was held by one hand at a time or by both hands simultaneously.

Stop and ask yourself ...

- In Sperry's study he ensured that his participants:
  · focused on the centre of the screen
  · were told only to speak when asked a direct question
  · only saw images flashed for one-tenth of a second
  · were shown images in left or right of the visual field
  · had their hands hidden from their view behind the screen

Can you explain why each of these controls was used in the study?
(Tip: what did they prevent happening?)

Links to methodological issues
- Experimental controls

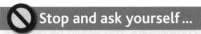

Stop and ask yourself …

- When Sperry tested normal subjects on any of these tasks, they had no problems performing them all correctly. Can you explain why?

- The subject would have no problems identifying an object by name if it was put in the right hand, but if it was put in the left hand they would have no conscious awareness of it. However, they would be able to find it by touch with the left hand in a bag full of objects.
- When the objects were placed in one hand, participants could point to what the object was with the same hand which had held the object.

Tests of the right hemisphere

- Participants were able to pick out semantically similar objects; for example, if they saw on the screen a picture of a wall clock in the left visual field (therefore right hemisphere) and the only related item in a tactile array was a toy wristwatch, this would be the object chosen.
- Right hemispheres were able to carry out simple mathematical problems.
- Left hands were able to sort objects by shape, size and texture.
- When participants saw the array of geometric shapes, they would giggle or look embarrassed when the picture of the nude appeared, even though they could not say to what they were responding. This non-verbal response suggests that the right hemisphere has a second conscious entity.

Conclusions

The study gave considerable support to the idea that the brain consists of two seemingly independent hemispheres, each with its own consciousness, and that there is no transfer of information between the two sides. For the participants studied, the dominant hemisphere was the left-hand side, which contains the speech centres. This explained why, when information was presented to the right hemisphere, they were unable to say what they had experienced. The final tests of the right hemisphere give further support to the idea that the two hemispheres have their own consciousness, whereby one responds in a typically human way, by giggling at the nude, while the other has no idea what is going on.

Have a go yourself

Imagine you had been given the opportunity to test a split-brain patient yourself. Using Sperry's tasks to help you, describe how you could conduct a visual task and a tactile task that would show the important role of the corpus callosum in the brains of people who have not undergone a commissurotomy.

Evaluation of the study by Sperry

Links to methodological issues

Research methods

- In order to demonstrate the effects of the surgical severing of the corpus callosum, Sperry tested the participants experimentally under strictly controlled conditions. Using this method, he was able to show evidence for brain lateralisation and work out what functions the two hemispheres of the brain perform. The strengths of carrying out research under highly controlled conditions are apparent in this study. For example, without the controls of using the screen to hide their hands from view, flashing the images only briefly and instructing the participants not to talk unless spoken to, the functions of the two hemispheres would not have been revealed. In addition, this was a quasi-experiment, comparing the split-brain patients to normal controls who had not had a commissurotomy. This enabled Sperry to conclude that the reasons why the split-brain patients could not perform the tasks was because their corpus callosum had been surgically severed. The comparisons between the normal controls and the split-brain patients suggested to Sperry that the corpus callosum plays an important role in communication between the two hemispheres.

Types of data

- Sperry reports his findings qualitatively, describing what the split-brain patients could and could not do in general. These rich data show a pattern of difficulties that enabled Sperry to map brain lateralisation. However, he does point out that in the split-brain patients, a small sample of 11 people,

# Practice questions

1. From Sperry's split-brain study, describe the apparatus used in the visual tasks. [2 marks]

2. In his split-brain study, Sperry writes '... one hemisphere does not know what the other hemisphere has been doing':
   (a) Give one piece of evidence to support this statement. [2 marks]
   (b) Explain why, in everyday life, these patients do not experience the problems identified in this study. [2 marks]

3. Explain why Sperry's split-brain study can be placed in the biological area. [2 marks]

4. Outline two experimental controls used in Sperry's split-brain study and explain why these two controls were necessary. [4 marks]

Casey et al. (2011)

Can you resist temptation? Do you have strong willpower and self-control? In a famous demonstration of deferred gratification (i.e. the ability to resist a reward in the present for a greater reward in the future), Mischel, one of Casey's co-authors in this study, demonstrated how some children could resist temptation while others could not. The way the study was typically conducted was that a child was tested individually by an adult researcher. The pre-school child was taken to a room that had no distractions and seated on a chair at a table. On the table an attractive treat (e.g. a marshmallow) was placed on a plate. The child was told that the researcher had to go out for a while, and that the child could have the marshmallow. However, they were also told that if they could wait and not eat the marshmallow then they would get two marshmallows when the researcher returned. The researcher was out of the room for about 15 minutes. The results showed that some children were high delayers, meaning they could wait and received the reward of two marshmallows, whereas others were low delayers who could not wait and took the immediate reward by eating the marshmallow. The ability to resist temptation depends on cognitive control, and it seems that some people have better self-control than others, and that this can be predicted by their performance as a young child on the Marshmallow Test.

Figure 4.10 Pre-schoolers demonstrate their self-control (or lack of it!) in the Marshmallow Test

Why can some children resist and others cannot? Casey et al. point out that, in the presence of such a highly rewarding treat, those who could not resist the marshmallow on their first 'go' could wait for longer when retested if taught to use 'cooling' strategies to reduce the appeal of the reward, so instead of focusing on the 'hot' cues (e.g. how sweet and delicious the marshmallow is), they might think of it as a cotton wool ball, or a cloud, or focus on just its shape. It seems that we respond to 'hot' and 'cold' cues differently in that we can resist 'cold' cues more than 'hot' ones.

Casey et al. quote research by Metcalfe and Mischel (1999) who proposed two interacting neurocognitive systems to explain resistance to temptation. They suggested that there is a 'cool' system which involves cognitive control-related neural circuitry, located in the prefrontal cortex, and brain imaging studies show that a particular area of the pre-frontal cortex – the inferior frontal gyrus (Figure 4.11) – is involved in deciding whether to resist or not.

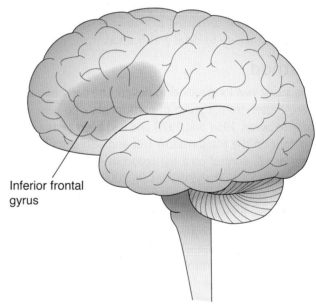

Inferior frontal gyrus

Figure 4.11 The location of the inferior frontal gyrus

Second, there is a 'hot' system which is related to emotion and desires and is related to emotional brain regions. For example, one part of the limbic system, the emotional region of the brain, is called the ventral striatum and this area is associated with rewards.

🚫 **Stop and ask yourself ...**

- What do the researchers mean in this study by 'hot' and 'cold' cues or stimuli?
- Where in the brain are the systems that respond to and process these types of stimuli, according to Metcalfe and Mischel?

Links to methodological issues
- Check your understanding

Aim

Casey *et al.* aimed to find out if participants who were low delayers on the Marshmallow Test at age four, and also reported low self-control on psychometric measures in their twenties and thirties (the 'low delayers'):

1. would show more errors on a Go/No-Go task if the stimuli were 'hot' (rewarding emotional faces) than those participants who had shown consistently high self-control (the 'high delayers')

The researchers predicted that fMRI brain scans while completing the Go/No-Go task would show that the low delayers:

2. would show lower activity in their right prefrontal cortex (the inferior frontal gyrus), suggesting lower response inhibition to stimuli, and
3. would show increased activity in the ventral striatum, where positive or rewarding cues are processed, than the high delayers.

The study would therefore show if there were regions of the brain that correlated with low self-control and diminished ability to defer gratification.

Method

This study was longitudinal in design. The participants were chosen from a group of participants who were all born between 1964 and 1970 and had been tested at age four on the Marshmallow Test and also completed tests of self-control on a self-report inventory in their twenties (in 1993) and thirties (in 2003). The original study at age four had tested 562 participants. The 1993 follow up was completed by 155 adults and 135 completed the 2003 self-control self-reports. This study identified those who scored consistently low on measures of self-control (the 'low delayers'), of whom there were 60 of the 135 who qualified in this category, and those who scored consistently high on self-control (the 'high delayers'), of whom 57 of the 135 qualified. The 117 potential participants were contacted and 59 participants agreed to be tested in this study. The 59 consisted of 27 low delayers (16 females and 11 males) and 32 high delayers (20 females and 12 males).

Procedure

The study reports two experiments.

Experiment 1 – Behavioural correlates of delay of gratification 40 years on

In experiment 1, all 59 participants were tested. Self-control was measured in the study by the use of a Go/No-Go task.

Go/No-Go tasks are used to measure people's response control. For example, a Go/No-Go task requires a participant to perform an action given certain stimuli (e.g. press a button when you see a yellow circle flash on a screen = Go) and not perform that action in response to other stimuli (e.g. not press that same button when you see a red circle flash on a screen = No-Go). Errors, or 'false alarms', in this test would be to 'Go' (press the button) when a No-Go stimulus appeared.

In this study, Casey *et al.* manipulated the 'hot' stimulus by the social cues of emotional faces. Happy faces, they suggested, would be a rewarding 'hot' stimulus, compared with the 'cool' stimuli of neutral or fearful faces.

Casey *et al.* wanted to find out if the low delayers would make more errors in the Go/No-Go tasks involving 'hot' stimuli (happy faces) than the high delayers because their brain would fail to control their response to the 'hot' cue.

The 59 participants each did four Go/No-Go tasks. The tasks involved faces being shown on the screen of a laptop which was delivered to participants' homes. Each face appeared for 500 ms, with a 1-s interval between faces. Before each task, instructions appeared on screen saying which face (male or female neutral face, fearful or happy face) was the target stimulus. Participants were told to press a button for the target face (Go) and not press the button for the other face (No-Go). Participants were also instructed to respond as quickly and accurately as possible.

Stop and ask yourself...

- Can you explain what a quasi-experiment is, using this study as an example?

Links to methodological issues
- Quasi-experiments

Stop and ask yourself...

- Can you give one reason why it would be a strength of this study to send laptops to the participants so they could do the study in their own home?
- Can you see any problems that might arise as a result of testing participants in this way?

Links to methodological issues
- Experimental controls

The Go/No-Go tasks were as follows:

- 'Cool' version, having to press the button whenever the male neutral face appeared, which it did 120 times out of the 160 pairs of faces seen (i.e. male neutral face = Go, and female neutral face = No-Go)
- 'Cool' version, having to press the button whenever the female neutral face appeared, which it did 120 times out of the 160 pairs of faces seen (i.e. female neutral face = Go, and male neutral face = No-Go)
- 'Hot' version, having to press the button whenever a happy facial expression appeared, which it did 120 times out of the 160 pairs of faces seen (i.e. happy facial expression = Go, and fearful facial expression = No-Go)
- 'Hot' version, having to press the button whenever a fearful facial expression appeared, which it did 120 times out of the 160 pairs of faces seen (i.e. fearful facial expression = Go, and happy facial expression = No-Go).

Results for experiment 1

Both groups of participants performed with a high level of accuracy on the 'Go' trials in both the 'cool' and 'hot' versions.

Both groups made more errors on the No-Go tasks, which Casey *et al.* measured as the percentage of false alarms. However, whereas they made a similar number of errors on the 'cool' task, the low delayers made more errors on the 'hot' task.

Further analysis showed that the two groups performed similarly on the fear face No-Go trials (Table 4.3), and that errors made by the low delayers in the 'hot' task were largely commission errors on the happy face No-Go trials.

Table 4.3 Comparative percentage of errors for low delayers and high delayers on the fearful face No-Go trials and happy face No-Go trials on the 'hot' task

Type of No-Go trial	Percentage errors for low delayers	Percentage errors for high delayers
Happy	15.7	11.2
Fearful	12	10.4

Casey *et al.* conclude that the low delayers who had shown more difficulty in delaying gratification at age four showed more difficulty suppressing responses to happy faces in their forties. These findings suggest that low self-control remains consistent in an individual. The findings also show that this depends on the rewarding nature of the stimulus in the task, as the low delayers had more difficulty only on the happy face 'hot' task than the high delayers.

Experiment 2 – Neural correlates of delayed gratification 40 years on

In their second experiment, Casey *et al.* aimed to investigate the regions of the brain that they predicted would be implicated in self-control. They did this using an fMRI scanner. Functional MRI scans (fMRI) differ from MRI scans in that fMRI scans investigate the physiognomy of the brain (how it works), whereas MRI scans are designed to investigate the anatomy of the brain (its structure). For this experiment, 27 of the 59 participants in study 1 agreed to be tested, while in an fMRI scanner (of these, one male participant was excluded from all analysis because of poor task performance). Of the 26 remaining participants, 15 were high delayers (10 female and 5 male) and 11 were low delayers (4 female and 7 male).

The participants each took part in a similar 'hot' Go/No-Go task as in experiment 1. The task differed from the first experiment in that:

- Instead of a 1-s delay between the presentation of faces, there was a 2–14.5 second delay (mean, 5.2 s) where participants rested while viewing a fixation crosshair.
- There were 48 trials per run, 35 'Go' and 13 'No-Go', giving a total of 70 'Go' and 26 'No-Go' trials for each expression, fearful and happy.
- Although the stimuli and instructions were identical to experiment 1, the apparatus was different as the stimuli were presented on a screen in the scanner and a different type of push button apparatus was used for responses.

Results for experiment 2

As in experiment 1, both groups scored highly on accuracy rates for the 'Go' trials, and again the low delayers showed more false alarms (low delay 14.5 per cent and high delayers 10.9 per cent).

Stop and ask yourself…

- Why do you think that only 27 of the participants from the first study agreed to be retested while in the fMRI scanner?

Links to methodological issues
- Sampling issues

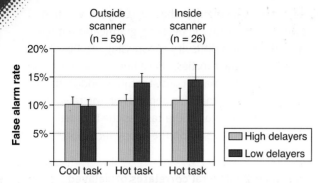

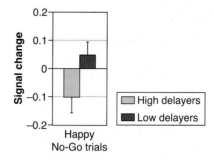

Figure 4.14 The low delayers showed higher activity in the ventral striatum than the high delayers on the happy 'No-Go' trials.

Figure 4.12 Casey *et al.*'s behavioural findings as percentage errors on the 'cool' and 'hot' tasks for experiment 1, and the 'hot' task in the scanner in experiment 2.

The imaging results showed two main differences between the low and high delayers.

First, the low delayers showed lower activity in the right inferior frontal gyrus than the high delayers on the No-Go trials. Casey *et al.* conclude that this suggests that this brain region plays an important role in the withholding of a response.

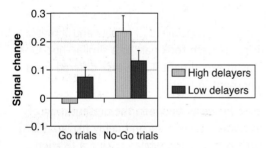

Figure 4.13 Casey *et al.*'s imaging study showed that the low delayers had lower activity in the right inferior frontal gyrus in the No-Go trials, which is involved in accurately withholding a response.

Second, the low delayers showed higher activity in the ventral striatum, specifically when the 'happy' faces were the No-Go stimuli. This suggests that the 'hot' or alluring features of this stimulus made this reward-related region more active and made it harder for them to 'resist', resulting in more errors, and shows that the alluring qualities of a stimulus affect cognitive control ability.

Casey *et al.* suggest that 'resisting temptation in favour of long term goals is important for individual, societal and economic functioning' (page 15001) (below under Links to debates: Usefulness of the research), and that the findings of this study show a neurobiological

basis for differences between people in their ability to show self-control and delay gratification.

Conclusions

In the discussion of their results, Casey *et al.*'s conclusions include:

- Resisting temptation (or not!) is a relatively stable individual characteristic. This was shown in the study over a 40-year span, as those who had been low delayers at age four years had more difficulty suppressing responses to socially alluring cues (the happy faces).
- The study suggests that delay ability is hindered by alluring cues specifically, and is not a general problem with cognitive control.
- The study provides empirical evidence for Mischel and Metcalfe's 'hot' and 'cool' processing systems in the brain that affect self-control. The 'hot' system is in the ventral striatum and the 'cool' system is in the inferior frontal gyrus. In this study, 'hot' stimuli interfered with the low delayers' self-control on the Go/No-go tasks, specifically in the happy face No-Go trials. Casey *et al.* conclude that:

... sensitivity to environmental cues influences an individual's ability to suppress thought and actions, such that control systems may be 'hijacked' by a primitive limbic system, rendering control systems unable to appropriately modulate behaviour (page 15001).

This was shown in the study with the low delayers showing less recruitment in the inferior frontal gyrus and exaggerated recruitment being shown in the ventral striatum when trying to resist alluring cues.

Have a go yourself

- How good are people at resisting temptation? Try putting together a self-report exercise in which participants are asked to rate on a 1–10 scale how well they think they could resist a bowl of apples with a 'help yourself' notice and also how far they could resist a bowl of small packets of chocolates in it with a similar 'help yourself' sign. They should imagine that these have been put out in the school or college common room or recreational area.
- Try doing this as a survey of 20 participants and then graphically present your data, calculating a suitable measure of central tendency and analysing the data statistically. (See Chapter 7, Research materials, for guidance on how to do this.)
- Are the responses of your participants in line with what the study by Casey *et al.* might lead you to expect? How do the concepts of 'hot' and 'cool' stimuli apply in this investigation?

Evaluation of the study by Casey *et al.*

Links to methodological issues

Research methods

- In order to investigate the behavioural correlates of deferred gratification, Casey *et al.* tested their participants experimentally under strictly controlled conditions. The experiments were quasi in design, as the participants either fell into the low delayer or high delayer conditions. The strengths of carrying out research using technical equipment are apparent in this study. In both experiments, the software used for the Go/No-Go tasks enabled the reactions of the participants to be recorded with split-second accuracy. In study two, the use of fMRI to measure brain activity gave detailed and objective observations of the brain activity in the areas of the brain associated with self-control and rewards, and enabled the researchers to draw conclusions about the differences between the low delayers and high delayers in their brain function.
- Casey *et al.* conducted their study longitudinally, as it was following up on a group of participants who had been tested at age four, in their twenties in 1993 and again in their thirties in 2003. This is a strength

 Stop and ask yourself...

- What does this study tell us in relation to the key theme of 'regions of the brain'?

Links to methodological issues
- Regions of the brain

of the study as it allowed the researchers to come to the conclusion that the ability to resist temptation is a relatively stable characteristic and that some people are consistently good at resisting and some people are not. However, longitudinal studies have problems associated with them in that they are affected by subject attrition and take a long time to conduct (see below under Validity and Reliability below).

Types of data

- Casey *et al.* present their findings quantitatively. For example, they show that in experiment 1 the low delayers at age 40 made the most errors on the 'happy face' Go/No-go trials (15.7 per cent). Quantitative data have the strength of being easy to summarise, for example, each condition's performance could be summarised as a single percentage of errors score. Another strength of quantitative data is that numerical values are easy to compare between conditions. Comparing the 15.7 per cent errors on the happy Go/No-go task with the other conditions showed that the low delayers group found it difficult to resist 'hot' (tempting) stimuli. The quantitative data gathered could also be analysed statistically to confirm the significance of this result. Quantitative data are also easy to summarise and present in graphical form, and Casey *et al.* used bar charts to demonstrate the difference between the low and high delayers, both in the number of errors made on the No-Go task and in the levels of activation shown in the ventral striatum from the brain scans in experiment 2. This makes the data easy to read and the conditions easy to compare. Finally, quantitative data have the advantage that the study could be easily repeated and tested to see if it is reliable or not, using correlational analysis of the findings from the original and repeated studies.

Ethical considerations

- The study was conducted ethically as the participants consented to be studied, no deception was used and they were neither harmed nor unduly stressed by the experimental tests. The fact that a number of participants who had taken part in experiment 1 chose not to take part in experiment 2 demonstrates that they clearly had the right to withdraw.

Validity

- Casey *et al.* conducted their study under controlled conditions, using standardised instructions, testing and procedures. This high level of control means that the study is high in design validity, as extraneous variables that could impact on the study have been strictly controlled.
- There are problems with the sample of Casey *et al.*'s study that make us question the study's population validity (see below under Sample).

Ecological validity

- In terms of ecological validity, the Go/No-Go tasks in this study are contrived tests that do not have a direct equivalent in everyday life. While the momentarily flashed static image of a happy face may elicit a realistic response from the participant, it is possible that it may not. Therefore Casey *et al.*'s findings might not tell us how people respond under normal conditions. Similarly, being scanned in an fMRI scanner while doing a Go/No-Go task is not something that a person would have to do every day and the strangeness of it could have had an impact on the performance of the participants on the test.

Reliability

- One of the weaknesses of longitudinal studies that are conducted over decades (as in this study) is that they are not time- and cost-effective to replicate. For instance, if we wanted to repeat Casey's study to establish its reliability, we would have to start out with four-year-olds and follow them through into their forties. It would therefore not be easy to establish the reliability of Casey's research (also see above under Types of data).

Sample

- At age four, a sample of 562 children had been studied, 155 of these completed the 1993 follow-up self-report study, and 135 of these were further tested in 2003. For the purposes of this study, 117 of the remaining 135 were deemed eligible for this study based on the authors' criteria for high delayers

(57/135) and low delayers (60/135). Of these invited 135, only 59 agreed to be in Casey *et al.*'s study. This is known as subject attrition, where in a longitudinal study people choose not to continue, or do not want to take part in follow-up studies. This means that the sample of the study reduces in size and may not be as generalisable as the original sample, as those people who continue to volunteer to be in studies may differ in many ways from those who do not. We must also be cautious before assuming that the brains of all the low and high delayers would be the same as those 26 who were tested in experiment 2 in the fMRI scanner. For example, of the 11 low delayers tested, there were just four females, and this is a very small sample from which to make judgements about the brains of all 'low delayer' females.

Ethnocentrism

- On the one hand, since Casey's study tells us that self-control and deferred gratification is affected by the anatomy and physiognomy of our brain, we could argue that Casey's study is not ethnocentric as it was investigating a species-specific behaviour. On the other hand, the research was only conducted in America, and it may well be that being raised in a culture of capitalism and consumerism, which puts temptation in people's way more than other cultures might, means that there may not be as many 'low delayers' in other cultures. This would mean the findings of this study were ethnocentric and we should be cautious in assuming that a lack of self-control is either 'natural' or a universal human trait.

Links to debates

Psychology as a science

- Casey *et al.* carried out a controlled laboratory experiment and this method fulfils the scientific criteria of theory, control, evidence and replication. As with many biological area studies, this supports the claim that psychology is a scientific discipline.

Usefulness of the research

- Casey *et al.*'s point out that 'resisting temptation in favour of long-term goals is important for individual, societal and economic functioning' (page 15001). Studies have linked being a high delayer aged four years to the development of better social-cognitive and emotional coping in adolescence and it also protects against physical and mental health problems in middle age, e.g. 'high BMI, cocaine/crack use, features of borderline personality disorder, anxious overreactions to rejection, and marital divorce/separation' (page 15001). Casey suggests that such predictions are significant. Perhaps if we could create strategies to train the brains of low delayers aged four years (remember they did better on their second go with the marshmallow when they were taught to use 'cooling' techniques) might we help to protect them from vulnerability to these problems in later life?

Nature–nurture debate

- Casey et al.'s study raises the question of whether we are born destined to be 'low delayers' or 'high delayers'. The difference can be clearly seen in the Marshmallow Test at age four years, and Casey's study, among others, shows the stability of this lack of self-control over time. On the other hand, by the time we are four we have learned a great deal about the ability of our environment to reward us, and will also have seen others modelling resisting temptation or not by that age, so nurture could also have an influence. Could nurture, through some programme of intervention or training, change a 'low delayer' at age four years into a 'high delayer', and thus avoid the future negative effects on mental and physical health that being a 'low delayer' seems to predict?

Free will and determinism

- Are we determined by our biology? Are we born with brain differences that mean that some of us can easily resist temptation and work towards long-term goals and others of us are pre-wired to become 'low delayers' and vulnerable to a range of threats to our mental and physical health later in life?

Links to areas/perspectives

- Casey et al.'s study falls within the biological area as it is investigating whether there are specific regions of the brain that impact on our ability to resist the temptation of rewarding stimuli. Specifically, it provided empirical evidence that our biology has a significant part to play in our ability to defer gratification.
- Casey et al.'s study can also be considered to be an individual differences study, as the study suggested that there are individual differences, present from early childhood and stable across decades, in people's ability to resist temptation and defer gratification.

Links to the key theme

- In relation to the key theme of regions of the brain, Casey et al.'s study revealed that there are two regions of the brain that have an impact on our ability to resist temptation and defer gratification. Specifically, the study found empirical evidence for Metcalfe and Mischel's 'hot' and 'cool' processing systems in the brain that affect self-control. The 'hot' system is in the ventral striatum and the 'cool' system is in the inferior frontal gyrus.
- In terms of the extent to which Casey et al.'s study changes our understanding of the key theme of 'regions of the brain', it can be seen as adding to Sperry's research by telling us about the role that other regions of the brain appear to play (apart from the corpus callosum); it also suggests other ways to research regions of the brain (e.g. by using fMRI scanning).
- How does the contemporary study by Casey et al. change our understanding of individual social and cultural diversity?

Casey et al.'s study does not change our understanding of cultural diversity, since both Sperry and Casey were studying the brain structure or function of individuals in America, and their studies were not concerned with social or cultural differences. However, Casey et al. were studying typical participants whereas Sperry's were atypical, having suffered severe epilepsy and having had a commissurotomy. Casey's work confirmed that there are individual differences in brain structure in the general population which could influence their behaviour. In this way, Casey's study changed our understanding of individual diversity as it suggests that there are brain differences in typical people in the areas of self-control that can explain individual differences in response to a range of 'tempting' stimuli in the environment.

Comparison with the classic study

- In what ways is the study by Casey et al. similar to the study by Sperry?
  - The studies both included highly controlled laboratory experiments.
  - The studies both demonstrate the functions of specific regions of the brain, with Sperry showing that the corpus callosum plays an important role in the communication between the two hemispheres and Casey showing that the ventral striatum and inferior frontal gyrus are important in self-control.

- The studies were both conducted ethically.
- It would be difficult to establish the reliability of either study. It would not be possible to find a suitable sample for a replication of Sperry's study since commissurotomy is no longer commonly used as a treatment for epilepsy. Casey's study would also be difficult to replicate as it was a longitudinal study testing participants from age four years through to their forties.

- In what ways is the study by Casey *et al. different from* the study by Sperry?
  - Whereas Casey studied the brains of normal adults, Sperry's research was conducted on abnormal subjects, so Casey's research may be more generalisable than Sperry's research.
  - Casey's study was a longitudinal study, whereas Sperry conducted a snapshot study.
  - Casey's study was able to benefit from the technology now available using brain imaging techniques (fMRI) and was able to scientifically observe the functioning of the regions of the brain they were interested in. Sperry's classic study from the 1960s did not have the benefit of this technology, so any activity from the right hemisphere could only be inferred from what the split-brain patients could or could not do.

Questions arising from Casey *et al.*'s study

Casey *et al.*'s study raises the question of whether resisting temptation is pre-wired in our brains, and also makes us question whether or not 'low delayers' could be trained to become 'high delayers', and if so, when and how?

Practice questions

1. For Casey *et al.*'s study (neural correlates of delay of gratification), describe the initial delay of gratification task as given to the children at age four years and explain what it measures. [4 marks]
2. For Casey *et al.*'s study, identify one area of the brain that the researchers investigated and outline what their results show in relation to this area of the brain. [3 marks]
3. Casey *et al.*'s study used a longitudinal design. Give one strength and one weakness of conducting this study longitudinally. [4 marks]
4. Outline one way in which the studies by Sperry (split-brain study) and Casey *et al.* (neural correlates of delay of gratification) are similar to each other and one way in which they are different from each other. [4 marks]

Brain plasticity Ⓐ

How flexible are our brains? Our brains, or parts of them, can actually change size (or rather shape or structure) in order to accommodate new information.

Jacobs et al. (1993) looked at the portion of the human cerebral cortex responsible for understanding words (Wernicke's area), using deceased individuals who had given their consent prior to death. They compared the effects of enrichment in tissue from individuals who had received a college education with others who had left education after secondary school. The results demonstrated that the nerve cells in the college-educated participants showed more dendrites than those in the secondary school population. Further experiments on human tissue have supported the findings of animal research and the conclusion that the brain does change in response to enrichment, in both animals and humans.

It is likely that you have been told at some time that you only have the brain cells you were born with, and as you get older they begin to die off, with alcohol and other damaging substances causing you to lose them more quickly. More recent research indicates that brain cells can actually regenerate. For example, Eriksson et al. (1998) identified the fact that the human hippocampus retains its ability to generate new neuronal cells throughout life, through a process known as 'neurogenesis'.

Studies have established the neuroplasticity of the brain: brains can change in response to external stimuli. Imagine a piece of plasticine. It changes in response to the pressure or moulding that is applied to it. This is what happens with the brain; it changes and responds to the demands placed on it by increasing the cell dendrites and therefore the number of synapses available, in order to meet increased processing demands. These changes can be both functional (e.g. changes in neurotransmitters) and structural (changes in the size and number of synaptic connections between neurones).

Studies of brain plasticity have considered the developing brain's responses to the environment, as Blakemore and Cooper do in our core study by investigating brain plasticity in the visual sense of kittens from birth. Studies of brain plasticity in adult humans have also been conducted and the core study by Maguire et al. on the plasticity of the hippocampi in taxi drivers is an example of this.

The hippocampus is a very important brain structure for all types of memory. The hippocampus is linked to the conversion of information from short-term to more permanent memory. The impact of a damaged hippocampus is that memories of the past are retained, but new memories are not stored (known as 'anterograde amnesia'), although individuals with a damaged hippocampus can learn new skills. This suggests that there may be different types of memory stores for different types of information. Another function of the hippocampus is to connect memories with each other, thus giving them meaning. For example, the hippocampus may connect the memory of a visit to a certain location with the information about where you went and how it looked and sounded.

The hippocampus is also associated with the memory of spatial relationships, the location of places or objects, and the distances and routes between them. It is this function of the hippocampus on which Maguire et al.'s study focuses. If we have to learn a great deal of information to help us find our way around a complex environment, what happens to our hippocampus? Maguire et al. chose to study London taxi drivers in order to try to answer this question.

Blakemore and Cooper (1970)

Working at the University of Cambridge, Blakemore and Cooper conducted a study into the effect of the environment on the development of the brain in cats. The background to this study includes work by Hirsch and Spinelli at Stanford University in California where the researchers reared kittens with one eye viewing vertical stripes and the other eye viewing horizontal stripes and found that most of the neurones of the visual cortex were monocularly driven (driven by one eye) and the preferred orientation of the neurones reflected the pattern experienced in that eye. This suggested that the neurones of the visual cortex showed plasticity in that they developed according to the environment experienced.

Blakemore and Cooper's study was related to this but in their study they raised kittens by exposing them to an environment of either horizontal or vertical stripes which the kittens experienced binocularly (with both eyes).

Aim

The aim of this study was to limit the visual experience of kittens to one orientation – either vertical stripes or horizontal stripes – and to compare the behavioural consequences of this restricted visual environment on the kittens. The study also aimed to investigate the neurophysiological effects on the neurones in the kittens' visual cortex. This study would therefore investigate the responses of the kittens' brain development to their environment and illustrate brain plasticity in their developing visual sense.

Procedure

The sample used for this study was kittens, from birth to approximately one year old.

The visual environment in which the kittens were raised was strictly controlled:

- From birth, the kittens were housed in a completely dark room.

- From the age of about two weeks, the visual experience of the kittens was manipulated by exposing them to either a completely vertically oriented or a completely horizontally oriented environment. This was achieved by placing the kitten in a specially designed piece of apparatus (Figure 4.15) which was cylindrical in shape and in which there was a clear glass platform halfway up the cylinder on which the kitten was placed. The cylinder was 46 cm in diameter and about 2 m high.

The inside of the cylinder, as far up and down as the kitten could see, was decorated either with vertical high contrast black and white stripes or horizontal high contrast black and white stripes. The stripes were of a variety of widths. The kittens spent about 5 hours a day in this apparatus. They wore a wide black collar so that they could not see their own bodies and this limited their vision to about 130 degrees. A top cover, or 'lid', was placed on the cylinder. The stripes were illuminated from above by a spotlight beneath the top cover.

- Blakemore and Cooper reported that while in the apparatus the kitten could not see beyond its 'world of stripes' (page 477).

- Blakemore and Cooper report that the kittens 'did not seem upset by the monotony of their surroundings and they sat for long periods inspecting the walls of the tube' (page 477).

Figure 4.15 The apparatus used by Blakemore and Cooper to control the visual environment of the kittens, in this example an environment entirely vertically oriented.

Stop and ask yourself …

- Why do you suppose that it was important to house the kittens in the dark from birth and for most of the time during the study?
- Why do you think Blakemore and Cooper did not want the kittens seeing their own bodies?
- What is the independent variable in this study?

Links to methodological issues
- Experimental controls
- Independent variables

- Why do you think Blakemore and Cooper want us to know that the 'kittens did not seem upset by the monotony of their surroundings'?

Links to methodological issues
- Ethical considerations

- The daily exposure to either the vertically or horizontally striped visual environment came to an end when the kittens were about five months old. By this time, the kittens would have passed through the 'critical' or 'sensitive' period for visual development.

Results

Behavioural findings

From five months old, the cats were taken for several hours a week from their dark room home to a well-lit room that was furnished with chairs and tables. In this room, the cats were observed to see the behavioural consequences of their restricted visual experience.

- When first exposed to the well-lit room, both the horizontally raised and vertically raised cats showed visual deficits. Although they had normal pupillary reflexes, they showed no startle response when an object or hand was thrust towards them. In addition, they did not demonstrate what is known as visual placing. If you hold a cat and move it towards a ledge or table, it will put out its feet to meet the edge of the ledge or table. The visually restricted kittens did not do this, and they only put out their feet once they had detected the edge of the table by touch. In addition, the kittens navigated their way round the room by touch, and showed a fear response when, for example, they reached the edge of the table or chair they were walking on.
- After about ten hours of exposure to the well-lit room, however, these deficits disappeared and they began to show visual placing, startle responses, and would jump easily from a chair to the floor.
- Some deficits remained, however. Their visual tracking of moving objects was with clumsy, jerky head movements and they often tried to reach for objects moving across the room and way out of their reach. They often bumped into things as they scurried about exploring the room.

Differences between the horizontally raised and vertically raised cats were also observed. Blakemore and Cooper report that 'they were virtually blind for contours perpendicular to the orientation they had experienced' (page 478). In other words, the horizontally raised kittens did not see vertical lines and the vertically raised kittens failed to see horizontal lines. This was apparent in two tests conducted:

1. A sheet of Perspex with thick black and white lines was presented to the kittens. They showed no reaction if it was presented to them in the 'wrong' orientation, but would respond to the 'right' orientation with a startle response if the Perspex sheet was presented to them.
2. A rod was shaken in front of the kittens, a likely game to play with kittens who will try to catch and chase the rod. If the rod was presented horizontally to two kittens, one which had been raised in a horizontally striped environment and one which had been raised in a vertically striped environment, only the horizontally raised kitten would respond to the rod. The other kitten ignored it. This was reversed if the rod was shaken vertically, as this time the vertically raised kitten would follow and chase the rod while the horizontally raised kitten ignored it, as if it did not see it.

Neurophysiological findings

In a normal cat, the visual neurones demonstrate a 'preferred orientation' and on experiencing the world a normal cat's pattern of neurons would have a balance of horizontal and vertical neurons. If you imagine a clock face, a normal cat would have neurones 'around the clock', covering both the horizontal and vertical orientations. However, in the diagram in Figure 4.16, you can see that in the horizontally raised kitten (left) there were no neurones in the vertical orientation and in the vertically raised kitten there were no neurones in the horizontal orientation. These distributions of preferred orientation are totally abnormal. This was what Blakemore and Cooper discovered when they operated on two of the cats at seven and a half months old.

Conclusions

Blakemore and Cooper conclude that 'Evidently the visual experience of these animals in early life has modified their brains, and there are profound perceptual consequences' (page 478). This study showed that the development of the brain, at least of the visual sense, responds to the environment that is experienced. Cells that had begun with a preferred 'vertical' orientation changed to a horizontal preference when the environment presented was only horizontal. This example of brain plasticity demonstrates the role of nurture in the development of vision, at least in cats.

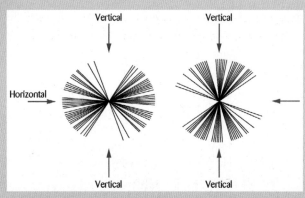

Figure 4.16 These bipolar histograms show the distributions of optimal orientations for 52 neurones from a horizontally experienced cat on the left and 72 from a vertically experienced cat on the right. The slight torsion of the eyes, caused by the relaxant drug was assessed by photographing the pupils before and after anaesthesia and paralysis. A correction has been applied for torsion, so the polar plots are properly orientated for the cats' visual fields. Each line shows the optimal orientation for a single neurone. For each binocular cell, the line is drawn at the mean of the estimates of optimal orientation in the two eyes. No units have been disregarded except for one with a concentric receptive field and hence no orientational selectivity

Evaluation of the study by Blakemore and Cooper

Links to methodological issues

Research methods

- Blakemore and Cooper conducted their experiment under highly controlled laboratory conditions. They were able to manipulate and control the type of visual environment in which each of the kittens were raised as an independent variable and, as a result, were able to conclude that it was the type of environment in which the kittens were raised that caused the kittens' observed perceptual difficulties and the atypical neurobiological findings.

Types of data

- Blakemore and Cooper present quantitative data in terms of the neurobiological findings in their study. Of 125 neurones studied in two cats, all but one was shown to favour the restricted orientation in which the cats were raised. These quantitative data provide scientific evidence of brain plasticity in the kittens. Collecting quantitative data also enables research to be repeated and tested for reliability, which strengthens the scientific value of the research.
- The authors also presented qualitative data describing the kittens' reactions, for example the fact that they had no startle response and bumped into things around the room, and that the horizontally

raised kitten ignored the rod shaken at them if it was presented vertically and the vertically raised kitten ignored a shaken rod that was presented horizontally. This qualitative data provides detailed descriptive examples of the differences observed in the kittens raised in the two different environments.

Ethical considerations

- The study was conducted within the strict ethical guidelines laid down by the Home Office for studies conducted on animals.

Validity

- The study was conducted with a high level of control so the researchers could be confident that the findings were caused by the restricted visual environment in which the kittens were raised. This means the study had high design validity.
- The researchers measured the effects of the restricted visual environments in which the kittens were raised using both behavioural and neurophysiological measures. These measures both showed evidence that the kittens raised in the horizontal visual environment did not see in the vertical orientation and that the opposite was true of the kittens raised in the vertical environment. These findings are concurrently valid and each supports the researchers' claims that the development of the kittens' brains had been influenced by their environment.

Reliability

- As the study was conducted under controlled conditions and the researchers give detailed descriptions of their procedure then it would be possible for this study to be repeated and tested to see if it had test–retest reliability.
- The study does not explicitly state the sample size, just that two kittens — one raised in a vertical environment and the other in a horizontal environment — were used for the neurological part of the study. Ideally, the study would have been carried out on a larger sample of cats, to establish that these were not 'fluke' results.

Sample

- The evidence presented came from a small number of kittens, in fact only two cats reported on in the neurophysiological findings, and it could therefore be the case that the findings would not be generalisable to all cats. Of course, we would have to be very cautious about extrapolating from this research to try to make claims about the influence of environment on the developing brains of other species, including humans.

Ethnocentrism

- This study is from comparative psychology and studied cats. It is not relevant, therefore, to the discussion of ethnocentrism in research.

Links to debates

Nature–nurture debate

- The study by Blakemore and Cooper showed that the development of visual orientation in cats was a product of both nature and nurture. Nature provided the kittens with neurones with a preferred orientation, but the restricted visual environment in which the kittens were raised meant that nurture had a strong effect on how their brains developed in terms of orientation of their vision. The kittens' visual neurones adapted to the environment that the kittens experienced.

Psychology as a science

- Blakemore and Cooper carried out controlled laboratory observations and experiments and these fulfil the scientific criteria of theory, control, evidence and replication. As with many biological area studies, this supports the claim that psychology is a scientific discipline.
- In theory, it would be possible to prove false what Blakemore and Cooper are saying about the impact of the visual environment on the visual neurones of kittens by replicating their study with a fresh sample of kittens; as such, their work is falsifiable.

Ethical considerations

- This study was conducted ethically according to guidelines for animal research. However, studies of this type raise questions about the ethics of animal experimentation in general.

🔍 Find out more

- Research the ethical guidelines for conducting studies with animals. When, if ever, can research using animals be justified, do you think?
- Search on the internet for video footage from Blakemore and Cooper's research.

Links to areas/perspectives

- Blakemore and Cooper's study falls within the biological area as it is investigating the effect of the environment on the developing brain in cats. Specifically, it demonstrated the plasticity of the kittens' brains as neurones originally primed to prefer either a horizontal or vertical orientation would switch to prefer the opposing orientation when the early visual environment the kitten experienced seemed to require this adaptation.

Links to the key theme

- In relation to the key theme of brain plasticity, Blakemore and Cooper's study demonstrated that in the developing brains of cats the visual neurones will change their preferred orientation such that a cat raised in a restricted horizontally oriented environment will develop horizontal vision only and a cat raised in a restricted vertically oriented environment will develop only vertical vision.
- Questions arising from Blakemore and Cooper's study:
  - Would limitations on the visual environment of human infants lead to similar changes in the visual neurones? Of course, this could not be investigated for ethical reasons.
  - Despite their exposure to a normal world of both horizontal and vertical orientation, the cats raised in a restricted environment did not adapt and continued to experience serious perceptual difficulties. Once the critical stage of development is passed, is the brain 'fixed' and unchanging?
  - Ethical questions can be raised about animal experimentation of this type – does the end justify the means?
  - What can we really learn, if anything, about the plasticity of the human brain from comparative studies of animals? The contemporary study by Maguire *et al.* answers some of these questions in that it aimed to investigate the possibility of brain plasticity in human adults.

📝 Practice questions

1. From Blakemore and Cooper's study (Impact of the visual environment on cats' brains):
   (a) Explain what is meant by 'brain plasticity'. [2 marks]
   (b) Outline what Blakemore and Cooper's findings tell us about the key theme of brain plasticity. [2 marks]
2. From Blakemore and Cooper's study, describe how the visual experience of the kittens was manipulated as an independent variable. [3 marks]
3. From Blakemore and Cooper's study, outline the behavioural findings. [3 marks]
4. From Blakemore and Cooper's study, outline the neurophysiological findings. [3 marks]
5. Suggest two ways in which the study by Blakemore and Cooper could be said to be valid. [4 marks]

Maguire *et al.* (2000)

Maguire *et al.*'s core study investigates neuroplasticity in one structure of the brain, the hippocampus (Figure 4.17). This is a bilateral brain structure, which means there is a hippocampus on the left of the brain and a hippocampus on the right of the brain. The plural of hippocampus is 'hippocampi'.

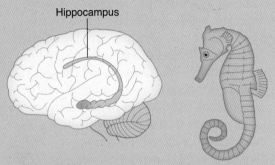

Figure 4.17 The brain structure: the hippocampus (left) is so-called because anatomists thought it resembled a sea horse, and the Greek for seahorse is *hippocampus*.

The hippocampus helps us to navigate; that is, to find our way round both familiar and new environments. This means that this area of the brain plays an important part in our spatial memory.

If the needs of our spatial memory change or increase, will the hippocampus change to accommodate this? Maguire *et al.* suggest that it will, and provide evidence to support their theory from animals and birds: 'in some species hippocampal volumes enlarge…during seasons when demand for spatial ability is greatest'. They also point to reported evidence that brain differences exist between humans with different skills, for example musicians and non-musicians, who place different demands on their brains. Maguire's claims that studies to date have not provided evidence as to the source of these differences. Is it that people with certain types of brains (predetermined by biology) become musicians? Or is it that the brains of musicians change in response to environmental stimulation and learning? In this study, Maguire aimed to investigate plasticity of the brain (neuroplasticity – the ability of the brain to change or adapt as a response to learning) in London taxi drivers.

Someone who wants to be a London taxi driver has to pass exams set by the police in order to get their taxi driver's licence. This is known as 'being on The Knowledge' and involves approximately two years spent learning how to get around London. This requires them to make increasing demands on their spatial memory. It is for this reason – the increased environmental demands on their spatial memory as they acquired 'The Knowledge' – that they were considered excellent participants for this study.

Aims

To investigate the differences in the brain, especially in the hippocampus, in London taxi drivers, and to establish whether, compared to controls, differences in hippocampal volume would be observed. The study also aimed to further investigate the functions of the hippocampus in spatial memory.

Method

Method and design

The study was an experiment using an independent measures design, comparing the brains of London taxi drivers with controls who were not taxi drivers.

In addition, correlational analysis was carried out to see if hippocampal changes increased with time as a taxi driver and were therefore likely to be environmentally determined.

Participants

Taxi drivers

- Sixteen right-handed male London taxi drivers, aged 32–62 (mean age, 44 years).
- All had been licensed London taxi drivers for at least 1.5 years (mean time as a taxi driver, 14.3 years; range, 1.5–42 years).
- The average time they had spent 'being on The Knowledge' was two years.
- All had healthy general medical, neurological and physiological profiles.

Control group

- Fifty right-handed males, aged 32–62 years, who had been scanned for the MRI database at the Wellcome Department of Cognitive Neurology, University College London.
- They were selected so that no females, no left-handers, no under-32s or over-62s, and no one with health problems was included.

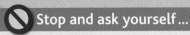

Stop and ask yourself…

- Can you give three reasons why we would need to be cautious before making generalisations about the brains of people in general from this sample?

Links to methodological issues
- Sampling issues and generalisability

Procedure and measurement

The taxi drivers' brains were scanned using an MRI scanner. These were structural MRI scans designed to investigate the anatomy of the brain (its structure), as opposed to functional MRI scans which investigate the physiognomy of the brain (how it works).

Their scans were analysed and compared with the scans of the control participants.

The measurement of brain differences used two techniques:

1. VBM (voxel-based morphometry) was used to measure the grey matter volume and indicate general brain differences between the two conditions. A voxel is a three-dimensional measurement of volume that allows a computer program to calculate the volume of area, in this case the grey matter in the brain in structural MRI scans.

2. Pixel counting was carried out on the scans of the taxi drivers and 16 age-matched controls taken from the 50 control participants. Pixel counting was carried out by 'one person experienced in the technique and blinded to the participants' identity as taxi drivers or controls and the outcome of VBM analysis'. A pixel is a two-dimensional measurement of area. It was possible to calculate differences by pixel-counting 'slices' of the scan. The scan was separated into 26 slices and 24 of these focused on the hippocampus, as follows:
   (a) posterior (rear/back) hippocampus, six slices;
   (b) hippocampus body, 12 slices;
   (c) anterior (front) hippocampus, six slices.

VBM thus confirmed a structural difference in the hippocampi of taxi drivers compared with controls.

What did the pixel-counting analysis of the results show?

Pixel-counting analysis revealed that there was no difference in the overall volume of the hippocampus between taxi drivers and controls.

However, it did show a regionally significant difference by side (right and left) of the hippocampus (see Table 4.4 and Figure 4.18).

Table 4.4 Results from the pixel-counting analysis of the MRI scans of taxi drivers and controls

Anterior hippocampus	The non-taxi drivers (controls) had higher hippocampal volume in the right anterior hippocampus than in the left
Hippocampus body	The taxi drivers showed no difference in overall volume in the hippocampus body compared with controls, but analysis by side showed non-taxi drivers had higher volume in the right side
Posterior hippocampus	The taxi drivers had a generally higher volume in their posterior hippocampus than the non-taxi drivers

Results

What did the VBM analysis of the scans show?

VBM analysis showed that in the taxi drivers there was an increase in grey matter in only two areas of the brain: the left and right hippocampi. There was an *increase* in grey matter bilaterally (that is, on both the left and right sides) of the *posterior* hippocampi, but a *decrease* in grey matter bilaterally in the *anterior* hippocampi.

Figure 4.18 Volumetric analysis findings. (Top right inset) The orientation of the slices measured in the volumetric analysis with respect to the hippocampus (A, anterior; B, body; P, posterior). (Upper) The mean of the cross-sectional area measurements (uncorrected for ICV) for the three regions of the left hippocampus (LH). (Lower) The means for the right hippocampus (RH): taxi drivers had a significantly greater volume relative to controls in the posterior hippocampus, and controls showed greater hippocampal volume in the anterior; there was no difference between the two groups in the hippocampus body ($*p < 0.05$). *Source*: Maguire *et al.* (2000). Copyright 2000 National Academy of Sciences, USA.

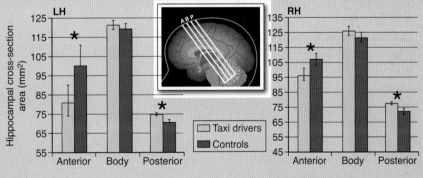

 Stop and ask yourself ...

- Why is it good that the researchers used both pixel counting and VBM to measure the differences between the taxi drivers' and non-taxi drivers' brains?

Links to methodological issues
- Concurrent validity

Correlational analysis of changes to the hippocampus with navigational experience in taxi drivers

The authors carried out a correlational analysis to see if there was a correlation between the VBM analysis of hippocampal volume and time spent as a taxi driver ('time spent' included time spent 'being on The Knowledge' and time practising as a taxi driver after qualifying).

The correlational data showed a positive correlation between one brain area only, namely the right posterior hippocampus, with time spent as a taxi driver (see Figure 4.19). There was a negative correlation between time spent as a taxi driver and the volume of the anterior hippocampus. (The authors report that data were removed from this analysis for one taxi driver who had been in the job for 42 years. Given that the next highest length of time in the job was 28 years, the subject was removed from the analysis for statistical reasons as an outlier. The authors report that evidence from this subject was nonetheless consistent with their general findings from the taxi drivers.)

Conclusions

The authors conclude that 'the data presented in this report provide evidence of regionally specific structural differences between the hippocampi of licensed London taxi drivers and those of control subjects'. Correlational analysis also confirmed that this difference was related to environmental stimulation. Increases/decreases of hippocampal volume in the posterior/anterior hippocampi of taxi drivers with time supports the idea that the brain has changed in response to the demands of being a taxi driver, rather than the idea that people choose to be taxi drivers because they have pre-existing brain differences.

Discussion

The fact that the hippocampal volume correlated positively with the length of time as a taxi driver suggests that the hippocampal changes occur in line with the demands on spatial memory made by their job. This suggests that the human brain has plasticity, the ability to change (at least locally in the hippocampus) to meet the demands of the environment.

The authors report that their findings are consistent with findings from animal studies of rodents and monkeys, as well as studies of patients with brain damage (lesions). Findings from brain-damaged patients where the posterior hippocampus is not damaged demonstrate that the patients can recall cognitive maps they knew before the lesions were present.

In terms of how the hippocampus contributes generally to our spatial memory, the authors suggest that their findings indicate different roles in spatial memory for the anterior and posterior hippocampi. They suggest that the posterior hippocampus is involved when we are using previously learned information, and the anterior hippocampus (along with the posterior hippocampus) is more involved when we are learning about new environmental layouts.

The fact that the right and not the left hippocampal volume correlated with years of taxi driving experience suggests that the left and right sides of the hippocampus have separate functions. The authors suggest that the right holds 'mental maps' and the left holds memories and events not dependent on using such cognitive maps.

The authors suggest that the increased tissue volume in the posterior hippocampus in the taxi drivers occurs to accommodate their vast knowledge and mental map of the layout of London and how to find their way round the city.

In evolutionary terms, the authors point out that the hippocampus is an 'old' part of the brain which may have evolved to deal with navigation. Although in humans it is also adapted to be involved in other types of memory, such as episodic memory (memory

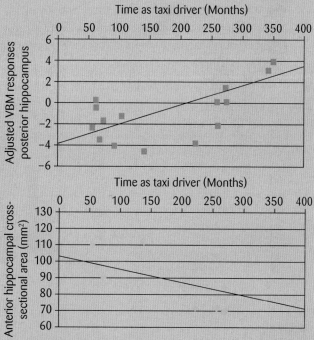

Figure 4.19 Correlation of volume change with time as a taxi driver: in VBM analysis, the volume of grey matter in the right hippocampus was found to correlate significantly with the amount of time spent learning to be and practising as a licensed London taxi driver, positively in the right posterior hippocampus and negatively in the anterior hippocampus. *Source*: Maguire *et al.* (2000). Copyright 2000 National Academy of Sciences, USA.

Stop and ask yourself...

Links to methodological issues

- If the researchers had simply compared taxi drivers and non-taxi drivers' brains experimentally then it might not be clear whether being a taxi driver had really had an influence on the taxi drivers' hippocampi or if the differences had been caused by other factors, or had indeed always been there.

  Can you explain how the correlational evidence supports the idea that being a taxi driver has led to changes in the taxi drivers' hippocampi? (see Discussion on previous page to check your thinking.)

- Check your understanding

Have a go yourself

Put a picture of the hippocampus in the centre of a piece of A4 paper, then map the findings from this study around it to show what was found in terms of differences in the taxi drivers' hippocampi, and what the researchers suggest that this means about the functions of the hippocampi.

for events), it 'retains an ability to store large-scale spatial information'. While the hippocampus does not operate alone, but works with other areas of the brain to support navigation, the key role of the hippocampus seems to be 'crucial to the storage and use of mental maps of our environments'.

The authors concede that structural MRI does not reveal exactly what is happening in the hippocampus to lead to the changes they observed in taxi drivers. However, they offer the theory that what happens is an 'overall reorganization of hippocampal circuitry'.

The study has implications for the rehabilitation of people who have suffered brain damage. The findings show that, at least in certain areas, the brain is capable of adaptation in response to environmental stimulation. People who have suffered brain damage or disease might be helped in the future if it could be shown that areas of the brain other than the hippocampus could respond and change.

Evaluation of the study by Maguire *et al.*

Links to methodological issues

Research methods

- This study was a highly controlled laboratory experiment. It had a quasi-design, as the participants were either taxi drivers or not. A quasi-design is a between-subjects design and could have been affected by subject variables; however, a number of controls were put in place to ensure that the taxi drivers and the non-taxi driving controls were similar to each other (see below under Validity).

- Physiological methods of measurement, such as brain-imaging techniques, are the only method available for this kind of study of the structure of the brain (you cannot self-report about the volume of your hippocampus and it is not directly observable to the naked eye in living participants). The use of technical equipment can be costly, both in terms of equipment and the amount of specialists' time it takes to carry out the tests and analyse the results.

- The use of correlational analysis helped to establish a *relationship* between volume of grey matter in the hippocampus and time spent as a taxi driver, but it could not confirm (for instance) that it was time spent as a taxi driver that was the *cause* of the data for hippocampal volume.

Types of data

- The laboratory setting for the scans enables the use of highly technical equipment (MRI scanning suite) and allows for precise measurement of data. Both the VBM and pixel-counting analysis provided quantitative data (in mm^3) about the volume of grey matter/volume of the hippocampus. Without quantitative data, statistical analysis of the differences between the two groups or analysis of the correlation between VBM measurements and time spent as a taxi driver would have been impossible to establish. Quantitative data enable the reliability and validity of the research to be established. In this study, for example, comparison of the pixel-counting data with the VBM data showed concurrent validity and it would be possible to replicate the study and test its reliability as a result of collecting quantitative data.

Ethical considerations

- The study was carried out according to the British Psychological Society's (1993) ethical guidelines, so there are no ethical concerns: the participants were not deceived; they gave their informed consent; they had the right to withdraw; and they were not negatively affected by their experience.

- Also, given that the study points towards (albeit probably in the distant future) implications for the rehabilitation of brain-damaged patients, we could describe the study as ethically worthy.

Validity

- Matching of the gender, handedness, good psychological and physical health, and age of taxi drivers and control participants for the pixel counting gave a high level of control over the study and means that the study is high in design validity.
- The volume differences in the hippocampus were established by two concurrently valid independent measures (VBM and pixel counting), supporting the validity of the findings.
- The authors had theorised that the hippocampal changes occurred because of being a taxi driver and not because people who already possessed differences in their hippocampi would choose to become taxi drivers. The validity of this theory is supported by the correlational evidence, which showed that the changes in hippocampal volume correlated with time spent as a taxi driver. Changes in the hippocampus were more marked as time spent as a taxi driver increased.
- The validity of the findings is also supported by the fact that evidence from comparative studies with animals and brain-damaged patients are consistent with the findings from the taxi drivers.

Ecological validity

- In terms of ecological validity, being scanned in an MRI scanner is not something that a person would have to do every day. However, in this case, the variable being measured (hippocampal volume) would not be one that the participants could actually falsify, so the data are unlikely to be affected by responses to demand characteristics or the artificiality of the laboratory setting, so it does not affect the outcome of the study if the process of being given an MRI scan lacks ecological validity.

Reliability

- As this was a highly controlled laboratory experiment that collected quantitative data, this study could be repeated and tested to see if it had test–retest reliability

Sample

- A reason to question the validity of this plasticity of the hippocampus being typical of everyone is that the sample is not exactly typical of the general population. It may be that not everyone's brain could or would respond in the same way to the environmental demands of doing 'The Knowledge' and being a taxi driver in London. For a start, there is a clear gender bias in the sample and we cannot assume that female and male brains operate similarly in terms of spatial memory.

Ethnocentrism

- On the one hand, since brain plasticity in the hippocampus in response to the spatial demands of our environment is affected by the anatomy and physiognomy of our brain, we could argue that Maguire et al.'s study is not ethnocentric as it was investigating a species-specific behaviour. On the other hand, it could be that there is something unique to the experience of being on The Knowledge, or something different about those cab drivers who succeed on the course when many drop out, that might mean that the results are in fact only representative of London cab drivers. If this is the case, then the study could be considered to be ethnocentric and we should be cautious in making the assumption that everybody's hippocampus has a similar capacity for brain plasticity.

Links to debates

Psychology as a science

- Maguire et al. carried out a highly controlled experiment and this method fulfils the scientific criteria of theory, control, evidence and replication. As with many biological area studies, this supports the claim that psychology is a scientific discipline. In addition, the data were gathered using an MRI scanner and this objective method of measurement also means that this study can be considered to be highly scientific.

Nature–nurture debate

- Maguire et al.'s study shows how nurture in the form of the environmental demands placed upon the spatial memory of black cab London taxi drivers led to brain plasticity in their hippocampi. Their spatial knowledge improved with experience and as their experience increased so their hippocampi changed to accommodate the demands placed on their spatial memory.

Usefulness

- The study is useful in that it furthers our understanding of how the brain works, and provides evidence about the plasticity of the brain. As the authors suggest, there are implications for brain-damage sufferers in what this study reveals about neuroplasticity: rehabilitation of individuals who have suffered brain damage might be assisted if it was clear which areas of the brain are capable of adaptation and what environmental cues might stimulate them to change.
- The MRI scan is one of a number of brain-imaging techniques that represent relatively new technological advances in science, and are enabling researchers to map the functions and observe the structure of the human brain. As advanced as the technology is, however, it remains limited. As the authors point out, the changes can be observed and quantified, but as yet the underpinning causes of the changes can only be theorised about, and this perhaps limits the usefulness of the study.

Links to areas/perspectives

- Maguire et al.'s study falls within the biological area as it is investigating neuroplasticity in the brains of adult human subjects. Specifically, it demonstrated the plasticity of the hippocampi in London taxi drivers. The study also used an MRI scanner to gather data and this gives biological data. In this case, a structural MRI scanner was used to measure grey matter volume in the hippocampi of the participants.

Links to the key theme

- In relation to the key theme of brain plasticity, Maguire et al.'s study demonstrated that the fully developed adult human brain could change and adapt to environmental demands placed upon it. Specifically, the study showed brain plasticity in the hippocampi of taxi drivers in London on 'The Knowledge', with the hippocampi reducing in volume in the anterior hippocampus and increasing in volume in the posterior hippocampus with time spent as a black cab London taxi driver. This neuroplasticity was explained by the researchers as the hippocampus having to adapt to enable the taxi drivers to meet the very high demands placed on their spatial memory by their job.

- In terms of the extent to which Maguire et al.'s study changes our understanding of the key theme of 'brain plasticity', it clearly adds to Blakemore and Cooper's study in confirming that brain plasticity can occur, but this time in humans rather than cats and in the hippocampus rather than in visual neurones.
- How does the contemporary study by Maguire et al. change our understanding of individual social and cultural diversity?

Since the study by Blakemore and Cooper was conducted on animals rather than humans, the Maguire et al. study cannot be compared with it to show changes in our understanding of individual, social and cultural diversity. However, what Maguire's study does show is that new technology has enabled us to work not only with animals but also with humans when investigating the anatomy and physiognomy of the brain. Brain imaging techniques, such as structural and functional MRI scans, allow research to be carried out to study the live and active human brain, and to identify individual differences in participants' brains that may help to explain individual diversity. For example, the taxi drivers were able to develop their extensive knowledge of London because their hippocampus was able to adapt in order to accommodate the demands placed on their spatial memory.

Comparison with the classic study

- In what ways is the study by Maguire et al. similar to the study by Blakemore and Cooper?
  - The studies both included highly controlled laboratory experiments.
  - The researchers aimed to gather objective evidence. Maguire achieved this by using MRI scans to objectively measure grey matter in the hippocampi of the taxi drivers and Blakemore and Cooper took neurophysiological measures of the visual neurones of the kittens.
  - The studies gathered quantitative data.
  - The studies both constitute examples of brain plasticity.
  - The studies were conducted ethically.
- In what ways is the study by Maguire et al. different from the study by Blakemore and Cooper?
  - Maguire's study was on the human brain, whereas Blakemore and Cooper were studying the brains of cats.

- Maguire's study was a snapshot study, whereas the study by Blakemore and Cooper was longitudinal in design.
- Maguire *et al.* were studying the hippocampus, whereas Blakemore and Cooper were studying visual neurones.

Questions arising from Maguire *et al.*

- What questions are we left with after studying the research by Maguire *et al.*? It would be interesting to find out if learning 'The Knowledge' affects female taxi drivers and left-handed taxi drivers in the same way as it seems to affect male right-handed taxi drivers. It would also be interesting to know if plasticity occurs in other parts of the brain apart from the hippocampus.

 Find out more

- If the studies on regions of the brain and brain plasticity have interested you, you may want to reread the introduction to Chapter 4, The biological area, and you might also want to look in to whether a university degree course in cognitive neuroscience might be something that would interest you.

Practice questions

1. The Maguire *et al.* study on taxi drivers' hippocampi used MRI scans (magnetic resonance imaging):
   (a) Explain what an MRI scan measured in this study. [2 marks]
   (b) Outline one piece of evidence that suggests the brains of taxi drivers are different from the brains of non-taxi drivers. [2 marks]

2. In the study by Maguire *et al.* of taxi drivers' hippocampi:
   (a) Describe two features of the sample. [2 marks]
   (b) Outline one limitation of this sample. [2 marks]

3. From Maguire *et al.*'s study of taxi drivers' hippocampi:
   (a) Identify two controls used in this study. [2 marks]
   (b) Explain why it was important to use controls in this study. [2 marks]

4. Outline one way in which the studies by Blakemore and Cooper (on impact of the visual environment on cats' brains) and Maguire *et al.* (taxi drivers' hippocampi) are similar to each other and one way in which they are different from each other. [4 marks]

5. Suggest one way in which the study by Maguire *et al.* changes our understanding of the key theme of brain plasticity. [3 marks]

Chapter 5

The individual differences area

The other areas of psychology can be characterised as investigating *patterns* in human behaviour (e.g. faced with a particular social situation, or brought up in a particular way, how will people *typically* behave?). To put this another way, their focus is on the ways in which people are *similar*. By way of contrast, the psychology of individual differences is unique in being interested in the ways in which people *differ* and the reasons for these differences. For instance, why do some people have a crippling fear of heights while others don't? Why do some people appear to have much less intellectual ability than others? Why, even, do some people refuse to give 450 volt electric shocks in Milgram's experiment, while others go ahead and do this?

As psychologists working in this area focus more on those whose behaviour falls outside the 'normal', typical or expected range of behaviour, this area is sometimes known as 'abnormal psychology'. This, of course, raises the question of what counts as 'normal' behaviour, and arguments have raged about whether this is a matter of statistics (i.e. what is 'normal' is what is true of the majority of people) or whether it is a question of cultural expectation (i.e. behaviour is 'normal' if it conforms to what society expects of someone of that age, sex, etc.). Neither definition is satisfactory – people with exceptionally high levels of intelligence may be statistically rare, but do we want to describe them as 'abnormal'? Do we want to say that the first people to campaign for women to get the vote or for slavery to be abolished were 'abnormal'? – but questions of how to measure differences between people and of how to understand mental disorders have helped to define the subject matter of this area of psychology.

It is important to note that whilst to some extent this area of psychology has a distinct body of material that it studies (e.g. mental disorders, intelligence and psychometric testing), nonetheless the central thought that sits behind it – namely, that we should focus on how people differ as much as on how they are similar – can be applied to research in all areas of the subject, meaning that the psychology of individual differences is as much of an approach as it is a distinct area of study.

The particular individual differences studies we will be examining are as outlined in Table 5.2.

Table 5.1 Strengths and weaknesses of the individual differences area

Strengths of the individual differences area	Weaknesses of the individual differences area
It enables psychologists to find out about a wider range of human behaviours because all behaviours, not just average ones, are studied.	As it lacks a set of defining beliefs about why people behave the way they do, it is arguable that there is more disagreement within this area than within other areas.
It can have great social benefit, improving our understanding of mental disorders and suggesting treatments.	With much of the research in this area being socially sensitive, it has the potential to be put to harmful use.
It can help to inform the free will–determinism debate, suggesting the extent to which we have control over our behaviour.	The tools for measuring differences that are developed may not always be valid.

Table 5.2 Individual differences studies

Key theme	Classic study	Contemporary study
Understanding disorders	Freud (1909) Little Hans	Baron-Cohen *et al.* (1997) Autism in adults
Measuring differences	Gould (1982) A nation of morons Bias in IQ testing	Hancock *et al.* (2011) Language of psychopaths

Further reading

Baron-Cohen, S., Jolliffe, T., Mortimore, C. and Robertson, M., 1997, 'Another Advanced Test of Theory of Mind: Evidence from Very High Functioning Adults with Autism or Asperger Syndrome'. *Journal of Child Psychology and Psychiatry*, vol. 38, 813–822.

Freud, S.J., 1909, 'Analysis of a Phobia in a Five-Year-Old Boy'. *The Pelican Freud Library, Vol. 8, Case Histories I*, 169–305.

Gould, S.J., 1982, 'A Nation of Morons'. *New Scientist*, vol. 6, 349–352.

Hancock, J.T, Woodworth, M.T., and Porter, S., 2011, 'Hungry Like the Wolf: A Word-Pattern Analysis of the Language of Psychopaths'. *Legal and Criminological Psychology*, vol. 18, no 1, 102–114.

Understanding disorders

People behave in a wide range of ways. Some of these we may find a bit strange and perhaps even worrying. For instance, what if someone couldn't leave the house because they were so concerned about picking up an infection from the world around them? What if someone couldn't remember things that had been said to them only the day before? What if someone were consistently 'flat' in their mood and couldn't be cheered up even by doing things they had always enjoyed in the past?

We may be less troubled by their behaviour if there seems to be a reason for it, but this requires an understanding of how different factors (e.g. physical illness, or devastating events occurring in a person's life) can be the cause of a particular behaviour. How can such an understanding be achieved? Those following a biomedical model of health will seek explanations in terms of single-factor physical causes, while those following a biopsychosocial model of health will argue that a purely biological account of behaviour is too narrow and that it is necessary and appropriate to take account of psychological and social factors as well (Banyard, 2002).

Separate from the question of understanding people's behaviour is the question of whether it is appropriate to describe unusual behaviour as a disorder. To a large extent, the practice of doing this can be traced back to the work of Emil Kraepelin in the late nineteenth century. Following a biomedical model of health, he observed that certain groups of symptoms tended to appear together on a sufficiently regular basis for it to be possible to view them as having an underlying physical cause. He proposed two main groups of severe mental disorder – dementia praecox (an early name for schizophrenia, which Kraepelin believed to be caused by a chemical imbalance) and manic-depressive psychosis (which he believed to be caused by an irregularity in metabolism) – thereby beginning the process of trying to classify mental disorders (Davison and Neale, 2001).

Today, many different systems of classification are used, with two of the most commonly used being the International Classification of Diseases (ICD, currently in its tenth edition), and the *Diagnostic and Statistical Manual of Mental Disorders* (DSM, currently in its fifth edition). Such manuals help with the diagnosis of a disorder, but they rest on an understanding being achieved of what it means to experience a particular disorder, how one disorder differs from another and what causes a particular disorder to develop. How (in terms of research methods) can such an understanding be achieved, and what concepts are the best ones to draw upon to explain the development of a disorder?

It is at this point that we need to turn to our two core studies. In our classic study, Sigmund Freud will use the case study method and psychodynamic principles to explain phobias. In our contemporary study, Simon Baron-Cohen will use the quasi-experiment method and cognitive principles to explain autistic spectrum disorders. Whilst these two studies will seem very different from each other, nonetheless it is important to keep in mind that in many ways they are engaged in the same enterprise – namely, a desire to understand the disorders on which they are focused. Where they differ is in the methods and concepts through which they seek to do this.

Freud (1909)

There are many things of which young children can be afraid. For example, they may be fearful of thunderstorms, of clowns, or of drowning in the bath. Why do children develop the fears that they do, and are such fears a normal part of growing up or are they pathological (i.e. a disorder requiring treatment)? Different psychologists give very different answers to these questions, but none has given answers that have aroused more controversy than Sigmund Freud. For him, there is always a deeper meaning to the fears that children have, with the fears being merely the surface expression of inner conflicts relating to a child's psychosexual development. If a psychoanalyst can help to decode a child's fears and explain to the child what it is that he is really afraid of, Freud believes this will be the way to overcome the child's fears. For him, then, fears/phobias have meanings and it is the job of the psychoanalyst (rather like that of a detective) to discover these meanings and bring them out into the open.

Background

To be able to understand the case study of Little Hans, it is necessary to know a bit about Freud's theory of psychosexual development. This was a theory that he was developing at about the same time, and as the case study of Little Hans was seen by Freud to provide evidence in support of his theory, so the theory gave Freud ideas that were used in the treatment of Little Hans.

Freud believed in the existence of a sexual instinct and, according to him, sexual impulses are '... already present in the new-born child' (7; page 92) and usually emerge '... in a form accessible to observation round about the third or fourth year of life' (7; page 92). In children, the sexual instinct '... is not directed towards other people, but obtains satisfaction from the subject's own body' (7; page 97) through a series of 'pre-destined erotogenic zones' (7; page 100), as follows:

- **The oral stage** – Freud regards thumb-sucking as '... a sexual manifestation' (7; page 97). For him, '... sucking at his mother's breast, or at substitutes for it' (7; page 98) will have been the child's 'first and most vital activity' (7; page 98) and thumb-sucking is seen as a way of experiencing this pleasure all over again, with the child's lips behaving '... like an erotogenic zone' (7; page 98) that gains 'sexual satisfaction' (7; page 98) from the 'rhythmic character' (7; page 99) of the sucking process.
- **The anal stage** – erotogenic zones are defined by Freud as parts '... of the skin or mucous membrane in which stimuli of a certain sort evoke a feeling of pleasure' (7; page 99), and the anus is another such part of the body. According to Freud, if a child is '... holding back their stool till its accumulation brings about violent muscular contractions' (7; page 103), then this is a sign that the child is gaining pleasurable sensations from his anus.
- **The phallic stage** – the third stage in '... this early efflorescence of infantile sexual life (between the ages of two and five)' (7; page 158) centres on the genital zones which, 'even during their earliest infancy' (7; page 105), children are likely to have noticed are capable of producing pleasurable feelings. Boys can be expected to manipulate their genitals frequently during this stage, and they can also expect to find that '... adults do not approve of this behaviour' (7; page 316), with a threat being announced that his penis will be taken away from him. During this stage, boys and girls both notice (perhaps through sight of siblings or playmates) that it is only boys who possess a penis, and they will develop theories to make sense of this. One such theory is that girls lack a penis because they have been castrated. The fear that this could happen to them becomes particularly real to young boys because, during this stage, children see their parents as sexual objects with '... the son being drawn towards his mother and the daughter towards her father' (7; page 150). During this stage (which is known as the Oedipus complex), the boy '... regards his father as a disturbing rival and would like to get rid of him and take his place' (7; page 333). However, he has such an intense fear that he will be punished for his desires through castration that his Oedipal desires are 'literally smashed to pieces' (7; page 341) and the boy channels his energies elsewhere.
- **The latency stage** – following the destruction of the Oedipus complex, '... the onset of sexual development in human beings '... is interrupted by the period of latency' (7; page 158) in which the child's energies are '... diverted, wholly or in great part, from their sexual use and directed to other ends' (7; page 94). Examples might include a growing interest in sport, hobbies or friendships.
- **The genital stage** – with the onset of puberty, '... the sexual instinct emerges with greater intensity' (7; page 95); however, this time, the child's sexual inclinations will be 'diverted away' from their parents on to other people, albeit '... other people who resemble them' (7; page 159).

Aim

Freud's theory of infantile sexuality had been developed on the basis of treatment of adults. However, Freud recognised the need for a '... more direct and less roundabout proof' (8; page 170) of his theories than making inferences about what might have been the cause of his adult patients' symptoms. In particular, he believed that it must be possible to observe '... in children at first hand and in all the freshness of life the sexual impulses and wishes which we dig out so laboriously in adults from among their own debris' (8; page 170). The case of Little Hans, therefore, can be seen as an attempt by Freud to provide evidence in support of his theory of psychosexual development, with the 'results' from the case study consisting of the various fantasies and dreams that Little Hans reported himself as having.

For Little Hans' parents, their aim was to use psychoanalysis to gain access to the boy's 'repressed wishes' (8; page 275) and thereby overcome the 'nervous disorder' (8; page 185) he had developed.

Sample

Given his aim (above), Freud had been urging his pupils and friends 'to collect observations of the sexual life of children' (8; page 170). Freud had had a connection with Hans' parents since the time when his '... beautiful mother fell ill with a neurosis as a result of conflict during her girlhood' (8; page 298), and he describes Hans' parents as both being among his 'closest adherents' (8; page 170). The first reports he received about Hans dated from '... a period when he was not quite three years old' (8; page 170) and those early observations began 'to rouse an expectation that much, if not most, of what Little Hans [would show would] turn out to be typical of the sexual development of children in general' (8; page 171). Hans had been born in April 1903 and lived with his parents in Vienna, Austria. It was in 1906 that Freud first received reports about him, although the actual analysis (treatment) of Little Hans lasted from January 1908 until May 1908.

Research method

As this investigation comprised an in-depth study of a single individual (Little Hans), it can be described as a case study. While the case history is published in Freud's name, it is important to note that the actual analysis of Little Hans was conducted by the boy's father. He would send written reports to Freud of conversations he had had with Little Hans, and Freud would write back to him suggesting alternative interpretations of Hans' dreams and fantasies, as well as directions in which to take the conversations with Hans. For most of the case history, it was weekly reports that Freud received from Little Hans' father.

During the course of the analysis, Freud only met Little Hans once, on 30 March 1908. The consultation was described by Freud as 'a short one' (8; page 203) but, after it, he '... received almost daily reports of the alterations in the little patient's condition' (8; page 205). It is worth noting that Hans was very aware that his father was writing to Freud about his 'nonsense' (as Little Hans' father described his anxieties), and on many occasions he wondered aloud what 'the professor' would make of his dreams and fantasies.

🚫 Stop and ask yourself...

- What do you think of the fact that Little Hans was aware that his father was writing to Freud about him? What is good about this? What is less good about it?

Links to methodological issues
- Validity/ethics

Case history and analysis

The letters that Little Hans' father sent to Freud showed him to have a lively interest in his 'widdler'. When he was three and a half years old, his mother found him with his hands on his penis and threatened him by saying, 'If you do that, I shall send for Dr A to cut off your widdler.' For Freud, this was when Little Hans' anxieties would begin as from this date he began to fear loss of his penis; however, the effects of this castration complex would not emerge straight away but instead come out later.

At the age of four and a half, Hans made what Freud described as the first of two attempts at seducing his mother. He was given his usual daily bath by his mother. Afterwards, she was powdering around his penis and taking care not to touch it. Hans said, 'Why don't you put your finger there?' (8; page 182). His mother replied, 'Because it's not proper.' Hans then said, laughing, 'But it's great fun.' The second seduction attempt occurred soon afterwards when Hans climbed into his mother's bed one morning and said, 'Do you know what Aunt M said? She said, "He *has* got a dear little thingummy"' (8; page 186).

🚫 Stop and ask yourself...

- Is Freud correct to interpret these comments as attempts by Little Hans at seducing his mother? Is that what is going on here?

Links to methodological issues
- Validity

It was at this same time that Little Hans became a 'case' requiring treatment when, in January 1908, he suddenly developed such a fear of being bitten by horses that he became afraid of going out into the street. It turned out that Little Hans had previously heard someone say, 'Don't put your finger to the white horse or it'll bite you', which might be thought to explain where his fear had come from. However, for Freud, it wasn't this simple; instead, what Freud thought Little Hans was really afraid of was not so much being bitten by a horse as having his widdler cut off: 'the threat of castration made to him by his mother some fifteen months earlier was now having a deferred effect upon him' (8; page 278).

In late March 1908, Little Hans surprised his parents one night by climbing into their bed. The next day, he explained why he had done this, 'In the night there was a big giraffe in the room and a crumpled one; and the big one called out because I took the crumpled one away from it. Then it stopped calling out; and then I sat down on top of the crumpled one' (8; page 199). He hadn't been afraid and he was adamant that it had been something he had thought of, rather than a dream. As he had visited Schönbrunn zoo five days earlier, it might be thought that Hans' giraffe fantasy could be easily explained as a memory of animals seen there. However, Hans' parents weren't prepared to settle for such an easy explanation. Instead, Hans' father decoded it as follows: 'The big giraffe is myself, or rather my big penis (the long neck), and the crumpled giraffe is my wife, or rather her genital organ ... Thus the solution ... is this: he was seized in the night with a longing for his mother, for her caresses, for her genital organ, and came into our bedroom for that reason' (8; page 201).

Shortly after this incident, the visit to Freud took place. It was during this short consultation that Freud learned that Hans '... was particularly bothered by what horses wear in front of their eyes and by the black

Figure 5.1 Little Hans' giraffe fantasy

 Stop and ask yourself...

- What do you think about this as an interpretation of the giraffe fantasy? Is Little Hans' father right to ignore the easy explanation for Hans' fantasy and to opt for this more sexualised interpretation instead?

Links to methodological issues
- Validity

Figure 5.2 Little Hans was afraid of horses, particularly disliking their blinkers and muzzle

round their mouths' (8; page 203). Freud immediately interpreted this as a fear of Little Hans' father, with the horses' blinkers being like his father's glasses and their muzzle being like his father's moustache.

Further conversations with his father now revealed that Hans' fear of horses was even more wide-ranging than had previously been thought. He admitted that he was also afraid of carts, furniture vans and buses because he was worried that when they turned they would fall over. Yet again, there was a straightforward explanation for these fears that could have been accepted – namely, that when he had been out with his mother he had seen a bus-horse fall down and kick out with its feet. However, the question Hans' father asked Little Hans suggested that he thought there was more going on in these fears than this. He asked, 'When the horse fell down, did you think of your daddy?' Hans' reply was 'Perhaps. Yes. It's possible' (8; page 213).

 Stop and ask yourself...

- What do you think of the way Little Hans' father posed this question? Do you see any problems with it? Are there any other (better) ways in which he could have worded it?

If it was beginning to appear as if horses represented his father and Hans had a wish that his father would fall down in the same way that the horse had done, it got more complicated when Hans confessed that he was '… very much afraid of coal-carts, too … because they're so heavily loaded' (8; page 216).

At this same time, it emerged that Hans was preoccupied with 'lumf' (faeces), and this became a point of discussion between Hans and his father. Under questioning from his father, little Hans admitted that he had often been in the toilet with his mother and also with Berta, '…one of the girls he had been playing with' (8; page 183). He said that he liked 'very much' (8; page 224) being there when his mother either 'widdled' or did 'lumf.' In many ways, his preoccupation with 'lumf' could easily be explained as he had 'trouble with his stools from the very first' suffering from 'habitual constipation' (8; page 217) until, under medical advice, he had reduced his food intake. However, Little Hans' father saw more significance to it than this, believing that his 'fear of defecation and his fear of heavily loaded carts is equivalent to the fear of a heavily loaded stomach' (8; page 226).

For Freud, Little Hans' father was now 'beginning to get a glimmering of the true state of affairs' (8; p226) as what seemed to be happening was that Hans was grappling with the question of where babies come from and he was hypothesising that they come from inside the mother's body like a 'lumf'. This idea – that, for Hans, children were 'lumfs' – seemed to be supported by the way he invented the name 'Lodi' for a child that he talked about. A 'saffalodi' is a kind of sausage and, as Hans' father pointed out to him, saffalodi sausages look like lumf. Could it be that the heavily loaded horses that little Hans feared were symbolic not only of his father but of his mother in childbirth, delivering a new baby? This would fit with Freud's theory that 'it would be possible to trace back Hans' phobia to thoughts and wishes occasioned by the birth of his baby sister' (8; p235).

On 11 April 1908, Hans reported the first of two plumber fantasies. Hans said, 'I was in the bath, and then the plumber came and unscrewed it. Then he took a big borer and stuck it into my stomach' (8; page 226). Later on that day, he admitted that when he was in the big bath he was afraid that his mother would let him go and that his head would go under

the water. His father asked, 'Perhaps it was because you'd been naughty and thought she didn't love you anymore?' Hans replied, 'Yes.' Hans' father then asked, 'When you were watching Mummy give Hanna [Little Hans' younger sister] her bath, perhaps you wished she would let go of her so that Hanna should fall in?' Hans replied, 'Yes.' (8; page 227). His fear of the bath was seen, then, as a fear that he would be punished for the death-wish he had towards his sister – a death-wish that was claimed to arise from a desire to have his mother all to himself.

By 26 April, Hans' father was able to report that Hans' anxiety had almost completely disappeared, although he still liked to remain in the vicinity of their house. Four days later, while Hans was playing with his imaginary children, he explained to his father that he was the children's daddy, that his mummy was their mummy and that he (Hans' father) was their granddaddy. As Freud put it, 'Things were moving towards a satisfactory conclusion. The Little Oedipus had found a happier solution than that prescribed by destiny. Instead of putting his father out of the way, he had … made him a grandfather and married *him* to his own mother too' (8; page 256).

On 2 May 1908, Hans now reported a final fantasy. 'The plumber came; and first he took away my behind with a pair of pincers, and then gave me another, and then the same with my widdler' (8; page 257). Hans' father sought clarification about this. 'He gave you a *bigger* widdler and a *bigger* behind.' Hans replied, 'Yes.' Hans' father then said, 'Like Daddy's; because you'd like to be Daddy.' Hans replied, 'Yes, and I'd like to have a moustache like yours and hair like yours [pointing to the hairs on his father's chest].' (8; page 257). This fantasy was seen as a new version of the previous plumber fantasy, with both being interpreted as an overcoming of his castration complex – in both fantasies, Hans was accepting that the doctor (the plumber) did indeed come and take away his penis, but the outcome was a happy one as in both cases it was only to exchange it for a bigger version.

Have a go yourself

Try representing the case study of Little Hans in cartoon strip format. Build in as many actual quotes as you can.

Conclusions

From Freud's perspective, he claims to have '... learnt nothing new from this analysis, nothing that [he] had not already been able to discover (though often less distinctly and more indirectly) from other patients analysed at a more advanced age' (8; page 303). As such, Little Hans' story was that of '... a little Oedipus who wanted to have his father "out of the way", to get rid of him, so that he might be alone with his beautiful mother and sleep with her' (8; page 269). Although Little Hans was able to resolve his Oedipus complex in a happy way (instead of gaining access to his mother by getting rid of his father, he elevated him to the role of grandfather), nonetheless Freud would like to see this case as '... being a type and a model' (8; page 303).

Discussion

Freud anticipated two main criticisms that would be made of his work. In the first place, he anticipated critics arguing that Little Hans was not a normal child, meaning that it would not be legitimate to '... apply to other, normal children conclusions which might perhaps be true [only] of him' (8; page 260). Freud replies to this point by describing Little Hans as '... a cheerful, amiable, active-minded young fellow' (8; page 298) whose '... illness may perhaps have been no more serious than that of many other children who are not branded as "degenerates"' (8; page 299).

The other 'more uncompromising objection' (8; page 260) he anticipated being made was that, with the analysis of Little Hans being conducted by his father, critics would say that Hans was just giving his father the material that he wanted to hear 'out of gratitude to his father for taking so much notice of him' (8; page 261) and that, therefore, his dreams and fantasies were simply the product of 'suggestion' and the whole case history was '... devoid of any objective worth' (8; page 260). Freud has three replies to this. In the first place, Freud accepts that '... during the analysis Hans had to be told many things that he could not say himself, that he had to be presented with thoughts which he had so far shown no signs of possessing' (8; page 262), but he would defend this on the grounds that it is central to the 'interpretative technique' (8; page 278) that the psychoanalyst is 'a step in front of him [the patient] in knowledge' (8; page 278), and this is particularly true of children who may, on account of the small development of their intellectual systems, require 'especially energetic assistance' (8; page 263). Second, Freud argues that

Hans '... gave evidence of enough independence to acquit him upon the charge of 'suggestion'' (8; page 263). Third, Freud does not '... share the view ... that assertions made by children are invariably arbitrary and untrustworthy' (8; page 261), and feels that 'statements made by adults offer no greater certainty' (8; page 262).

Finally, he is at pains to emphasise that this analysis did not do Little Hans any harm. Contrary to the risk of 'wicked instincts ... [being] strengthened by being made conscious' (8; page 300), Freud claims that '... the only results of the analysis were that Hans recovered, that he ceased to be afraid of horses, and that he got on to rather familiar terms with his father' (8; page 301). As further evidence of this, Freud reports how, in 1922, 'a strapping youth of nineteen' (8; page 304) introduced himself to Freud and informed him that he was 'Little Hans'. This young man 'could remember nothing' (8; page 304) of the psychoanalysis, but '... declared that he was perfectly well, and suffered from no troubles or inhibitions' (8; page 304).

Evaluation of the study by Freud
Links to methodological issues
Research method

- As this was a case study, it raises the issue of generalisability that Freud himself anticipated. You will need to decide for yourself the extent to which Little Hans was a boy whose feelings and experiences were typical of those of other children, such that he can help to give validity to the theories of infantile sexuality that Freud developed.
- Another problem that can arise with case studies is that of such a close bond developing between the people involved that the researcher can lose objectivity and the person being studied can be keen to give the researcher what they want to hear. Given that in this case it was a father analysing his son, this could be expected to be a particular concern.

🚫 Stop and ask yourself...

- Can Freud have this both ways? Can Little Hans be both someone who was unwell enough to need treatment and someone whose experiences are typical of all children? Is he someone from whom it is possible to generalise?

Links to methodological issues
- Sample

Usefulness

- In Freud's own words, he describes the aim of psychoanalysis as being '... to enable the patient to obtain a conscious grasp of his unconscious wishes' (8; page 278), replacing '... the process of repression ... by a temperate and purposeful control on the part of the highest agencies of the mind' (8; page 301). It certainly aims to be of use to those in receipt of it and, according to Freud, Little Hans seemed to benefit from it.

Links to areas/perspectives

- Freud's study falls within the individual differences area because it is investigating a way in which people differ – namely, by experiencing phobias.
- It can also be seen as coming from the psychodynamic perspective because of the way in which Freud explains Little Hans' behaviours (his phobias as well as his fantasies) as arising from unconscious forces, in this case the psychosexual stages of development through which he was progressing.
- Freud's study could also be seen as developmental because it is concerned with something that affects how a child grows up – namely, how they progress through the psychosexual stages.

Links to the key theme

- In relation to the key theme of understanding disorders, Freud's study would appear to tell us that this can be done through an understanding of unconscious conflicts.
- However, there are many questions that arise from Freud's study, such as:
  - Is it only in psychodynamic terms that phobias can be understood? (As we have seen, behaviourists and followers of John Bowlby would both claim that there are other, non-psychodynamic, ways in which anxiety disorders can be explained.)

- Would a psychodynamic approach be appropriate in the understanding of other disorders (such as autism)?
- Is the case study method the best, or only, way to try and achieve an understanding of disorders? (Is it not possible, for example, to use the experimental method?)
- It is because of questions like this that it will be helpful to look at the study by Baron-Cohen *et al.* as this suggests other ways in which to try understanding disorders.

🔍 Find out more

- Fancy a day out? If you live anywhere near London, you could make a visit to the house in which Freud lived after he fled Vienna in 1938. It is in Hampstead and contains wonderful artefacts, such as a pair of Freud's spectacles and the couch on which patients would lie. The shop also contains souvenirs that make great (if slightly odd) presents.

📝 Practice questions

1. From Freud's study of Little Hans:
   - (a) Outline Little Hans' giraffe fantasy. [2 marks]
   - (b) Outline how Little Hans' giraffe fantasy was interpreted by his father. [2 marks]
2. From Freud's study of Little Hans:
   - (a) Suggest one strength of the case study method used in this study. [2 marks]
   - (b) Suggest one weakness of the case study method used in this study. [2 marks]
3. Outline one reason why Freud's study of Little Hans may be considered to lack validity. [3 marks]
4. Suggest why Freud's study of Little Hans can be placed within the individual differences area. [2 marks]

Baron-Cohen et al. (1997)

Autism is described by the National Autistic Society on their website as '... a lifelong developmental disability that affects how a person communicates with, and relates to, other people. It also affects how they make sense of the world around them.' It is described further as '... a spectrum condition, which means that, while all people with autism share certain difficulties, their condition will affect them in different ways.' The difficulties they share are sometimes known as the 'triad of impairments' and these are generally divided into three groups:

- Difficulties with social communication (e.g. people with autism may not 'read' a person's facial expression or tone of voice; they may also struggle to understand jokes and sarcasm, and even everyday expressions such as 'That's cool').
- Difficulties with social interaction (e.g. people with autism may behave in ways that others will see as inappropriate, such as standing too close to another person or starting up a conversation 'out of the blue'.
- Difficulties with social imagination (e.g. people with autism may find it hard to predict what might happen next or to anticipate danger).

People with autism may also have a love of routines, sensory sensitivity, and very keen interests in particular fields. It is thought that around 1 in 100 people in the UK have autism, and it seems to occur more often in males than in females. While autism can co-occur with learning disabilities, people can also be diagnosed with 'high-functioning autism'. Asperger syndrome (AS) is another disorder on the autistic spectrum. This is very similar to high-functioning autism, with the main difference seeming to centre on the way in which people with high-functioning autism will (and people with Asperger syndrome typically won't) have experienced a delay in their language development when younger.

There is much that remains unknown about autism. For example, while it is currently believed that autism arises from genetic and environmental factors that combine to cause changes in brain development, nonetheless the cause of autism is still not known for certain. There is also no known 'cure' for autism, although there are various interventions that can help in alleviating symptoms. As a further indication of how little has been known about autism, what Simon Baron-Cohen has engaged with in his work has been perhaps the most fundamental question of all – namely, trying to understand exactly what it is, and whether there is a single feature of it (a core deficit) that applies to all people diagnosed with the disorder.

Aims

Baron-Cohen himself had shown in previous research that children with autism have impairments in the development of a theory of mind, by which he means the ability to infer what another person is thinking or feeling. More recent research (e.g. Bowler, 1992; Ozonoff et al., 1991) had, however, appeared to suggest that adults with autism could succeed even on so-called second-order theory of mind tests (Table 5.3).

Table 5.3 First- and second-order theory of mind tests

First-order theory of mind tests	These test the ability of the participant to work out the thoughts that another person might have.
Second-order theory of mind tests	These test the ability of the participant to work out the thoughts that another person might have about the thoughts of someone else.

Baron-Cohen et al.'s concern with this research was that the tests they used were not sufficiently complex and that, as children with normal intelligence pass second-order theory of mind tests at about six years of age, using such tests on adults with autism could produce a ceiling effect. To put this another way, just because an adult with autism might be able to succeed on a test designed for a six-year-old doesn't automatically mean that they don't have a problem with theory of mind as the tests will place a cap on what they can or can't show.

Francesca Happé had recognised this problem and, in research conducted in 1994, she had tested adults with autism or AS on an 'advanced' test of theory of mind in which participants were presented with a story and had to make inferences about a character's mental state. While this so-called Strange Stories task was undoubtedly more advanced than previous tests of theory of mind, nonetheless even this test was pitched at the level of a normal eight- to nine-year-old child so imposed a 'ceiling' of its own on what participants could show.

Consequently, one of Baron-Cohen et al.'s aims in their 1997 study was to develop another 'advanced' test of theory of mind, but this time one that would properly test the theory of mind competence of adults. The test that Baron-Cohen would develop was known as the 'Reading the Mind in the Eyes' Task, or the Eyes Task for short. It would require participants to look at photographs of the eye region and make a forced choice between which of two words best described what the person in the photograph might be thinking or feeling. It would be used with three groups of participants.

Participants

Group 1 consisted of 16 people with either high-functioning autism (four of them) or Asperger syndrome (12 of them). They were all of normal intelligence (i.e. they scored >85 on the Wechsler Adult Intelligence Test, revised edition [WAIS-R]) and could be considered as cases of 'pure' autism as their disorder was not confounded by additional learning difficulties. They had a mean age of 28.6 years (range, 18–49 years) and were recruited from a variety of clinical sources, as well as from an advertisement placed in *Communication*, the magazine for the National Autistic Society. There were 13 males and three females in this group.

Group 2 consisted of 50 'normal' adults (25 male and 25 female). They were assumed to all have intelligence in the normal range, and they had a mean age of 30.0 years (range, 18–48 years). They came from the general population of Cambridge (excluding members of the university) and were selected at random from a subject panel held in the university department. They had no history of any psychiatric condition.

Group 3 consisted of ten adults with Tourette syndrome (eight male and two female). A short version of the WAIS-R was administered on these participants to confirm that they were all in the normal IQ range. Their mean age was 27.77 years (range, 18–47 years), and they were recruited from a tertiary referral centre in London.

Why were groups 2 and 3 included?

The people in group 2 were included largely as a control group so that Baron-Cohen *et al.* could establish what a 'normal' level of performance on the Eyes Task would be for an adult. In addition to this, though, there was a secondary hypothesis that they wanted to test (see below), which is why they included relatively large numbers of 'normal' people in their sample.

The people in group 3 were included because Tourette syndrome has a number of similarities with autism and Asperger syndrome. In particular, they are all childhood-onset disorders that cause disruption to both normal schooling and normal peer relations; on top of this, they all seem to have a strong genetic basis to them which is believed to involve abnormalities in the frontal regions of the brain; they also all affect males more than females.

Hypotheses

Baron-Cohen *et al.* had two main hypotheses:

1. They predicted that the participants with autism or AS, in spite of being adults of normal or above average intelligence, would show a significant impairment on the Eyes Task relative to the other two groups.
2. They predicted that, in line with 'folk psychology', the normal females would perform significantly better on the Eyes Task than would the normal males.

Procedure

Participants were tested individually in a quiet room either in their own home, in the researchers' clinic, or in a laboratory at the university. There were four tasks that the participants were given to do, with these being presented to them in a randomised order.

The four tasks were as follows:

1. **The Eyes Task**: Participants were shown 25 photographs for 3 seconds each. The photographs were taken from magazines, were all in black and white, and were all standardised to the same size of 15 × 10 cm (Figure 5.3). The photographs were of the eye region of a person's face and, in the case of each pair of eyes, participants were asked, 'Which word best describes what this person is thinking or feeling?' Underneath each photograph, there were two mental state terms that they had to choose from, and these were always semantic opposites (as shown in Table 5.4) on p.161. The photographs were all of different faces (male and female) and the maximum score was 25.

Figure 5.3 The Eyes Task

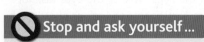

Stop and ask yourself…

- What do you think about the numbers of participants in each condition? Are the numbers large enough? Is it realistic to expect Baron-Cohen *et al.* to be able to obtain more participants than they have?
- Does it matter that all participants were from the UK?

Links to methodological issues
- Sample

How was the Eyes Task developed?

The photographs were shown to four judges (two male and two female) and, in open discussion, they reached a decision about the mental state behind each pair of eyes. This was described as the 'target' word. For a 'foil' (distracter) word, the semantic opposite of the target word was always selected.

These pairs of words were then tested on a panel of eight additional judges (four male and four female) who were all independent raters and blind to the hypotheses in the study. There was complete agreement between them on the target words.

Table 5.4 The target words used for the Eyes Task, and their foils

Target word	Foil
Concerned	Unconcerned
Noticing you	Ignoring you
Attraction	Repulsion
Relaxed	Worried
Serious message	Playful message
Interested	Disinterested
Friendly	Hostile
Sad reflection	Happy reflection
Sad thought	Happy thought
Certain	Uncertain
Far away focus	Near focus
Reflective	Unreflective
Reflective	Unreflective
Cautious about something over there	Relaxed about something over there
Noticing someone else	Noticing you
Calm	Anxious
Dominant	Submissive
Fantasising	Noticing
Observing	Daydreaming
Desire for you	Desire for someone else
Ignoring you	Noticing you
Nervous about you	Interested in you
Flirtatious	Disinterested
Sympathetic	Unsympathetic
Decisive	Indecisive

Have a go yourself

Try creating your own version of Baron-Cohen *et al.*'s Eyes Task using the same target and foil terms.

2. **The Strange Stories Task**: The way this task operates is described by Francesca Happé in her book *Autism*. It involves participants being presented with two examples of each of 12 story types. These include Lie, White Lie, Joke, Figure of Speech, and Irony. In each story, a character says something which is not literally true, and the participant is asked to explain why the character said what he or she did. An example would be as follows: *'One day, while she is playing in the house, Anna accidentally knocks over and breaks her mother's favourite crystal vase. Oh dear, when mother finds out she will be very cross! So when Anna's mother comes home and sees the broken vase and asks Anna what happened, Anna says, "The dog knocked it over, it wasn't my fault!"'* (In this case, the correct answer would be that she's telling a lie.) Answers on the Strange Stories task are scored as either correct or incorrect, and as either involving mental states/psychological factors (e.g. 'Said it to fool her') or involving physical states (e.g. 'Because the dog is big').
3. **Gender Recognition Task**: This task involved the participants looking at the same sets of eyes that were used in the Eyes Task, but this time their task was to identify the gender of the person in each photograph. The maximum score on this task was 25.
4. **Basic Emotion Recognition Task**: In this task, participants were shown photographs of whole faces (Figure 5.4). Six faces were used and they displayed the six basic emotions (based on the categories proposed by Ekman in 1992). These were happy, sad, angry, afraid, disgust and surprise.

Stop and ask yourself ...

- What do you think of the way in which the Eyes Task was constructed (particularly the fact that it required those taking the test to choose from one of two semantically opposite words)?
- Why did Baron-Cohen *et al.* bother to include 25 pairs of eyes in the test, instead of (say) ten?
- Why did Baron-Cohen *et al.* bother to test the pairs of words on eight additional judges?

Links to methodological issues
- Validity

- Reliability

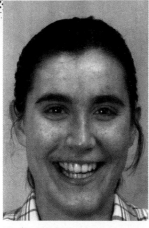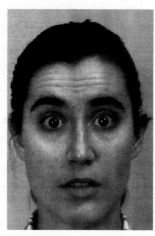

Figure 5.4 Examples of basic emotions

Why were these other tasks included?

- The Strange Stories Task was included in order to validate the Eyes Task as a theory of mind task. As Baron-Cohen *et al.* put it, 'If the Eyes Task was indeed tapping theory of mind, then performance on the Eyes Task should correlate with performance on Happé's strange stories.'
- The other two tasks were included as control tasks, enabling Baron-Cohen *et al.* to check whether deficits on the Eyes Task were due to other factors.

Results

In relation to Baron-Cohen *et al.*'s first hypothesis, performance on the Eyes Task was as outlined in Table 5.5.

Table 5.5 Perfomance on the Eyes Task in relation to the first hypothesis

Condition	Mean score (max 25)	Standard deviation	Range
High-functioning autism or Asperger syndrome	16.3	2.90	13–23
Normal	20.3	2.63	16–25
Tourette syndrome	20.4	2.63	16–25

In relation to Baron-Cohen *et al.*'s second hypothesis, performance on the Eyes Task was as outlined in Table 5.6.

Table 5.6 Perfomance on the Eyes Task in relation to the second hypothesis

Gender of people in the normal group	Mean score (max 25)	Standard deviation	Range
Males	18.8	2.53	16–22
Females	21.8	1.78	20–25

Conclusions

Baron-Cohen *et al.* conclude from their findings that adults with autism or Asperger syndrome, despite being of normal or above average intelligence, have subtle deficits in their mindreading ability. They also conclude that, within the normal population, adult females are significantly better at mindreading than adult males.

Discussion

In the case of both hypotheses, the results from the experiment supported Baron-Cohen *et al.*'s predictions.

In relation to the first hypothesis, while there was no significant difference in performance on the Eyes Task between the normal participants (combined male and female) and the Tourette syndrome group, both groups performed significantly better on this task than the group with high-functioning autism or Asperger syndrome. As we are told that the participants with autism or AS were also significantly impaired on Happé's Strange Stories Task (relative to the other two groups), Baron-Cohen *et al.* interpret their findings as providing experimental support for subtle theory of mind deficits in individuals with autism or AS at later points in development and at higher points on the IQ continuum than had previously been demonstrated.

In relation to their second hypothesis, the difference in performance on the Eyes Task between normal females and normal males was statistically significant. The fact that this had not been seen in previous studies of theory of mind is attributed by Baron-Cohen *et al.* to the use by other researchers of mostly all-or-none, pass-or-fail type tests. In terms, though, of whether the female advantage on the mind-reading task reflects either genetics or socialisation, more research needs to be done.

Evaluation of the study by Baron-Cohen *et al.*

Links to methodological issues

Research method

- Baron-Cohen *et al.*'s study can be seen as using a quasi-experimental method, with the naturally occurring independent variable being whether the participants had been diagnosed with high-functioning autism or Asperger syndrome (group 1), were 'normal' (group 2), or had been diagnosed with Tourette syndrome (group 3).
- It can be seen as having an independent measures design as, although efforts were made to ensure

that the participants in each group were similar in key respects (especially their age and IQ levels), they were not formally matched in triplets before being assigned to their condition.

- The inclusion of the two control groups helped to isolate the extent to which it was autism or Asperger syndrome that was affecting adults in their ability to recognise the emotion in a person's eyes.

Data

- The answers that participants gave on the various tasks were expressed in numerical or quantitative form (e.g. the number of correct answers, out of 25, on the Eyes Task).
- This made it possible for results to be compared across the different conditions of the experiment, but qualitative data might have been helpful in illuminating *why* the participants chose the particular mental state words that they did.

Ethics

- It can be assumed that the participants gave their consent to take part but it is unclear what they were told about the tasks they were given to do. As it would have meant explaining the very concept that the participants on the autistic spectrum were hypothesised to have difficulties with, it is possible that the participants were not fully informed about the purpose of the tasks.
- The fact that the Eyes Task presented participants with options to choose from may have reduced any potential for harm by enabling them to give an answer each time. However, it is possible that some may have been concerned that they were giving the wrong answers.
- In terms of withdrawal, presumably the participants could have just stopped answering the questions, but it is not made clear if they were told this at the start.
- With regard to debriefing, the original article doesn't mention this. Whilst it would not have been difficult for Baron-Cohen et al to have done this with the 'normal' and Tourette syndrome groups, it might have been harder to do this with those participants on the autistic spectrum as it would have meant explaining something – namely, theory of mind – that the results of the study had just confirmed them to have difficulty with.

Validity

- A great deal was done to make this study as valid as possible. Regarding the sample, the fact that participants in the different groups were matched for mean age and intelligence levels helped the researchers to be able to rule these out as possible

extraneous variables. Also, the inclusion of people with Tourette syndrome helped the researchers to establish that it wasn't just the fact of having a developmental neuropsychiatric disorder that caused impairment on the Eyes Task; rather, it was something specific to autism/AS.
- Regarding the tests the participants were given to do, the inclusion of the Strange Stories Task helped the researchers to confirm (through a process of concurrent validity) that it was actually theory of mind that they were measuring in the Eyes Task. On top of this, the inclusion of the two control tasks helped confirm that poor performance on the Eyes Task was likely to be because of impairment in theory of mind rather than, say, an inability even to recognise a person's gender and/or an unfamiliarity with even the most basic of emotions.
- With regard to the Eyes Task itself, this was designed with care to be as 'pure' a test of theory of mind as it could be. In particular, looking at the eyes alone required no ability to use context to work out a person's mental state (i.e. no 'central coherence component') and no skills of attention switching, inhibition, planning, etc. (i.e. no 'executive function component'). Furthermore, it deliberately included terms describing cognitive mental states (e.g. certain or uncertain) so was more than just an emotion perception test.
- In terms of how the tests were administered, the fact that different participants took the four tests in different orders helped control for order effects, while taking them individually in a quiet room helped to control for peer pressure or noise as possible extraneous variables.
- However, in spite of all of this, some issues with the validity of this study remain. In the first place, the fact that participants were given words to choose from in the Eyes Task meant that the researchers couldn't find out the mental state that they really thought was being shown in the eyes: participants had to choose from the options they were given rather than being able to say what they genuinely thought. Second, the fact that the choice was between one of two words meant that there was a likelihood that results could reflect successful (50:50) guesses rather than accurate knowledge. Moreover, because the words were opposites as opposed to being near-synonyms may, again, have made it easier for participants to guess the right answer. (It is interesting to note that when the test was revised for Baron-Cohen's book *The Essential Difference* (2003), each pair of eyes was accompanied by four words and these were not based around semantic opposites).

Figure 5.5 A still from the film *Rain Man*, which is about a man with autism.

Find out more

To find out more about autism and Asperger syndrome, you could:

- Visit the website of the National Autistic Society
- Read the novel *The Curious Incident of the Dog in the Night-time* by Mark Haddon
- Read *Freaks, Geeks & Asperger Syndrome* by Luke Jackson
- Watch the film *Rain Man*.

To find out more about the Strange Stories task, consult Francesca Happé's book *Autism – An Introduction to Psychological Theory*.

Practice questions

1. From Baron-Cohen *et al.*'s study into autism in adults, explain what is meant by the term 'Theory of Mind'. [2 marks]
2. From the Baron-Cohen *et al.* study into autism in adults, explain why people with Tourette syndrome were included. [2 marks]
3. From Baron-Cohen *et al.*'s study into autism in adults:
   (a) Identify one of the hypotheses in this study. [2 marks]
   (b) Outline the findings in relation to one of the hypotheses in this study. [2 marks]
4. Suggest one way in which the study by Baron-Cohen *et al.* (autism in adults) changes our understanding of individual, social or cultural diversity in relation to the key theme of understanding disorders. [3 marks]

Measuring differences Ⓐ

People differ in many ways. Some of these – their height or weight, for example – can be measured with relative ease. While it might be thought that this is because these are physical characteristics, it is worth noting that other physical characteristics – e.g. the colour of people's hair – are not so easily measured and, instead, we have to rely on descriptive categorisation (e.g. whether someone's hair is dark brown or light brown). Bearing this in mind, it should come as no surprise that the enterprise of trying to measure ways in which people differ psychologically (e.g. in terms of their level of 'intelligence', or their 'personality') has proved to be extremely difficult. Furthermore, because decisions about a person's schooling or employment may rest on the results of the tests that are used, the whole process of trying to measure differences between people is extremely socially sensitive.

There are many different approaches that are taken to measuring differences between people. For instance, people may be given measuring devices to complete themselves (as commonly happens with intelligence tests or personality questionnaires) or trained professionals may complete the measuring devices on the people they are assessing (as happens in the case of Hare's Psychopathy Checklist).

In terms of the measuring devices people complete themselves, these may vary considerably, as intelligence tests will typically comprise tests that people are given to do, whereas personality questionnaires (e.g. the Eysenck Personality Questionnaire) will typically comprise a series of statements with respondents being instructed to say which ones are or aren't generally true of them. If creating a test and then getting people to take it, these will often be psychometric (i.e. the tests will endeavour to express a psychological construct in numerical form), but the big challenge for the people creating the test will be to have a clear understanding of the psychological construct they are trying to measure and then confidence that their test is (in a valid way) genuinely measuring that construct and that construct alone. It is also crucial that every person taking the test does so under the same conditions so that they all have an equal chance of doing well on it. As we will see in the core study by Gould, these challenges are harder to overcome than might be thought.

Another way of measuring differences between people centres on professionals using measuring devices to assess others. This approach is illustrated in the core study by Hancock *et al.* in which the language people use is subjected to computer-based analysis. The participants were not given a special test to do; rather, what happened was that one of their habitual ways of behaving (i.e. how they speak) was subjected to analysis and measurement. For such an approach to work, the participant clearly has to be unaware of the detail of what is going to be happening (to avoid them altering their behaviour in a 'socially desirable' way) and care needs to be taken to ensure that the analysis is not affected by researcher bias (i.e. the researcher being able simply to find what they want to find).

Whichever approach is taken, the measuring devices that are used are likely to be assuming that the psychological construct being measured is stable over time and situation (will they be?), and there is the difficulty of isolating the construct that the researchers want to measure. While technology may help with ensuring that tests are analysed in an objective way, it will do little to help with the challenge of ensuring that tests are equally accessible to all different types of people (irrespective of such things as their age, gender or cultural background).

Gould (1982)

Is it meaningful to say that some people are more 'intelligent' than others? To be able to do this, the first step would presumably be to define what is meant by intelligence. Then, if the aim was to compare one person against another (to be able to say which of the two is the more intelligent), it would presumably be necessary to devise some way of measuring how far people possess it. As we are going to see in the core study that follows, not only is the whole enterprise of trying to measure intelligence extremely difficult, but it also raises bigger issues about the extent to which a person's level of intelligence can be altered by environmental factors such as education and how (or whether) the findings from psychological research should be made use of by society as a whole.

It is important to note from the start that, although this core study is attributed to Stephen Jay Gould, what he is doing is describing work carried out by someone else – namely, Robert M. Yerkes. Like Gould, it will be Yerkes' work upon which we will be focusing, and it will be Yerkes' work that we will be evaluating.

Aims

Robert Yerkes was a Professor of Psychology at Harvard University in the USA. He had been a lecturer there since 1902, but by 1915 he was becoming frustrated at the way in which his subject was viewed as a 'soft' science, if a science at all. His primary aim was to prove that psychology could be as rigorous a science as physics, by which he meant it could be just as focused on numbers and quantification. For Yerkes, the area of psychology that offered the most promising means by which to do this was the field of mental testing which, at the time, was only just beginning to develop.

Sample

The First World War gave Yerkes the opportunity to build up the large pool of data that he craved as he succeeded in persuading the US army to test the intelligence levels of all its recruits. As Colonel Yerkes, he would end up presiding over the administration of mental tests to 1.75 million men during the First World War.

Design of the tests

Between May and July 1917, Yerkes worked with Lewis Terman, H.H. Goddard and other colleagues to produce the army mental tests. In their attempt to 'measure native intellectual ability', the scheme they developed included three types of tests:

- **The Army Alpha**: This was a written examination to be given to literate recruits. It included eight parts, took less than an hour, and could be given to large groups. Most of the items in the test comprised such tasks as filling in the next number in a sequence, unscrambling sentences, and analogies (e.g. 'Washington is to Adams as first is to ...'). It also included a series of multiple-choice questions such as:
  - Crisco is a: patent medicine, disinfectant, toothpaste, food product.
  - The number of a Kaffir's legs is: 2, 4, 6, 8.
  - Christy Mathewson is famous as a: writer, artist, baseball player, comedian.
- **The Army Beta**: This was a test designed for illiterates and men who had failed the Army Alpha. It included seven parts and, like the Army Alpha, took less than an hour and could be given to large groups. Items included maze running, cube counting, finding the next symbol in an X-O series, and translating numerals into symbols (Figure 5.6). Another of the tests, pictorial completion, required those being tested to draw in whatever was missing from the pictures (Figure 5.7).
- **Individual examination**: Failures in the Army Beta were to be recalled for an individual examination.

Following these tests, army psychologists would then grade each man from A to E (with plusses and minuses) and offer suggestions for proper military placement. Yerkes suggested that recruits with a score of C− should be marked as 'low average intelligence' and be recommended for the rank of 'ordinary private'.

> ### 🚫 Stop and ask yourself...
> - What are the strengths and weaknesses of the sample that Yerkes used for his research?
>
> **Links to methodological issues**
> - Sample

> ### 🚫 Stop and ask yourself...
> - What do you think of these as tests of 'native intellectual ability'? Are these tests really assessing people's raw intelligence (irrespective of how much schooling and/or cultural knowledge they have behind them)?
>
> **Links to methodological issues**
> - Validity

Administration of the tests

Although (as you may already have worked out) there were serious problems with the way the tests were designed, there were also major problems with the way the tests were administered. Yerkes' protocols stated that men who were illiterate in

Figure 5.6 The Army Beta test: pictorial completion test

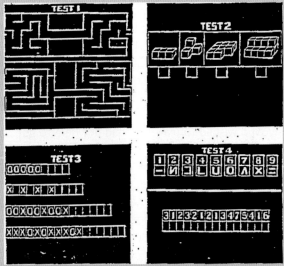

Figure 5.7 The Army Beta test: tests 1–4. More examples from the Beta test for army recruits. Test 1: running a maze. Test 2: count the number of cubes. Test 3: find the next in the series. Test 4: translate the numerals into symbols. Remember, this was a test for recruits who were illiterate – and they had to write their answers.

English should have been automatically assigned to take the Army Beta examination; similarly, men who failed the Army Alpha examination should have taken the Army Beta examination. However, persistent logistical difficulties meant that in many camps these protocols were not followed.

In the first place, it turned out that recruits and draftees had, on average, spent fewer years in school than Yerkes had anticipated. This meant that the queues of men lined up to take the Beta examination began to lengthen. To avoid a bottleneck, at many camps the definition of 'literate' was lowered so that men could be sent to take the Alpha test instead (e.g. in one camp, it was enough to have been schooled to third grade; in another, men were counted as literate if they said they could read, at whatever level). Inevitably, many of these men scored either zero or next to nothing on the Alpha test.

Yerkes' protocols stated that these men should have been given a retest on the Beta examination. However, under pressure of time and in the face of hostility from regular officers, Yerkes' protocols were rarely followed and so men who had incorrectly taken the Alpha test often didn't get a chance to take the Beta test. Furthermore, the requirement that men failing the Beta test should be given an individual examination was rarely met.

🚫 Stop and ask yourself...

- Why, for the men taking these tests, was it such a problem that they often didn't get given the correct test to take?
- Why, for Yerkes himself, was it such a problem that the men taking these tests often sat a test that was inappropriate for them?

Links to methodological issues
- Validity/ethics
- Validity/reliability

Results

From all the data collected, E.G. Boring selected 160,000 cases for analysis. After converting the scales of the three different tests (Alpha, Beta and individual examination) to a common standard, Boring reported three 'facts':

1. The average mental age of white American adults was 13. This meant that they were only just above the level expected of a moron.
2. With regard to immigrants from Europe, the darker people of southern Europe and the Slavs of Eastern Europe were found to be less intelligent than the fair people of western and northern Europe. The average Russian had a mental age of 11.34; the Italian, 11.01; the Pole, 10.74.

3. Black Americans lay at the bottom of the scale with an average mental age of 10.41.

These findings were taken up by politicians who used the 'facts' that Boring had extracted from Yerkes' data to lobby not just for limits to immigration but for changing its character by imposing tight quotas against nations deemed to be of inferior genetic stock. This lobbying eventually led to the Immigration Restriction Act of 1924 which limited new arrivals each year to 2 per cent of the foreign-born of any nationality as shown in the 1890 census (with this particular census being used because immigration from southern and eastern Europe had been relatively rare before then). It is estimated that, as a consequence of these harsher quotas, up to six million southern, central and eastern Europeans were barred entry to the USA between 1924 and the outbreak of the Second World War.

Discussion

For discussion of Yerkes' mental tests, we need to turn to Gould as in many ways the whole point of his article is to draw out the lessons to learn from this whole episode. There are many points that he raises in relation to Yerkes' tests.

With regard to the design of the tests, Gould regards as 'ludicrous' (page 349) Yerkes' claim that his tests were measuring 'native intellectual ability' when they included whole sections that presupposed familiarity with American ways (e.g. the multiple-choice questions in the Alpha test, and the picture-completion test in the Beta examination). This makes the tests culturally biased. Gould also draws attention to the way in which the Beta examination required pencil work and, on three of its seven parts, a knowledge of numbers and how to write them. Given that many of the men taking this test had never before held a pencil in their hands, Gould comments that, 'Yerkes had overlooked, or consciously bypassed something of importance' (page 350).

In relation to the administration of Yerkes' tests (particularly the way in which illiterate men were often sent to take the Alpha test and then not given retests on the Beta examination), Gould points out that the men who were most likely to be illiterate in English were either black men (who would have had less schooling due to segregation, poor conditions in black schools, and poverty that made it necessary for many black children to go out to work) or those who had only recently migrated to the USA. For this reason, Gould makes the claim that 'the persistent logistical difficulties imposed a systematic bias that substantially lowered the mean scores of Blacks and immigrants' (page 350). Furthermore, as the examinations were conducted in an almost frantic rush on men who must have been 'either utterly confused or scared shitless' (page 350), Gould struggles to see how 'recruits could have been in a frame of mind to record anything about their innate abilities' (page 350).

With regard to how the results of Yerkes' tests were interpreted, Gould emphasises the extent to which Yerkes and his followers were so in thrall to hereditarian explanations (in terms of people's genetic inheritance) that they failed to see alternative explanations for the 'facts' that they presented. For example, in spite of the accomplishments of many Jewish scholars, statesmen and performing artists, the army tests had assessed Jews as quite low in intelligence. Instead of recognising that this might be a reflection of many of them being recent immigrants who were unfamiliar with American ways, Carl Brigham (one of Yerkes' followers) suggested that Jews might be more variable than other groups and that we really notice it when Jews are successful because this is so exceptional.

Finally, in relation to the way in which the findings from Yerkes' army tests were used to justify tighter limits on immigration to the USA from southern, central and eastern Europe, Gould points out that the consequence of this was almost certainly to consign many would-be immigrants to their deaths at the hands of the Nazis: 'We know what happened to many who wished to leave but had nowhere to go' (page 352)

Conclusions

Gould ends his article with this sentence: 'The paths to destruction are often indirect, but ideas can be agents as sure as guns and bombs.' It would be his conclusion that some ideas – of which Yerkes' idea of carrying out mental tests on army recruits in the USA during the First World War would be one – can have consequences every bit as tragic as more deliberate and direct attempts to do harm.

➡ Have a go yourself

Try designing yourself a way of testing intelligence that presupposes neither a certain level of education nor a familiarity with your culture.

Evaluation of the study by Yerkes/Gould

Links to methodological issues

Research method

- The way Boring analysed the data collected by Yerkes would suggest that Yerkes' study can be seen as following a quasi-experimental method, with the naturally occurring independent variable being the ethnic origin of the participants (e.g. white American, black American, Russian, Italian, Polish) and the dependent variable being the average mental age of the recruits from the various ethnic backgrounds, based on their results in the tests of 'native intellectual ability'; however, this was certainly not a tightly controlled quasi-experiment given all the variation in how the tests were administered.
- Gould can be seen as having carried out a review of Yerkes' work; as such, it is legitimate to question the objectivity with which he has selected his evidence as it could have been chosen to support the argument that he wants to put forward.

Data

- Yerkes' tests yielded numerical values (i.e. quantitative data) for the number of correct answers scored by recruits on the tests. 'Army psychologists would then grade each man from A to E (with plusses and minuses) ...' (page 349).
- Boring's analysis of the distribution of scores on the tests produced additional quantitative data – namely, the 'average mental age' of people from different ethnic backgrounds.
- Boring's analysis would enable him to produce statistics that allowed comparison on the basis of the men's ethnic backgrounds; however, whether these quantitative data were valid is the hugely important question being raised by Gould.

Ethics

- In terms of consent, the army recruits '... were told nothing about the examination or its purposes' (*The Mismeasure of Man*, page 235); it can reasonably be assumed that they were unable to withdraw from taking the tests.
- When taking the tests, the army recruits had to fill in '... their names, age, and education (with help for those too illiterate to do so)' (page 234), meaning that their results were not anonymous.
- Regarding protection from harm, it is likely that many recruits were in a state of heightened anxiety as they took the tests given their inability to make sense of what they were being asked to do and the rushed and chaotic conditions in which many of the tests were administered.
- On top of this, with some camps stipulating that no man scoring below a C could be considered for officer training (page 350), it is likely that the results from these tests would have led some men with the potential to be officers to be held at the level of private and recommended for more dangerous military placements as a consequence.
- Of arguably greatest significance in terms of harm (albeit not to the people actually taking the tests) was the way in which the data from these tests was used to justify the 1924 Immigration Restriction Act. If the estimates are correct that the quotas barred up to six million southern, central and eastern Europeans from emigrating to the USA between 1924 and the outbreak of the Second World War, then this whole episode has to go down as perhaps the most shameful in the history of psychology: people who wished to leave countries in these parts of Europe but had nowhere to go will have ended up suffering at the hands of the Nazis as a consequence.

Validity

- As Gould points out, there are major problems with the claim that Yerkes' tests were an accurate measure of intelligence. Instead, then, of a person's score on the tests representing their 'native intellectual ability', it was more likely a measure of such things as how much schooling they had had (something that was out of their control), how long they had been in the country for (such that they might be familiar with what Crisco was or who Christy Mathewson was), or how much money and leisure time they had (to be familiar with lawn tennis, record players and electric light bulbs).
- A person's score could also, of course, reflect which army camp a recruit happened to be in, and whether the definition of 'literate' had been lowered so far as to mean that people who ought really to have taken the Beta test were reassigned to the Alpha test.

Hancock *et al.* (2011)

One dimension upon which people are thought to differ is that of psychopathy, with it being estimated that approximately 1 per cent of the general population are psychopaths. What, though, does it mean to describe someone as a psychopath? Psychopaths can be described as people who exhibit a wholly selfish orientation and profound emotional deficit; however, in spite of appearing to have little or no 'conscience', they exhibit no apparent deficits in intellect.

It has been claimed that psychopathy has a biological basis to it and evidence from neuroimaging research has suggested structural and functional abnormalities of the brain, including reduced grey matter in frontal and temporal areas (de Oliviera-Souza *et al.*, 2008), and anomalies in the prefrontal cortex, corpus callosum and hippocampus (Raine *et al.*, 2003, 2004). However, the whole concept of psychopathy is hugely controversial because it suggests that such people might not be fully responsible for their crimes and also that efforts at rehabilitation may not work with them. Also controversial is the claim that many successful business leaders may be psychopaths. However, insofar as it may be a dimension upon which people differ, how can we tell whether someone is a psychopath or not? The intriguing suggestion from the study by Hancock *et al.* (2011) is that it may be possible to identify psychopaths from the way they speak.

Aims/hypotheses

The aim of the study was to examine the language characteristics of psychopaths (when describing their violent crimes) on three major characteristics:

1. As psychopaths appear to view the world and others instrumentally as theirs for the taking, Hancock *et al.* were interested in seeing if this would be reflected in their speech in the form of *more usage of subordinating conjunctions* (e.g. 'because', 'since', 'as', 'so that'). These words are associated with cause-and-effect statements and would suggest offenders whose crimes are premeditated and motivated by the achieving of an external goal and are, therefore, open to the use of causally framed explanatory language.

2. It seems to be the case that satisfying their basic physiological and material needs (e.g. for food, sex and shelter) matters more to psychopaths than satisfying higher level needs for meaningful relationships, spirituality or self-esteem. Bearing this in mind, Hancock *et al.* were interested in seeing whether their narratives about their crimes would (relative to other criminals) contain *more semantic references to food, drink, clothing, sex and resources (money) and fewer semantic references reflecting higher level needs such as love, family and spirituality*.

3. Psychopaths exhibit a generalised deficit in their ability to experience emotions themselves and to recognise the emotions that other people are feeling. Hancock *et al.* hypothesised that this emotional deficit might lead psychopaths to (a) *produce fewer and less intense emotional words*, (b) *produce more disfluencies* (e.g. 'uh', 'um'), reflecting the increased cognitive load being placed on them by the challenge of describing what had happened in a manner that appears appropriate (i.e. impression management), and (c) *use language that reflects increased psychological 'distancing' from and a lack of personal responsibility for the crime, such as a higher rate of past tense and fewer present tense verb forms, and a higher rate of articles (e.g. 'a', 'the')* in line with more use of concrete nouns.

Participants

The sample consisted of 52 men who were being held in prison in Canada for murder. All had admitted their crime and all volunteered to take part in this study. Their mean age at the time of the murder for which they had been imprisoned was 28.9 years.

 Stop and ask yourself …

- What do you think about Hancock *et al.*'s expectations? Does it sound plausible to expect that psychopaths would use language in these ways? (Are all three expectations equally plausible?)

Links to methodological issues
- Face validity

 Stop and ask yourself …

- How generalisable is this sample? Do you see any problems with it?

Links to methodological issues
- Sample

Procedure

To ascertain which of the men were psychopathic and which were non-psychopathic, assessments were made using the Psychopathy Checklist-Revised (PCL-R; Hare, 1991, 2003). On the PCL-R, which is the most widely used tool for assessing psychopathy in criminal settings, psychopathy is characterised by 20 criteria scored from 0 to 2 for a maximum score of 40. Items on the PCL-R measure traits in two broad areas: Factor 1 items assess interpersonal and affective traits, such as superficial charm, lack of remorse, and pathological lying; Factor 2 items assess traits that indicate an anti-social lifestyle, such as early behavioural problems, impulsivity and irresponsibility.

For 39 of the men, assessments were completed by extensively trained prison psychologists. However, for the other 13 men, assessments were not available in their prison files so a researcher who was well trained in the coding of the PCL-R completed these. To check that the different raters were consistent with each other in how they had arrived at the PCL-R scores for the prisoners they had assessed, a trained graduate student recoded ten case files selected on a random basis. Results indicated a high level of agreement between the raters in their codings ($r = 0.94$; $p < 0.001$).

The cut-off point for a clinical diagnosis of psychopathy is a score of 30 or above. However, in line with practice in research by other psychologists, a person was classified as a psychopath in this study if they had a score of 25 or above. On this basis, 14 of the offenders were classified as psychopathic and 38 were non-psychopathic. The two groups did not differ significantly either in age or the amount of time since the murder was committed (Table 5.6).

Table 5.6 Mean age and mean amount of time since the murder was committed for psychopaths and non-psychopaths

	Mean age	Mean amount of time since the murder was committed
Psychopaths	39.71 years (SD = 7.53)	11.87 years (SD = 7.78)
Non-psychopaths	39.91 years (SD = 9.76)	9.82 years (SD = 6.78)

To collect data from the participants, an interview was arranged with all 52 men. These were led by two senior psychology graduate students and one research student. All were blind to the psychopathy scores of the offenders. At the start of each interview, the purpose of the study (i.e. to examine the manner in which homicide offenders recall their homicide offence) was explained to each offender verbally, as was the procedure that would be followed. Participants were then asked to describe their homicide offence in as much detail as possible, from beginning to end, omitting no details. Interviews were audiotaped and lasted approximately 25 minutes. Afterwards, the narratives were turned into typed transcripts, with efforts being made to make these as verbatim as possible.

Data analysis

Two text analysis tools were used to analyse the transcripts:

1. The first was a 'corpus analysis' program called 'Wmatrix' in which the speech produced by all 14 of the psychopaths was brought together and analysed as one in comparison to the speech produced by all 38 of the non-psychopaths. To analyse these two 'corpora' (i.e. 'the psychopath corpus' – the body of speech produced by the psychopaths – and 'the non-psychopath corpus'), two features of Wmatrix were used – namely, its ability (1) to tag parts of speech (e.g. nouns, verbs, adjectives, etc.), and (2) to analyse semantic concepts (e.g. language and communication, social actions, states and processes, time, etc.). The extent to which there is a significant difference in word usage between text corpora is expressed in Wmatrix as a 'log-likelihood ratio'.

2. The other text analysis program that was used was the Dictionary of Affect in Language (DAL). This is a dictionary-based tool that assesses the emotional properties of language. On this program, each participant's transcript was analysed individually, with a score being given for the pleasantness and intensity of emotional language in each statement.

 Stop and ask yourself ...

Links to methodological issues
- Validity

- Why might it be a problem that Hancock *et al.* classified people as psychopathic if they had a score of 25 or above on Hare's PCL-R?
- Why was it important that those conducting the interviews of the offenders were unaware of the offenders' psychopathy scores?

Results

The 14 psychopath narratives together amounted to a 'corpus' of 29,562 words (averaging 2,201.5 words per participant), while the 38 non-psychopath narratives together amounted to a 'corpus' of 97,814 words (averaging 2,554.3 words per participant). With regard to the three characteristics of the offenders' language that Hancock *et al.* analysed, they found the following:

1. **Instrumental language analysis**: As predicted, the psychopaths produced significantly more subordinating conjunctions than the non-psychopaths. Such words made up 1.82 per cent of the words used by the psychopaths, but only 1.54 per cent of the words used by the non-psychopaths.

2. **Hierarchy of needs analysis**: Again, results were in line with expectations. The psychopaths used significantly more words connected to food, drink, clothing and money (i.e. basic physiological needs) than did the non-psychopaths. By way of contrast, the non-psychopaths used significantly more words connected to family and religion (i.e. social needs) than did the psychopaths.

3. **Emotional expression in language**: As expected, the speech produced by the psychopaths contained approximately 33 per cent more disfluencies (e.g. 'uh', 'um') than the speech produced by the non-psychopaths. With regard to psychological distancing, yet again results were in line with predictions as the psychopaths used a significantly higher percentage of verbs in the past tense (e.g. 'stabbed'), the non-psychopaths used a significantly higher percentage of verbs in the present tense (e.g. 'stab'), and articles (e.g. 'a', 'the') made up a significantly higher percentage of the speech produced by the psychopaths. With regard to the emotional content of language, examination of the DAL scores revealed no significant differences between the two groups; however, when the DAL scores were analysed again based not on each participant's total PCL-R score but simply their Factor 1 score (the part within the PCL-R which assesses interpersonal and affective deficits), it was found that there was a negative correlation between Factor 1 scores and both the pleasantness and intensity of emotional language used by the participants.

Conclusions

Hancock *et al.* conclude from the 'idiosyncratic' way in which psychopaths describe powerful emotional events (their crimes) that they operate on a primitive but rational level.

Discussion

The findings from this study were generally consistent with the predictions that the researchers had made, suggesting that psychopaths describe powerful emotional events (their crimes) in an idiosyncratic manner. In particular, narratives by psychopaths included a higher level of instrumentality and more explanation themes, focused on self-preservation and bodily needs, and were more disfluent, past-orientated and had less emotional intensity relative to non-psychopathic offenders.

It must be considered, though, whether the use of language shown by the psychopaths in this study is necessarily the product of psychopathy. For example, where emotional negativity was shown, this might reflect their general state of mind during imprisonment, experiencing it (even more than some non-psychopaths) as placing restrictions on their ability to fulfil many of their basic and thrill-seeking drives. Similarly, the more frequent use by the psychopaths of the past tense could just be a reflection of a greater ability on their part to follow instructions and to be more compliant.

Beyond this, there are two noteworthy limitations that should be kept in mind when interpreting the results from this study. First, it was only on narratives about one type of event – a murder – that the statistical text analysis was conducted, and this is clearly an unusual type of event, especially in terms of its emotional content. Second, there was no objective evidence (e.g. videotapes) relating to the events the offenders were describing and it is quite probable that the psychopaths may not have been honest in their accounts of what happened.

These points aside, as the stylistic differences in language use of the psychopaths are likely to be beyond conscious control and are difficult to alter intentionally, Hancock *et al.* put forward the claim that their findings on speech may '... begin to open the window into the mind of the psychopath, allowing us to infer that the psychopath's world view is fundamentally different from the rest of the human species' (page 112).

> ### ➡ Have a go yourself
>
> Try role-playing the interview part of this study. Two people could be interviewees, with one pretending to be psychopathic and the other non-psychopathic. The interviewer has to work out, from their use of language alone, which is which.

Evaluation of the study by Hancock *et al.*

Links to methodological issues

Research method

- Hancock *et al.*'s study can be seen as following a quasi-experimental method, with the naturally occurring independent variable being whether the participants were psychopaths or non-psychopaths. It can be seen as having an independent measures design.
- This study used self-report in the form of semi-structured/open-ended interviews (the Step-Wise Interview technique) to gather data in relation to the language of psychopaths and non-psychopaths who had committed murder.
- It can also be seen as a content analysis, given the quantitative analysis they carried out of verbal information obtained during interviews.
- As a content analysis, it is possible to question the content that Hancock *et al.* chose to analyse. Hancock reported various ways in which psychopaths use language differently from non-psychopaths. However, it is possible that there were other ways in which they expected psychopaths to use language differently, but it turned out that they didn't. It would be interesting to know if there were aspects of language where their null hypothesis was supported (i.e. they expected to see a difference, but didn't).

Data

- The prisoners' descriptions of their crimes were analysed in a way that generated quantitative data. This was helpful in enabling Hancock *et al.* to confirm if the differences in language use between the psychopaths and non-psychopaths were statistically significant (i.e. beyond any difference that would be expected anyway).
- These data were collected through interviews (as opposed to the participants having to fill in anything themselves). It is arguable that this should have led to natural behaviour revealing itself.

Ethics

- The participants were not deceived regarding the purpose of the interviews, but it's unclear whether the prisoners knew that they were being assessed for psychopathy or that they were being compared against another group of prisoners.

- The participants volunteered to take part, so they gave their consent to be involved (although it can be questioned whether this consent was fully informed).
- There is no mention of the offenders being told that they could withdraw their data.
- Confidentiality/anonymity was maintained.

Validity

- What Hancock *et al.* wanted to measure was how their participants use language and whether there are any measurable differences in this between psychopaths and non-psychopaths.
- The validity of their study was helped by the offenders appearing not to be told about either the independent variable in the study or the precise aspects of language the researchers were interested in investigating, making it less likely that participants had modified their normal ways of speaking. It was also helped by the results being kept anonymous and by the use of a double-blind procedure (which reduced the dangers of researcher bias in analysis of the data).
- However, the validity of this investigation can be questioned in a number of ways. First, with prisoners being classified as psychopathic if they scored 25 or above on Hare's PCL-R (instead of the usual 30 or above), it is arguable that not all of the prisoners classified as psychopathic were actually psychopathic. Second, it is important to keep in mind that the study was not examining the participants' general language usage so much as their use of language in one specific context – namely, when describing a murder. Third, it is possible that the way language is used could reflect other things apart from psychopathy. For instance, it could reflect their level of education (e.g. the extent to which someone is in the habit of providing justifications for their behaviour might be related to their highest level of education), the culture they are from, or even how pedantic they are (in terms of being disfluent because they want to find the right words). Finally, the extent to which any of their descriptions of their crimes would have been accurate can be questioned – and this would apply whether the account came from a psychopath or a non-psychopath.

Reliability

- In many ways, the reliability of this study was good. There was an inter-rater reliability check in relation to the coding of the PCL-R assessments.

Interviews with prisoners all followed the same 'step-wise' interview procedure. The use of computer programs to analyse the prisoners' language would also have helped ensure that the data from each participant were approached in a consistent way. On top of this, looking at several different aspects of language (as opposed to just the one) will have helped improve the reliability of the findings as they could then be compared to see if they are all telling the same (consistent) 'story'.

- However, as the interview procedure was open-ended in style, it is likely that the narratives generated by the prisoners would have varied in such matters as which parts of their crime they described in most detail. Also, whether a sample size of 14 psychopaths is large enough to establish a consistent effect is questionable.

Sample

- There are a number of ways in which the sample in this study can be seen as of limited generalisability. In particular, there were only 14 psychopaths, they were all men, they were all drawn from the same country (Canada), they were all criminals (unlike those who are psychopathic but not criminals), and they had all been convicted of the same crime – namely, murder.
- As the men in this study volunteered to take part, it can be seen as having used a self-selected sampling method.

Ethnocentrism

- With the men in this study all being drawn from the same country, it can be argued that this research is ethnocentric as it is quite possible that people in other countries would use language in different ways according to the nature of the language (e.g. whether it uses articles in the same way) or the nature of the culture (e.g. the extent to which physiological needs are a preoccupation in a particular culture).
- In Canada, there are two official languages-namely, English and French. The research paper by Hancock et al. does not make it clear whether the participants that they studied were English speakers, French speakers, or speakers of both languages. The research would be less ethnocentric if it was based on speakers from both language traditions but, as this isn't mentioned, it is probably reasonable to assume that they were all English speakers as such people form the majority within the Canadian population.

Links to debates
Free will/determinism

- In so far as it is meaningful to talk about psychopaths as a distinct group of people, the question arises of whether the characteristics assigned to psychopaths are beyond their control.
- The suggestion that '… the psychopath's diminished capacity for moral sensibility appears to have biological underpinnings' (page 103) would lend support to a determinist position, as would the (more psychodynamic) claim that '… psychopaths have unique drives and socioemotional needs' (page 104).
- However, also central to the concept of psychopathy is the suggestion that such people are 'highly manipulative' (page 103). Hancock et al. tell us that '… psychopaths typically are skilled conversationalists and use language to lie to, charm, and ultimately "use" others for material gain, drugs, sex or power' (page 103). If they are able to manage how they are perceived by others, then this would suggest they have control over their behaviour to at least some degree.

Usefulness

- Hancock et al.'s claim that their '… findings on speech begin to open the window into the mind of the psychopath' (page 112) suggests a new way of detecting psychopaths (i.e. by listening to how they use language).
- Potentially, this could be extremely useful. For instance, in a prison context, it could be used when trying to work out the best rehabilitation schemes to give to inmates. No doubt others would argue that it could even be used in non-prison contexts, such as at school, to identify those children (the 1 per cent of the population) with psychopathic tendencies.
- However, before rushing to analyse the language of convicted offenders or children in the ways that Hancock et al. describe, it is vital to be certain that their language assessment techniques are valid as indicators of psychopathy. Furthermore, we'd need to think through how we'd want to make use of the findings from analysis of people's language. If we found, for instance, a certain proportion of convicted criminals who use language in the way that psychopaths do, then how should we deal with them? Also, what if language analysis of children revealed those with psychopathic tendencies? Should the aim then be to use education to try and

change them (assuming this is possible)? Would this be appropriate, though, given that many will not go on to become criminals? (That said, if Hare is correct in saying that, 'Corporate and political and religious psychopaths ruin economies. They ruin societies' [quoted in Ronson, page 117], non-criminal psychopaths may be no less dangerous to society).

Socially sensitive research

- As the above comments should bring out, research of this kind can be regarded as socially sensitive.
- Given the potential applications of its findings, it is vital that research such as that by Hancock *et al.* is both valid and reliable.
- It is also vital that its findings are not misapplied. Quite aside, then, from the sorts of potential (societal) uses discussed above, it is conceivable that people who are disfluent in their language, who have a tendency to use the past tense when describing their actions and who use a lot of subordinating conjunctions could find themselves being labelled as psychopaths. On top of this, it is conceivable that employers could screen out people who use language in this way even before they get to interview.
- Psychologists need to anticipate how their findings might be latched onto and take all measures that they can to avoid their work being used inappropriately.

Links to areas/perspectives

- Hancock *et al.*'s study falls within the individual differences area because it is investigating a way in which it might be possible to measure differences between people – in this case, their use of language. The enterprise of measuring differences is a central theme within this area of psychology.
- It can also be seen as coming from the psychodynamic perspective. Throughout the research paper, there are references to psychodynamic concepts. For instance, the suggestion that the stylistic differences in how psychopaths use language are 'likely beyond conscious control' (page 112) invokes the idea of an unconscious element to each of us that is responsible for at least some of our behaviour. This impression is reinforced by the way in which Hancock *et al.* suggest that it is because of the way in which prison restricts the ability of the psychopaths to fulfil many of their 'basic and thrill-seeking drives' (page 110) that they use less emotionally pleasant language. Furthermore,

the expectation (in their third hypothesis) that psychopaths would 'use language that reflects increased psychological "distancing"' (page 104) such as higher rates of past tense usage can be seen as a kind of ego defence mechanism. On top of this, some of the research that Hancock *et al.* cite in the course of their study makes reference to psychodynamic concepts. Thus, Endres (2004) refers to psychopaths as possibly being 'stuck in the lowest stage of ego development', while Huprich *et al.* (2004) made use of the Rorschach 'inkblot' test (a projective test which presupposes the existence of the unconscious) in finding out that psychopaths show little need for interactions or dependency on others (page 104).

- Hancock *et al.*'s study also makes explicit reference to the humanistic perspective in the context of Maslow's hierarchy of needs.

Links to the key theme

- In relation to the key theme of measuring differences, Hancock *et al.*'s study suggests that it is possible to carry out a quantitative analysis of how people use language and that, if doing this, psychopaths use language in measurably distinctive ways.
- In terms of the extent to which Hancock *et al.*'s study changes our understanding of the key theme of measuring differences, it suggests that instead of getting respondents completing tests or questionnaires on themselves, an alternative way of measuring differences could be to have professionals analyse what people do anyway (e.g. use language). It also suggests that there can be a role for technology in this process (e.g. the use of programs such as Wmatrix and DAL). However, it is important not to attach undue significance to the use of computer programs in Hancock's study as these only draw out from their participants' use of language what the researchers have instructed the programs to draw out, and so issues of validity still remain in terms of whether they genuinely are measuring something that is a reflection of psychopathy and psychopathy alone.
- In terms of the extent to which Hancock *et al.*'s study changes our understanding of individual, social and cultural diversity, it extends our understanding of individual diversity by drawing our attention to psychopathy and how this might be revealed by the language that people use. It seems as if it analyses people from a narrower

range of ethnic backgrounds than the Gould study but, by studying people from Canada, it teaches us about people from another country (i.e. Canada, as opposed to the USA).

Comparison with the classic study

● In what ways is the study by Hancock *et al. similar to* the research carried out by Yerkes (and described by Gould)?
  ● Both pieces of research were conducted on all-male samples.
  ● Both pieces of research were carried out in 'institutional' settings (data for Yerkes' research were collected in army camps; the interviews in Hancock's study were conducted within a prison setting).
  ● Both pieces of research were trying to capture the psychological construct they were investigating (intelligence; psychopathy) in numerical/measurable form.
  ● Both Yerkes' research and the study by Hancock can be seen as following a quasi-experimental method.
  ● Both studies used the self-report method to gather data.
● In what ways is the study by Hancock *et al. different from* the research carried out by Yerkes (and described by Gould)?
  ● In terms of generalisability, whereas Yerkes' sample was in many ways quite varied (the army recruits certainly came from different backgrounds in terms of their cultural origins), the sample in Hancock's study was very specific (i.e. they had all committed the same crime of murder).
  ● The sample sizes were very different: Yerkes studied 1.75 million people, whereas Hancock studied 52 people (of which 14 were classified as psychopathic).
  ● In terms of how data were collected, in Yerkes' study the researchers gave the army recruits a specific, researcher-created task to do (i.e. fill in – or attempt to fill in – an intelligence test) and then analysed how well they were able to do this; in the study by Hancock analysis was made of the normal behaviour of the prisoners (in terms of the language they used when describing their crime).
  ● The study by Hancock made use of technology (the Wmatrix and DAL programs) to help them in the analysis of their data.
  ● The study by Hancock was conducted under more controlled conditions that were the same for all participants.

Questions arising from the study by Hancock *et al.*

● What questions are we left with after studying the research by Hancock *et al.*? Clearly, before any use could be made of Hancock's study, it would need to be replicated on larger samples (and preferably samples of psychopaths in other countries, including people who have committed crimes other than murder, people who haven't committed any crimes at all, and women) to confirm that the findings from this study are not just a 'one-off' but, instead, have exposed something reliable. However, if this work were done, Hancock's study would then raise the intriguing question of whether it might be possible to detect any other psychological constructs (apart from psychopathy) through the ways in which people use language.

Find out more

● Use the internet to find out more about the Psychopathy Checklist-Revised (PCL-R).
● Use the internet to find out more about the two text analysis tools used in this study.
● Read Jon Ronson's book *The Psychopath Test*.
● Use the internet to find out more about Maslow's hierarchy of needs.

Practice questions

1. From the study by Hancock *et al.* (language of psychopaths), outline one feature that the researchers expected to find in the language used by psychopaths.   [2 marks]
2. Outline one way in which Hancock *et al.* analysed the use of language by participants in their study.   [2 marks]
3. Suggest one reason why the study by Hancock *et al.* may be considered to have an ethnocentric bias.   [2 marks]
4. Suggest why Hancock *et al.*'s study of the language of psychopaths can be considered to take the psychodynamic perspective.   [3 marks]
5. Suggest one way in which the study by Hancock *et al.* changes our understanding of the key theme of measuring differences.   [3 marks]
6. Outline two ways in which the study by Gould ('A nation of morons') and the study by Hancock *et al.* (on the language of psychopaths) are different.   [4 marks]

Chapter 6

Exam guidance for Component 2

A Level

Unit 2 is worth 35 per cent of the full A Level. The exam for Unit 2 will be two hours long and there are 105 marks available for the exam paper as a whole. It is divided into three equally weighted sections as shown in Table 6.1.

Table 6.1 Three sections of the exam for Unit 2

Section	Format	Content
Section A (35 marks)	A series of short-answer questions about the core studies	You can expect to be asked questions on a combination of the following: ● Individual studies – the detail of a core study (i.e. its background, method [design, sample, materials/apparatus, procedure], results, conclusions) ● Core studies in their pairs – how the two studies are similar or different; the extent to which the contemporary study changes our understanding of the key theme or of individual, social and cultural diversity ● Methodological issues – you could be asked to comment on (or evaluate) a core study in relation to its research methods and techniques, the type(s) of data collected, ethical considerations, validity, reliability, sampling bias, ethnocentrism ● Key themes and areas of psychology – how a core study relates to its key theme, and how it relates to the area of psychology within which it is placed
Section B (35 marks)	A structured question in several parts focusing on one or more of the areas, perspectives or debates; this will build up to an essay-style question; psychological research (e.g. core studies) should be referred to in order to illustrate points being made	You can expect to be asked questions on one or more of the following: ● Areas – social, cognitive, developmental, biological, individual differences ● Perspectives – behaviourist, psychodynamic ● Debates – nature/nurture, free will/determinism, reductionism/holism, individual/situational explanations, usefulness of research, ethical considerations, conducting socially sensitive research, psychology as a science For each of these, you need to be able to: ● Identify its defining principles and concepts ● Cite relevant supporting research (of an area or perspective; of particular sides within a debate) ● Outline different positions that can be taken up in relation to it (e.g. strengths and weaknesses of an area or perspective; the different sides of a debate) ● Suggest and evaluate ways in which an area or perspective or a particular position within a debate could be applied ● Say how each area, perspective or debate is similar to or different from the other areas, perspectives or debates
Section C (35 marks)	A structured question in several parts focusing on the practical applications of psychology	You can expect to be presented with some written stimulus material (e.g. an extract from a newspaper or magazine article) and then be asked questions requiring you to do the following: ● Recognise the psychological content in the source ● Make evidence-based suggestions in relation to the source ● Consider the strengths and weaknesses of the suggestion(s) you are making

Section A

Hopefully, it should be clear how the textbook has been preparing you for Section A of the exam for Unit 2. The summaries of each core study should enable you to 'tell the story' of them, and the evaluative comments should help you to see the methodological issues raised by each of the core studies as well as how they relate to their key theme, area and paired study. We will provide some further guidance about Section A questions shortly.

Section B

With regard to Section B, you do not need to know any additional research beyond the core studies (although it is entirely permissible for you to refer to other studies in support of points you are making). The only additional knowledge you need to have is about the areas, perspectives and debates (e.g. what they entail, and the different positions that can be taken up within them). You then need to use psychological research to illustrate points about these areas, perspectives or debates. To this end, the evaluative comments made about each core study should help you to see ways in which they relate to the various areas, perspectives and debates. The introductory chapter to the book gave definitions of the different debates, as well as an overview of the two perspectives and their strengths and weaknesses, while the opening pages of each chapter attempted to capture the defining features of each area, as well as suggesting strengths and weaknesses of them. In the pages that follow, we will attempt to give some guidance about techniques for how to answer the questions you might be asked.

Section C

Section C does not require any additional knowledge on your part as the point of this section of the exam is to see how you can apply what you know in a practical context. What you will need to do is practise applying psychology to novel sources (i.e. seeing the psychological assumptions being made in them, making practical suggestions that are grounded in psychological evidence, and then evaluating the suggestions that you yourself have made). Later in this chapter, you will be given the opportunity to do this, along with suggestions about how to approach exam questions in this section.

AS Level

The exam for Unit 2 of the AS Level is quite similar to that for Unit 2 of the A Level. It differs in that it is worth 50 per cent of the AS Level (instead of 35 per cent of the A Level) and it is 1½ hours long (instead of 2 hours). Also, there are 75 marks available (instead of 105). Beyond these differences, though, the two exams are very similar, with the same three sections and the same equal weighting for each (albeit the total for each section is 25 marks, rather than 35).

The main difference between the AS Level and the A Level is in terms of the content being assessed, rather than in the way in which it is assessed. For the AS Level, students look at ten core studies, rather than 20. The ten that are looked at are as shown in Table 6.2.

Apart from this, students following the AS Level course are expected to have the same grasp of methodological issues, areas, perspectives and debates as students following the A Level course. What this means is that the guidance about how to approach the Unit 2 exam can be assumed to apply to both the AS and A Level courses.

Table 6.2 The ten core studies which are the focus of AS Level

Area	Key theme	Classic study	Contemporary study
Social	Responses to people in authority	Milgram (1963) Obedience	Bocchiaro et al. (2012) Disobedience and whistle-blowing
Cognitive	Memory	Loftus and Palmer (1974) Eyewitness testimony	Grant et al. (1998) Context-dependent memory
Developmental	External influences on children's behaviour	Bandura et al. (1961) Transmission of aggression	Chaney et al. (2004) Funhaler study
Biological	Regions of the brain	Sperry (1968) Split-brain study	Casey et al. (2011) Neural correlates of delay of gratification
Individual differences	Understanding disorders	Freud (1909) Little Hans	Baron-Cohen et al. (1997) Autism in adults

Guidance about how to approach exam questions

Below, we will attempt to offer some guidance about how to approach questions in the various sections of the Unit 2 exam. It is important to bear in mind that, at the time of writing, the only examples of potential exam questions that were available were the specimen assessment materials (SAMs), and even these were only in draft form. While SAMs were available for both the A Level and AS Level courses, at the time of writing there were no actual past exam questions for reference. This is important because exams tend to evolve over time and so it would be misleading to suggest that actual exam question papers would be precisely like the SAMs.

When you are preparing for your exams, you would be well advised to **refer to OCR's website for both past question papers and past mark schemes** as these are extremely helpful. The purpose of the mark schemes is to guide the examiners in what they should be looking for in the exam scripts that they read and to ensure consistency (reliability) between them so that it doesn't matter which examiner marks your work as they would all mark it in the same way. The most recent mark schemes will be the best ones to refer to as they will confirm the directions that the exam seems to be heading in.

Given the limited range of sample questions available at the time of publication, the guidance given below is deliberately quite general. That said, the points that are being made can be assumed to hold good as general examining principles that are unlikely to change.

Section A

The focus of questions in Section A is on the core studies. Questions in this section can be expected to ask about different aspects of the core studies, as the following should make clear.

They may, for instance, ask about detail from a single core study, such as the following question from the AS Level specimen materials:

- From Bandura *et al.*'s study of transmission of aggression, outline how the model displayed aggressive behaviour. [3 marks]

They may also ask questions testing your understanding of why a Core Study followed the procedure that it did, such as the following question from the A Level specimen materials:

- From the Baron-Cohen *et al.* study into autism in adults, describe the purpose of the Basic Emotion Recognition Task (Emotion Task). [2 marks]

Something else they could do is ask what a particular core study has taught us, such as the following question from the A Level specimen materials:

- Outline one conclusion that can be drawn in relation to visual inattention from Simons and Chabris' study. [2 marks]

They could also ask a question inviting evaluation of some aspect of a core study, such as the following question from the AS Level specimen materials:

- Baron-Cohen *et al.*'s study into autism in adults gathered quantitative data. Explain one strength of gathering this type of data in this study. [3 marks]

They could also assess your ability to see how a particular core study relates to its key theme, such as the following question from the A Level specimen materials:

- With reference to Milgram's study of obedience, describe what the study found in relation to how individuals respond to people in authority. [4 marks]

They could also assess your ability to see how a particular core study relates to its area, such as the following question from the A Level specimen materials:

- Suggest how Freud's study of Little Hans is relevant to the area of individual differences. [3 marks]

They could, beyond this, assess your ability to compare or contrast the two studies (one classic, the other contemporary) that are paired together in relation to a key theme, such as the following question from the AS Level specimen materials:

- Outline one difference between Sperry's split brain study and Casey *et al.*'s study of neural correlates of delay of gratification. [3 marks]

This is probably not an exhaustive list of the kinds of demand that could be made on you in this section of the Unit 2 exam, but it provides a flavour of what you can expect. For all questions, the key will be doing precisely what the question asks of you – no less, but no more – and adjusting (slightly) the amount that you write to the number of marks available. Furthermore, responses will need to draw on detail from the study or studies in question, so that you are giving answers that are in context rather than producing bland generalities that could be about any study.

Section B

The focus of section B is on areas, perspectives and debates, with psychological research coming in only to back up the points that are being made in relation

183

to these areas, perspectives and debates. It can be expected that the questions that will be asked are likely to make reference to a mixture of different areas, perspectives and debates.

Questions in Section B of Unit 2 can be expected to follow a format similar to this (which was published by OCR in their Specimen Assessment Materials for the A Level):

1. Describe the difference between an individual explanation for behaviour and a situational explanation for behaviour. [4 marks]
2. Explain how one psychological study can be considered as providing an individual explanation for behaviour. [5 marks]
3. Evaluate the usefulness of providing a situational explanation for behaviour. Support your answer with evidence from one appropriate psychological study. [6 marks]
4. Discuss ethical considerations in relation to the study of individual differences. Support your answer with evidence from appropriate psychological studies. [20 marks]

As ever, the key to answering questions like these will be to do precisely what the questions are asking of you – no less, but no more – and to adjust the amount that you write in line with the number of marks available. Furthermore, for questions 2, 3 and 4, responses would need to be backed up with examples of relevant psychological research, with appropriate details being referred to from within these studies.

It is important to note that in this section of the exam it is entirely permissible to refer to studies beyond the specified core studies, so if you have done additional reading or you wish to use research from Unit 3 then that is permitted by the specification.

When answering questions, a good tip is to pay close attention to the injunction at the start of the question. If, therefore, you are asked to 'Describe' something (as in question 1 above), don't bother doing any evaluating (e.g. saying what is good or bad about something) as this will not be creditworthy within the mark scheme. Similarly, if asked to 'Discuss' something (as in question 4 above), don't waste time on description – instead, take your cue from the question and get a discussion going, exploring different sides to the debate and supporting them with examples of appropriate research. The same would apply to an injunction like 'Evaluate' in question 3, for which you would need to consider ways in which situational explanations of behaviour are and aren't useful, with both sides of the debate being supported with carefully chosen examples of psychological research. A question such as question 4

should be treated as, in effect, a kind of essay question, requiring a response that is tightly focused on the demands of the question, considers different sides of the debate (backed up with examples), is carefully structured, and comes to a considered (and defensible) conclusion.

The specimen assessment materials published in relation to Section B of the AS Level specification were as follows:

1. Outline how biological psychology explains behaviour. [2 marks]
2. Suggest one strength of claiming that behaviour is only due to nature. Support your answer with evidence from one appropriate core study. [3 marks]
3. Suggest one weakness of claiming that behaviour is only due to nature. Support your answer with evidence from one appropriate core study. [3 marks]
4. Explain how any one core study can be considered to be located within the area of social psychology. [5 marks]
5. Discuss the extent to which psychology can be viewed as a science. Support your answer with evidence from core studies. [12 marks]

Obviously these add up to 25 marks, rather than 35, and it can probably be assumed that a consequence of the smaller mark total is that students taking the AS Level course are unlikely to be set a 20-mark essay-style question. That said, question 5 should be treated as an essay question in the same way that question 4, in particular, would have needed to be treated in the A Level paper.

It is also worth bearing in mind a few points thrown up by these SAM questions that can be assumed to apply to both courses. First, a question like question 4 doesn't have to be answered by only citing those studies officially designated as falling within the social area – as both the specification and the mark scheme make clear, it is entirely legitimate to refer to other studies provided you can justify why they should be seen as falling within the social area. Second, what questions 2, 3 and 5 bring out is that sometimes questions might restrict you in terms of the studies you are permitted to refer to (e.g. for these questions, it was only core studies that could be used, not studies from extra reading or Unit 3). Third, what questions 2 and 3 also bring out is that it would be worth going into the exam equipped with knowledge of strengths and weaknesses of different positions within the various debates, rather than having to try and think of these on the spot.

Exam preparation exercise

For each debate, you need to be able to define what it is all about. On top of this, you might find it helpful to fill in grids such as the one shown in Table 6.3, perhaps including examples of research that you'd want to refer to in support of the particular arguments you'd be putting forward.

Table 6.3 Grid depicting strengths and weaknesses of research

	Strengths	Weaknesses
'Nature' explanations of behaviour	1.	1.
	2.	2.
'Nurture' explanations of behaviour	1.	1.
	2.	2.
	Strengths	**Weaknesses**
Free will	1.	1.
	2.	2.
Determinism	1.	1.
	2.	2.
	Strengths	**Weaknesses**
Reductionism	1.	1.
	2.	2.
Holism	1.	1.
	2.	2.
	Strengths	**Weaknesses**
Individual explanations of behaviour	1.	1.
	2.	2.
Situational explanations of behaviour	1.	1.
	2.	2.
	Strengths	**Weaknesses**
Research being useful	1.	1.
	2.	2.
	Strengths	**Weaknesses**
Research staying within ethical guidelines	1.	1.
	2.	2.
	Strengths	**Weaknesses**
Conducting socially sensitive research	1.	1.
	2.	2.
	Strengths	**Weaknesses**
Psychology being scientific	1.	1.
	2.	2.

As an example of the kinds of points you could make, Table 6.4 is a completed version of part of Table 6.3.

Table 6.4 Example of a completed version of part of the grid in Table 6.3

	Strengths	Weaknesses
Psychology being scientific	1. It is likely to lead to psychology receiving more respect as an academic subject (e.g. Baron-Cohen *et al.*)	1. It is likely to lead to more lab experiments, which may lack ecological validity (e.g. Bandura *et al.*)
	2. It may be useful in helping to predict, or even change, human behaviour in the future (e.g. Casey *et al.*)	2. It can mean other research methods (e.g. case studies) being undervalued even though they can provide great insight (e.g. Freud)

Section C

The focus of questions in Section C is on applying your knowledge of psychological research to a novel written source (e.g. an extract from a newspaper or magazine article). Questions in Section C can be expected to follow a format similar to this (which was published by OCR in the A Level SAMs):

Is Peppa Pig making toddlers naughty?
Parents despair as children copy cartoon by answering back

With her cheeky smile, and even cheekier attitude, she has become a hit with children. But it seems a growing number of parents are turning against television character Peppa Pig, claiming she is a 'bad influence'. Many complain their sons and daughters have started to copy the 'naughty' behaviour of the cartoon pig and her younger brother, George, by answering back to their parents.

Some have even banned the programme because they claim it has made their children misbehave.

One father spoke of his despair at how his four-year-old son had taken to splashing in what he gleefully called 'muddy puddles' on his way to school, copying Peppa's favourite pastime.

A mother reported 'My daughter kept saying "No" and "Yuk" in a really high and mighty way, just like Peppa does, and generally answering back when I ask her to do something.'

Psychologist Dr Aric Sigman said that in recent years there had been a 'significant increase' in children using 'adversarial, snide, questioning, confrontational and disrespectful behaviour' they had copied from cartoons. He added, 'Some 80 per cent of brain

185

In one particular case, a Locket user locked and unlocked their phone up to 900 times.

During peak hours, when users are most active, between 5 and 8 p.m., over 75 per cent of people unlock their phones and actively use them.

During off peak hours – between 3 and 5 a.m. – this figure drops to 24 per cent but still shows a quarter of people are using their devices in the early hours.

At peak times, the average person checks their device around nine times an hour. Off peak, this drops to four times an hour.

Source: www.dailymail.co.uk

Suggested possible answers

Source one
Links to psychology

- Levine *et al.* (the fact that the story comes from Singapore, which was ranked twenty-first in Levine's overall helping index).
- Piliavin *et al.* (the fact that it involves reference to someone being helped on public transport; the idea that people don't help because they don't want to be inconvenienced – this suggests a weighing up of costs and rewards when it comes to helping out).
- Bocchiaro *et al.* (the claim that Singaporeans are becoming more outspoken could arguably be linked to the concept of 'whistle-blowing').

Management

- Bandura *et al.* (the Singapore Government could run a campaign celebrating as role models people who have helped those in need or speak up to challenge anti-social behaviour).
- Chaney *et al.* (the Singapore Government could give out rewards to people who help those in need or speak up to challenge anti-social behaviour).
- The old woman on the bus could move to a *simpatico* culture where it would be less unusual for her to receive help when in need (Levine *et al.*).

Problems with these suggestions

- People might start challenging anti-social behaviour, but those whose behaviour they challenge might respond violently.
- People could start staging fake situations in which one friend behaves in an anti-social way and then another friend 'challenges' this in order to get money from the government.
- The old woman on the bus may not have the financial means (or inclination) to move abroad.

Source two
Links to psychology

- Moray or Simons and Chabris (this article suggests an inability to divide our attention).
- Casey *et al.* (inability to defer gratification on the part of those taking phone calls while driving).

Management

- Moray or Simons and Chabris (the Government could ban the use of any kind of phone by people while driving motor vehicles, including hands-free phones).
- Bandura *et al.* (the Government could run a safety campaign in which the first thing a respected role model does when getting into the driver's seat of their car is turn off their phone).

Problems with these suggestions

- It would be very difficult for the police to enforce a ban on drivers using mobile phones, especially hands-free ones, as even if they used CCTV cameras there would be too many cars to keep watch over.
- Any safety campaign run by the Government would cost money; there would also be challenges involved in making sure it reached its target audience (particularly in a multi-media age) and that the way in which the message was framed was one that the recipients responded to sympathetically.

Source three
Links to psychology

- Chaney *et al.* (the positive reinforcement that people get from their phones, in terms of feedback from friends, etc.).
- Casey *et al.* (inability to delay gratification).
- Maguire or Casey *et al.* (it could be speculated as to whether this pattern of behaviour could be having an effect on the brain).

- Research process: ethics (monitoring without consent?); reliability (sample size); sampling method.

Management

- Bandura *et al.* (a respected role model could show him/herself turning off their phone and demonstrating all the things they are able to do by not spending their time constantly monitoring their phone).
- Chaney *et al.* (schools could offer rewards to children who can demonstrate that they are not constantly checking phones).
- Carry out some further research into this through self-report, asking people how often they check their phones (for quantitative data) and why they do this (for qualitative data).

Problems with these suggestions

- No role model is likely to appeal to everyone, so they would have to be chosen with care to ensure that they genuinely appeal to the specific audience being targeted.
- Schools may not have the resources to be able to pay for rewards for children not constantly checking their mobile phones, and it would be hard for them to check up on this. (It would also be open to abuse as children could, for example, have one phone that they never check but then another phone that they are always checking.)
- Collecting data through self-report could be helpful in producing qualitative data but, unless participants were encouraged to keep a tally of every time they check their phone, it would be difficult to see how this could lead to the collection of valid quantitative data, and if people knew that their behaviour was being measured (which they would do) then this awareness could affect their behaviour anyway.

The three sources here are just examples of ones that you could relate to psychology. The specification advises teachers to prepare you for Section C of the Unit 2 exam by giving you a variety of sources to consider, but you don't need to wait for your teacher to do this. You could build up a 'cuttings file' of articles which you think connect to psychology, and you could even share these with the other students in your class, seeing if they can identify the psychology that you think lies within the article or – better still – identify psychology that you didn't see yourself. The more practice you have at doing this, the better. When you start to see psychology everywhere you turn, you'll know either (a) that you're ready for the exam, or (b) that the course has started to have a strange effect on you ...

Part 2

Research methods

Chapter 7

Research methods

Planning and conducting research

Hopefully you will enjoy the practical aspect of psychology, using your knowledge to carry out mini research activities and therefore experiencing the problems psychologists may have when they do their research. However, it is very important that before you conduct *any* piece of research you check it with your teacher to ensure that you are not breaking any ethical guidelines. As a rule, we wouldn't expect you to research people under the age of 16 years, or to cause any stress or offence, for example by asking personal questions which may cause some people anxiety or by setting up uncomfortable situations. In the core studies, you look at research which has varying degrees of ethical concerns, but as an A Level student you need to ensure that you are carrying out ethical research every time. The 'Have a go yourself' activities are all acceptable for you to carry out without consulting your teachers, but remember to not use children under 16 as your participants.

When conducting their research, psychologists use a range of research methods, data gathering methods, designs, and sampling methods, taking a number of methodological and general issues into account in their research. A range of techniques is also used to present and analyse the data that have been gathered. The methods and techniques selected depend on what and whom the researcher is investigating, and, as you will see in this chapter, can be influenced by both ethical and practical considerations.

OCR examinations

For both the Research methods examination (Unit 1) and the Psychological themes through core studies examination (Unit 2), you need to be able to identify, describe, apply and evaluate psychological research methodology.

Unit 1 aims to develop your knowledge and understanding of the process of carrying out psychological research across a range of experimental and non-experimental methodologies using a variety of data gathering techniques. You then consider a range of evaluative concepts to help you assess each piece of research. In the Research methods examination, you are expected to know about all of the aspects of carrying out psychological research and to be able to apply this knowledge to examples of research given to you in the exam (the 'source material'). What you learn in the core studies (Unit 2) will help you in this examination – you are also expected to know about them in this examination, with the emphasis on research methodology.

In Unit 2 of the AS and A Level specifications, the core studies introduce you to a range of methods used in psychological research, including experiments carried out either in the psychology laboratory or under controlled conditions, such as Baron-Cohen *et al.*'s Eyes Task; field experiments carried out in natural settings, such as Chaney *et al.*'s study about the Funhaler; observations, such as Milgram's obedience study; and case studies such as Freud's study of Little Hans. You will also need to use your knowledge from Unit 1 Research methods to make links with the content of Unit 2 (and Unit 3 for the A Level). For example, you may be asked to evaluate the method used in a particular core study, or use an evaluation issue to judge the background knowledge in Unit 3 of the A Level.

The Research methods specification requires that you learn about four general methods:

1. Experiments
2. Observations
3. Self-reports, and
4. Correlations as they are used in psychological research.

One of the difficulties students often have is working out the difference between a research method, a data-gathering method, a design, and a methodological issue. Table 7.1 will help you as you go through the sections in this chapter.

Table 7.1 Differences between a research method, a data-gathering method, a design and a methodological issue

Research methods	Data-gathering methods	Designs	Methodological and general issues
The experimental method	Self-report methods (e.g. questionnaire, interview, asking questions, psychometric tests)	The experimental designs: repeated measures, matched participants, independent measures (groups)	Making generalisations: sampling methods Control
Case study	Observations (e.g. using an observation schedule to code and categorise behaviours, content analysis)	Longitudinal and snapshot (or cross-sectional) designs	Use of qualitative and quantitative data Subjectivity Generalisability
Correlation Observational methods* Self-report methods* (e.g. interview, survey)	Physiological measures (e.g. structural MRI scan; EEG) and biochemical measures (e.g. testing saliva for levels of cortisol, as a measure of stress)		Validity and reliability Ethical considerations Social desirability Demand characteristics Researcher bias

*This may seem confusing, as self-reports and observations appear in two columns, but as you will learn, psychologists use these data-gathering methods in experiments, correlations and case studies. So for the method, always work out if it is an experiment, case study or correlation before asking if it is an observational research method or a self-report research method!

Experiment

The experimental method is a research method that can establish causal (cause-and-effect) relationships between variables. If psychologists change one feature (variable) of a situation, then this can cause a change in the behaviour of the people in that situation. A hypothesis (prediction) is formulated to predict the effect of changing one variable, known as the independent variable (IV), on another variable, known as the dependent variable (DV).

Often, people in an experiment are in one of two situations (conditions) with one group in the experimental condition (with the IV manipulated) and the other group are in the control (or normal) condition, where no change has been made.

 Let's look at an example …

If a psychologist was interested in seeing if listening to music helped or hindered a student's revision, then that psychologist could set up an experiment. The normal or control condition is no music, and the independent variable would be the music. A hypothesis could suggest that music would hinder the revision of the student. The strength of the revision (dependent variable) could be measured by a multiple choice test of the information being revised.

If psychologists saw worse performances on the test when the music was playing during revision, psychologists could assume that the music caused the student to revise less well. Our prediction would be supported.

 Have a go yourself

Try to revise a list of 20 words with music playing. You could use 20 words from a dictionary. See how many you can recall in a set time, say 15 seconds. Then try the same thing with a different set of words with no music playing. Is there any difference in the number of words you recalled in each condition?

What psychologists are saying is that experiments are more than just 'investigations' – they have key features that must be present, including:

- The fact that the effect of independent variable(s) on dependent variable(s) is being tested
- Controlled conditions that are established, e.g. using standardised procedures
- The possible replication of the procedures, which is an important element of science, in order to test the reliability of the findings.

The specification requires that you know the definitions of each experimental method and be able to evaluate their strengths and weaknesses.

Laboratory and field experiments

Experiments can be carried out under controlled laboratory conditions (laboratory experiments) or in a natural setting (field experiments – not actually in a field!). The choice of location reflects a balance between strict control in laboratory conditions, and ensuring that the study has sufficient ecological validity (is enough like real life) for the results to be generalised to a real-life setting. Field experiments can offer a more realistic setting for a study, and therefore can be more ecologically valid when psychologists are studying social behaviour. However, the control in a laboratory (lab) experiment is necessary to produce scientific research, with all the other extraneous factors (variables) – which might influence behaviour – controlled to ensure that the variable which we are manipulating is really the *only* thing affecting the behaviour. Biological and cognitive research in psychology will often be based in laboratory settings. Both lab and field experiments have a place in psychological research. Loftus and Palmer (eye-witness testimony) used the lab experiment in their research into the effect of words on memory, with controls set up to ensure that every participant saw the same clips, had the same questions and that the *only* difference was the verb used to describe the car crash. Chaney *et al.*, on the other hand, carried out a field experiment – the participants were in their own home, and there could have been any number of factors about their home or what had happened over that period of time (such as holidays, illness, etc.) which could have impacted on their use of the Funhaler and normal inhaler.

Experiments can also be quasi-experiments, where the IV occurs naturally or is already established and can't, for either ethical or practical reasons, be manipulated by the experimenter, and only the resulting behaviour can be observed by the experimenter. Confusingly, these are sometimes known as natural experiments, because of the naturally occurring IV. For example, if the IV is age, gender or ethnicity, this obviously cannot be changed by the experimenter for the purpose of the experiment. An example of this type of quasi-experiment is the Baron-Cohen *et al.* (autism) study, where people already had autism, Tourette's syndrome or 'normal'. This type of experiment can limit the amount of control the experimenter has over all the other variables, such as how society treats different genders, or people with disorders such as Tourette's syndrome. The strength of this method is that it allows us to study the effects of the variables psychologists can't manipulate or change, using as controlled a method as is available to us (Table 7.2).

The following questions will test your knowledge and understanding of this topic, and reflect the type of questions which could be asked in psychology examinations. You will find this feature appearing throughout this chapter to help you.

 Stop and ask yourself...

- Can you explain each of the three types of experiments and identify the strengths and weaknesses of each?

Table 7.2 Strengths and weaknesses of experimental methods

Type of experiment	Strengths	Weaknesses
Laboratory experiment	Control in a laboratory experiment will produce scientific research, which ensures that the variable which we are manipulating is really the only thing affecting the behaviour.	Lab experiments have less ecological validity, as they are artificial settings which do not reflect real life, so therefore the behaviour seen may also be artificial.
Field experiment	Field experiments can offer a more realistic setting for a study, and therefore can have more ecological validity.	Lack of control can mean it is difficult to assume that the variable manipulated was actually influencing behaviour and that it wasn't something else.
Quasi-experiment	It allows us to study the effects of the variables psychologists can't manipulate or change on behaviour.	There is no control over the participants, in terms of social setting, how they were brought up, life style, etc., and these may be confounding variables which influence behaviour.

Practice questions

1. Which of these is the independent variable? [1 mark]
   (a) The variable measured
   (b) A variable which might confound the data
   (c) The variable being manipulated
   (d) The prediction of what will happen.

2. Which of these is a strength of field experiments? [1 mark]
   (a) Lack of control
   (b) Natural behaviour likely to be shown
   (c) Naturally occurring IV
   (d) Less extraneous variables.

3. What differentiates a quasi-experiment from a field experiment? [1 mark]
   (a) Natural setting
   (b) Lack of control
   (c) Naturally occurring IV
   (d) Less extraneous variables.

Observation

In psychological research, observational methods can be used on their own as a method in themselves. For example, Milgram carried out a controlled observation in his obedience study. They can also be used as a way to gather data within an experimental design, as used by Bandura *et al.* in their study on transmission of aggression.

There are a number of different types and settings for observations, and the researchers can have different roles to play.

The specification requires that you know the definitions of observation types and be able to evaluate their strengths and weaknesses.

Have a go yourself

Try making a note of everything that happens during five minutes of your favourite television programme, or from an internet video or film. Now try concentrating on one person for five minutes and tally their behaviours on your list, then observe another character for five minutes, and so on.

Naturalistic observation is observation which is carried out in the field. If you wanted to carry out an observation into mobile phone use by students, you would set yourself up in a natural (for students) setting, such as a college or on a school bus. This gives you the chance to observe natural behaviour.

A controlled observation controls all the possible factors which might alter the behaviour, and which might therefore hide (or confound) the behaviour caused by the IV. Bandura *et al.* made sure that the toys in the third room were set up in the same place for each child, so that if they were tempted to play with the first thing they saw, it was always the same toy.

Participant observation is a method of gathering data through observation, where the observers are part of, or are pretending to be part of, the group they are observing. For example, if you decided to observe a group of your friends in the café, and you were sitting talking with them with them, noting their behaviour, you would be carrying out a participant observation.

The alternative to participant observation is called non-participant observation where the observer is not a member of the group being studied or playing a part of another person in the group.

In an unstructured observation, the researcher/observer continuously records and reports on behaviour, noting everything that happens. You will get a lot of data with this 'observe and report everything' method, and a number of problems can arise.

In order to focus the observation and increase the usefulness and objectivity of the study, researchers plan and carry out structured observations. This means they impose a structure on their observation to meet the aim of their observation (what behaviours in particular they are interested in recording), and the observational systems they will use for recording the data.

Let's look at an example ...

If a psychologist is interested in seeing how people react when their personal space is invaded, then they might set themselves up in a shopping centre and look at how people react when sitting on a bench. Do they sit away from anyone else already on the bench? Do they protect their space using a bag? What happens if someone sits next to them? Do they get up? How long do they stay? Does their body language change?

195

These may include the designing of a coding system or a category checklist against which the observations will be made. For example, in the Bandura *et al.* (Bobo doll) study, for each child, the observer noted if the child displayed physical aggression such as punching the Bobo doll, or verbal aggression such as saying, 'Sock it to him'. The third behaviour observed was the number of times the mallet was used to show aggression other than hitting Bobo, and the final type of behaviour noted was aggression shown by the child that was not an imitation of the role model's behaviour, such as shooting Bobo.

Covert observation is where the participant (the person being observed) does not know that he/she is being observed.

Overt observation is where the participant knows that he/she is being observed, and has either given their consent or is aware of being observed because of the observer's presence. This method makes it possible to carry out ethical research.

> ### ➡ Have a go yourself
>
> Set yourself up to observe in a public space, such as on a bus, or in a college or sixth form café (not in a school as there will be under 16s) and try out the various types of observation to see the pros and cons for yourself. Does the type of observation you choose affect your results?

Strengths and weaknesses of observation methods

In unstructured observations, there might be too much going on and so many things to record that the observation isn't very successful. The data gathered may be too dense and detailed to reveal anything to the observer. It would be difficult to summarise and present the data and it would be difficult to make comparisons between different participants or situations being observed.

The structured approach allows comparisons to be made across each observation and for trends in the data to be more easily seen. However, once you start only noting down some behaviours then you are at risk of missing something important. Suppose you had a list of six behaviours, but a seventh behaviour was happening a lot more often. You would have very skewed data if you didn't note that seventh behaviour.

In naturalistic observations, while you may see normal realistic behaviour, the lack of control means there could be other factors influencing the behaviour. In the example of observing student mobile phone use, these could be the bus going through a signal-free zone, which might cause very little phone use, which is not necessarily natural for students. If the college has banned the use of phones in the café, then you would only be observing the phone use of disobedient students, which might not be the natural behaviour of all students.

In controlled observations, the control of everything usually means the situation is somewhat artificial. The children in Bandura *et al.*'s research were not in their normal play room at the nursery, so this may in itself make their behaviour unusual. How does your behaviour change if you are eating at a friend's or relative's house instead of eating at home?

One advantage of being a participant observer is that you have a good vantage point for your observations. However, your presence may change the course of the events you are observing, particularly if your friends know you are observing and noting their behaviour. Another advantage of participant observation is that as an 'insider' you can get an insight into the experience yourself, and also gather detailed information about the situation if you are observing over an extended period of time. However, it is also possible that if you are observing as a participant observer for a long period of time, you may become too involved in the group to be really objective about your observations. You could think, 'well I know that person would not normally be so quiet', and therefore you could ask a direct question to make that person speak.

The advantage of non-participant observation is that you may remain more objective about what is being observed, but you may not have the same level of insight into the behaviour as you would if you were a participant observer. Imagine sitting outside the café looking in through the window and noting the groups' behaviour. What difference would it make to the data you collect?

Covert observations are useful because it means that 'natural' behaviour can be observed, especially if the study is carried out in the field. In a controlled laboratory-based study, observation is often carried out in the psychology laboratory through the use of a one-way mirror. This is what Bandura *et al.* did. However, observing participants without their consent – and therefore possibly invading their privacy – raises ethical issues. Do you think it would be acceptable to observe people on a train if they didn't know their behaviour was being noted? What difference would it make if they knew they were being observed? The problem with covert observation is that the participant may not display 'natural' behaviour if they become aware of being observed, and may respond to demand characteristics or behave differently because of social desirability bias.

The advantage of covert observation then, is that you are sampling 'real' behaviour, uncontaminated by the subject reactivity. Some researchers believe that the only valid way to sample typical human behaviour is by covert observation in a field setting.

Stop and ask yourself ...

Can you define the different observation types and identify the strengths and weaknesses of each? Draw up a revision table to help you collate your notes.

Designing observations

The specification also requires you to know how to design observations and how to collect the data.

There are various ways of sampling behaviour during an observation. The observers can note behaviour in one of the following two ways.

First, event sampling is where an event is recorded each time it happens. For example, an observer may want to find out if more male or female students take up the offer of free fruit at break times at their school. They could observe children at break time and tally how many males and females come and collect fruit. This gives them two 'events' to observe for: 'male student collecting fruit' and 'female student collecting fruit'. In event sampling, observers use observation schedules, or observation categories.

Second, time sampling, has two meanings. One is time point sampling, where the observer records what the participant is doing at fixed intervals, for example, every five seconds over twenty minutes, as in the Bandura *et al.* study (imitating aggression). The other is time event sampling, where a fixed period of time is set for observation, for example, if the first ten minutes of every hour is allocated to observe the number of people using a café over a working day.

Using time sampling means that the observer has a manageable way of sampling the behaviour they are interested in. However it is possible that, in the time periods they are not observing, they may miss some behaviours, and therefore end up with data that aren't valid.

Behavioural categories are necessary in structured observations, when the researcher will devise an observation schedule, so that what is going to be observed and how it is going to be observed is all decided before the observation takes place. This is a form of event sampling. First, it is necessary to establish categories of behaviour to observe, for example, 'punching Bobo'; 'imitative verbal aggression' (Bandura *et al.* study).

Advantages of using categories in observations are that they provide quantitative data which can be fairly easily compared between subjects or groups, easlly presented and summarised and can also be analysed statistically.

However, observation using categories has a main weakness. It may give a very restricted view of what is actually happening. This is especially true if time-point sampling is also used. The researcher may miss important behaviour, and the data are not as in-depth as simply observing and recording all behaviour as it is occurring.

Coding frames are useful as they will enable psychologists to analyse qualitative data (data in the form of words rather than numbers). The researcher in an observation needs to observe the behaviour and identify key features of the behaviour and code them. This can be done in stages. Initially, this involves observing and noting how the participant e.g. a child behaves when alone, when in a subservient position such as talking to the teacher, and when playing in the playground with peers. Then, categories of behaviour can be identified. The observation can then continue with the behaviour being noted in the appropriate category. Finally, analysis can be carried out, and comparisons can be made, such as seeing if the child is shy with peers but not when with authority figures. In interviews, the psychologist will note conversations and then read the text to identify specific key concepts. The researcher will then have several categories and will re-read the text identifying the parts of the text which relate to each category. This gives a clearer view of, for example, sibling relationships in comparison to peer relationships. A therapist may look at a client's conversation about their childhood, identifying specific segments of interest, such as the client's relationship with their siblings, parents or extended family, their friendships, and their behaviour in school.

 Let's look at an example ...

Psychologists might want to see the behaviour of children and parents when they are looking at gender differences in behaviour. They might identify behavioural categories, such as playing with parent, playing alone, playing with another child, playing with cars, playing with a doll, playing with a train set. This would give them the number of times each activity happened. Or they might note everything the child does without using the behavioural categories, and just write down as the child moves about, and then look for the key words such as parent, alone, another child, cars, doll, train set. This would allow for the observer to record any interaction with the parent, including playing, but also arguing, cuddling, etc.

Content analysis

An observer can code written material (such as articles in a newspaper) or filmed material (such as television adverts or soap operas), and this kind of observation is called a content analysis. This method eliminates the ethical concerns that arise when studying human participants, as the information being observed is already in the public domain.

Content analysis can also be used to code and observe qualitative data to turn it into quantitative data. In one of the A Level studies, Hancock interviewed murderers who scored highly on the psychopath rating about their crime, and he compared the words they used to non-psychopathic murderers. He was looking at their use of words such as cause-and-effect descriptors (e.g. because), material needs (e.g. money) and social needs (e.g. family), plus their use of past and present tenses.

Self-report

As with observational methods, self-report methods can be used on their own as a method in themselves, for example a survey could be carried out to find out why students love psychology so much(!), or self-report techniques can be used as a data-gathering tool, to measure behaviour (the dependent variable) within an experiment or for a correlation.

Self-report data range from participants' responses to being asked simple questions, such as, 'Did you see any broken glass?' in the Loftus and Palmer study on eyewitness testimony, to the detailed notes of interviews presented in case studies; such as the notes Little Hans' father made for Freud.

The specification requires you to know the different techniques for collecting data via self-report designing self-report questions, plus the strengths and weaknesses of all of these.

Questionnaires are sets of questions that are usually completed as pen and paper tests, but can also be done over the internet or telephone.

An advantage of questionnaires is that they enable a great deal of data to be gathered from a large sample very quickly, making this a cost- and time-effective method of data collection. However, asking the right question in the right way is very difficult, and researchers have to be careful to frame their questions carefully using language their respondents will understand.

Interviews, as the name of this self-report method suggests, is where participants are interviewed, usually face-to-face, and their responses recorded. They may be written down 'on the spot', or recorded on audiotape or videotape and later written up (transcribed).

There are several types of interview, but the three you need to know are structured interview, semi-structured interview and unstructured interview.

A structured interview is where the same set of questions is asked to each participant in the same order. Often researchers will not show any expression or interest, for fear of influencing the answers. It is often written down and the interviewer works his or her way through the questions. An advantage of this is that it is easier to gather quantitative data than in an unstructured interview, making it possible to analyse the data and draw out trends from participants' responses.

A disadvantage, however, is that the structured nature of this type of interview is artificial, and the respondent may not feel free to add to or explain their answers. This may mean the data gathered are limited and superficial.

Being asked a list of questions in this way is not a natural activity and so lacks ecological validity.

An unstructured interview is where the researcher has topics to discuss but these don't have to be in the same order for each participant and is more like a conversation. One point may follow on from what the interviewee has just said and answers can be more detailed, and participants can be asked to clarify or explain points they make. Hans' father used this type of interview to question Hans on his dreams, feelings and thoughts. An advantage of this type of interview is that a lot of detailed information, often qualitative data, can be gathered using this method.

Another advantage is that this type of interview is more like a regular conversation and is therefore higher in ecological validity than the structured interview. A disadvantage, however, is that because a broad range of topics can be discussed in detail it can be difficult to summarise the data, to analyse the data for trends or to make comparisons between participants.

A mixture of the two is the semi-structured interview where the interviewer has a list of questions, but can ask for clarification for example, and can be a bit more friendly and sociable. However, there is still the list of questions which have to be asked. This interaction is likely to be seen by participants as more trustworthy and therefore there may be more detail, but there is still some quantifiable data to analyse, often in addition to the qualitative (wordy) answers given to clarify.

Stop and ask yourself …

- Can you list the strengths or weaknesses of different self-report methods?

You could put these on a revision card.

Designing self-reports

The specification requires that you know how to design self-reports and collect data.

Open questions or free response questions allow the participant freedom to respond and give them the opportunity to explain their answers. For example, 'Why do you think some people don't obey the law and continue to use their mobile phone, without using a hands-free kit, while they are driving?'

Open questions provide qualitative data, and the advantage of this is that psychologists get rich, detailed information. Here psychologists have increased realism (validity), as respondents aren't forced to respond in a particular way and this allows them to qualify their responses rather than just give 'Yes/No/Don't know' answers. Freedom to respond removes the negative feelings respondents have when forced to choose from a limited range of responses.

However, it is harder to analyse and compare responses to open questions, as the data need to be coded or quantified in some way to do this and this may not be easy. It is therefore difficult to establish the reliability of qualitative responses.

Closed questions or fixed/forced response questions, on the other hand, give the respondent to the question or questionnaire a limited fixed range of responses to choose from. For example, Do you think that the early experiences people have as children have an effect on them in later life? Yes/No/Don't know

Closed questions provide quantitative data, and an advantage of this is that the results can then be easily summarised, presented and compared between participants or conditions. It is also easier to test the reliability of data where quantitative measures have been used. This type of question can lack ecological validity, however, due to the forced choices of answers available.

The researcher is only gathering limited information, and important information may be missed where respondents are unable to qualify or explain their answers. Respondents may feel frustrated or constrained by the limited number of responses available and this may affect their attitude towards the research.

Baron-Cohen *et al.* used these questions in their two words choice for participants to choose one to describe the emotion in the Eyes Test. However, closed questions are also likely to frustrate respondents where forced choice responses are the only option (e.g. Yes/No are the options, but I want to say 'sometimes'!).

➡ Have a go yourself

Ask two friends to describe their favourite place. Can you compare their answers, and see *any* similarities between the two? Now ask them to rate their psychology lessons on a scale of 1–5 with 1 being 'hate them' and 5 being 'love them'. Is this easier to compare?

Variables can also be measured on rating scales, providing a quantitative measure. Often this is used in self-report questionnaires and structured interviews.

For example, on a scale of 1–10, where 0 is very miserable and 10 is ecstatically happy; circle the number that indicates how happy you are at the moment:

1	2	3	4	5	6	7	8	9	10

Likert scales can also be used. A Likert scale is where people are given a range of answers from which they select the one that represents the extent to which they like/dislike something or agree/disagree with something. For example, psychology is a fascinating subject and I am very glad I chose to study it.

Strongly agree	Agree	Not sure/ Don't know	Disagree	Strongly disagree

A Likert scale can increase the ecological validity of a rating scale, since people have a range of verbal options to choose from, and this is not as artificial as, say, choosing from a simple numerical scale of 1–10.

By assigning numerical values to the responses, e.g. 1 for disagree strongly, 2 for disagree, 3 for don't know, 4 for agree, 5 for agree strongly, it is possible to generate quantitative data from Likert scales.

A semantic differential scale is used to put something on a scale between two descriptive words, such as strong and weak. To create a scale, psychologists take two words which are opposite each other, and which reflect what is being measured. So psychologists researching leadership might consider: decisive vs indecisive, bold vs fearful, active vs passive. Then there are a number of spaces on the continuum for the person to mark their rating. This could be a

scale of 7 or 5. Usually no more than twelve lines would be used, as after this, participants may get bored, or just tick the middle rather than think about their response.

Let's look at an example ...

Psychologists could compare ratings of one person or product with another: comparing 'Chocco chocolate bar' with 'Chocish chocolate bar' for example, on cost, taste, satisfaction, value for money, etc. A visual display of the responses could show consumers' preferences or provide psychologists with a focus for an advertising campaign.

Ratings for Chocish chocolate bar

Tastes good	✓						Tastes bad
Too big						✓	Too small
Expensive		✓					Cheap
Value for money					✓		Not value for money

One problem is that as the rating scale is based on words, participants have to have a reasonable vocabulary and there may be cultural limitations. Children would find this difficult to complete, unless simplified enough.

Because the data from rating scales are quantitative, all the strengths and weaknesses of quantitative data apply. As with all rating scales, Likert scales and semantic differential scales are basically closed or fixed response questions, and so the strengths and weaknesses of this type of questions also apply to these methods.

Strengths and weaknesses of self-report methods

The advantages of using self-report data are that psychologists are able to measure cognitive variables, such as memory, knowledge and attitudes, which cannot be either observed directly or tested for in any biological test. Without self-report, the study by Loftus and Palmer on memory and language would not be possible, for example.

However, the validity of self-report data can be questioned where participants are able to deliberately falsify their answers. This can be because they are responding to demand characteristics present in the study or because of evaluation apprehension: they lie to give a socially desirable answer to avoid being judged negatively.

Stop and ask yourself ...

● Have you understood the methods of collecting data through self-report, and their respective strengths and weaknesses?

Try making revision notes on these.

 Practice questions

A researcher has become interested in studying stress associated with driving and wishes to conduct an investigation to assess stress levels of motorists in England using the self-report method.

1. Write an appropriate question using a rating scale, which could be used in this study. [2 marks]
2. Outline one strength of using this question in this study. [3 marks]

Correlation

Correlational studies in psychology use a statistical technique that can tell us about the way two variables are related to each other. They may be positively or negatively correlated or not correlated at all. A correlational study in psychology, then, is a study that investigates whether a relationship (or correlation) exists between two variables.

 Let's look at an example ...

Psychologists may wonder if there is a relationship between height and intelligence, or number of hours spent playing computer games and exam results. They will then gather the data, via IQ tests and measurements or self-reports of hours spent playing computer games, and exam results. They can then compare these two data sets and see if the person who is the tallest has the highest IQ and the person with the lowest IQ is also the shortest. Everyone else would fit on the line between these two, although of course it is only a relationship that is being looked at and there may be the occasional tall person with low IQ and vice versa.

The specification requires that you know what the different types of correlation mean, how to collect correlational data, as well as the strengths and weaknesses of the correlational method.

Because correlation is a mathematical technique, correlation requires that two variables be measured quantitatively in order for any correlation between them to be established. So when obtaining data

for correlation only numerical data are used. Data for correlations are gathered by self-report, or observation or by physiological measures for example brain cell development which can be correlated with age.

There are two types of correlation or relationship. A positive correlation is where as one variable increases so the other one does. In the case of IQ and height, the taller the people are, the more they score on an IQ test. A negative correlation is where one variable increases as the other one decreases. So as the number of hours playing computer games increases, so the exam results decrease. If there is no real link between the two, for example number of pets and shoe size, then we would say there is no correlation.

 Have a go yourself

Try and think what variables might correlate either positively or negatively with aggression.

There are some descriptive statistics that are only used for correlations, including the use of scatter diagrams (or scattergraphs) to pictorially represent the relationship, and correlation coefficients, which describe numerically the relationship between two variables.

Strengths and weaknesses of correlational evidence

Correlation is a useful tool in psychology as it allows us to measure the relationship between variables which it would be difficult or unethical to manipulate experimentally.

 Let's look at an example ...

Psychologists might be interested in investigating the impact of student debt in university students on their general health.

Psychologists could not ethically put a group of students into debt for comparison with a group of students whom psychologists had financed through their studies. However, psychologists could correlate the level of debt a student has in their third year of university with a measure of their general health. Psychologists would take all of the participants and put their debt into rank order and then question them about their health. Psychologists could then see if those who rated themselves as less healthy had more debt. This correlational method would give us an ethical way to measure the relationship between student debt and health.

A common use of correlational analysis in psychological research is as a test for either reliability or validity. This can be carried out where quantitative data have been gathered and where a study can be easily repeated (replicated), as most laboratory studies can be. If the data gathered by one observer in a study is the same as that gathered by the other observer in the study, then there would be a relationship/correlation between the two, and therefore psychologists could conclude that the observed data are consistent and therefore have inter-observer reliability (Bandura *et al.* did this with the observers in their study on Bobo doll). Concurrent validity is, for example, if the data in one test is related to the data in another test. So if you did well in one IQ test you would expect to see a relationship in your score on another IQ test. Correlation can therefore be used to support the scientific credibility of research.

The major problem with correlational evidence is that correlation does not mean causation. In other words, just because two variables are correlated this does not mean that one of them has caused the other one to change. For example, if there was a correlation between student debt and health does this mean that having an overdraft makes you ill? Possibly not. It could be that being ill gives you an overdraft as you can't work. Or there could be a third variable, such as poor students live in draughty run down houses, and so get ill.

Have a go yourself

What could the explanations be for a rise in ice cream sales being linked to a rise in murders?

Stop and ask yourself ...

- Can you explain positive, negative correlations and what it means if there is no correlation? Do you know how to collect correlational data and the strengths and weaknesses of the correlational method?

Other research methods

Case studies

Case studies are research that focus on one participant or a small group of participants with a specific characteristic, such as one class in a school, or followers of a certain religion. Freud's study on Little Hans is a single subject case study as it was carried out on one participant. The key point is that the study is in depth, and will usually contain a lot of data either from one point of view, such as Han's father, or from several points

 ## Practice questions

1. Which of these best describes a positive correlation? [1 mark]
   (a) Where one variable increases, the other variable increases.
   (b) Where one variable increases, the other variable doesn't change.
   (c) Where one variable increases, the other variable decreases.
   (d) There is no relationship between the two variables.
2. Which of these is a strength of the *weakness* correlational analysis? [1 mark]
   (a) It is very complicated.
   (b) It doesn't show cause-and-effect.
   (c) It is only displayed on a scatter diagram.
   (d) It is only quantitative.
3. Which of these is a possible explanation for the rise in rioting in summer? [2 marks]
   (a) As the temperature rises, so does aggression.
   (b) As the temperature rises, aggression is reduced.
   (c) As temperature rises, there is no impact on aggression.
   (d) As aggression rises, so does the temperature.

of view. The information from Hans was also important. You could consider Sperry's research a case study as it was on a very small group of unusual participants and there was much research, not just his observations, but also the data collected from using the apparatus.

Case studies will use a variety of methods of data collection, such as unstructured interviews, observation, psychometric test results or medical notes. These are all then used to gain a useful holistic overview of the participant. However, case studies tend to result in subjective analysis of the data as often the researchers have a close relationship with the participant(s) and are trying to support their own theories of behaviour. If you read the original case of Little Hans, you will see how Freud interprets seemingly innocuous comments by Hans in line with his own theory. Nevertheless, case studies are useful for gaining an insight into unusual behaviour and by using several sources an in-depth analysis of the behaviour can take place. One problem of having only one participant or a small group of participants is that case studies will tend to lack generalisability. There are rarely people with exactly the same behaviours, after all, not every boy with a phobia of horses would have felt the threat to his widdler that Little Hans had.

Longitudinal and snap shot studies

In a snapshot design, different groups of people are tested at the same point in time and their performances compared. Examples from the core studies include Bandura *et al.*'s, where the children of all ages were tested at the same point in time (it may take a few days to carry out the research but each participant was only tested once) and Baron-Cohen *et al.*'s study on the Eyes Test.

The advantages that snapshot studies have over longitudinal studies is that they are relatively quick and inexpensive to carry out, can be easily replicated to test the reliability of findings and are relatively easy to modify. This final point means that if design faults become apparent, the study can be repeated with modifications to eliminate them. It also means that variations of the study can be easily carried out to investigate fully the variables that may affect behaviour, such as Milgram's variations.

In a longitudinal study, one participant or one group of individuals is studied over a long period of time, for example, taking periodic samples of behaviour. This design allows us to track development and enables us to monitor changes over time, for example in Freud's analysis of Little Hans, the changes in the behaviour of Hans were seen as he developed from three to five years. An advantage of the case study method is a reduction in participant variables as the same person/people are being studied.

Let's look at an example ...

If psychologists were interested in the decline of memory in middle aged to elderly people, they could conduct a longitudinal study which monitors a group of people over time and then participant variables, such as innate memory skills, are eliminated. If someone had a poor memory to start with then their decrease in memory skills may be less than someone who had a high memory score at the beginning, so the actual differences over time can be measured.

Psychometric tests

Psychometric tests are instruments (e.g. pen-and-paper tests, one-to-one tests) that have been developed to measure mental characteristics, e.g. intelligence tests (IQ tests), brain damage/brain function, creativity, personality, job attitudes, aptitude and skills. Although they often provide quantitative measurements that are attractive to psychologists, as this makes comparison between participants and analysis of data possible, there

are some problems associated with psychometric tests. They are often completed as self-reports, so data may be falsified. This affects their internal validity.

Validity is a problem in general for these tests. Are they really testing what they say they are testing? It is very difficult to design a test that does not contain cultural biases and can be used for people in general.

Reliability is also important. If participants do not score significantly similar results on an equivalent test, then the tests are not reliable. Psychometric tests need to be administered and assessed by trained individuals. In the wrong hands they can be misinterpreted, for example, low IQ scores used to 'label' someone as stupid, and treating them accordingly!

Physiological measures

Psychologists can measure behaviour as the change in cell activity in just the same way as by looking at changes in observable behaviour, such as aggression. Studies which take a biological approach will often look at physiological measures of activity to assess the impact of the independent variable, or to look at a correlation for example between cortisol levels in saliva and self-reports of stress. In Casey *et al.*'s study, for example, he looked at functional imaging of the brains of some of his participants and found that the prefrontal cortex differentiated between No-go and Go trials more in high delayers, whereas greater ventral striatal activity in low delayers was seen relative to high delayers. By looking at which behaviours the respective areas of the brain are thought to be responsible for gives some understanding of how the brain can affect resistance to temptation.

Cross-cultural research

Cross-cultural research is a research method where the purpose is the study of participants in various cultural groups. Culture is the shared ways of living in a group of people. This can be based on such diverse considerations as country, district, type of setting (urban, rural), social class, ethnicity, religion or any other feature of a group which distinguishes it from another group.

Often there is predicted to be a difference in behaviour which can be attributed to the cultural background and upbringing. Therefore research studies need to be carried out to see if the predictions are justified or not. However, there is also the case that research may be looking for similarities in behaviour which can then be assumed to be universal features of human behaviour.

One of the issues with cross-cultural research is bias. This might be in the use of materials, the way the research is carried out or in the interpretation of data. The way of gathering data in different cultures may not be exactly the same but it has to be equivalent.

If you use a questionnaire in one setting, then using a questionnaire where people are not used to writing may lead to lack of validity. However, the equivalent method may be an interview (although we all know the differences between answering questions face to face and on paper).

Aims and hypotheses and how to formulate these

The specification requires you to know how to identify research aims and questions, and how to formulate hypotheses from these.

Psychologists can start off with research questions, which are questions posed about human and animal behaviour. Milgram's research arose when the question was posed, 'Are Germans different to Americans?' A research question can be suggested by an event, such as the Holocaust in Milgram's case, or based on previous research, such as Sperry's split-brain research. Psychologists are involved in trying to understand the cause of behaviour, and a research question might arise out of previous theories, such as Chaney *et al.*'s research question based on operant conditioning inherent in the Funhaler, and if this is likely to cause adherence behaviour to increase.

Once the research question has been identified, then the next step is to be a bit more specific and identify the research aim. For example, if a psychologist was interested in the research question about the nature of obedience, then the research aim might be to see if obedience is shown when an authority figure is present.

> **→ Have a go yourself**
>
> For the following research questions, try to identify a specific research aim:
>
> 1. Do children learn to be aggressive from television?
> 2. Can dogs learn to dance through operant conditioning?
> 3. What therapies might help drug addiction?
> 4. Does car choice reflect the personality of the driver?

In terms of the main features of science, the hypothesis is the prediction based on a theory or observation, and testing the hypothesis is how psychologists get data to support their theories.

A hypothesis for a correlation is a prediction about the relationship between two variables (for example, the younger you are, the better you will score on a memory test).

In a research study, the alternate (or experimental, if it is an *actual* experiment) hypothesis will predict the effect of the independent variable on the dependent variable (see page 206 for more information on independent and dependent variables), e.g. 'children shown an aggressive role model (IV) will show more aggressive behaviour (DV) than children shown a non-aggressive role model.' The hypothesis in a correlation is always called an alternate hypothesis as a correlation is never an experiment.

- A shorthand way of writing the alternate hypothesis is H_1
- The alternative or experimental hypothesis can also be known as the research hypothesis.
- Alternative and experimental hypotheses can be either one-tailed or two-tailed.

In a one-tailed hypothesis, a specific effect is predicted. This is also known as a directional hypothesis. One-tailed hypotheses have *only one possible true outcome*. For example, 'Students who listen to music while studying will score higher in their end of term test than those who study without music.' Those who listen to music must do better in order for this hypothesis to be true. If all the previous research points to a certain outcome, it is logical to have a one-tailed hypothesis.

In a two-tailed hypothesis, an effect is *predicted but not specified*. This is also known as a non-directional hypothesis. Two-tailed hypotheses have two possible true outcomes. For example, 'Listening to music while studying will affect a student's performance in their end of term test.' Now those who listen to music can do better *or* worse to make this hypothesis true. If there is no previous research or conflicting research then it might be logical to have a two-tailed hypothesis.

One-tailed (directional) alternate hypotheses for correlations say what kind of correlation is predicted, either positive or negative: 'There will be a positive correlation between the amount of independent study students complete and their A Level grades (the more they study, the better their grades will be).'

Two-tailed (non-directional) alternate hypotheses for correlations just say that a correlation is predicted, no direction is predicted: 'There will be a correlation between the number of hours' paid work a week students do in term time and their A Level exam scores.'

For statistical purposes (which will become clear in the study of inferential statistics), it is important to know how to formulate a null hypothesis.

The null hypothesis tells us that the independent variable will *not* have the predicted effect on the dependent variable.

- A shorthand way to write the null hypothesis is H_0
- It always states there will be no difference between conditions, regardless of whether the alternate hypothesis is one- or two-tailed.
- Therefore, it is never one-tailed. For example, 'There will be no difference in the number of errors made on the eyes task between "normal" adults and adults with HFA or AS even if the research hypothesis predicted fewer errors in "normal" adults.'

The null hypothesis will always predict no relationship in a correlational study.

- There will be no correlation between the amount of independent study completed by students and their A Level grades.
- There will be no correlation between the number of hours' paid work a week students do in term time and their A Level exam scores.

Psychologists do tests and experiments (psychology is a science), but psychologists are not trying to prove their hypothesis to be true, instead psychologists are trying to see if it can be proved false or not.

Karl Popper proposed the definition that phenomena, such as Theory of Mind, can be considered scientific if it can be objectively tested and proved (or not proved) to be false. That means that the aim of science is to see if phenomena can be falsified.

This is a problem for psychologists as they have an alternative hypothesis that they don't want to be false. In fact, psychologists very much want it to be true. So what psychologists do now is begin their study with the assumption that the hypothesis is not true, and that is why psychologists need the null hypothesis. Psychologists then set about *trying to show that the null hypothesis is not true*.

If psychologists can provide evidence that the null hypothesis is not true and can be rejected, then this means psychologists have supported the alternate

Practice questions

1. A psychologist was interested in the relationship between the number of books a student read and their mathematical ability. She used a correlational analysis to investigate this in a self-selected sample of 40 student participants. Each participant completed a maths test which involved several calculations and then they had to state how many non-study-related books they had read during the previous six months. The psychologist's hypothesis predicted a significant negative correlation.
   (a) Using this information, explain what she was expecting the results to show. [2 marks]
   (b) Write a null hypothesis for this study. [3 marks]
2. You have been asked to carry out an experimental study to investigate the differences in children's television adverts aimed at boys and girls. This will be a quasi-experiment doing a content analysis on the words used in ten television adverts aimed at girls and ten television adverts aimed at girls.

Write an alternative hypothesis for your investigation. [3 marks]

hypothesis and have in fact got scientific evidence for their theory.

A bit of a convoluted to way to say that if the hypothesis isn't wrong then it must be right!

Variables and how they are operationalised

When psychologists carry out research they are often asking the questions, 'Why or how does this behaviour

Stop and ask yourself...

Can you:

1. Explain the difference between a one-tailed and a two-tailed hypothesis.
2. Identify whether the following five alternate hypotheses are one-tailed or two-tailed:
   (a) Dog owners are more physically fit than cat owners.
   (b) Boys score differently on a test of aggressiveness from girls.
   (c) People given twenty emotionally charged words to learn will remember significantly more words than people given twenty emotionally neutral words to learn.
   (d) Students who have a computer at home for their own exclusive use do better in their exams than students who do not.
   (e) Doing more than ten hours' part-time paid work affects students' exam performance.
3. Identify the IV and the DV for each of the five examples above.

happen?' Loftus and Palmer wanted to know how memory could be influenced by post-event information, Bandura *et al.* wanted to know why children might show aggression. In order to carry out a scientific study, psychologists need to conduct research where they carefully control anything which might affect the behaviour but which is not being studied (such as the severity of the car crash or the gender of the child). They then have to manipulate the variable they think *will* influence the behaviour (the verb used in the question, the type/gender of role model). Then the variation in behaviour is recorded and compared to the participant's baseline behaviour or the control group's normal behaviour.

The specification requires you to know what the independent variable and dependent variable are, plus what extraneous variables are and how to control them.

In psychological terms, the variable which psychologists are testing, as they predict that it will influence behaviour, is the independent variable. The behaviour which they are measuring and recording is the dependent variable (it depends on the independent variable whether it is shown or not).

- The DV is always the effect, so to find the DV look for the results of the study.
- When explaining an IV or DV, state it in a way that can be measured, e.g. by saying 'amount of' or 'number of' or 'level of'. Where the IV is one of two types, for example gender, state it as categories, e.g. 'whether the participant is male or female'.

Hypotheses need to state variables in an operationalised format. This means that the variable that is being manipulated and the variable that is being measured are described in detail. For example, the prediction that eating chocolate improves exam performance could have several different variations.

For example, what does the researcher mean by 'eating chocolate' and 'exam performance'?

An operational hypothesis makes it clear exactly how these variables will be measured. For example, 'Participants who eat 200 g of 70 per cent cocoa chocolate twenty minutes beforehand will score higher in their mock GCSE maths exam than those who eat no chocolate.'

If a variable is to be studied scientifically (or objectively) then it must be operationalised. This is a benefit as it means a variable must be defined and measured in a way which is unambiguous, so anyone using that measurement to measure that variable in a given situation would come up with the same result.

For example, if the research hypothesis was age affecting memory, the variable 'memory' could be operationalised in any number of ways, such as 'the number of words a person can freely recall from a list

of 100 words learned in two minutes' or 'the number of pictures recalled after being shown 20 images for 30 seconds', or 'the number of characters' names recalled after watching a 15 minute film clip'.

As long as psychologists use the same list of words, images or film clip, all the participants can be equally tested and get comparable 'memory' measures.

All the other variables which might influence the behaviour are extraneous variables, and these need to be controlled as far as possible. This is known as controlling extraneous variables or applying experimental controls in an experiment. All the extraneous variables that psychologists want to control will fall into one of two categories:

1. Participant variables or personal factors: these are factors *within* a person that can vary over time or vary with a situation, for example, 'Being bored when studying maths but interested when studying psychology'; 'Feeling alert mid-afternoon but tired late at night'. Subject variables can also vary *between* people: the best time of the day for being alert for one person is late at night, whereas for another it is early afternoon. More obvious differences between people include age, gender and ethnicity.

2. Situational variables or environmental factors: these are factors which can vary in the environment including level of noise in a room; number of people present in a situation; time of day; the way an experimenter behaves towards the participants; and the procedure of a study (the way participants are tested).

It is essential that psychologists control extraneous variables in research because if any extraneous variable is not controlled then it will spoil the study by becoming a confounding variable. This is any extraneous variable which has not been controlled but has operated alongside the independent variable in the experiment, and it is this second variable which has caused any change in the dependent variable. This uncontrolled extraneous variable has confounded the study, which means that because of this variable, psychologists cannot isolate the IV as the cause of any change in the DV.

There are a number of strategies for controlling extraneous variables. These include standardisation, randomisation and counterbalancing.

Standardisation means keeping the test conditions the same for every participant. It is a method of controlling situational variables, or environmental factors, which might have an influence on the participant's behaviour. To keep all extraneous variables constant across experimental conditions, researchers use standard

Let's look at an example ...

If psychologists wanted to know whether students achieved better grades in a college compared to a school, they could set up two groups of students and look at their A Level results. However, there may be some differences which would impact on the exam results. The entry requirements may be different, so only students with five grade Bs at GCSE were accepted to the school sixth form, but five Cs at GCSE was enough to get into the college. Then there might be a difference in subjects chosen. Would students studying physics be different from students studying performing arts? How might this impact on their results? And what about gender differences, ethnicity, social class, parental involvement, place in the family (eldest or youngest child, for example). All of these might impact on the A Level results quite apart from the school/college variable. These extraneous variables need to be controlled to ensure the only real difference between the two groups is their place of learning.

 Have a go yourself

In the example of sixth form and college students, how do you think you could make sure the two groups were as similar as possible?

apparatus, standard instructions and procedures, standard locations. In fact, as an experienced student you have often been tested in standardised conditions, such as during your GCSEs.

Randomisation or random allocation, is where participants are allocated to experimental conditions on a chance basis, by drawing lots or tossing a coin, for example. Random allocation can be used to avoid experimenter bias (whether conscious or unconscious) when allocating participants to conditions for a study.

Counterbalancing is a method of controlling variables, especially order effects in repeated measures designs. This is done systematically varying the order of presentation of tasks to participants. For example, alternating the test procedure so that half take the control test first and the other half take the experimental test first. This spreads out the effects of order of presentation across the test conditions.

Populations, samples and sampling techniques

The entire population psychologists are interested in studying, for example children under five or adults

with autism, is usually too many to study and so just like a doctor wouldn't drain you of blood to test your blood, psychologists don't test *every* five-year-old, but

🚫 Stop and ask yourself ...

- A researcher wanted to investigate if there was a gender difference between women and men in their risk-taking behaviour. A questionnaire was devised and administered to all the participants.
- All 200 students in a school sixth form assembly at a local school were asked to take part in the study and were each given the questionnaire. They were asked to complete the questionnaire over the next 24 hours and post it into a box in their common room by the end of the next day.

Can you:
- Identify one experimental control that was used in this study and explain why it was used.
- Suggest one further experimental control that ought to be used in this study and explain why it ought to be used by the experimenter.

take a sample. Psychologists use a sample in research when they cannot, for practical reasons (e.g. cost- and time-effectiveness), study the entire target population in which they are interested. The target population is the section or group of people whom psychologists want to study. For example, Bocchiaro *et al*. studied undergraduates, and Baron-Cohen *et al*. had a target population of autistic and normal adults and Tourette syndrome and then a sample from each group was chosen to actually take part in the research.

Psychologists choose a sample and try to achieve a balance between:

1. Getting as representative a sample as they can. They can then make generalisations from the findings and establish general rules about the target population being studied and
2. Being cost- and time-effective when conducting the study.

It is also important to avoid any bias so that it is not only people who are likely to show the expected behaviours that are used, or only people with certain characteristics that are used in the research.

Usually a sample size between 30 and 50 is considered enough for a psychological study, although if you are distributing a questionnaire you can have a sample size of hundreds if your target population is very big, and if you are doing an in-depth case study you may have a sample of a single participant.

There are several techniques for obtaining a sample of people, all of which try to balance the needs identified above, but no sample is ever perfect.

The specification requires you to know the definitions of each sample type and how psychologists select each of these samples from a target population. You should also be able to evaluate the strengths and weaknesses of these sampling methods, in the context of a particular psychological investigation or study.

In a random sample, every member of the target population must have an equal chance of being selected to be in the sample. To obtain such a sample, there has to be a clear and finite target population where a full list of members can be drawn up, and then a random sample can be taken from this list. This can be done with a small target population by putting the names in a hat and drawing out the number of subjects required. For a large target population, a researcher can use a random number generator (RNG) computer program to select the sample.

 Let's look at an example ...

If psychologists wanted to see how college students felt about changes to the timetable, they could put all of the names into a hat, and pull out 50 names. Of course if the college is large, then it might be easier to use a random number generator to generate 50 numbers in the range and find out which students have that college ID number. One problem with this is that by chance they could just pick out all male students names, which would make it unrepresentative of all students. However, there is no researcher bias as the researchers can't influence who they ask.

A snowball sample is a particularly useful technique to gather a group of people to research if they are few and far between. The psychologist will find one participant and once they have been studied, the researcher will ask if they know anyone (a friend perhaps) in the same situation, who might be interested in taking part in the research. This person is then contacted and the researcher will collect their data, and then ask if they know anyone who might be interested, so the sample grows in much the same way as a snowball gets larger as each clump of snow is added. The usefulness of obtaining a sample of difficult to locate people is offset by the bias of the sample. Often these people will all have similar characteristics: they may be the same age or from the same place.

An opportunity sample is also known as a convenience sample. The researcher selects the most convenient people to study. In their research on eye witness testimony, Loftus and Palmer studied students.

 Let's look at an example ...

A psychologist might want to study homeless people and will go on the streets at night and talk to one person, sheltering in a doorway. Then that person might know someone else who would be willing to be studied, and direct the researcher to them. That person, after taking part in the research can then point the researcher in the direction of two other people sleeping outside, and so on.

As Elizabeth Loftus was a university lecturer we could assume that these were university students who happened to be available. Of course, they could have been volunteers, Palmer and Loftus don't tell us. Often research is carried out on undergraduates as these are a readymade group of participants, who need the money and sometimes are given credit towards their degrees if they take part in lecturers' research. Obviously this can lead to a biased sample, as lecturers are unlikely to choose the students they think won't take it seriously, or a psychologist might choose to study students in a college library rather than a café, due to the noise. This would mean that the sample isn't really representative of the whole student population. Also if lecturers only use the students at their university, they may be limited by the type of university and things such as entry criteria. Opportunity samples do give researchers access to large numbers of easy-to-access participants, even if there is possibly an inherent bias in whom they choose.

 Let's look at an example ...

Psychologists might be interested in people who use the public library and so go to the library on a certain day to interview the people using the library that day. However, it could be biased because if someone is concentrating on using the internet, the researcher might not want to interrupt them, or there may be several local villages who don't have a bus service into town that day, and so they will be unrepresented in the sample.

A self-selected sample is also known as a volunteer sample. Here people will choose to take part or volunteer to take part in the research. Typical ways of getting such a sample include putting an advert in a newspaper or a notice on a notice board, and sending out postal questionnaires. Those who respond to the ad or notice and those who fill in and return the questionnaires are volunteering to take part in the study. A problem with this method is that only people who read that particular newspaper, or pass that board, would be given the opportunity to take part, so it may not be representative. For example, what differences do you think there would be in people who read the *Independent* and those who read *The Sun* newspaper? There may also be certain characteristics about people who volunteer, they may have more time on their hands, they may be keen on psychology and they could just want the money if payment is offered. On the other hand, with a volunteer sample you can rely on them more to take part in a lengthy study as they signed up for it in the first place. This was one reason why Milgram thought his participants might have continued giving the shocks.

Let's look at an example ...

Milgram gained his sample by sending out a mailshot and putting an advert in the local paper. Milgram tried to overcome the inherent bias of only selecting from one town, by then selecting men who were from a variety of careers, had a range of educational experiences and were aged between 20 and 50.

Have a go yourself

Design an advert or poster to recruit participants for Chaney *et al.*'s research (see page 89, Chapter 3).

Strengths and weaknesses of sampling techniques

A sample should be representative of the target population from which it is drawn. If a sample is representative, this allows us to generalise the findings: to establish general rules about the behaviour of the target population based on the behaviour of the sample.

A sample that is not representative of its target population or of people in general is called a biased sample. There are a number of biasing factors that can limit the generalisability of findings from a sample.

First, sample size has to be considered. Can Baron-Cohen *et al.*'s 25 males and 25 females drawn from a subject panel from Cambridge University truly represent 'normal males and females' in general? Is Little Hans a typical 3–5-year-old boy? Samples that are not large enough to represent their target population mean psychologists must be cautious about making generalisations from them. Similarly, psychologists must be cautious making generalisations where only one type

of person is selected to represent a diverse population, e.g. one region, one culture, one occupation, age group or gender is selected to be in the sample. These biases are known as ethnocentric biases.

- **Gender bias.** A sample of all males or all females is clearly not representing the omitted gender (consider Milgram's obedience study and Freud's case study of Little Hans which both had all male samples). Having all males (and assuming that they will represent normal behaviour) is known as androcentric bias.
- **Age bias.** If certain age groups are omitted, then the sample will not be representative of people in general. It is seen in any study where students are used to represent adults or people in general, as students are generally young. Consider how Loftus and Palmer's sample would be biased towards non-experienced drivers.
- **Culture bias.** Only one country/area is represented. Milgram's study was conducted in one place, New Haven in the United States and so can only say something about the obedience of men aged 20–50 years from New Haven.

Stop and ask yourself...

Can you:
- Make up a chart with a definition of each sampling method, how you would obtain one from a target population (e.g. students at college) and then the strengths and weaknesses of each method.

Experimental designs

Once psychologists have identified and chosen their sample, they have to identify which participants will be in each condition. There are often two conditions in a research study, the normal or control condition and the experimental condition, where the independent variable has been manipulated. The control group will be used to see what behaviour is like if there is no manipulation. Bandura *et al.* had a large control group and several experimental groups. The control group was used to get the baseline aggression of children not exposed to either aggressive or non-aggressive role models. Therefore he could statistically compare the behaviours shown in the other conditions to that baseline measure.

Often there are individual differences between each person, known as participant variables. Psychologists have three experimental designs to try and minimise these variables, where possible.

Practice questions

A researcher wants to carry out a study to see if drinking coffee helps you to concentrate better in lessons. The researcher chooses to study sixth formers in a large school in the UK where the sixth form has a population of 500 students. A sample of 50 students in total needs to be selected to take part.

The psychologist wants to use a random sample for her research.

1. Explain one strength and one weakness of using a random sample for this study. [6 marks]
2. Name and outline one other sampling technique for selecting these participants. [2 marks]
3. Describe one strength and one weakness of using the sampling technique you have chosen in this study. [6 marks]

The specification requires you to know how participants are allocated in each of these designs and the strengths and weaknesses of each of these designs. You should be able to relate this to any research context given in the exam.

In a repeated measures design, each participant is tested in every condition – thus each subject provides their own comparison (control) scores. A repeated measures design is therefore a related design as each pair of scores is from one participant. The strengths and weakness of a repeated measures design are shown in Table 7.3.

Table 7.3 Strengths and weaknesses of a repeated measures design

Strengths of a repeated measures design	Weaknesses of a repeated measures design
By comparing each person with themselves the likelihood that individual differences between subjects will confound the study is reduced. This is the best design, therefore, for controlling subject variables in an experiment.	The repeated measures design can be affected by order effects such as practice, fatigue, and boredom, so it requires counterbalancing to control for these.
This design can use fewer participants than a matched participants or independent measures design so may be more cost- and time-effective.	If subjects are tested twice or more they may work out the independent variable (they do this by picking up on the demand characteristics in the study) and may try to behave according to what they believe is expected.

Counterbalancing. Remember, this is a method of controlling variables, such as order effects in repeated measures designs. It is done by varying the order of the conditions to participants. For example, condition one is given to half of the participants first and condition two

to the other half first. Then the groups swap conditions. This spreads out the effects of order of presentation across the test conditions.

 Let's look at an example ...

If psychologists were studying memory of words and pictures, they would first give half of the participants the test with words and the other half the test with pictures. Then they would swap, so that the ones who did the words test now did the picture test and vice versa. That way if participants were just better the second time they did a test as they had already had one test, half would be better on the word test and half on the picture test. This would balance out the order effects of practice.

An alternative to a repeated measures design is to use a matched participants, or matched pairs, design (Table 7.4). Here each participant is paired up with someone else in the sample on the basis of the variables that matter to the study, e.g. gender, age, position in the family, level of aggression, intelligence, level of skill or experience at doing something. One of the pair is tested in the experimental condition and the other one is tested in the control condition. This is also a related design, as each score in the experimental condition is compared with its related score in the control condition.

 Let's look at an example ...

Bandura et al. did this with a matched participants design. Each group who saw either a male or female role model and aggressive or non-aggressive role model, had the same average age, the same gender and the same aggression rating from the teacher's original observation. This means that the resulting behaviour was not influenced by participant variables. It wasn't that all the aggressive boys observed the aggressive male role model because of the group they were put in. The aggressive boys were spread out among all of the groups.

Table 7.4 Strengths and weaknesses of a matched participants design

Strengths of a matched participants design	Weaknesses of a matched participants design
A matched design avoids some of the problems that a repeated measures design presents, for example a matched participants design isn't affected by order effects and is less likely to be affected by demand characteristics as each participant is tested only once.	The matched participants design isn't often used as it is very time consuming to match participants.
A matched design controls participant variables better than an independent measures design as participants are matched on the variables important to the study.	It is impossible to match participants on enough variables to be sure that there are no possible extraneous individual differences that might confound the study.

⏩ Have a go yourself

What would you consider to be the key characteristics which should be matched in all research? What specific characteristics might you add for:

● Children's educational performance?
● Teenagers' driving skills?
● Adults' drinking habits?

In an independent measures design (Table 7.5), a sample is allocated to either the experimental condition(s) or the control condition, usually in equal numbers. Each participant is tested in only one condition. The scores for each group are compared with the scores for the other group. For example, a group of students could be selected to take part in the study, and they could then be allocated to conditions, as in the Loftus and Palmer study. Random allocation to conditions is assumed to spread out any individual differences across conditions.

Since this method compares the whole experimental condition's scores against the whole control condition's scores, this is known as an unrelated design.

📋 Practice questions

1. Which of these is a strength of matched pairs design? [1 mark]
   (a) It is difficult to arrange.
   (b) It controls participant variables.
   (c) It has different people in each condition.
   (d) It encourages order effects.
2. Which design is this: each person undertakes both condition A and condition B. [1 mark]
   (a) Independent measures design
   (b) Correlational design
   (c) Matched participants design
   (d) Repeated measures design
3. What is counterbalancing? [1 mark]
   (a) Giving half the participants condition (a), then condition (b) and the other half condition (b), then condition (a)
   (b) Giving half the participant condition (a) and the other half condition (b)
   (c) Giving each person a matched participant in the other group
   (d) Giving each person a rest after condition (a) before they start condition (b)

Table 7.5 Strengths and weaknesses of an independent measures design

Strengths of an independent measures design	Weaknesses of an independent measures design
An independent measures design isn't affected by order effects as each participant is tested only once in one condition.	An independent measures design does not control extraneous participant variables effectively, so individual differences between the participants may confound the findings.
This design is also less likely to be affected by demand characteristics than a repeated measures design as each person is tested only once and has less opportunity to work out the hypothesis being tested and act accordingly.	Large samples are often needed in order to be sure that any effect of the independent variable is caused by the dependent variable and not by individual differences.
This design is possibly less time consuming to conduct than a matched participants design.	

- Could you explain how to allocate participants to each condition using the different designs, and what the strengths and weaknesses of these designs are?

Data recording, analysis and presentation

In this section, **the specification requires** you to know how psychologists collect, analyse and present data, and how this might be different for the different research methods, as well as the associated strengths and weaknesses of these techniques. You will also need to be able to carry out some calculations (see Appendix 1, page 241).

There are various mathematical symbols used, which have specific meanings in psychology. Table 7.6 is a list of the symbols you need to know and understand. There is a reference to the page on which these symbols are used, which might help to you understand their use in a psychological context.

Table 7.6 Table of mathematical symbols

Symbol	Meaning	Page
<	Less than	221 & 225
<<	Much less than	217
>	Greater than	225
>>	Much greater than	217
~	Approximately	
∝	Proportionality	228

Raw data

The data that psychologists collect for each participant are known as the raw data. This might be the time taken for each participant to complete a test, or the number of items recalled for each participant in a memory test. It won't have been subjected to any kind of mathematical analysis, so it will simply be the number of right answers, or the time taken, to complete a task.

In order to be able to record data, psychologists need to have raw data recording tables in which to note down their results. The type of data recorded will suggest the best type of recording table.

The following table shows the simplest table based on a tally chart which will summarise nominal data in terms of how often that behaviour was shown.

	Not buying fruit in the college café	Buying fruit in the college café
Male students	16	18
Female students	9	22

The results from each participant can be recorded with ordinal or interval data (Table 7.7).

Table 7.7 Number of hours slept the night before and the score on a memory test

Participant	Number of hours slept the night before	Score on memory test out of 20
A	5.5	18
B	8.1	15
C	6.3	11
D	9.4	14
E	8.3	16
F	7.5	17
G	5.5	19

These data tables can be used to get an overview of the data and to identify any anomalous data (which don't match the other data) so that the appropriate measure of central tendency can be used. Each table should have clear labels, for example 'Score on memory test out of 20' or 'Buying fruit in the college café', not simply labelled 'Condition A' and 'Condition B', or 'Memory test'. Participants are usually anonymised, i.e. identified by letters or their initials, to keep the data confidential.

Mathematicians will deal with extremely large and small numbers and it is necessary for them to be able to write these in shorthand form which is known as standard form. The number 300,000 (not necessarily outside the scope of psychological research) can be written as 3×10^5 which means $3 \times (10 \times 10 \times 10 \times 10 \times 10)$. Also mathematicians might consider 10^{-5}.

Psychologist rarely work with standard form. It is also not very often that psychologists will work in whole numbers. Once any analysis of data is carried out, the whole numbers tend to disappear and decimal form tends to become the normal way of presenting data. The median (see page 216) for '2, 3, 4, 5' would be 3.5 or a correlation coefficient (see page 226) could be 0.367. Probably the most frequent use would be when analysing statistical significance with probability levels of 0.05 (see page 225). These three numbers 3.5, 0.05 and 0.367 are all in decimal form. However, they all have a different number of decimal places, one (3.5), two (0.05) or three (0.367). Sometimes numbers have many more decimal places. You will probably be familiar with the figure pi (π) (used in geometry) which is 3.14159265358979932384626433 ... (the dots show it hasn't finished or been rounded up or down to a significant figure). Rather than write such a long number the number is limited to a significant figure (number of digits).

Let's look at an example ...

Using π as our example, to get to the significant figure you count from the left hand digit (in this case 3) and then on until you get to the digit which represents the significant figure you need. So for four significant figures it is 3.141.

However, the final digit has to represent the next digit, so if the next digit is 5 or higher, then the final significant digit is rounded up. So 3.1415 becomes 3.142 to four significant figures.

- π to four significant figures is 3.142
- π to three significant figures is 3.14 (because digit 4 is only 1 so doesn't increase digit 3).

Stop and ask yourself ...

- What is the value of π to five significant figures?
- What is the value of π to ten significant figures?

Just one word of warning: if the first number is 0.659 then the zero doesn't count towards the significant figures so 0.659 is three significant figures (not four as the zero doesn't count). However, if the zero appears in the number e.g. 4.706 then it does count so this has four significant figures.

Again psychologists rarely get bogged down in these kinds of data, using 3 as the maximum number of significant figures, depending on the context, and the scale used. For example, if the range of answers is from 4 to 63, then the decimal places are not necessarily going to be very important, however if correlation coefficients are calculated these can only be in the range +1 to −1 the decimal places could be needed to really show the level of difference.

Psychologists are more interested in statistical analysis than estimating from data, but it could be that by looking at a set of grouped data psychologists might want to estimate a mean (see page 216), if they didn't have individual scores.

Let's look at an example ...

In the data table below, psychologists might want to estimate the mean number of hours slept. We could ask the question:

'How many hours did you sleep last night?' (please circle one)

0–4	5–9	10–14	14–19	19–24

This would be the data in raw form:

Number of hours slept	0–4	5–9	10–14	15–19
Number of participants recording this number of hours of sleep	3	7	6	2

To estimate the mean, we assume each participant slept the middle number of hours (midpoint).

For 0 to 4 hours, the midpoint would be 2, for 5–9 hours it would be 7, for 10–14 hours it would be 12 and for 14–19 hours it would be 17.

Number of hours slept	Number of participants	Midpoint	Midpoint × number of participants
0–4	3	2	6
5–9	7	7	49
10–14	6	12	72
15–19	2	17	34
Total			161

Then we have to multiply each midpoint by the number of people in that box. And add up all the means. In this case, this gives us a total of 161. This is then divided by the number of participants 161/18 which gives an estimated mean of 8.9.

Another symbol which shows a general relationship rather than an accurate figure is the symbol $\approx$ which represents 'almost equal to'. If the means for two sets of data of scores on an IQ test were calculated and they were 112.6 and 113, then, in the scale of IQ tests, these are almost equal. To show this, psychologists might write 112.6 $\approx$ 113 in their descriptive statistics, showing that the two means are almost equal. They could go on to say that this would suggest that there is no significant difference. Of course they would still carry out a statistical test for their inferential statistical analysis.

Another mathematical calculation which psychologists might occasionally need to know is in an order of magnitude calculation where if an estimate is made then psychologists need to know that the order of magnitude is correct.

 Let's look at an example ...

If psychologists looked at a memory test with a maximum score of 100, carried out on a sample of 39 people, and found that the total of the scores was 3618, then an estimate of the mean gives 3600/40 = 90. If you got an answer near 900 or 9 then a mistake has been made because the order of magnitude is too big (answer is thought to be 900) or small (answer is thought to be 9). Psychologists have to know that an estimate gives an answer that is in the right area (whether it's 0.something, 10s, 100s or 1000s etc.)

Levels and types of data

The most basic type of data psychologists can gather is nominal level data which is simply categories of behaviour and how often they occur, for example, the number of male and female students who buy fruit in the café or the number of students in the class who have or do not have iPhones.

	Not buying fruit in the college café	Buying fruit in the college café
Male students	16	18
Female students	9	22

In the table above, the categories of behaviour were buying fruit and not buying fruit. The frequency of these behaviours for males and females was recorded. One problem with this type of data is that it doesn't tell us how much fruit each person bought or how often the person bought fruit (was it lots of times in one day?).

 Have a go yourself

Ask your friends if they have a smart phone and create a survey of gender differences in smart phone ownership.

If psychologists record the behaviour for each participant individually then the data will either be ordinal or interval data. Ordinal level data are individual data which show which participant did the behaviour most or least and indicates the position of a participant in the group. Psychologists know from Table 7.8 that participant G got the highest score in the memory

test (19) and participant C got the lowest (11). Psychologists can then rank each person and put them in order of how well they did on the test.

These data, however, don't show how much of a gap there is between each participant in term of how large it is. Psychologists can't suggest that participant D who scored 14 compared to participant C who scored 11 (a difference of three) has three times as good a memory

Table 7.8 Results given as ordinal level data

Participant	Number of hours slept the night before	Score on memory test out of 20
G	5.5	19
A	5.5	18
F	7.5	17
E	8.3	16
B	8.1	15
D	9.4	14
C	6.3	11

as participant G who scored 19 compared to participant A who scored 18 (a difference of one). The gap between the rating points is not fixed or equal.

Interval level data has equal intervals. This type of data gives more than just order, they also show how much difference there is between the first and second, the second and third, and so on, these equal intervals could, for example, be centimetres or kilograms or seconds.

A measurement of time not only tells psychologists which participant is quickest, or slowest, but also by how much. And psychologists know that someone who took three seconds more than another participant really did take three times as long as someone who was one second slower. This type of data is quite detailed, and tells us the most about differences in behaviour of the three levels.

As a rule of thumb, if a machine can be bought which will measure the dependent variable, for example a clock, thermometer, blood pressure machine, then the data are likely to be interval data. If the gap (interval) is measurable and is always the same, for example seconds or degrees of temperature, then the data are interval data if there is an *arbitrary zero*. One refinement of interval data is data which has a *true zero*. A temperature of 0°C does not mean there is no heat in something. So temperature readings are interval data. However 0 seconds does indicate no time. Data with a true zero, such as time, are known as ratio level data, but are generally treated as interval data when it comes to statistical analysis at A level.

🚫 **Stop and ask yourself ...**

● Can you identify the level of data the researcher gained in the core studies you have covered?

When psychologists think of measurement, they tend to assume that this means that numbers will be used to tell us how much or how many of something there were. This is precisely what you get with quantitative data. An advantage of using numbers to measure variables is that it allows for easy comparisons to be made between participants, e.g. on a memory test, subject one scored 10 out of 100 and subject two scored 90. Psychologists can also summarise quantitative data easily, using averages or percentages. For example, Milgram found that 65 per cent of his participants went up to 450 volts.

It is easier to establish the reliability of results when quantitative data are collected, as you can repeat the test to see if the findings are replicated (repeated) or not.

Quantitative data alone can be quite narrow and may not reflect how we would respond in everyday life, so could lack ecological validity. For example, if you ask someone, 'How are things with you?', they are more likely to say, 'Pretty good, thanks', rather than, 'On a scale of 0 to 100, where 0 is terrible and 100 is unqualified bliss, I'd say today was scoring 65.'

In order to increase the level of detail and the validity of findings, qualitative data can be gathered. This usually consists of descriptions in words of what was observed or what a participant is feeling. For example, Milgram tells us subjects were seen 'to sweat, tremble, stutter, bite their lips ... [and] these were characteristic rather than exceptional responses to the experiment' (Milgram, 1969, page 375). This tells us a lot more about the experience of subjects in the study than just the fact that 65 per cent of subjects went to the end on the shock generator.

Qualitative data can also be reports of interviews, responses to open questions in questionnaires and reports of what participants said and did during a study. Using this type of information gives a richness and detail to the findings and is more valid. However, it is harder to make comparisons between participants' responses or to summarise qualitative data.

In experiments, however, researchers tend to measure their variables quantitatively to allow analysis of the findings to be carried out.

When psychologists carry out their research and gather data directly from the participants, such as observed behaviours, results on a test, answers to questionnaires then these data are called primary data. An advantage of this type of data is that they are collected to specifically inform the psychologists' research. The researchers know how they were gathered and what controls were put in place to ensure validity. However, sometimes psychologists can't actually carry out the research themselves and have to use data already collected, for example by Government departments. Information on hospital admissions and alcohol consumption, for example, would be difficult and costly to gather for a psychologist interested in studying addiction, but the data are already gathered as part of the information the NHS collects and so psychologists can access this. This is called secondary data. The main advantage is that these are data that would be impossible or too expensive to collect by the psychologists and often they are data from a period of time so that trends over time can be analysed. However, secondary data may be included in other information, and may not have been collected in a valid or reliable way and there may have been extraneous variables which have not been considered.

Practice questions

1. Which is an example of ordinal level data? [1 mark]
   (a) The number of pixels in an MRI scan of the hippocampus
   (b) The rating on a scale of how stressed someone is
   (c) How many novels males and females read in the last year
   (d) The time taken to read a list of taboo words.
2. Which of these is an advantage of using qualitative data? [1 mark]
   (a) It is easy to analyse.
   (b) It is difficult to collect.
   (c) It lacks depth and detail.
   (d) It has high levels of depth and detail.

Descriptive statistics

Once psychologists have gathered their data, they will use descriptive statistics to present, summarise and describe their findings.

Imagine psychologists have carried out a study to see the effects of age on memory. Subjects/participants have learned 30 items in two minutes and then freely recalled the items to give their memory score out of 30. The researcher predicted that a younger age group would do better on the test. The groups are split into 30–45 years old and 55–70 years old with 20 participants in each condition.

Table 7.9 shows what the raw data might look like.

Table 7.9 The number of items recalled out of 30 for the 30–45 years old condition and the 55–70 years old condition

Age group	Scores out of 30 on the memory test
30–45 years old	15, 15, 15, 15, 16, 17, 17, 17, 18, 18, 18, 20, 20, 21, 21, 23, 27, 28, 28, 30
55–70 years old	9, 10, 10, 11, 11, 13, 13, 15, 15, 15, 16, 16, 16, 21, 22, 22, 23, 23, 24, 24,

From the raw data, psychologists can see some things, for example the lowest score (9) was in the older age group and the highest score (30) was in the youngest age group, but if psychologists want to compare the groups more easily, they may want to use statistics to summarise the data. This is where psychologists can calculate information such as the averages to summarise the data so that they can make comparisons between the groups' scores to see if they support the researcher's predictions.

The mathematical term x is used to represent any variable which is measured. In psychology we could use this to represent the dependent variable, but by convention would probably use the abbreviation DV. However in a data set such that above x could represent the scores out of 30 on the memory test. So for the 30–45 years old age group it could be written that the scores of the test (x) = 15, 15, 15, 15, 16, 17, 17, 17, 18, 18, 18, 20, 20, 21, 21, 23, 27, 28, 28, 30.

Data sets which are gathered during research can tell us many interesting facts about human and animal behaviour. One way of analysing data is to calculate a measure of central tendency. These will help to show the middle point or most frequent number. They can tell us something about the 'normal' or average participant in any data set. However, they can also sometimes have problems if they are influenced by anomalous (very unusual) data.

The mean is calculated by adding up all the scores in the set and dividing by the number of scores. For example, to calculate the mean for the 30–45 years old condition in the memory test you need to add all their scores and divide by 20. If you do this, the answer you will get is 19.95. If you then calculate the mean for the older age group you will get 15.3.

By comparing the mean scores, psychologists can see that the results do give evidence for the prediction that the younger group would score higher than the older group, as indicated by the higher mean score of the 30–45 years old condition.

If psychologists were measuring things like time, weight or height or anything where decimal accuracy has real meaning, then the mean average is the best and most accurate measure of central tendency with which to work.

However, there is a problem with the mean here, as it can give us what is called 'spurious accuracy'. For example, is it possible to remember 19.95 items? What would the recall of 0.95 of an item be like?! Also on a data set, one outlier or score which is very different from the rest can skew the mean. For example, if the mean age of 20 students in the class is 16 years 6 months, then to find the mean age of people in the room simply adding in a nearing retirement age teacher's age of 58 years 6 months will skew the mean to 21, which doesn't really reflect anyone in the group.

The symbol $\bar{x}$ is used to signify the mean of the scores from a sample, which is known as sample mean. If you see this, it is demonstrating that the mean of the scores has been calculated. So, for example, the sample mean for the 30–45 years old condition is 19.95, so $\bar{x} = 19.95$, and for the older age group $\bar{x} = 16.9$.

Where psychologists are measuring in whole numbers often a more useful measure of central tendency is the median. The median gives us the central point of a set of scores.

The median is worked out by putting all the scores in size order (this is done for you in the table) and finding the central point. If there is an even number of scores in the set you take a midpoint of the middle two scores to find the median.

To find the median, then for the 30–45 years old scores, psychologists have to find the central two scores since there is an even number of scores, so psychologists find the tenth and eleventh numbers. These are both 18, the midpoint of these is 18, so the median for this set is 18.

Psychologists now have a whole number to represent a set made up of whole numbers. In this case, it even represents at least three of the actual scores, so in this instance the median is a better measure of central tendancy than the mean. The median of the 55–70 years old scores is 15.5 as the midpoint is between scores of 15 and 16. In this case, the median is also a better (more representative) measure of central tendency than the mean.

Psychologists could also calculate the mode for the sets of scores. This tells us the most typical score since the mode is simply the number that occurs most frequently in the set. For the 30–45 years old group, the mode is 15, then, and for the 55–70 years old group there are two modes (bimodal), 15 and 16. The mode will always represent at least two scores in the actual set of scores, but loses its meaningfulness if there are more than two modes. Of course, if each score occurs only once in a set then there is no mode, so this measure of central tendency is not useful where all items are different in the set. However, on the plus side, it is the only measure which can deal with non-numerical (qualitative) data. You could record the words said most often in a content analysis, or the most frequent eye colour, which you wouldn't be able to do with the mean or median.

 Stop and ask yourself ...

- Ask people how long it takes them to get to school in minutes, then work out the mean, median and mode for your data. Which is the most appropriate to use?

As well as being able to summarise a set of scores by looking at central, average or typical scores, it is also useful to know how widely dispersed or spread out the scores are. There are several measures of dispersion.

To calculate the range of a set of scores, you simply subtract the lowest score in the set from the highest score and add 1. For our example, then, the range for the 30–45 years old group is calculated by subtracting 15 from 30 and adding 1, so the range for that set of scores is 16.

When comparing descriptive statistics we could use the symbols >> to mean much greater than e.g. 17>>6 or << to mean much smaller than e.g. 17<<54.

 Stop and ask yourself ...

Can you:
- Work out the range for the 55–70 years old scores.

📖 Practice questions

1. Which of these would be least affected by anomalous data? [1 mark]
   - (a) Mean
   - (b) Median
   - (c) Variance
   - (d) Range

2. Here are the scores (x) of a memory test of 20 objects carried out by ten people aged over 90 years. Calculate the $\bar{x}$. [2 marks]

Scores (x) of a memory test
12
14
13
15
13
14
13
16
14
11

3. Explain one situation when you would not use the mean as a measure of central tendancy.

In statistics, variance measures how much a set of numbers is spread out. A variance of zero indicates that all the values are identical. A small variance indicates that all of the scores are very close to the mean and hence to each other, while a high variance indicates that the data are very spread out around the mean and away from each other.

To calculate the variance, follow these steps:
- a) Work out the mean.
- b) For each participant, subtract the mean from their score. This gives the difference (d).
- c) Square the result (multiply it by itself). This gives the squared difference (d^2).
- d) Work out the mean of those squared differences.

On its own, the variance gives an idea of how spread out the scores are from the mean, but it really comes into use when calculating the standard deviation.

Standard deviation is directly related to the variance and is simply its square root. It is more useful as you can refer to the standard deviation in terms of the original category, for example the standard deviation may be a number of correct spellings.

These are the number of spellings ten children got right in their end-of-week spelling test (Range = 18 − 12 + 1 = 7). To calculate the variance:

a) Work out the mean (12 + 15 + 13 + 18 + 17 + 16 + 14 + 16 + 18 + 15)/10 = 15.4.

Child	Number of correct spellings out of 20
A	12
B	15
C	13
D	18
E	17
F	16
G	14
H	16
I	18
J	15
Mean	15.4

b) Subtract the mean from each score e.g. 15.4 − 12 = −3.4 (difference, *d*).

Child	Number of correct spellings out of 20	Score − mean (*d*)
A	12	−3.4
B	15	−0.4
C	13	−2.4
D	18	2.6
E	17	1.6
F	16	0.6
G	14	−1.4
H	16	0.6
I	18	2.6
J	15	−0.4

c) Square the difference (*d*) = *d*²
d) Mean of the squared differences.

Child	Number of correct spellings out of 20	Score–mean (*d*)	*d*²
A	12	−3.4	11.56
B	15	−0.4	0.16
C	13	−2.4	5.76
D	18	2.6	6.76
E	17	1.6	2.56
F	16	0.6	0.36
G	14	−1.4	1.96
H	16	0.6	0.36
I	18	2.6	6.76
J	15	−0.4	0.16
Mean	15.4		36.4/10 = 3.64

The variance for this data set is 3.64.

If the scores were more spread out the variance is much greater (Range = 20 − 5 + 1 = 16):

Child	Number of correct spellings out of 20	Score–mean (*d*)	*d*²
A	9	−3.9	15.21
B	15	2.1	4.41
C	5	−7.9	62.41
D	20	7.1	50.41
E	19	6.1	37.21
F	8	−4.9	24.01
G	11	−1.9	3.61
H	14	1.1	1.21
I	10	−2.9	8.41
J	18	5.1	26.01
Mean	12.9		23.29

For this data set, the variance is 23.29.

If the variance in the first data set is 3.64, the standard deviation is √3.64 = 1.91. In the second data set, the variance of 23.29 gives a standard deviation of √23.29 = 4.83.

Standard deviation can tell us much more detailed information about how spread out the data is around the mean, median and mode. In a curve of normal distribution, 34 per cent of people will score 1 standard deviation above and 34 per cent will score 1 standard deviation below the mean. The percentage of people in the second standard deviation is 13.5 per cent, so you can estimate how many people will score plus or minus 2 standard deviations. 34 + 13.5 above + 34 + 13.5 below the mean = 95 per cent.

For three standard deviations, it is 99.7 per cent. You can't assume that no-one will be more than three standard deviations from the mean, but it is only 0.3 per cent of the scores.

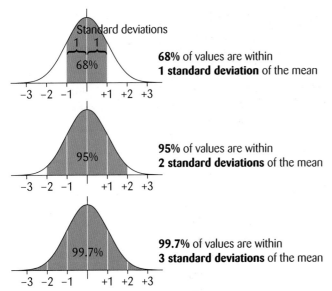

Standard deviations

68% of values are within **1 standard deviation** of the mean

95% of values are within **2 standard deviations** of the mean

99.7% of values are within **3 standard deviations** of the mean

Figure 7.1 Percentage of scores found in standard deviation

Let's look at an example ...

In a curve of normal distribution, if the mean score on a memory test is 50/100 and the standard deviation is 2, then 34 per cent of the people will have scored between 50 and 52, and 34 per cent will have scored between 48 and 50. So 68 per cent will have scored between 48 and 52, showing that most people scored around the mean.

However, if the standard deviation is 8, then 68 per cent of the people will have scored between 42 and 58 showing a much more wide distribution of scores.

Stop and ask yourself ...

- See if you can work out the minimum and maximum score for the 68 per cent of people who are one standard deviation away from the mean in the worked example. Mean = 15.4 and standard deviation = 1.91. Now try the other data set (mean = 12.9 SD = 4.83) and see how many the people within 2 standard deviations from the mean would have scored.

Ratios, as used by psychologists, are a way of expressing proportions of a whole population. They are written in the form 1:4 (read as 1 to 4) where for every five people we can see the proportion of people who have a certain characteristic. In this case, for every one person who has a certain characteristic, there will be four who won't have it. This could be shown as 1 in 5.

Let's look at an example ...

Here are some statistics from the Mental Health Foundation regarding Mental Health in the UK:

- One in four people will experience some kind of mental health problem in the course of a year. This means that for every four people in the UK, one will have a mental health problem and three won't.
- About 10 per cent of children have a mental health problem at any one time. If this were written as a ratio, it would be 1:9.
- Depression affects one in five older people. For every five people, one person has depression, a ratio of 1:4.
- Self-harm statistics for the UK show one of the highest rates in Europe: 400 per 100,000 population or 400:99600. This could be written as 4:996 which simplified is 1:249.
- Only one in ten prisoners has no mental disorder, which means nine out of ten or 90 per cent of prisoners have a mental disorder.

If psychologists have two groups of people that are an uneven number, for example Baron-Cohen *et al.* had 50 'normal' adults and 14 adults with Asperger's, just comparing how many errors were made would not necessarily tell us anything. If seven adults with Asperger's couldn't identify an emotion, and ten normal adults couldn't identify it, does this mean that normal adults are less able to identify emotions? No, of course not. It means $\frac{1}{2}$ (a fraction) or 50 per cent (a percentage) of adults with Asperger's couldn't identify it, but only $\frac{1}{5}$ or 20 per cent of normal adults couldn't. So, as a proportion of the total group, seven out of 14 is much more than 10 out of 50. This analysis is also very useful when producing graphical representation in the form of pie charts.

Psychologists might need to consider data in a different form to how it is presented, such as a percentage as a fraction, or what actual number a fraction represents of the total. There are some simple formulae to remember:

A Convert fractions to percentages: divide the top of the fraction by the bottom, multiply by 100.

B To convert a percentage to a fraction: write down the percentage over 100. Simplify (or reduce) the fraction. If the percentage is not a whole number, then multiply both top and bottom by 10 for every number after the decimal point. (For example, if there is one number after the decimal, then use 10, if there are two then use 100, etc.) e.g.
$\frac{7.2}{100} = \frac{72}{1000} = \frac{9}{25}$.

C To find the actual number a percentage of an amount represents divide the amount by 100 and multiply by the percentage.

D To find the actual number represented by a fraction of an amount, divide the amount by the denominator (number under the line in a fraction i. e. the 5 of $\frac{1}{5}$) and multiply it by the numerator (the number above the line in a fraction i. e. the 1 of $\frac{1}{5}$).

Let's look at an example ...

One hundred participants are sent a questionnaire, and $\frac{3}{4}$ of them reply.

A What percentage of the participants replied?
$\frac{3}{4} \times 100 = 75$ per cent (= 75 replies.)

B Of the 75 replies, 20 per cent are male and 80 per cent female.
What fraction of the replies came from males?
$\frac{20}{100} = \frac{1}{5}$.

C How many replies were from females?
$\frac{75}{100} \times 80 = 60$ replies.

D If $\frac{1}{5}$ of the 75 replies were from males how many males replied?
$\frac{75}{5} \times 1 = 15$ replies from males.

Have a go yourself

Try calculating the remaining percentages, ratios and fractions for each of the mental health statistics.

When the raw data are simple as in the examples on the previous page then quite often trends or differences can be seen fairly easily. However, data can be presented in a visual form to show more clearly the key information contained within data sets. There are a variety of methods for presenting data, and these will often depend on the type of data which has been gathered. What is important is that it should be clear to see what the data show, there shouldn't be so much data that the whole thing is muddled.

Practice questions

1. What percentage of people would have scores 2 standard deviations from the mean? [1 mark]
    (a) 13.5 per cent   (b) 34 per cent
    (c) 47.5 per cent   (d) 95 per cent.

2. If 200 school children take part in an observation and 3/5 are males how many boys take part?   [1 mark]
    (a) 40   (b) 60
    (c) 80   (d) 120.

3. Which of these represents 5×10^5?   [1 mark]
    (a) $5 \times 10 \times 5$
    (b) $5 \times 10 \times 10 \times 10 \times 10 \times 10$
    (c) $5 \times (10 \times 10 \times 10 \times 10 \times 10)$
    (d) 5.0000000000

4. What would 4.0487 be to three significant figures?   [1 mark]
    (a) 4.049
    (b) 4.04
    (c) 4.05
    (d) 4.49

A simple way of presenting data would be to show the actual tally of behaviour, for example in an observation using a frequency table (tally chart, Table 7.10).

Table 7.10 Observational data of aggression shown in playground

Behaviour	No. of times shown
Kicking	///////////
	//////////
Punching	///////////
Biting	//////////////
	///

However, even this type of tally chart can be made clearer, if the number of times a behaviour shown is grouped into fives (Table 7.11).

Table 7.11 Clearer depiction of counting in fives

Behaviour	No. of times shown
Kicking	卌 卌 卌 卌 III
Punching	卌 卌 卌 III
Biting	卌 卌 卌 III

Displaying data

A **line graph** would be particularly useful to show behaviour over time. For example, the line graph in Figure 7.2 shows the number of boys and girls talking at 15-minute intervals throughout the day. The red line (the girls) shows more girls talking for most of the day, with the boys talking more at times which coincide with playtime and lunchtime. This could suggest girls talk more when working, but this doesn't show if it is the same girls talking or why they are talking.

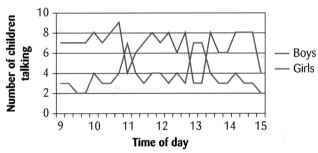

Figure 7.2 A line graph

Pie charts are helpful to show each behaviour as a proportion of total. The pie chart in Figure 7.3 shows how much of the time children are being aggressive during the day.

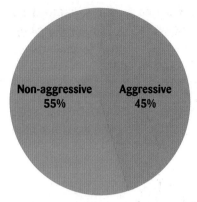

Figure 7.3 Pie chart showing percentage of time aggressive behaviour observed

However, a pie chart can sometimes hide other information. For example, Figure 7.4 shows what the make up of the aggressive behaviour is.

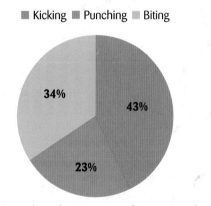

Figure 7.4 Pie chart showing types of aggression observed

But, if there was another set of data with non-aggressive behaviours included, this might show something else, as in Figure 7.5.

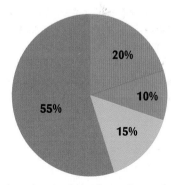

Figure 7.5 Pie chart showing behaviours observed

Now the aggressive behaviour is also seen as a proportion of the overall behaviour.

Although there are many ways of displaying pie charts, for example 3D or without the percentages shown, one is always enough to show the same data.

> **➡ Have a go yourself**
>
> Collect information on the social media used by your friends in the last week or two days, then display the data using a pie chart.

Bar charts are a useful and meaningful way of presenting data from an experiment providing that you *keep it simple!* For example, a useless and meaningless bar chart might look like Figure 7.6.

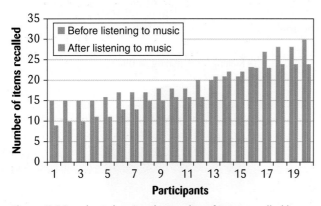

Figure 7.6 Bar chart showing the number of items recalled by participants before and after listening to music

This doesn't tell us anything at a glance, and since psychologists use the graph to clarify results for the person reading about them, then psychologists need a simpler graph to show what they have found.

In order to achieve this simple bar chart, you should draw a bar chart using a measure of central tendency for each condition, such as the mean or median, and use two bars to show any observed difference between the two conditions. It is easy to draw conclusions from a simple two-bar bar graph. Psychologists can now see if the data appear to support the alternative hypothesis or not (see Figure 7.7).

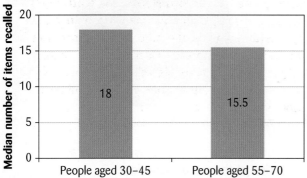

Figure 7.7 Bar chart showing the median scores for the number of items correctly recalled out of 30 for people aged 30–45 years and people aged 55–70 years

It is important to show the whole possible scale as in the chart in Figure 7.7 the scale from 0 to 20 shows the difference, but in the chart in Figure 7.8 starting the scale at 15 and ending at 18.5 (which is easily done using software) shows what appears to be a much larger difference for exactly the same data.

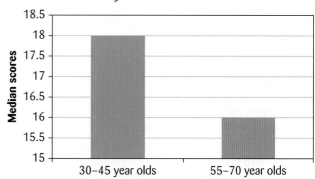

Figure 7.8 Bar chart showing the median scores for the number of items correctly recalled out of 30 for the two age condition – distorted scale

Histograms look like bar charts, but can only be used if the data are continuous.

For example, for a data set as shown in Table 7.12 the number of hours slept are grouped as continuous data for less than 3 hours of sleep to under 15 hours of sleep.

Table 7.12 Mean score of recall of 30 items after number of hours slept

Number of hours slept	Mean score of recall of 30 items in memory test
Less than 3 hours	7
3 to <6*	8
6 to <9	26
9 to <12	18
12 to <15	0

*Mathematical symbol < means less than. This means anyone who slept 5 hours 55 minutes would be in the second row and anyone who slept 6 hours would be in the third row

Then the histogram would look like as in Figure 7.9.

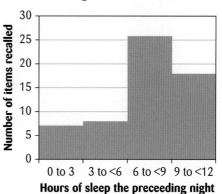

Figure 7.9 Histogram showing mean number of items recalled after number of hours slept

Stop and ask yourself...

Can you:

● Sketch a histogram for the number of hours of homework you do for each day of the week.

The graph that psychologists draw to represent a correlation is called a scatter diagram or scattergraph.

By the pattern that the scores make on the graph psychologists can work out:

1. The *direction* of the correlation, that is, whether it is positive or negative, and
2. The *strength* of the correlation, that is whether it is strong or weak.

The direction of the correlation is indicated by the pattern of the scores plotted on a scatter diagram.

If scores go 'uphill' from left to right on the scatter diagram, this indicates a positive correlation (Figure 7.10).

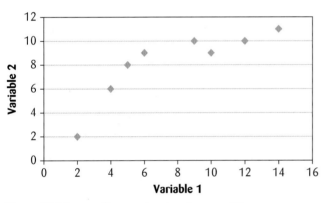

Figure 7.10 Scatter diagram showing strong positive correlation

Scores that go 'downhill' from left to right indicate a negative correlation (Figure 7.11).

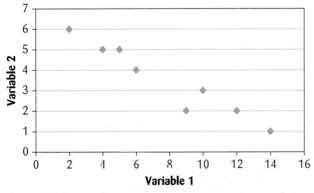

Figure 7.11 Scatter diagram showing strong negative correlation

The closer the scores are to falling in a straight line, the stronger the correlation is, and the more spread out the scores, the weaker the correlation.

 Have a go yourself

Conduct a survey of how many hours of television was watched the night before (or how many hours spent on social media, or working, or sleeping) and how alert the person rates themselves on a scale of 1–10. Display this data in a scatter diagram. Is there a correlation?

In addition, the scatter diagram will also show any anomalous scores, or outliers, which do not follow the general pattern, showing if the relationship is not true in all cases and if there are exceptions to the general trend observed in the data.

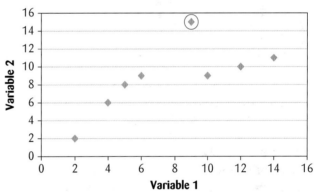

Figure 7.12 Scatter diagram showing anomalous data

In the scatter diagram in Figure 7.12, you can see a trend in general towards a strong positive correlation between the two variables. The anomalous score of 9, 15 however shows that this is not true for all cases and there are exceptions to the general trend.

Proportionality (∝) means that a correlation has a linear property, i.e. when plotted the scatter diagram shows as a straight line. As one variable increases by a certain amount the other variable increases by the same proportion. For example if one variable doubles the other variable will also double. Inverse proportionality means if one variable doubles the other variable halves.

Let's look at an example ...

If an educational psychologist wanted to see how the amount of time spent on revision was related to test results, and found that if the time spent revising doubled the scores on the test doubled it would show as a linear graph. This correlation shows proportionality.

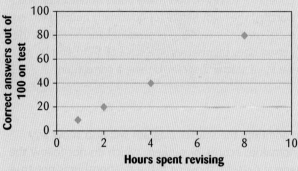

Figure 7.13 Scatter diagram to show proportionality

Inverse proportionality

A psychologist might want to find out if the number of hours spent on social media each week has a correlation with the number of phone calls made, to find out whether an increase in one is linked to a reduction in the other. Inverse proportionality would be where as the number of hours spent on social media doubled the number of phone calls made would be halved.

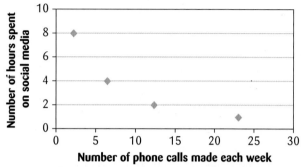

Figure 7.14 Scatter diagram to show inverse proportionality

📖 Practice questions

1. A researcher carried out a study to see if the more times a day teenagers use their mobile phone, the higher number of friends they have (Table 7.13).

Table 7.13 Research results

Participant	Number times used mobile phone	Number of participant's friends
1	17	15
2	26	29
3	26	19
4	19	17
5	22	16
6	12	9
7	27	22
8	15	16
9	30	18
10	39	23

(a) Sketch a scatter diagram to illustrate the correlation of this data. [3 marks]
(b) What type of correlation does the scatter diagram appear to show? [2 marks]
(c) What does the anomalous data (point 26, 29) tell you? [2 marks]

2. A psychologist tested the effects of temperature on the ability of students to revise for a test. She used matched pairs and one half of the students revised in a room where the temperature was 16°C, and the other half revised in a room where the temperature was 23°C. Each student was then given the same test on the revised material. The psychologist presented her findings in the bar chart in Figure 7.15.

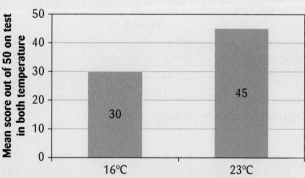

Figure 7.15 Bar chart showing the mean scores on test for students revising in room temperature 16°C and room temperature 23°C

(a) Summarise the findings from the bar chart. [2 marks]
(b) Explain why a bar chart is appropriate for presenting these data. [2 marks]
(c) Calculate the percentage of the total available marks the mean of each group represents. [4 marks]

Inferential statistics

Inferential statistics allow us to go beyond describing the data (descriptive statistics) and actually infer or deduce from the data whether our alternative hypothesis can be supported.

The specification requires you to know how psychologists use distribution curves to consider data. You will also need to know about statistical analysis, why we use it, what significance levels we use and what this tells us about probability. Also, you need to know which test (out of five named tests) you would use in any piece of given research and why you would or would not use parametric tests. You also need to know about type 1 and type 2 errors.

Data about any behaviour from a representative sample of the target population will tend to fall into a curve of normal distribution. You would have come across this curve of normal distribution in standard deviation (see page 218). Most scores are around the midpoint and then fewer and fewer participants are seen as the behaviour becomes more or less than the midpoint. For example, a curve of normal distribution of memory recall could look something like this.

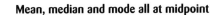

Mean, median and mode all at midpoint

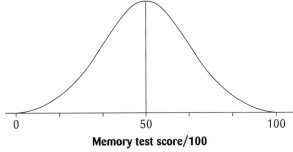

Memory test score/100

Figure 7.16 The curve of normal distribution

A 'true' normal curve is when all measures of central tendency occur at the highest point in the curve.

A curve of normal distribution would be what would be expected from a normal target population, which covered a range from lowest to highest memory score.

However, if the distribution curve was representing data from a skewed or unusual data set, then the result would be a skewed distribution curve. The mean would be different from the mode, and there would be more or fewer low scores or high scores.

If the distribution was plotted for the results of a test such as the memory scores of A Level students, who on average would have better memory scores (all that revising!) than the whole of the population, the curve would look like Figure 7.17 and the spread of scores would not be symmetrical.

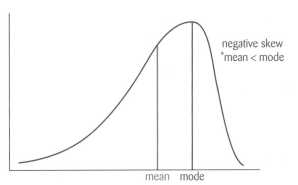

negative skew
*mean < mode

mean   mode

Figure 7.17 A skewed distribution curve. *Mathematical symbol < means 'less than'

This is known as a negative skew or a skew to the left. There are fewer people at the lower end and more at the higher end of the scores. The mean and mode are not the same, the mean is less than the mode (most frequent score was high).

We can also have a positively skewed curve if the population has more low scorers than high scorers. For example, if we looked at the memory recall of older people, where on short-term memory tests they would probably do worse than the normal population, the curve of distribution would look like Figure 7.18. The mean is higher than the mode (most frequent score was low).

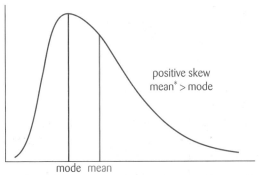

positive skew
mean* > mode

mode mean

Figure 7.18 A positively skewed curve. *Mathematical symbol > means 'greater than'

In skewed distribution, the standard deviation cannot be used.

Have a go yourself

Ask your psychology class to rate their interest in working with people in the caring/medical sector as a career. Plot the curve for the number of people in each rating from 1–10. Is there a skew? Maybe more people studying psychology would be interested in working with people in the caring/medical sector than those studying another subject?

One of the key concepts psychologists have to know about is probability. As psychology looks at trends not certainties in behaviour, there is never going to be a data set where *everyone* in one condition does exactly the same as everyone else. Individual differences will always mean the data is *never* going to show 100 per cent of the participants showing *exactly* the *same* behaviour. However, if the independent variable really does affect behaviour, most people will show that trend to a greater or lesser extent. Psychologists want to know what the probability is that the independent variable did affect the dependent variable.

Probability is the likelihood of something happening. If a coin is spun for heads and tails, there is a 50 per cent chance that it would be heads, and 50 per cent chance it would be tails. If a die (singular of dice) is thrown then there is a one in six chance of any one number showing on the top. Both of these are ways of expressing probability.

Psychologists carrying out research would want to have an idea of what they will accept as the probability of the independent variable influencing the dependent variable. We know it won't be 100 per cent and obviously if there is only a 50 per cent chance of the independent variable affecting the dependent variable, then psychologists won't accept this as good enough to say with any certainty that the independent variable affected the dependent variable and that they can reject the null hypothesis. The usual level of significance – which is the level at which psychologists will reject the null hypothesis – is 95 per cent. So there is a 95 per cent probability of the independent variable having affected the dependent variable and 5 per cent likelihood of it being simply due to chance. Probability always adds up to 100 per cent.

Psychologists can vary their significance level. While 95 per cent is the norm, if there was a need to be as certain as possible – for example, if the results are going to impact greatly on society – then psychologist can set the level at 99 per cent (or even higher, but never 100 per cent). Conversely, if there is a small sample or unusual data, then the significance level could be set lower at 90 per cent as a difference at this level in a small group is likely to be significant.

Psychologists do have a shorthand way of writing this in research. The usual way to display the significance level which the psychologist has set is:

$p < 0.05$

where p = the probability of the results being due to chance

$<$ = is less than

0.05 = 5 per cent.

The probability of the results being due to chance is less than 5 per cent, therefore the probability of the results being due to the independent variable is 95 per cent or more.

We could set it at $\leq$ which means equal to or less than:

$p \leq 0.05$.

The probability of the results being due to chance is 5 per cent or less, and the results being due to the independent variable is 95 per cent or more.

In order to find out if results are significant (meet the set significance level), statistical tests are used to analyse the data according to formulae. Psychologists don't have to worry about proving the formulae as they just use them to analyse their data.

Once the formula has been used, the final result is the calculated value (calculated by applying the formula).

Usually, on their own, these calculated values are not very helpful, but in the case of correlations even without any further analysis, correlation coefficients can show something about the results.

A correlation coefficient is a number between −1 and +1 that describes the direction and extent of a correlation. The closer the number is to 1 or −1, the stronger the correlation. The signs + and − tell us whether it is a negative or positive correlation. A score of, or close to, zero indicates no correlation between the variables.

Let's look at an example ...

Examples of correlation coefficients:

Table 7.14 Examples of correlation coefficients

	Indicates	Scatter diagram looks like this
Positive correlation coefficient		
+0.957	Very strong positive correlation	
+0.823	Strong positive correlation	
+0.359	Very weak positive correlation	
Negative correlation coefficient		
−0.868	Very strong negative correlation	
−0.796	Strong negative correlation	
−0.226	Very weak negative correlation	

📖 Practice questions

1. If a correlation co-efficient is calculated to be 0.1 and the value of zero correlation is 0, which of the following is true? [1 mark]

   (a) 0.1 < 0, so there is a small negative correlation

   (b) 0.1 ≈ 0, so there is a very little correlation

   (c) 0.1 = 0, therefore there is no correlation

   (d) 0.1 >> 0, therefore there is a strong positive correlation.

In some of the statistical tests, the calculated value has to be less than the critical value, to achieve that particular significance level. Also some tables will refer to df (degrees of freedom). See Appendix 2 (page 244) for the critical value tables for each of the named tests.

Tests of significance come in many shapes and sizes, some work out correlation, some differences, each used for a different set of criteria. As a general rule, for the basic tests used at A Level, the key criteria are:

- What level of data is being used, nominal, ordinal, interval/ratio?
- Is it a test of difference or correlation?
- If it is a test of difference, does it have repeated or independent design?

Table 7.15 shows the criteria for using a specific non-parametric inferential test.

Table 7.15 Criteria for using a specific non-parametric inferential test

Type of data	Independent design in test of difference	Repeated design in test of difference	Test for correlation
Nominal	Chi Square test	Binomial Sign Test	*
Ordinal	Mann-Whitney U test	Wilcoxon Signed Ranks test	Spearman's Rho Correlation Coefficient
Interval/ratio**			

*You couldn't have a correlational test with nominal data.

**To use a test for this level of data you need to have parametric data.

However, even with a correlation coefficient, we cannot be sure that the result meets the significance level without reference to critical tables.

Using statistics and tables of critical values enable psychologists to compare the calculated value, based on their data, with the *critical values* mathematicians have identified to be the value at which data are significant. The factors which impact on the critical values are the significance level set ($p < 0.05$), the sample size (n) and sometimes whether the research is investigating a one- or two-tailed hypothesis.

In Table 7.16 for the correlation test Spearman's rho, the calculated value of the correlation coefficient is compared to the appropriate critical value.

➡️ Have a go yourself

Take one of the data tables in this chapter and work out which test you would carry out. Using the internet or any statistical package you have in your school or college, test for significance at 95 per cent.

To consider interval or ratio data as parametric and therefore be able to use appropriate parametric tests of difference or correlation, the data have to meet the criteria for using a parametric test. These are that:

- The data have to be interval or ratio.
- The data have to have a curve of normal distribution.
- The variances should be similar.

At A Level psychology, we can't usually make the assumption about normal distribution as our samples are likely to be unrepresentative of the general population, so will be skewed. Therefore, we treat the data as non-parametric (and ordinal) and would use one of the named tests in the Table 7.15.

It is possible for psychologists to set their significance level too high or too low, and therefore they accept their alternative hypothesis when there isn't really a significant difference, or they reject their alternative hypothesis when they should really accept it, as there is a significant difference. In the first instance, the alternative hypothesis is accepted and the null hypothesis is rejected, and the behaviour shown was really due to chance, this is called a type 1 error. In the second case, the rejection of the alternative hypothesis and the acceptance of the null hypothesis when the independent variable really is having a significant impact on the dependent variable, is called a type 2 error.

It is difficult to eliminate the possibility of either of these. If we try to avoid the type 1 error by setting our significance level higher, i.e. 0.01, then we are more likely to make a type 2 error. The practical application of the research may dictate which is the better error to make.

	The null hypothesis is really true. The results really are due to chance	The alternative hypothesis is really true. The IV has affected the DV
The alternative hypothesis is supported by research at $p < 0.05$ and accepted, and the null hypothesis is rejected	Type 1 error $\alpha = 5\%$	
The null hypothesis is supported by research at $P < 0.05$ and accepted, alternate hypothesis is rejected		Type 2 error

Figure 7.19 Hypotheses testing outcomes and type 1 and type 2 errors

Let's look at an example ...

For 0.05 ($p < 0.05$) with a sample size (n) of 10. The critical value is 0.648. If the calculated value is equal to or greater than the critical value (i.e. if it was 0.724), then the results are significant at the 0.05 level of significance. If, however, the calculated value were less than the critical value (i.e. 0.543), the correlation would not be significant at the 0.05 level. There might still be a correlation, but we couldn't be sure it was a strong enough relationship to be 95 per cent certain the two variables were linked.

If the significance level had been set at $p < 0.01$ (99 per cent certain there is a significant relationship between the two variables and only 1 per cent this is due to chance), the column headed 0.01 would be used to identify the critical value (Table 7.16). In this case the critical value would be 0.833.

Table 7.16 Table of critical values (Spearman r_s for the 0.05 and 0.01 levels of significance)

n	0.050	0.01	N	0.050	0.01
6	0.05	0.01	19	0.462	0.608
7	0.886	–	20	0.450	0.591
8	0.738	–	21	0.438	0.576
9	0.683	0.881	22	0.428	0.562
10	0.648	0.833	23	0.418	0.549
11	0.623	0.818	24	0.409	0.537
12	0.591	0.794	25	0.400	0.526
13	0.566	0.780	26	0.392	0.515
14	0.545	0.716	27	0.385	0.505
15	0.525	0.689	28	0.377	0.496
16	0.507	0.666	29	0.370	0.487
17	0.490	0.645	30	0.364	0.478
18	0.476	0.625			

If we are going to change the education system completely then we might rather make a type 1 error and reject the alternative hypothesis incorrectly, than a type 2 error and accept the alternative hypothesis incorrectly, change the education system and then find out it doesn't impact on the behaviour in the way we wanted it to. If however it is a minor impact and any likelihood of something affecting behaviour is a good thing, then we could set our significance level lower 0.1 (10 per cent due to chance) and risk making a type 2 error. For example, using a technique to try and help reduce criminal reoffending rates it might be better to try it and if it doesn't really help then nothing is really lost.

 Stop and ask yourself ...

Can you explain and use all of the terms on the specification?
Make a check list of all the items on the specification under inferential statistics and then tick (or put a smiley face) for each one you are able to explain. Use the exam-style questions to check you can use these in an exam.

📖 Practice questions

1. Which inferential test should a researcher use to decide whether a difference found in research with ordinal data and a repeated design is significant? [1 mark]
   (a) Chi Square test
   (b) Mann–Whitney U test
   (c) Spearman's Rho test
   (d) Wilcoxon Signed Ranks test.

2. Which of these is a requirement of a parametric test? [1 mark]
   (a) Data are at nominal level.
   (b) Mode scores are significantly different.
   (c) Sample is drawn from a positively skewed population.
   (d) Dispersion for each condition is not significantly different.

3 a. Look at the scatter diagram in Figure 7.19: Which is the best estimate of the correlation coefficient for the above data? [1 mark]
   (a) 0.9
   (b) 0.3
   (c) −0.9
   (d) −0.3

3 b. Which test would the researcher use to test for significance? [1 mark]
   (a) Binomial sign test
   (b) Spearman's Rho test
   (c) Mann–Whitney U test
   (d) Chi Square test.

4. A psychologist looked at the difference between males and females and their choice of fruit or not fruit in the college cafe. He predicted females would buy more fruit than males. His data looked like this.

	Not buying fruit in the college cafe	Buying fruit in the college cafe
Male students	16	18
Female students	9	22

The Chi Square test was used to analyse the data. Give two reasons for this choice of test with reference to the study. [2 marks]

5. The Chi Square test gave a calculated value of 3.80. Level of significance is $p < 0.05$ for a one-tailed test, df = 1.

Significance level	0.05	0.025	0.01
Critical value	2.71	3.84	5.41

Using the above critical values, explain whether the psychologist had found a significant difference or not; give reasons for your answer. [4 marks]

6. The psychologist was concerned about making a type 2 error. Outline what is meant by a 'type 2 error'. [2 marks]

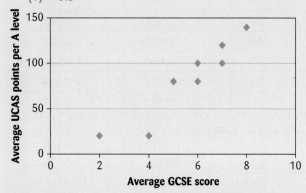

Figure 7.20 Scatter diagram showing relationship between students' GCSE scores and A Level grades

Methodological issues

The aim of the research is to make a sample represent the target population as far as possible, with the same mix of gender, age and ethnicity as the target population. If the sample is similar in make up to the target population then it can be said to be representative. It is difficult, if not impossible, to select a sample that contains no bias and is representative of all people. If a sample is not representative, then psychologists must be cautious before they can say that the findings of the study can be used to predict behaviour in a broader population. For example, if there is a heavy gender bias as the study is done on male participants, then it can't be used to predict the behaviour of females in the target population. Therefore, the ability to generalise the result to the target population is limited and the results lack generalisability. It is important to remember that *samples lack representativeness* and *results lack generalisability*.

 Stop and ask yourself ...

- Why do you think it is so difficult to obtain a sample that truly represents the target population? What type of bias might occur when researchers are obtaining their sample?

The implications of a biased sample for validity and usefulness of the study are that if the generalisability of the findings is low, psychologists say that the study has low population validity: the sample fails to represent its intended population. If a study is low in population validity, this in turn limits the usefulness of the study's findings as psychologists will be less certain that any findings from the sample truly represent behaviours demonstrated by people in the population.

Reliability refers to the consistency of research or findings, or whether a test can be used more than once and produce consistent results.

Internal reliability refers to the consistency of results of a test across items within that test. For example, does the first half of a test give the same results as the second half of the test? If I was assessing IQ, then I would want to know that the first ten questions of a twenty questions test gave a similar score to the second set of ten questions.

The way to test internal reliability of a test is to use a split half method. I would test one half of the questions and gain a score and then the other half of the questions to see if the same level of score was achieved on both halves. The first half could be the first questions, every other question or the first and third

quarter of questions. It shouldn't matter which ones I choose, the results should be consistent and therefore prove the test to be reliable.

 Have a go yourself

Find a questionnaire (from the internet or a magazine) and give it to a sample of your friends. Calculate whether their scores on the first half of the test correlate with the scores on the second half of the test.

External reliability refers to the extent to which a test score varies from one time to another. If I gave an IQ test to someone today would it give the same reading as if I gave the test in six months' time?

To test external validity of a questionnaire or a piece of research the test–retest method can be used to see if the same results are achieved. A high level of standardisation would make a piece of research replicable (i.e. repeatable) and this would test for reliability. Simply making it replicable doesn't make it reliable; it makes it testable for reliability. Just as using a test a second time won't make it reliable, it will allow us to test the reliability of that test. The same results on a retest will, however, show external reliability.

In order to avoid observer bias, that is, an observer applying ratings or counting categories in a subjective rather than objective fashion, inter-rater reliability needs to be established. This means that two observers consistently rate or observe the same behaviour and the two sets of ratings are correlated. If a significant positive correlation is seen (as a rule of thumb, psychologists would look for a correlation of +0.8 or higher), inter-rater reliability has been established and the objectivity of the results confirmed.

In the Bandura *et al.* study (imitating aggression), inter-rater reliability was established to prevent any conscious or unconscious bias occurring on the part of the teacher or experimenter in their assessment of the children's general aggression prior to the children being allocated to the test conditions. A positive correlation of +0.89 was found between the teacher and the researcher's ratings of the children's aggressiveness.

Validity is how accurate a piece of research or test is at measuring what it aims to measure. For example, a test of IQ which measures the circumference of a person's head as an indicator of IQ (the larger the head the higher the IQ) is not a valid test of intelligence.

In the same way, a piece of research which has lots of extraneous variables may not actually be testing the effect of the independent variable on the dependent variable, there may be something else (noise, time of day, hunger) affecting behaviour, so the research is not accurately measuring the influence of the independent variable. This would cause low internal validity.

If results of research can be generalised to other settings, because they were done in realistic settings, or have a representative sample, or didn't have any bias in the method or interpretation of the results, then the research can be said to have high external validity.

There are different ways in which we can assess the validity of research or measurement tools.

- Face validity is how good the test or research looks to be at testing what it is meant to be testing. For example, the measurement of intelligence by measuring the circumference of a person's head falls at this first hurdle. It doesn't look like it measures IQ. However, a test of logic, or knowledge could be considered, at face value, to test intelligence. We would then have to look at other ways to assess the validity.
- Construct validity is where a test or study measures the actual behaviour it sets out to measure, so a test for intelligence shouldn't assess general knowledge, or memory. The results of a test could be correlated with other tests of the same construct, so a test of intelligence would give the same results as other tests of intelligence.
- Concurrent validity is where a test or piece of research gives the same results as another test or study, which claims to measure the same behaviour. So if a study gave the same results as a previous study then the study would have high concurrent validity. Loftus and Palmer's first experiment gave the same results for estimation of speed as the second experiment, giving an example of concurrent validity.
- Criterion validity refers to how much one measure predicts the value of another measure. It can include concurrent validity and predictive validity, which is where the test or research can predict certain behaviours, such as an IQ test predicting success in education, or a particular occupation. To test for predictive validity, a group of people would be tested and then tested at a later stage in their life to see if the predictions were correct. Using the A Level grades to predict success on a degree course (and therefore giving a place at a university) would be assuming predictive validity of A-levels.
- Population validity is how accurately the test or study measures behaviour in the general population. A study may have been carried out on a group of people from one city, or one country and not be an accurate

measure of behaviour in other cities or countries and therefore may lack population validity. A test such as an intelligence test may be a standardised test, such as one for adults over 16 so we wouldn't expect it to test intelligence in children under 16, but we would expect it to test intelligence in *everyone* over the age of 16. Some tests will have inherent culture bias, such as tests of general knowledge or linguistics which are usually culture specific, and these would not be tests of intelligence for everyone. They have, however, been used where they have been standardised to certain populations, such as western, English-speaking cultures, but they only have population validity for that population. Culture fair tests, such as logic tests of intelligence, can be used on people from any culture, without any bias.

💡 **Let's look at an example …**

- Culture fair:
In Figure 7.21 which piece fits the missing shape?

Figure 7.21 Culture fair test

or

- Not culture fair:
Fish is to swim as bird is to ....

Finally, ecological validity is considered to be how like real life a piece of research is. If we consider it as a form of validity, is it accurately measuring real life? If the setting is in a laboratory then it isn't, as we don't live our lives in laboratories, so lab experiments have low ecological validity, whereas field experiments have high ecological validity. We can also consider if the task given to the participant is like that which would be met in real life. For example, Milgram asked participants to shock people, which is not something we would encounter in real life, so again his research lacked ecological validity, not only for the setting but also for the task.

Artificial settings and artificial tasks may result in artificial behaviour and so this can limit the usefulness of the research. Questionnaires could be considered to lack ecological validity as it is not a normal state for us to be asked lots of questions one after the other, but observations, particularly naturalistic observations, can have high ecological validity due to their natural settings, which gets natural behaviour.

🚫 Stop and ask yourself …

- Which of the core studies that you have studied do you think has the highest and lowest ecological validity?

There are many types of bias which could affect the reliability and/or the validity of research. Participants will often try to present a good image to researchers. If the participant guesses the aim of the research, either because it is obvious, or they are in a repeated design and the second condition makes it clear what is being tested, they may act in the way they think the researcher wants them to act. Chaney et al.'s participants could have worked out that the Funhaler was meant to increase adherence (particularly as he couldn't counterbalance this study) and so the mothers used the Funhaler more frequently. This behaviour is known as demand characteristics. It can be avoided if the person is not aware they are taking part in research, or if they are not told what the research is about. If someone displays demand characteristics it is not an accurate reflection on their behaviour so will reduce the validity. They are also unlikely to show the same behaviour next time, as they may think they should show something different, and therefore the reliability can be reduced.

Social desirability bias is shown by participants who want to present an image of being a good member of society. So trying to behave in the way society wants or answer questions in a way that reflects society's norms, but not necessarily accurately reflecting true behaviour. This could have been shown in Chaney et al.'s research as the mothers had to complete a questionnaire on the use of the inhalers with their children, and it is quite likely that the mothers didn't want to admit to not using the inhalers, particularly in the first condition with the standard inhalers. They may have lied to make themselves look more like socially acceptable mothers. This would therefore not reflect their true behaviour and so the validity would be lowered. Also if they are not showing true behaviour, it is likely the next time they would show a different behaviour, and therefore the reliability could also be lessened.

It is not only the participant who may show bias in his or her behaviour, but the researcher or observer could show bias when collecting and when analysing their data. If a researcher wants to see a particular behaviour, for example if Bandura et al. wanted to see more aggression in boys than girls to support their hypothesis, they could have interpreted the behaviour of some of the boys as being aggressive, whereas the same behaviour in the girls might not have been interpreted as such. It would be easier in some situations to gain objective data, for example if the observer didn't know if the child had seen an aggressive or non-aggressive model, then the results would be more objective, but for something like gender this wouldn't be possible. To avoid this bias, Bandura et al. did use inter-rater reliability to make sure that both observers were noting things consistently. However, this doesn't preclude bias being present in both observers. Not telling the observer what the research is about would be one way of reducing observer bias. However, once the data are gathered, it is also possible for researchers to impose their bias on the interpretation of such data. This is more difficult with numerical quantitative data, which is less liable to bias, but with qualitative data such as in Freud's study on Little Hans, Hans' father and Freud were able to manipulate the data in a biased way – Freud asking leading questions, Hans' father only writing what he thought Freud would want to hear – interpreting it to support Freud's theory of psychosexual development.

The participants can be influenced by the researcher's presence, and these researcher/observer effects can make someone act very differently to normal. You only have to think about how school or college changes when OFSTED are in to see how behaviour can change when someone is being observed or studied. If you are aware of being observed you will behave differently, and it also depends on the researcher. In interviews, the gender or age of the researcher may influence the results of the questions asked. After all, would you want to talk about your peer relationships to someone old enough to be your grandma? Or would someone old enough to be your grandma want to talk to someone your age? So just knowing you are being watched, or the characteristics of the researcher can affect your behaviour, and might reduce the validity of the research if the results don't accurately reflect your true behaviour.

Over the years, research in psychology has become more constrained by ethical considerations to ensure the protection of the participants, and also to protect the status of psychology, and the psychologists undertaking the research. Each country has its own ethical guidelines, and these will reflect the society or culture

233

with which they are associated. In the UK, the British Psychological Society (BPS) produced the Code of Ethics and Conduct which are used for all research taking place by psychologists, from GCSE students to internationally renowned psychologists, and each piece of research should consider the ethical guidelines, and be scrutinised by an ethics committee, which might be a teacher or a university committee or representatives from the BPS. In the USA, the American Psychological Association is the body which governs the ethical guidelines for researchers in America. Current BPS guidelines published in 2009 have identified four areas of responsibility psychologists should consider when planning and carrying out research. These are Respect, Competence, Responsibility and Integrity. They include the previous guidelines, such as the respect of a participant's confidentiality, but also go beyond into more contemporary areas, such as respect for sexuality, ethnicity and other individual and cultural differences.

Most of the research covered in Units 2 and 3 will have been carried out prior to the introduction of clear ethical guidelines or in line with the previous guidelines. The current (2015) guidelines are:

- The area of RESPECT considers the necessity for gaining consent from participants and/or their representatives, allowing participants to withdraw from situations they find distressing and maintaining confidentiality wherever possible.
  - **Informed consent**. Consent should be gained from all participants where possible, and informed as far as possible as to what the research will involve. If a person is too young or incapable of giving consent, then the consent of a responsible adult, e.g. parent, should also be sought. However, the right of the participant is paramount and even if consent is gained from a parent, then the right of the child not to take part must be considered. Bandura *et al.* used children from Stanford University nursery, so while the parents hadn't given explicit permission for the Bobo study, they probably agreed when their child joined the nursery that he or she could be used as participants in psychological research. Teachers can give consent in place of parents. This is known as *in loco parentis*.
  - **Right to withdraw**. At any time, participants should have the right to withdraw from the study, and although it is often considered that the use of the prods in Milgram prevented people from withdrawing, they could (and did) leave at any time they wished. They didn't even forfeit their payment. It may be that at the end of the research a participant wants to withdraw their data from the results and they also must have the right to do so if they wish.

  - **Confidentiality**. Participants have the right to their data being kept entirely confidential. They should not be identified by any means, and the use of initials, numbers or letters to denote participants is the most usual way to do this. Little Hans' real name was not actually Hans.
- COMPETENCE reflects the need for psychologists to work within their own capabilities, not giving advice to participants if not qualified to do so, and to check their research with peers. It clarifies the need for psychologists to monitor their own and others' competence in carrying out research appropriately.
- RESPONSIBILITY. The standard of responsibility is concerned with the need to protect participants from harm, and to ensure that participants are fully debriefed.
  - **Protection of participants**. No matter what the situation regarding deception, the participants should be protected from all physical and psychological harm. Bandura *et al.* could be accused of changing children's behaviour to be more aggressive, and Milgram's participants did seem to suffer some psychological and, in some cases, some physical harm. However, Milgram did follow up a year later to ensure there was no lasting psychological harm.
  - **Debrief**. This is more a method to deal with the issues arising from the guidelines above. The participant should leave the research in the same state of mind as they arrived. So any deception should be removed, they can legitimately be told the aim of the study. They are again given the right to withdraw, assured of confidentiality, and can ask any questions. Researchers may refer them to other agencies if they feel it is needed, but participants should be assured that their behaviour was perfectly acceptable, whether it was predicted or not, if they showed it, then it was OK to do so.
- INTEGRITY. Psychologists should have high standards regarding honesty, accuracy, clarity and fairness when carrying out research and avoid deception wherever possible.
  - **Deception**. Often it is not possible to gain fully informed consent, as this would inevitably lead to demand characteristics or social desirability bias, but deception should be kept to a minimum and as soon as possible the real situation should be made clear to the participant. Milgram's participants were deceived in many ways, from the aim of the study through the drawing of lots with a stooge pretending to be another participant, the shock generator and the feedback from the 'learner'. It wouldn't have made it more ethical to remove deception by using a real shock generator! There are also guidelines on using animals as participants – for more detail, see the BPS's guidelines on working with animals.

Practice questions

1. Which of these statements defines the BPS code of respect? [1 mark]
   (a) Psychologists to work within their own capabilities.
   (b) The participant should leave the research in the same state of mind as they arrived.
   (c) Deception should be kept to a minimum.
   (d) Gaining consent allowing withdrawal and maintaining confidentiality.
2. What is meant by the term inter-rater reliability? [1 mark]
   (a) Whether a test gives the same results if used again.
   (b) If observers see the same behaviours in participants.
   (c) If the results are accurate.
   (d) If the results show a positive correlation.
3. Which issue will be affected by social desirability bias shown by participants? [1 mark]

   (a) Ecological validity
   (b) Inter-rater reliability
   (c) Validity
   (d) Research bias.
4. Which of these methods would be most likely to prevent researcher effects? [1 mark]
   (a) Gaining qualitative data
   (b) Conducting participant observation
   (c) A controlled lab experiment
   (d) Conducting an interview.
5. Which ethical issue would be used to avoid demand characteristics? [1 mark]
   (a) Gaining informed consent
   (b) Deceiving the participant
   (c) Allowing the participant to withdraw
   (d) Debriefing the participant.

Report writing

The specification requires you to know the conventional way psychologists report their research, and demonstrate an understanding of the role and purpose of each of the main sections and subsections in a practical report.

Sections and subsections of a practical report

From the Core studies you will be familiar with the outline of a psychological report on a piece of research. These articles are usually published in academic journals, having been reviewed and accepted by peers as being of a good enough standard to warrant publication. There is an accepted format in which psychological research should be written, although there are sometimes slight variations in the headings or the order. However, it is important that each section is written in full so that the research has a good theoretical background which is explicitly detailed; that the method is replicable, for other researchers to carry out and test the reliability and validity of the research; that the data are presented in an unambiguous and unbiased way and subjected to stringent appropriate statistical analysis. The discussion should reflect how the study compares with the background research and also consider the limitations of the research to provide future research ideas to improve or extend the current piece of research. All research referred to in the article should be referenced so that it can be accessed by anyone reading the article who may

want to know what else has been found in that area. Appendices contain supplementary information, such as a copy of the materials used, raw data collected and often calculations or additional information.

The abstract is a summary of the research, outlining the aim, method, participants, results and conclusions. Although it is the first section of the report it is written at the end when the results have been analysed. It doesn't contain any evaluation, but is a brief summary of the study.

Have a go yourself

Look up the original articles of the core studies (look on the internet or ask your teacher if they have copies). Read the abstract. Does it give you a good overview of what happened in the study and what the results were?

The introduction considers the area of psychology in which the study is located, such as memory or obedience, and then focuses on previous research which has been carried out in the same area. This may include conflicting research, which the current research aims to clarify, or previous research which is being extended, i.e. in scope of population or using different techniques. It will justify the current research and identify the aim of the research. It will probably end with the alternative and null hypothesis.

The method is a lengthy section which includes all the details necessary for someone to be able to carry out

235

exactly the same research in the same conditions. It will include the method, such as observation, interview or experiment, together with information on the sample, the technique for obtaining it (explained in detail) together with features such as number, age range, gender, so that a sample as similar as possible could be obtained by the reader of the article. Then you would include the experimental design (repeated, independent, matched pairs) and show how you would allocate participants to the conditions. In order to replicate the research, a copy of all of the materials/apparatus would be needed in the appendices, such as word lists, tests, stimulus material, and these would be outlined in the method and the reader referred to the appendices to see the materials for him or herself. Finally an outline of the procedure, how the participants were approached, what was said, timings and what actually happened in the research. Remember the idea is to provide a replicable study.

🚫 Stop and ask yourself…

- Why would researchers want to replicate a study? Which methodological issue would they be testing?

The results will refer to the raw data and provide verbal summaries and descriptive statistics, such as measures of central tendency, measures of dispersion and graphical representation.

The graphs should provide easy to see comparisons of the conditions and the same data displayed in several different types of graphs is rarely, if ever, a good idea. Inferential statistics will then provide evidence for the acceptance of either the alternative or null hypothesis, and this will be summarised at the end of the result section.

The discussion will focus on what the study has discovered, relating it to the research in the introduction. Evaluation and alternative explanations plus suggestions for how to move the research on in terms of improvements or new ideas to pursue will complete the discussion.

All the works cited in the article should be clearly referenced so that anyone reading the article will be able to locate the book or article referred to in order to read for him or herself the original words being summarised.

The last selection will be the appendices, labelled and referred to in the body of the article, and these will contain materials, maybe calculations, raw data, and anything else the reader needs to fully understand and repeat the research.

Psychological research follows certain conventions when it comes to the writing up of research. It should be written in the third person ('it was', not 'I did') and in the past tense ('it was', not 'it will be'). Also one of the most serious misdemeanours an academic can commit is to plagiarise

another person's work. This is where you copy from books, articles or the internet and pass it off as your work, by not acknowledging where it came from and referencing it. If you quote directly from another source, whatever it is, this should be shown by the use of quotation marks (" ") and the source identified and referenced.

Citing academic references

There are many ways of citing academic work mentioned in a research article or book. The one that is most commonly used in psychology is the Harvard method of referencing. You will need to become familiar with citing academic research using this system of referencing. What is important is that every detail is included, these include the author(s), the date of publication, the title, the publisher, and where it was published if referring to a book. If the reference is to an article then the name of the journal in which it was published comes after the article title, followed by the volume, issue and page numbers. It is just as important to reference all internet sites used (remember: to avoid plagiarism you must acknowledge *any* source of information) and here you would need the URL (website address) and the date it was accessed. DVDs, videos, reports, conference proceedings all have to be acknowledged within the references. Most often, the date and author will appear in the body of the work and the full reference at the end of the article. The references will appear in alphabetical order at the end of the article.

💡 Let's look at an example …

In the text of the article, Milgram suggested that the participants 'reached extremes that are rarely seen in sociopsychological laboratory studies' (Milgram, 1963). This was seen by Baumrind as evidence that Milgram was more interested in his career than in the welfare of his participants (Baumrind, 1964).

References at the end of the article will read:
Baumrind, D. (1964) Some thoughts on ethics of research: after reading Milgram's behavioural study of obedience. *American Psychologist,* **19**(6), 421–423.

Milgram, S. (1963) Behavioral study of obedience. *Journal of Abnormal and Social Psychology,* **67**(4), 371–378.

➡️ Have a go yourself

Look up the original articles of your core studies on the internet or ask your teacher if they have copies. From the front page, use the information to write up the reference in the Harvard style. Check this with the references at the back of this book.

Peer review

Peers are people of the same standing as you, and in the world of scientific research peer review is the quality assurance process used to assess whether recently completed research has been carried out in an important area, in an acceptable manner with the appropriate methodology, and what the impact of the findings are. Peers in this case will be experts in the field of the research, and they will evaluate the new research before it can be published. Peer review could also be used before a piece of research is undertaken, when the plan of the research might be submitted to peers in order to satisfy the bodies providing the money that this would be a good piece of research to fund. Not all publications use peer review, but the most prestigious ones do, and they will usually accept the recommendation of the reviewer whether to publish the article or not. While peer review is important to retain the creditability of new research and ensure validity of publications, it is not always seen as positive. It can be a lengthy process, some reviewers may not 'pass' research which contradicts their own research, and it may not be possible to detect research which has used false data. But it does attempt to ensure that only the most relevant and methodologically robust research is published.

In psychology, for example, the study by Chaney *et al.* was published in the journal *Respirology*. This is part of a larger company Wiley, which publishes many journals and books. *Respirology* says on its website that it requires all submitted papers to be peer reviewed: 'both unsolicited and invited, are reviewed before publication by multiple independent (i.e. independent from the author) qualified experts.'

http://onlinelibrary.wiley.com/journal/10.1111/(ISSN)1440-1843/homepage/ForAuthors.html

Practical activities

The specification requires you to carry out your own small-scale research practicals in order to fully understand the process of undertaking research, using statistics and presenting data. You will need to be aware of ethical guidelines and ensure that your teacher has agreed your research methodology. Also, you need to make sure that you are aware of the risks and how to manage them. You can look at the Health and Safety Executive (HSE) website for guidance on this. Below are some examples of practical activities to give you some ideas. It is worth creating a portfolio of your research, with a write-up of each of the practicals you conduct. This can be word processed, so you might find creating a template with the headings for each section will help to guide you in your writing.

Experiment

1. Often in society we have to take notice of the colour red. Red traffic signs, red traffic lights, etc., are said to be eye catching. But is red more memorable than black. Try investigating the difference between memory of black and red words. You could have independent or repeated design. Give one group a list of twenty words in red and the other twenty words in black. If you are using an independent design, you could use the same words. If you are using a repeated design you could give them all of the words at the same time alternating red and black. Give each participant the list to memorise for one minute, then ask them to write down all they can remember. You could then look at

Practice questions

1. Which part of the practical report would contain an evaluation of the research? [1 mark]
   (a) Introduction
   (b) Method
   (c) Results
   (d) Discussion.
2. In the following academic reference, what is missing which should be included in Harvard references? [1 mark]

Chaney, G., Clements, B., Landau, L., Bulsara, M. and Watt, P. A new asthma spacer device to improve compliance in children: a pilot study. *Respirology*, **9**(4), 499–506.
   (a) The year of publication
   (b) The author's full name
   (c) The volume of the journal
   (d) The pages of the journal.
3. Explain why research which is published should be peer reviewed. [4 marks]

the measures of central tendency and display these graphically. A statistical test could be used to see if there is a significant difference.

2. The Stroop experiment was designed to see if we process information automatically when we look at something. Look up Stroop on the internet and you will find a list of words saying colours with the word written in the same colour ink, and a list with them written in a different colour ink. For example, red and red. The two conditions can be given in an independent or repeated designs (remember to counterbalance). Time how long it takes for each list to be read. Analyse and display your data appropriately. There are other Stroop tests with pictures and words of animals and food on the internet. Do these show the same effect? Is there a difference between mismatched colours and mismatched pictures?

3. Try investigating gender differences in behaviour, such as spotting errors in a picture or spot the differences. How long does it take for a person to find all the differences. Or gender differences in multi-tasking, such as answering quiz questions while completing a jigsaw puzzle. Can you find an answer to some of the questions about assumed gender differences?

Observation

1. Sit on a bench on a high street or in a park and make a note of the behaviours you see people doing. For example, talking to another person, talking on phone, walking in silence, listening to someone, sitting down. Then for ten minutes look at the behaviour of people passing by. You could look at gender differences in communication behaviour. Try this with a friend and check your results for inter-rater reliability. Remember you can only observe people where they would expect to be observed. No peeking in public toilets or through windows. You can record the behaviours for each gender as nominal data, and display this with a bar chart. Don't overcrowd the chart. Analysis with a statistical test would show if these differences are significant.

2. If you have access to a pet or local zoo, try observing an animal. List the behaviours the animal might display and every ten minutes throughout the day (set your phone or watch to remind you) make a note of the behaviour. Animals are never 'doing nothing', even if they are sleeping, do their ears twitch or are they breathing? If you have two pets,

do they display the same behaviours or are there any differences if you compare a cat with a dog?

3. Carry out a naturalistic observation to look at driving behaviour. This could be behaviour at traffic lights or wearing safety clothes such as cycle helmet, or unsafe behaviour such as using mobile phones. Remember to stand in a safe place.

Self-report

1. Compose a list of questions about your college or school. This could be closed questions or rating scales. For example, you might ask if they think the school is an equal opportunities school, or if they think the food is good quality. Give them to a sample of students and teachers and see if there is any difference in their perceptions of the college/school. Pie charts might display this information clearly, and a statistical test would show if their differences are significant.

2. Try interviewing people in authority. This could be your head girl/boy, student union president, principal, deputy head, supervisor at work, or friend or family member who has position of authority in their job. Try to find out what they feel are important attributes of being a leader. Use open questions, and see if you can find common traits. (You could compare this with what people not in authority think.)

3. Devise a questionnaire which looks at what people would value in a friend. Is there a gender difference?

Correlation

1. Does short-term memory get worse with age? Find a sample of people with different ages, say from your friends as teenagers through to grandparents. Give them a memory test (twenty words to learn in one minute and then recall) and correlate their age and score. Test for significance using a statistical test, and display your data in a scatter diagram.

2. Investigate the relationship between social media and social relationships. Ask people how many friends they have on their favourite social media (Facebook, Twitter, etc.) and how many times they went out with a friend each month. Is there a correlation between sociability and virtual sociability and, if so, is it positive or negative? Test these data for significance. Do you think there is a third variable which might influence these two variables?

3. Two observers gathered the data in Table 7.17 when observing behaviour in a university student common room over a two-hour period. Test for inter-rater reliability.

Table 7.17 Data gathered in a university student common room over a two-hour period

Behaviours observed	Observer 1	Observer 2
Eating/drinking	5	4
Reading	7	7
Talking/socialising	12	10
Studying	4	7
Using mobile phone	6	4
Sitting alone doing nothing	4	8
Playing games	12	10

How science works

Psychology is a science, and **the specification requires** you to know how we, as a society, use psychology to help develop our economy and society, and how we make decisions about research based on scientific principles.

The nature and principles of science

The British Psychological Society introduces psychology as 'the scientific study of human mind and behaviour' and it suggests that as a science 'psychologists study human behaviour by observing, measuring and testing, then arriving at conclusions that are rooted in sound scientific methodology.' Historically, psychology was seen as a social science, not quite as rigorous as some of the traditional sciences such as chemistry, and there are some clear differences. However, psychology is now recognised as a science and it is important to judge psychology against the principles of science to see how it measures up.

Stop and ask yourself…

- What do you think are the main differences between the hard sciences (biology, chemistry and physics) and psychology, which is sometimes seen as a 'soft science'?

One of the most eminent scientists in this field is Karl Popper, who in 1934 identified the keystone to scientific research which is falsification (Popper, 2002). However, there are other features of scientific enquiry and in order to consider psychology as a science it should be judged against these.

- **Cause-and-effect**. This is where research can – to any given significance level – show that one factor actually causes a change in behaviour (effect).

This can be seen in more scientific studies, such as Bandura *et al*, where it is reasonable to conclude that the behaviour of the adult model did cause a change in the behaviour of the child. The more standardised (see below) a study is, and the more control of extraneous variables, the higher the level of confidence we can have in the results showing cause-and-effect. Increased reliability will also help this confidence, as if the effect is seen many times when research is repeated, then we can be reassured that the change in the dependent variable is caused by the independent variable.

- **Deduction**. This is the logical conclusion based on irrefutable proof. So if we observe something in psychological research that is absolutely true and there is no other possible explanation, then we would deduce that the conclusion is correct. This is of course very difficult (if not impossible) to do in psychology as we would never see 100 per cent of the same results every time for every person. In Milgram's research, not every person went up to 450 Volts.
- **Induction**. This is the concept that we observe something and provide a theory for this. For example, we see that animals and humans appear to imitate behaviour shown by others, often older models. The theory then is that we learn from others through observation and imitation.
- **Hypothesis testing**. Once a theory has been identified based on observations, then in scientific enquiry a hypothesis is formulated and this can be tested in empirical research. For Milgram, the hypothesis would be that Americans would not commit acts of violence if told to do so.
- **Manipulation of variables**. The independent variable must be manipulated, so that we can see the results if it is or isn't present. Bandura *et al.*'s children were manipulated to see either a same sex or different sex role model, and within that either an aggressive or non-aggressive model, plus there was a control group who saw no model. This will enable us to see if there is any resultant effect on the behaviour.
- **Standardisation**. Keeping the test conditions the same for every participant. It is a method of controlling situational variables, or environmental factors, which might have an influence on the participant's behaviour. To keep all extraneous variables constant across experimental conditions, researchers use standard apparatus, standard instructions and procedures and standard locations. Milgram's set up was the same for each participant, including the feedback from the shock generator, and the verbal prods.

- **Replicability**. To be able to repeat and therefore support or refute the findings from another piece of research is important in the consideration of psychology as a science. Bandura *et al.*'s research was clearly replicable, with controlled settings, standardised procedures and observation schedules. Such replication can, if the findings prove the same time and again, provide a large body of evidence to support the scientific theory.
- **Controls**. For us to be clear on cause-and-effect (that the independent variable had impacted on behaviour), other extraneous variables have to be eliminated as far as possible. For Milgram, this was clearly the case from the standardised set up.
- **Quantifiable measurements**. Quantitative data, which is observable and objective should be used to identify the impact of the independent variable. It should not be data which rely on unobservable behaviour, such as belief. This is seen in the number of acts which each child displayed in Bandura *et al.*'s study.
- **Objectivity**. Allowing personal theories or expectations to cloud judgement in research will make it less scientific. All sources of bias should be eliminated. It is important that researchers remain objective. In Milgram's study the use of machinery to record the volts given was objective, however the interpretation of the laughter as 'nervous' was not necessarily objective.
- **Falsification**. It is important, however, that we should be able to falsify or prove wrong the claim. This can be done by assuming other explanations and then testing them. By testing them and not finding them to be true we can be more certain our theory is correct. Milgram looked at other explanations such as the surroundings, the learner being distant, no real authority figure, and he tested these in his variations, which showed these other explanations to be false, leaving the original theory of obedience due to an authority figure to be true.

All of these features work well in laboratory-based research, such as social experiments, behaviourist and cognitive studies, but tend to do less well when considered against something like Freud's psychodynamic theory.

- **Deduction**. This is the logical conclusion based on irrefutable proof. There is no irrefutable proof for Freud's theory and the conclusions are not necessarily logical.

- **Induction**. This is the concept that we observe something and provide a theory for this. Freud did this, trying to find out what caused the neuroses and constructing his psychodynamic theory.
- **Hypothesis testing**. Once a theory has been identified based on observations, then in scientific enquiry a hypothesis is formulated and this can be tested in empirical research. Freud didn't have a hypothesis, he used data to support his theory, but without predicting what the behaviour would be in any given case.
- **Manipulation of variables**. The independent variable is manipulated, so that we can see the variation in results depending on whether it is or isn't present. Freud didn't carry out research in which he could manipulate variables, he worked with case studies of evidence, over which he had little control.
- **Standardisation** means keeping the test conditions the same for every participant. None of Freud's case studies (the backbone of his evidence) used standardised procedures.
- **Replicability** refers to the ability to be able to repeat and therefore support or refute the findings from another piece of research. The lack of scientific evidence means that it is impossible to replicate any of Freud's case studies.
- **Controls**. For us to be clear on cause-and-effect, other extraneous variables have to be eliminated as far as possible. Freud's case studies have a wealth of extraneous variables, so even a study of the phobia of horses in another young child would lack control.
- **Quantifiable measurements**. Quantitative data, which is observable and objective should be used. Freud did not use quantifiable measurements. His data were subjective observations and conversations.
- **Objectivity**. Allowing personal theories or expectations to cloud judgement in research will make it less scientific. Freud was using his case studies to support his theory, so everything was interpreted in line with this theory and his expectations.
- **Falsification**. It is important, however, that we should be able to falsify or prove wrong the claim. It is impossible to falsify a concept such as Oedipus conflict.

Some areas of psychology may be more scientific than others and it is important not to lose sight of some of the major psychological theories which are not necessarily scientific, but which tell us much about the human mind and behaviour.

Practice questions

1. A researcher was interested in finding out about sleep deprivation and its effect on performance in a school test. He carried out a field experiment in which he arranged for participants to record their sleep using an app on their smart phone, and then gave them a concentration test the next day, together with a test on the work from the lesson the previous day.

Explain how the following principles of science could be applied to this research:

(a) Controls [3 marks]

(b) Quantitative data [3 marks]

(c) Deduction. [3 marks]

Appendix 1

Mathematic requirements for assessment in Unit 1

Table A1.1 shows the mathematical requirements which will be assessed in Unit 1. These are only examples and are in no way definitive of how each skill will be assessed.

Table A1.1 Mathematical requirements

D.0: Arithmetic and numerical computation		
D.0.1	Recognise and use expressions in decimal and standard form	For example, converting data in standard form from a results table into decimal form in order to construct a pie chart.
D.0.2	Use ratios, fractions and percentages	For example, calculating the percentages of cases that fall into different categories in an observation study.
D.0.3	Estimate results	For example, commenting on the spread of scores for a set of data, which would require estimating the range.
D.1: Handling data		
D.1.1	Use an appropriate number of significant figures	For example, expressing a correlation coefficient to two or three significant figures.
D.1.2	Find arithmetic means	For example, calculating the means for two conditions using raw data from a class experiment.
D.1.3	Construct and interpret frequency tables and diagrams, bar charts and histograms	For example, selecting and sketching an appropriate form of data display for a given set of data.
D.1.4	Understand simple probability	For example, explaining the difference between the 0.05 and 0.01 levels of significance.
D.1.5	Understand the principles of sampling as applied to scientific data	For example, explaining how a random or stratified sample could be obtained from a target population.
D.1.6	Understand the terms mean, median and mode	For example, explaining the differences between the mean, median and mode and selecting which measure of central tendency is most appropriate for a given set of data. Calculate standard deviation.
D.1.7	Use a scatter diagram to identify a correlation between two variables	For example, plotting two variables from an investigation on a scatter diagram and identifying the pattern as a positive correlation, a negative correlation or no correlation.
D.1.8	Use a statistical test	For example, calculating a non-parametric test of differences using data from a given experiment.

D.1.9	Make order of magnitude calculations	For example, estimating the mean test score for a large number of participants on the basis of the total overall score.
D.1.10	Distinguish between levels of measurement	For example, stating the level of measurement (nominal, ordinal or interval) that has been used in a study.
D.1.11	Know the characteristics of normal and skewed distributions	For example, being presented with a set of scores from an experiment and being asked to indicate the position of the mean (or median, or mode).
D.1.12	Select an appropriate statistical test	For example, selecting a suitable inferential test for a given practical investigation and explaining why the chosen test is appropriate.
D.1.13	Use statistical tables to determine significance	For example, using an extract from statistical tables to say whether or not a given observed value is significant at the 0.05 level of significance for a one-tailed test.
D.1.14	Understand measures of dispersion, including standard deviation and range	For example, explaining why the standard deviation might be a more useful measure of dispersion for a given set of scores, e.g. where there is an outlying score.
D.1.15	Understand the differences between qualitative and quantitative data	For example, explaining how a given qualitative measure (for example, an interview transcript) might be converted into quantitative data.
D.1.16	Understand the difference between primary and secondary data	For example, stating whether data collected by a researcher dealing directly with participants is primary or secondary data.
D.2: Algebra		
D.2.1	Understand and use the symbols: $=, <, \ll, \gg, >, \propto, \sim$	For example, expressing the outcome of an inferential test in the conventional form by stating the level of significance at the 0.05 level or 0.01 level by using symbols appropriately.
D.2.2	Substitute numerical values into algebraic equations using appropriate units for physical quantities	For example, inserting the appropriate values from a given set of data into the formula for a statistical test, e.g. inserting the n value (for the number of scores) into the Chi Square formula.
D.2.3	Solve simple algebraic equations	For example, calculating the degrees of freedom for a Chi Square test.
D.3: Graphs		
D.3.1	Translate information between graphical, numerical and algebraic forms	For example, using a set of numerical data (a set of scores) from a record sheet to construct a bar graph.
D.3.2	Plot two variables from experimental or other data	For example, sketching a scatter diagram using two sets of data from a correlational investigation.

Appendix 2

Tables of critical values

Chi Squared test

1. Identify the level of significance column for your test, look along the top row.
2. Find your degrees of freedom in the left-hand column. 'Degrees of freedom' is the number of categories in the research minus 1. This determines the row of the table you will use.
3. The critical value for your test is found at the intersection of the column and row you have identified.
4. If your calculated value of x^2 equals or exceeds this critical value, your result is statistically significant at the level you have chosen.

Table A2.1 Table of critical value

Degrees of freedom	Level of significance for one-tailed test					
	0.10	0.05	0.025	0.01	0.005	0.0005
	Level of significance for two-tailed test					
	0.20	0.10	0.05	0.02	0.01	0.001
1	1.64	2.71	3.84	5.41	6.64	10.83
2	3.22	4.60	5.99	7.82	9.21	13.82
3	4.64	6.25	7.82	9.84	11.34	16.27
4	5.99	7.78	9.49	11.67	13.28	18.46
5	7.29	9.24	11.07	13.39	15.09	20.52
6	8.56	10.64	12.59	15.03	16.81	22.46
7	9.80	12.02	14.07	16.62	18.48	24.32
8	11.03	13.36	15.51	18.17	20.09	26.12
9	12.24	14.68	16.92	19.68	21.67	27.88
10	13.44	15.99	18.31	21.16	23.21	29.59
11	14.63	17.28	19.68	22.62	24.72	31.26
12	15.81	18.55	21.03	24.05	26.22	32.91
13	16.98	19.81	22.36	25.47	27.69	34.53
14	18.15	21.06	23.68	26.87	29.14	36.12
15	19.31	22.31	25.00	28.26	30.58	37.70

Mann–Whitney U test

1. Determine whether you are conducting a one-tailed or a two-tailed test.
2. Identify the level of significance for your test.
3. Find your N_1 and N_2 value – the sample sizes for both conditions – in the left-hand column and top row.
4. The critical value for your test is found at the intersection of the column and row you have identified.
5. If your calculated value of U equals or is less than this critical value, your result is statistically significant at the level you have chosen.

Table A2.2 Table of critical values for Mann-Whitney U test. This table is for significance level $p < 0.05$, two-tailed test (two-tailed hypothesis)

N_2 / N_1	5	6	7	8	9	10	11	12	13	14	15	16	17	18	19	20
2				0	0	0	0	1	1	1	1	1	2	2	2	2
3	0	1	1	2	2	3	3	4	4	5	5	6	6	7	7	8
4	0	1	2	3	4	4	5	6	7	9	10	11	11	12	13	14
5	2	3	5	6	7	8	9	11	12	13	14	15	17	18	19	20
6		5	6	8	10	11	13	14	16	17	19	21	22	24	25	27
7			8	10	12	14	16	18	20	22	24	26	28	30	32	34
8				13	15	17	19	22	24	26	29	31	34	36	38	41
9					17	20	23	26	28	31	34	37	39	42	45	48
10						23	26	29	33	36	39	42	45	48	52	55
11							30	33	37	40	44	47	51	55	58	62
12								37	41	45	49	53	57	61	65	69
13									45	50	54	59	63	67	72	76
14										55	59	64	69	74	78	83
15											64	70	75	80	85	90
16												75	81	86	92	98
17													87	93	99	105
18														99	106	112
19															113	119
20																127

Wilcoxon signed ranks test

1. Determine whether you are conducting a one-tailed or a two-tailed test.
2. Identify the level of significance for your test. This determines which column you will use.
3. Find your *n* (sample size) in the left-hand column. This determines the row of the table you will use.
4. The critical value for your test is found at the intersection of the column and row you have identified.
5. If your calculated value of T equals or is less than this critical value, your result is statistically significant at the level you have chosen.

Table A2.3 Table of critical values for Wilcoxon signed ranks test

One-tailed significance levels	0.025	0.01	0.005
Two-tailed significance levels	0.05	0.02	0.01
n			
6	0	–	–
7	2	0	–
8	4	2	0
9	6	3	2
10	8	5	3
11	11	7	5
12	14	10	7
13	17	13	10
14	21	16	13
15	25	20	16
16	30	24	20
17	35	28	23
18	40	33	28
19	46	38	32
20	52	43	38
21	59	49	43
22	66	56	49
23	73	62	55
24	81	69	61
25	89	77	68

Spearman's rho correlation coefficient

1. Determine whether you are conducting a one-tailed or a two-tailed test.
2. Identify the level of significance for your test. This will determine the column you will use.
3. Find your n (sample size) in the left-hand column. This determines the row of the table you will use.
4. The critical value for your test is found at the intersection of the column and row you have identified.
5. If your calculated value of Rs equals or exceeds this critical value, your result is statistically significant at the level you have chosen.

Table A2.4 Table of critical values for Spearman's rho correlation coefficient

One-tailed level of significance	0.05	0.025	0.01	0.005
Two-tailed level of significance	0.10	0.05	0.02	0.01
n				
4	1.000	–	–	–
5	0.900	1.000	1.000	–
6	0.829	0.886	0.943	1.000
7	0.714	0.786	0.893	0.929
8	0.643	0.738	0.833	0.881
9	0.600	0.700	0.783	0.833
10	0.564	0.648	0.745	0.794
11	0.536	0.618	0.709	0.755
12	0.503	0.587	0.671	0.727
13	0.484	0.560	0.648	0.703
14	0.464	0.538	0.622	0.675
15	0.443	0.521	0.604	0.654
16	0.429	0.503	0.582	0.635
17	0.414	0.485	0.566	0.615
18	0.401	0.472	0.550	0.600
19	0.391	0.460	0.535	0.584
20	0.380	0.447	0.520	0.570
21	0.370	0.435	0.508	0.556
22	0.361	0.425	0.496	0.544
23	0.353	0.415	0.486	0.532
24	0.344	0.406	0.476	0.521
25	0.337	0.398	0.466	0.511
26	0.331	0.390	0.457	0.501
27	0.324	0.382	0.448	0.491
28	0.317	0.375	0.440	0.483
29	0.312	0.368	0.433	0.475
30	0.306	0.362	0.425	0.467

Binomial sign test

1. Determine whether you are conducting a one-tailed or a two-tailed test.
2. Identify the level of significance for your test. This will determine the column you will use.
3. Find your n (sample size, in this case the number of matched pairs) in the left-hand column. This determines the row of the table you will use.
4. The critical value for your test is found at the intersection of the column and row you have identified.
5. If your calculated value of S is equal to or less than the critical value your result is statistically significant at the level you have chosen.

Table A2.5 Table of critical values for binomial sign test

n	a = .005 (one tail) a = .01 (two tail)	a = .01 (one tail) a = .02 (two tail)	a = .025 (one tail) a = .05 (two tail)	a = .05 (one tail) a = .10 (two tail)
1	*	*	*	*
2	*	*	*	*
3	*	*	*	*
4	*	*	*	*
5	*	*	*	0
6	*	*	0	0
7	*	0	0	0
8	0	0	0	1
9	0	0	1	1
10	0	0	1	1
11	0	1	1	2
12	1	1	2	2
13	1	1	2	3
14	1	2	2	3
15	2	2	3	3
16	2	2	3	4
17	2	3	4	4
18	3	3	4	5
19	3	4	4	5
20	3	4	5	5
21	4	4	5	6
22	4	5	5	6
23	4	5	6	7
24	5	5	6	7
25	5	6	7	7

References

Bandura, A., Ross, D. and Ross, S.A., 1961, 'Transmission of Aggression Through Imitation of Aggressive Models'. *Journal of Abnormal and Social Psychology*, vol. 63, no 3, 575–582.

Banyard, P., 2002, *Psychology in Practice Health*, London: Hodder Education.

Baron-Cohen, S., Golan, O., Chapman, E. and Granader, Y., 2007, 'Transported into a world of emotion'. *The Psychologist*, vol. 20, no 2, 76–77.

Baron-Cohen, S., 2003, *The Essential Difference – Men, Women and the Extreme Male Brain*. London: Allen Lane, The Penguin Press.

Baron-Cohen, S., Jolliffe, T., Mortimore, C. and Robertson, M., 1997, 'Another Advanced Test of Theory of Mind: Evidence from Very High Functioning Adults with Autism or Asperger Syndrome'. *Journal of Child Psychology and Psychiatry*, vol. 38, 813–822.

Bartlett, F.C., 1932, *Remembering: A Study in Experimental and Social Psychology*. Cambridge: Cambridge University Press.

Baumrind, D., 1967, 'Child care practices anteceding three patterns of preschool behavior'. *Genetic Psychology Monographs*, vol. 75, no 1, 43–88.

Blakemore, C. and Cooper, G.F., 1970, 'Development of the Brain Depends on the Visual Environment'. *Nature*, vol. 228, 477–478.

Bocchiaro, P., Zimbardo, P.G. and Van Lange, P.A.M., 2012, 'To Defy Or Not To Defy: An Experimental Study of the Dynamics of Disobedience And Whistle-Blowing'. *Social Influence*, vol. 7, no 1, 35–50.

Bower, G.H., Black, J.B. and Turner, T.J., 1979, 'Scripts in memory for texts'. *Cognitive Psychology*, vol. 11, 177–220.

Bowlby, J., 1953, *Child Care and the Growth of Love*. Baltimore, MD: Pelican Books. Based upon the World Health Organization (WHO) Report Maternal Care and Mental Health by John Bowlby (1951). 182 pp.

Bowler, D.M., 1992, 'Theory of Mind in Asperger syndrome'. *Journal of Child Psychology and Psychiatry*, vol. 33, 877–893.

British Psychological Society, 1993, *Ethical guidelines*. Leicester: Ethics Committee of the British Psychological Society.

Broadbent, D.E., 1958, *Perception and Communication*, Oxford: Pergamon.

Carlson, N.R., 1986, *Physiology of Behaviour*, 3rd edition, London: Allyn and Bacon.

Casey, B.J., Somerville, L.H., Gotlib, I.H., Ayduk, O., Franklin, N.T., Askren, M.K., Jonides, J., Berman, M.G., Wilson, N.L., Teslovich, T., Glover, G., Zayas, V., Mischel, W. and Shoda, Y., 2011, 'Behavioral and Neural Correlates of Delay of Gratification 40 Years Later'. *Proceedings of the National Academy of Sciences of the United States of America*, vol. 108, no 36, 14998–15003.

Chaney, G., Clements, B., Landau, L., Bulsara, M. and Watt, P., 2004, 'A New Asthma Spacer Device to Improve Compliance in Children: A Pilot Study'. *Respirology*, vol. 9, 499–506.

Cherry, E.C., 1953, 'Some experiments on the recognition of speech, with one and with two ears'. *Journal of the Acoustical Society of America*, vol. 25, no 5, 975–979.

Dalton, P., 1993, 'The role of stimulus familiarity in context-dependent recognition'. *Memory & Cognition*, vol. 21, 223–234.

Darley, J.M. and Batson, C.D., 1973, 'From Jerusalem to Jericho: A study of situational and dispositional variables in helping behavior'. *Journal of Personality and Social Psychology*, vol. 27, 100–108.

Darley, J.M. and Latané, B., 1968, 'Bystander intervention in emergencies: Diffusion of responsibility'. *Journal of Personality and Social Psychology*, vol. 8, 377–383.

Davison, G.G. and Neale, J.M., 2001, *Abnormal Psychology*, 8th edn. New York: John Wiley & Sons.

Ekman, P., 1992, 'An argument for basic emotions'. *Cognition and Emotion*, vol. 6, 169–200.

Endres, J., 2004, 'The language of the psychopath: characteristics of prisoners' performance in a sentence completion test'. *Criminal Behaviour and Mental Health*, vol. 14, 214–226.

Eriksson, P.S., Perfilieva, E., Bjork-Eriksson, T., Alborn, A.M., Nordberg, C., Peterson D.A. and Gage F.H., 1998, 'Neurogenesis in the adult human hippocampus'. *Nature Medicine*, November, 4, no. 11, 1313–7.

Eysenck, H.J., 1970, 'Explanation and the concept of personality', in R. Borger and F. Cioffi (eds), *Explanation in the Behavioural Sciences*. Cambridge: Cambridge University Press.

Freud, S.J., 1909, 'Analysis of a Phobia in a Five-Year-Old Boy'. *The Pelican Freud Library, Vol. 8, Case Histories I*, 169–305.

Freud, S., 1977, *The Pelican Freud Library Volume 7 – On Sexuality – Three Essays on the Theory of Sexuality and other works*. Harmondsworth: Penguin Books.

Freud, S., 1977, *The Pelican Freud Library Volume 8 – Case Histories 1 – 'Dora' and 'Little Hans'*. Harmondsworth: Penguin Books.

Gazzaniga, M.S., LeDoux, J.E. and Wilson, D.H., 1977, 'Language, praxis, and the right hemisphere: Clues to some mechanisms of consciousness'. *Neurology*, vol. 27, 1144–1147.

Gibbs, J.C., 2003, *Moral Development and Reality: Beyond the Theories of Kohlberg and Hoffman*. Thousand Oaks, CA: Sage Publications.

Gilligan, C., 1982, *In a Different Voice, Psychological Theory and Women's Development*. Cambridge, MA: Harvard University Press.

Godden, D.R. and Baddeley, A.D.,1975, 'Context-dependent memory in two natural environments: on land and underwater'. *British Journal of Psychology*, vol. 66, no 3, 325–331.

Gould, S.J., 1982, 'A Nation of Morons'. *New Scientist*, vol. 6, 349–352.

Gould, S.J., 1996, *The Mismeasure of Man – Revised and Expanded*. New York: W.W. Norton.

Grant, H.M., Bredhal, L.C., Clay, J., Ferrie, J., Groves, J.E., Mcdorman, T.A. and Dark, V.J., 1998, 'Context-Dependent Memory for Meaningful Material: Information for Students'. *Applied Cognitive Psychology*, vol. 12, 617–623.

Hancock, J.T, Woodworth, M.T., and Porter, S., 2011, 'Hungry Like the Wolf: A Word-Pattern Analysis of the Language of Psychopaths'. *Legal and Criminological Psychology*, vol. 18, no 1, 102–114.

Happé, F., 1994, *Autism – An Introduction to Psychological Theory*. Hove: Psychology Press.

Hare, R.D., 1991, *The Hare Psychopathy Checklist – Revised (PCL-R)*. Toronto: Multi-Health Systems.

Hare, R.D., 2003, *The Hare Psychopathy Checklist – Revised*. Toronto: Multi-Health Systems.

Hirsch, H.V.B., and Spinelli, D.N., 1970, 'Visual experience modifies distribution of horizontally and vertically oriented receptive fields in cats'. *Science*, 168, 869–871.

Huprich, S.K., Gacano, C.B., Schneider, R.B. and Bridges, M.R., 2004, 'Rorschach oral dependency in psychopaths, sexual homicide perpetrators, and non-violent paedophiles'. *Behavioural Sciences and the Law*, vol. 22, 345–356.

Jacobs B., Schall, M. and Schneibel, A.B., 1993 'A quantitative dendritic analysis of Wernicke's area in humans. II. Gender, hemispheric and environmental change', *Journal of comparative neurology*, 327, 97–111.

Johnston, W.A., Heinz, S.P., 1978 'Flexibility and capacity demands of attention'. *Journal of Experimental Psychology: General*, Vol 107(4), Dec 1978, 420–435.

Kohlberg, L., 1968, 'The Child as a Moral Philosopher'. *Psychology Today*, vol. 2, no 4, 25–30.

Lee, K., Cameron, C.A., Xu, F., Fu, G. and Board, J., 1997, 'Chinese and Canadian Children's Evaluations of Lying and Truth-Telling'. *Child Development*, vol. 68, no 5, 924–934.

Levine, R.V., Norenzayan, A. and Philbrick, K., 2001, 'Cross-Cultural Differences in Helping Strangers'. *Journal of Cross-Cultural Psychology*, vol. 32, no 5, 543–560.

Loftus E.F., and Burns H.J., 1982 'Mental shock can produce retrograde amnesia'. *Memory & Cognition*, 10, 318—23.

Loftus, E.F. and Ketcham, K., 1994, *The Myth of Repressed Memory*. New York: St. Martin's Press.

Loftus, E. and Palmer, J., 1974, 'Reconstruction of Automobile Destruction: An Example of the Interaction Between Language and Memory'. *Journal of Verbal Learning and Verbal Behaviour*, vol. 13, 585–589.

Mack , A., and Rock, I., 1998 *Inattentional Blindness*, Cambridge, MA: MIT Press.

Maguire, E.A., Gadian, D.G., Johnsrude, I.S., Good, C.D., Ashburner, J., Frackowiak, R.S., and Frith, C.D., 2000, 'Navigation-Related Structural Change in the Hippocampi of Taxi Drivers'. *Proceedings of the National Academy of Sciences of the United States of America*, vol. 97, no 8, 4398–4403.

Martin, K.M. and Aggleton, J.P., 1993, 'Contextual effects on the ability of divers to use decompression tables'. *Applied Cognitive Psychology*, vol. 7, 311–316.

Metcalfe, J. and Mischel, W., 1999, 'A hot/cool-system analysis of delay of gratification: dynamics of willpower'. *Psychological Review*, vol. 106, 3–19.

Milgram, S., 1963, 'Behavioural Study of Obedience'. *Journal of Abnormal and Social Psychology*, vol. 67, no 4, 371–378.

Milgram, S., 1974, *Obedience to Authority – An Experimental View*. New York: Harper Collins.

Moray, N., 1959, 'Attention in Dichotic Listening: Affective Cues and the Influence of Instructions'. *Quarterly Journal of Experimental Psychology*, vol. 11, no 1, 56–60.

Neisser U., 1979 'The control of information pickup in selective looking', *Perception and its Development: A Tribute to Eleanor J Gibson* in Ed. A.D. Pick Hillsdale, NJ: Lawrence Erlbaum Associates pp. 201–219.

Neisser U., Becklen R., 1975 'Selective looking: Attending to visually specified events' *Cognitive Psychology* 7 480–494

de Oliviera-Souza R., Hare R.D., Bramati, I.E., Garrido, G.J., Azevedo Ignacio, F., Tovar-Moll, F. and Moll, J., 2008, 'Psychopathy as a disorder of the moral brain: fronto-temporo-limbic grey matter reductions demonstrated by voxel-based morphometry'. *Neuroimage*, vol. 40, no 3, 1202–1213.

Ozonoff, S., Pennington, B.F. and Rogers, S.J., 1991, 'Executive function deficits in high-functioning autistic individuals: Relationship to theory of mind'. *Journal of Child Psychology and Psychiatry*, vol. 32, 1081–1106.

Piliavin, I., Rodin, J. and Piliavin, J., 1969, 'Good Samaritanism: An Underground Phenomenon?' *Journal of Personality and Social Psychology*, vol. 13, no 4, 289–299.

Popper, K., 2002, *The Logic of Scientific Discovery* (1934). London: Routledge Classics.

Raine, A., Lencz, T., Taylor, K., Hellige, J.B., Bihrle, S., LaCasse, L., Lee, M., Ishikawa, S. and Colleti, P., 2003, 'Corpus callosum abnormalities in psychopathic antisocial individuals'. *Archives of General Psychiatry*, vol. 60, 1134–1142.

Raine, A., Ishikawa, S.S., Arce, E., Lencz, T., Knuth, K.H., Bihrle, S., LaCasse, L. and Coletti, P., 2004, 'Hippocampal structural asymmetry in unsuccessful psychopaths'. *Biological Psychiatry*, vol. 55, 185–191.

Rosenbith, J.F., 1959, 'Learning by imitation in kindergarten children'. *Child Development* vol. 30, 69–80.

Sears, D.O., 1986 'College Sophomores in the laboratory: Influences of a narrow data base on social psychology's view of human nature', *Journal Of Personality and Social Psychology*, 51, no. 3, 515–30

Sieber, J.E. and Stanley, B., 1988, 'Ethical and professional dimensions of socially sensitive research'. *American Psychologist*, vol. 43, 49–55.

Simons, D.J. and Chabris, C.F., 1999, 'Gorillas in Our Midst: Sustained Inattentional Blindness for Dynamic Events'. *Perception*, vol. 28, 1059–1074.

Sperry, R.W., 1968, 'Hemisphere Deconnection and Unity in Conscious Awareness'. *American Psychologist*, vol. 23, 723–733.

Treisman, A.M., 1964, 'Verbal Cues, Language, and Meaning in Selective Attention', *The American Journal of Psychology*, 77 (2): 206–219

Tulving, E., 1972, 'Episodic and semantic memory' in Eds. E. Tulving and W. Donaldson, *Organisation of Memory*, London: Academic Press

Watson, J., 1913, 'Psychology as the Behaviourist Views It'. *Psychological Review,* vol. 20, no 2, 158–177.

WHO, 2007, 'Early Child Development: A Powerful Equalizer', www.who.int/social_determinants/resources/ecd_kn_report_07_2007.pdf?ua=1.

Glossary

Abstract   A summary of a piece of research that outlines the aim, method, participants, results and conclusions presented at the start of the research paper.

Alternate hypothesis   A prediction that there will be an effect (e.g. of the independent variable on the dependent variable in an experiment; or that two variables will be related in a correlation study).

Altruistic behaviour   Selfless behaviour; behaviour that is unselfish in its concern for others.

Anonymity   Where the participants' data is kept private.

Appendices/appendix   A section that may appear at the end of the research paper which contains any of a list of materials, calculations, raw data, and anything else the reader needs to fully understand and repeat the research.

Arousal [state]   Heightened stimulation or excitement.

Biased sample   A sample that is not representative of its target population or of people in general.

Biomedical   A model of health that seeks to explain health in terms of single-factor physical causes.

Biopsychosocial   A model of health that seeks to explain health in terms of psychological and social, as well as physical, causes.

Bystander apathy   Where people do not offer help to a victim when others are present.

Case studies   Where a small group of participants are studied in depth; often the participants are unusual in some way.

Castration complex   Part of the Oedipus complex: a boy's fear, after seeing a naked female for the first time, that he will lose his penis.

Ceiling effect   The point at which the participant cannot achieve a higher score, e.g. on a test, although they have the capability to do so.

Classical conditioning   The principle that people learn to associate two stimuli.

Closed questions/forced response questions   Questions with a limited range of responses to choose from.

Coding frames   Groups of classifications that show how qualitative data has been converted into numerical data for analysis.

Concurrent validity   Where a test is validated against an existing measure, e.g. if we know that X causes Y, and the new test also shows that X causes Y, then we know that the new test has validity.

Conditions   In an experiment, the situation under which it is undertaken. Usually there is a control condition and an experimental condition and results from each condition are compared to determine the effect of the influence of the independent variable on the dependent variable.

Confidentiality   A set of rules to protect the privacy of participants by not associating their names with their responses.

Conscious   What we are currently thinking about.

Consent[ed]   An ethical requirement that ensures that all participants have agreed to take part in the procedure/experiment/research

Construct validity   Where a test or study measures the actual behaviour it sets out to measure.

Content analysis   Where researchers analyse text to look for patterns and repetitions

Controlled observation   An observation that controls all the possible factors which might alter the behaviour.

Controls   The aspects of research that are kept the same for each condition to ensure that the independent variable is the only variable effecting the dependent variable

Correlation studies   Where the researcher tests to see whether two variables are related.

Cost–reward [analysis]   Weighing up of the price of a behaviour or action versus the potential benefits.

Counterbalancing   A way of reducing order effects in a repeated measures design experiment by systematically varying the order of presentation of tasks to participants.

Covert observation   Where 'participants' are observed without their knowledge.

Criterion validity   How much one measure predicts the value of another measure.

Cross-cultural   Across and involving people from different cultures.

Cross-sectional study   Where data is collected at a specific point in time, but participants are people of different ages; it is a form of snapshot study with some of the benefits of a longitudinal study.

Culturally biased [cultural bias]   Bias towards people from a particular culture, in that people from other cultures may not understand the research in the same way.

Curve of normal distribution   On a graph, a symmetrical, bell-shaped curve which shows that most scores are around the midpoint and then fewer scores are seen as the behaviour becomes more or less than the midpoint.

Debrief   A discussion between participant and researcher, following an investigation, where the researcher ensures the participant will not be traumatised by the experiment.

Deception   In research, where participants are tricked into believing the investigation is studying something other than what it is.

Deductive   Research where the primary goal is testing theories.

Demand characteristics   Where participants interpret the aims of the experiment/research and change their behaviour to fit these aims.

Dependent variable   The measure of behaviour in an experiment. Assuming the experiment is properly controlled, it can be assumed to be affected by the independent variable.

Design   The procedure used to control the influence of participant variables in an experiment

Determinist   Belief that a person's behaviour is determined by factors beyond their control.

Diffusion of responsibility   Where there is a victim and lots of bystanders are present; individual bystanders may not feel enough responsibility to help the victim because the responsibility is shared between all the bystanders.

Discussion   The part of the research paper that focuses on what the study has discovered. It includes evaluation and alternative explanations as well as suggestions for how to move the research on in terms of improvements or new ideas to pursue in the future.

Disorder   An illness that alters normal physical or mental functions.

Double-blind   Where both the participants and the researchers (data collectors) are unaware of which condition the participants are in or the aims of the study

Ecological validity   Where research is true to life.

Empirical evidence   Evidence obtained from research into how things actually are (as opposed to how we might believe them to be).

Ethics   In research, moral principles that influence the way in which the research is carried out.

Ethnocentric bias   Where only one type of person is chosen to represent a diverse population.

Event sampling   Where an event is recorded each time it happens.

Experiments   Tests undertaken under controlled conditions in order to investigate the effect of the independent variable on the dependent variable.

External reliability   The extent to which a test score varies from one time to another.

External validity   Where research can be generalised to other setting.

Extraneous variable   An undesirable variable that might affect the relationship between the independent variable and the dependent variable.

Face validity   Where a study measures what the researcher wants it to measure.

Face validity   How good the test or research looks to be at testing what it is meant to be testing

Falsified [falsifiability]   Possible to prove wrong.

Field experiments   Experiments that occur in the natural environment of the people whose behaviour is being studied.

Free will   Acting according to personal choice, rather than necessity or fate.

Frequency table   A tally chart, where the frequency of particular scores recorded.

Frontal lobes   The areas of the brain which are responsible for all the higher-order and more complicated functions, such as thinking, planning and forming ideas.

Generalise   To take a specific research finding and apply it to the broader population.

Histogram   Similar to bar charts, but only used for continuous data.

Holistic   Where parts of a whole are considered to be interrelated so that the whole is more than just the sum of its parts.

Hypothesis   The research prediction, based on a theory or observation.

Inattentional blindness   The failure to see an event or object in your field of vision because you are so focused on other elements of what you can see.

Independent measures design   Where participants are randomly allocated to the different experimental conditions.

Independent variable   An aspect of the experiment that is manipulated to see its effect on a particular behaviour (see dependent variable) - the behaviour that is tested.

Individual differences   Variations between people.

Inductive   Where the primary goal is generating new theories.

Internal reliability   Consistency of results of a test across items within that test.

Internal validity   where research does not have lots extraneous variables and the effect of the independent variable on the dependent variable is truly being measured

Inter-rater reliability   where two observers consistently rate or observe the same behaviour and the two sets of ratings are correlated to ensure that observations are not subjective

Interval level data   Data that has equal intervals but does not have a true zero, e.g. temperature.

Introduction   A section at the beginning of a research paper that considers the area of psychology in which the study is located, then focuses on previous research carried out in the same area.

Laboratory experiments   Experiments that occur in a controlled setting, such as a research laboratory at a university.

Leading questions   Questions where the researcher, often unintentionally, may lead the participant to give a certain (possibly more desirable) answer.

Level of significance   The level at which psychologists will reject the null hypothesis.

Likert scale   A scale that provides a range of answers for people to select the one that represents the extent to which they like/dislike something or agree/disagree with something.

Longitudinal study   The collection of data from participants over a long period of time in order to investigate behaviour changes over time.

Matched participants design   Similar to an independent measures design except that participants are allocated to their condition based on some relevant characteristic. This is to ensure both conditions contain similar sorts of people.

Mean   A measure of central tendency which is calculated by adding up all the scores in the set and dividing by the number of scores.

Measure of central tendency   Ways of calculating central, average or typical scores.

Measures of dispersion   Ways of calculating how widely dispersed or spread out the scores are.

Median   A measure of central tendency which is calculated by putting all the scores from a set in numerical order and then taking the central point from this set of scores.

Memory   The ability to retain information and demonstrate retention through behaviour.

Method   A lengthy section of the research paper which includes all the details necessary for someone to carry out exactly the same research in the same conditions.

Mode   A measure of central tendency which records the most frequently occurring score in a set.

Moral development   The process by which people come to understand right and wrong.

Naturalistic observation   Observation that is carried out in the field.

Nature   Innate features, i.e. those that may be genetically determined.

Negative correlation   As one variable increases the other variable decreases.

No correlation   When there is no relationship between the variables.

Nominal level data   Categories of behaviour and how often they occur.

Non-participant observation   Observation in which the observer is not a member of the group being studied or playing a part of another person in the group.

Null hypothesis   A prediction that there will be no effect (i.e. in an experiment, the independent variable will not have the predicted effect on the dependent variable; in a correlation, the two variables will not be related).

Nurture   Features affected by circumstances such as education, upbringing or lifestyle.

Objective   Not influenced by personal feelings or opinions; factual.

Observation   Where the researcher observes the behaviour of the particpant/s and records it.

Occipital lobes   The areas of the brain (located at the back of the head) which receive the main input from the visual pathways.

Oedipus complex   A term developed by Freud to describe incestuous feelings supposedly felt by a son towards his mother, as well as the associated jealousy felt towards a father who is perceived to be a rival.

One-tailed hypothesis   Hypothesis where a specific effect is predicted (i.e. that results will go in one direction).

Open questions/free response questions   Questions where the participant may respond in their own words.

Operant conditioning   The principle that behaviour will be repeated if it is rewarded.

Operationalised [format]   Where the concept that is being investigated is made measurable so that it can be tested.

Opportunity sample   A group of participants who have been selected due to their availability.

Order effects   Where the order that an experimental task is carried out may affect the result; order effects include fatigue and practice.

Ordinal level data   Individual data that show which participant did the behaviour most or least and indicates the position of a participant in the group.

Overt observation   Where participants are aware that they are being observed, and have usually explicitly given consent. This is more ethical than covert observation.

Parietal lobes   The areas of the brain (located between the occipital lobe and the central sulcus) which are specialised to deal with information from the body such as touch and temperature, and help to interpret body position.

Participant observation   The method of gathering data through observation, where the observers are part of, or are pretending to be part of, the group they are observing.

Participant variables   Factors within a person that can vary over time or vary with a situation.

Participants   The subjects of the research; those whose behaviour is studied.

Population validity   How accurately a sample represents its intended population (such that the findings from a study can generalise to that population).

Positive correlation   As one variable increases the other variable does, too.

Positively skewed curve   On a graph, a curve representing data from a population that has more low scorers than high scorers.

Preconscious   A part of our mind that we can access with relative ease by retrieving stored memories.

Predictive validity   Where the test or research can predict certain behaviours.

Primary data   Data gathered directly from the participants by the researcher.

Primary motor cortex   The area of the brain responsible for movement.

Procedure   An outline of how the participants were approached, what was said, timings and what actually happened in the research.

Proportionality   Where a correlation has a linear property, i.e. when plotted the scatter diagram shows as a straight line.

Psychometric   A test which endeavours to express a psychological construct in numerical form.

Qualitative data   Data in the form of words, e.g. a description of what was observed or what a participant is feeling.

Quantitative data   Data in the form of numbers, e.g. how much or how many of something there is.

Quasi-experiments   Where the independent variable is naturally occurring as opposed to being created and controlled by the experimenter; they are referred to as 'quasi' because, as the experimenter does not control the independent variable, they are not technically experiments.

Questionnaire   Sets of questions answered by participants which can completed with pen and paper, face-to-face, on the telephone or internet.

Random sample   A group of participants from a a target population who all had an equal chance of being selected.

Randomisation   Where participants are allocated to experimental conditions on a chance basis.

Range   A measure of dispersion which is calculated by taking the lowest score from the highest score in a set and then adding 1.

Rating scales   A set of values or categories, ranging from one extreme to its opposite, which allow feelings and behaviours to be rated.

Ratio level data   Data that has equal intervals and a true zero, e.g. time.

Raw data   The data that psychologists collect for each participant.

Reductionist   Where behaviour can be explained by breaking it down into its constituent parts.

Related design   Where each score in the experimental condition is compared with the corresponding score in the control condition.

Reliability   Consistency of research or findings i.e., whether a test can be used more than once and produce consistent results.

Repeated measures design   Where all participants participate in all experimental conditions.

Replicable   Where the research could be repeated by following the same procedure.

Researcher/observer effects   Effects on participants (and their behaviour or responses) which are brought about by the researcher's or observer's presence.

Results   The part of the research paper which refers to raw data, verbal summaries and descriptive statistics.

Sample   A group of selected participants.

Sample size   The number of participants.

Scatter diagram/scatter graph   A type of graph used to represent correlation.

Secondary data   Data that has already been gathered by someone other than the researcher.

Self-report   Where the participants provide data about themselves (in response to the researcher's questions).

Self-selected sample/volunteer sample   A group of participants who have selected themselves, or volunteered, to take part in the research, often in response to an advertisement from the researcher.

Semantic differential scale   A scale in which people are asked to rate something in terms of its position between two opposite descriptive words, such as strong and weak.

Semi-structured interview   Where the interviewer has a list of questions but can ask for clarification of particular answers or responses.

Sensory cortex   The area of the brain responsible for receiving sensory information, such as touch.

Significant figure   The number of digits that are used to express a figure to a desired degree of accuracy, e.g. 3.2467 to three significant figures would be 3.25.

Single-blind   Where the participants do not know (are 'blind' to) the condition they are in or the aims of the study.

Situational variables   Factors that can vary in the environment.

Skewed distribution curve   On a graph, a curve representing data from a skewed or unusual data set.

Snapshot study   Where data is collected from participants at a specific point in time.

Social desirability bias   Where participants try to present an image of themselves as being good members of society.

Socially desirable   Socially desirable responses are responses that the participant feels will present him/her in a good light.

Socially sensitive   Where (in research) there may be social implications either for the participants participating in, or for the group represented by, the research.

Split half method   A measure of reliability within a test, where one, and then the other, half of questions are tested to ensure the same level of score is achieved on each half.

Standard deviation   A measure of dispersion which comprises the square root of the variance.

Standard form   In maths, shorthand form, e.g. 3×10^5.

Standardisation   The process of keeping the test conditions the same for every participant.

Structured interview   Where the same set of questions is asked to each participant in the same order.

Structured observation   The method in which the researcher imposes a structure on the observation to meet its aim.

Subjective   Influenced by personal feelings or opinions.

Systematic bias   The tendency of an experiment or process to support particular outcomes.

Target population   The section or group of people whom the researcher wants to research.

Temporal lobes   The areas (located on either side of the head, near the ears) which receive information from the ears about sounds and balance.

Test–retest method   A method of testing external reliability - to see whether the same results are achieved if the sample is retested.

Time event sampling   See time sampling

Time point sampling   See time sampling

Time sampling   Has two meanings: time point sampling is where the observer records what the participant is doing at fixed intervals; time event sampling is where a fixed period of time is set for observation.

Two-tailed hypothesis   A hypothesis where an effect is predicted but not specified i.e. results could go in either of two directions.

Type 1 error   Mistakenly accepting the alternative hypothesis when actually it is the null hypothesis that has been supported (also known as a false positive).

Type 2 error   Mistakenly accepting the null hypothesis when actually it is the alternative hypothesis that has been supported (also known as a false negative).

Unconscious   The part of our mind that is hidden from our awareness and hard (if not impossible) to access.

Unfalsifiable   Impossible to prove wrong.

Unrelated design   Where the whole experimental condition's scores from one group of participants are compared with whole control condition's scores from a different group of participants.

Unstructured interviews   Interviews where the researcher asks spontaneous, rather than wholly scripted, questions.

Unstructured observation   Observation in which the researcher/observer continuously records and reports on behaviour, noting everything that happens.

Validity   How accurate a piece of research or test is at measuring what it aims to measure.

Variance   A measure of dispersion which records how much a set of numbers is spread out from the mean.

Index